Telling Lives

Telling Lives

Women's Self-Writing
in Modern Japan

Ronald P. Loftus

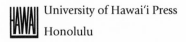 University of Hawai'i Press
Honolulu

Library of Congress Cataloging-in-Publication Data
Telling lives : women's self-writing in modern Japan / [edited] by
Ronald P. Loftus.
        p. cm.
Includes bibliographical references (p.) and index.
    ISBN 0-8248-2753-8 (acid-free paper) — ISBN 0-8248-2834-8 (pbk. :
acid-free paper)
    1. Autobiography—Women authors. 2. Women—Japan—Biography—History
and criticism. I. Loftus, Ronald P.
CT25.T45 2004
920.72'0951—dc22
                                        2003023277

Designed by University of Hawai'i Production Staff

Printed by The Maple-Vail Book Manufacturing Group

In memory of my parents,
John A. and Madelon B. Loftus
And my brother,
John J. Loftus

Contents

Acknowledgments

There are many people to thank for their support during this project. The United States Educational Commission in Japan provided essential support in the form of a Fulbright Research Grant during 1990–1991. Without their support, this project could not have been undertaken. During that year, I was affiliated with the Department of Comparative Literature and Culture, University of Tokyo, and had the distinct privilege to work under the supervision of Professor Hirakawa Sukehiro, from whose criticism and encouragement I benefited enormously. Professor Saeki Shōichi of Chūō University, Japan's foremost expert on autobiography, was also kind enough to meet with me on more than one occasion in order to provide me with his guidance.

Throughout the 1990s, I received summer support from the Atkinson Fund at Willamette University on numerous occasions. During visits to Japan, I had the privilege of being hosted by our sister institution, Tokyo International University. I owe a debt of gratitude to the director of the International Center, Kaneko Satoshi, and his excellent staff for their support on these occasions. During these visits I was able to gather valuable materials and spend time at the National Women's Education Center located in nearby Ranzan-machi, Saitama Prefecture.

While a visiting scholar at the Department of Comparative Literature and Culture, I was also privileged to participate in a reading group on feminism and women's studies at Ochanomizu Women's University under the direction of Professor Tachi Kaoru. I am very grateful to Professor Tachi and the other members of the group. Special thanks as well are due to Hori Hikari of Gakushuin University for her thoughtful responses to some of my ideas.

I have had numerous mentors in the Japan field to whom I owe an enormous debt. The first person to introduce me to the Japan field was George Packard. George Beckmann was my first Japanese history teacher, and I subsequently had the privilege to learn from George Bikle, a very thoughtful and reflective scholar and teacher. But it was Peter Duus who guided me to an understanding of how history works and how we can best learn from it.

There are two mentors in Japan who also helped me enormously over the years. Professor Nishida Masaru, emeritus of Hōsei University, has been a friend and unofficial adviser for thirty years. An expert on proletarian literature, among other things, Professor Nishida helped me far more than I can ever express. Professor Kano Masanao, retired from Waseda University, also helped me immeasurably. Professor Kano is a kind friend and peerless mentor. His knowledge of modern Japanese intellectual history is extremely deep and rich. He taught me about some of the many ways one can uncover the past and reflect upon the markings people leave from one era to another, whatever form these markings may take. As someone very interested in autobiography himself, Professor Kano pointed me in the right direction when I most needed it. I will never be able to repay the kindness he extended to me over the years.

Colleagues at Willamette University have also offered me much valued criticism and advice. Professor John Uggen of the Spanish department has listened attentively to the stories behind the lives that give this book its shape, while Michael Strelow in the English department always had useful insights about autobiography criticism. Suresht Bald of the politics department has kindly read early versions of several of my papers over the years and offered her thoughtful criticism. Professor Miho Fujiwara and Tomoko Harpster kindly helped me with some of my translations and offered insights into the overall project. Institutional and collegial support is invaluable.

Pamela Smith at Willamette provided essential support in preparing the manuscript. The two anonymous readers for the University of Hawai'i Press offered valuable critical insights that helped me shape the book in the final stages. I am also grateful to Patricia Crosby and her staff for making the manuscript much better. Of course, I alone am responsible for all errors and omissions.

Finally, I owe a great deal to my family. My wife Sylvia has supported me unstintingly over the years. She has listened, read parts of the manuscript, and offered her advice. There are times, I am sure, when my sons Joshua and Michael saw less of me than they deserved, but they nevertheless cheered me on. I am very grateful for their support and understanding. Jen, Amy, Leah Jo, Casey, and Jackson Ian all provided me with much-needed inspiration.

Introduction

Some critics believe that the age of autobiography is over, that autobiography is no longer relevant to our postmodern world. Others contend that all writing must be taken as autobiographical. Regardless of what critics proclaim, however, autobiography remains a remarkably popular and resilient mode of reading—and writing. Why is the act of reading autobiographies so appealing? Obviously, it affords the reader a unique insight into the "times" and into the worldview of the narrator. For the historian, the appeal of self-representational narratives may be rooted in what new historicist Stephen Greenblatt refers to as a "desire to speak with the dead."[1] As he explains, it was the fact that "the dead had contrived to leave textual traces of themselves" behind that initially drew him to the study of history. He comments:

> Many of the traces have little resonance, though *every one*, even the most trivial or tedious, *contains some fragment of lost life;* others seem *uncannily full of the will to be heard.*[2]

For anyone interested in recovering "some fragment of lost life" or in discovering voices that manifest this "will to be heard," then self-representational narratives are excellent resources to explore.

But there is more to the appeal of autobiographies than just mining them for their "content." Discerning readers may wish to reflect on the process by which autobiographical meaning or "truth" is constructed. In autobiography, there is a presumed relationship between a narrating subject and lived experience, between a self, its patterns of internal growth and development, and external reality. But it is now readily accepted that the "self" we observe remembering and recreating its past in a text is little more than a "fictive structure."[3] If the individual is nothing more than a discursive formation, then autobiography must be seen as one of the major forms of discourse by which myths about the individual and self-formation are produced and sustained. But autobiography has not always been perceived in this way. Initially, autobiography criticism was a thoroughly hegemonic practice, one that privileged "a teleological narrative enshrining the 'individual' and 'his' uniqueness."[4] This traditional view of autobiography, which was largely based on readings and critical analyses of such seminal texts as those by St. Augustine, Goethe, Jean-Jacques Rousseau, Henry Adams, and Benjamin Franklin, was thoroughly masculinist. The universalizing agenda that it embraced left little room for the kind of multiple, contradicted subjectivities that might be encountered in women's self-writing. Recognizing that reading is not a neutral or innocent act and that things like race, gender, class, and nationality shape how we approach a text, feminist scholars have challenged the traditional way of looking at autobiography, suggesting instead that self-writing can be seen as "a medium of resistance and counter discourse"[5] and that it has "provide[d] locations where subjects disrupted dominant conceptions of the bourgeois self."[6]

Feminist Criticism of Self-Writing

By introducing the notion of gender, then, this already complex, multi-layered discourse on autobiography revolving around individualism, the self, and identity instantly becomes much more complicated. Back in the late 1970s, when I first began exploring autobiography criticism, a bibliographic search on the subject would yield only a handful of monographs, almost all written by males and almost all of them exclusively about male autobiographers. But by the 1980s, feminist critics had begun to challenge the idea that a single, essentialist conception of the self is adequate to define the narrative practices of diverse subjects who struggle to find their voice from a position other than of the privileged center. The first person to focus attention on the absence of women's texts and to bring the feminist perspective to critical discussions of self-writing was Estelle Jelinek, who discovered in the late 1970s that there was "practically no criticism on women's autobiographies, except for that on Gertrude Stein's."[7] Her two works, *Women's Autobiography: Essays in Criticism* (1980) and *The Tradition of Women's Autobiography from Antiquity to the Present* (1986) did much to emphasize the discontinuous and fragmented nature of women's autobiographies. A central argument put forth by Jelinek but echoed by many others after her is that since there is a discernible difference in the lived reality of men and women, this must somehow translate into differences in their texts. One of the standard ways of conceptualizing this is to argue that male texts are thought to feature coherence and linearity while those by women are characterized by discontinuity, fragmentation, and a focus on personal or private matters as opposed to public ones. As Jelinek notes in *Women in Autobiography*,

> [I]rregularity rather than orderliness informs the self-portraits by women. The narratives of their lives are often not chronological and progressive, but disconnected, fragmentary, or organized into self-sustained units rather than connecting chapters.[8]

Obviously, signs of disruption, fragmentation, and discontinuity can occur in any autobiography regardless of the gender of the author. But, speaking in the broadest terms, many of the classical (male) texts do follow a chronological, linear path of development, culminating in the triumph of an individual over some circumstances, where those by females often do not. On the other hand, as this study will show, many autobiographies by Japanese women essentially follow a linear, chronological trajectory from birth to the narrative present, yet they are far from unmarked by disruptions and discontinuities.

Jelinek's pioneering effort was followed by Domna C. Stanton's *The Female Autograph: Theory and Practice of Autobiography from the Tenth to the Twentieth Century*, the preface of which states clearly that

> [t]he subject of this volume—female autobiographies memoirs, letters and diaries—represents one of those cases of maddening neglect that have motivated feminist scholarship since 1970.[9]

This collection of essays on women's autobiography includes Stanton's own classic introductory essay, "Autogynography: Is the Subject Different?" where she states her belief that there exists

> a fundamental deviance that pervaded autogynographies and produced conflicts in the divided self: the act of writing itself. For a symbolic order that equates the idea of author with a phallic pen transmitted from father to son places the female writer in contradiction to the dominant definition of woman and casts her as the usurper of male prerogatives.[10]

And further,

> Because of woman's different status in the symbolic order, autogynography, I
> concluded, dramatized the fundamental alterity and non-presence of the sub-
> ject, even as it asserts itself discursively and strives toward an always impos-
> sible self possession.[11]

Stanton points directly to differences not only in lived experiences, or in
the sociopolitical order, but also in the very act of writing itself. Specifically,
she alludes to a kind of difference in female self-writing that preserves the
"otherness" of the female voice and interferes with its full presence in the
text.

Frustration over the "maddening neglect" of women's self-writing inspired a number of other feminist scholars to turn their attention to
women's autobiography. The pioneering work of one of these scholars,
Sidonie Smith, stands out among all the others. In her first book, *The Poetics of Women's Autobiography* (1987), Smith notes that although "gender
ideologies and the boundaries they place around women's proper life
script, textual inscription and speaking voice" have operated to hamper
women's attempts at self-representation,

> there have always been women who cross the line between private and public
> utterance, unmasking their desire for the empowering self-interpretation of
> autobiography as they unmasked in their life the desire for publicity. Such
> women approach the autobiographical territory from their position as speak-
> ers at the margins of discourse. In so doing, they find themselves implicated in
> a complex posture toward the engendering of autobiographical narrative.[12]

This notion of female autobiographers as voices who must speak from the
margins of discourse—"always removed from the center of power within
the culture she inhabits"—is central to Smith's argument. Simply put,

> Autobiography is itself one of the forms of selfhood constituting the idea of
> man and in turn promoting the idea. Choosing to write autobiography,
> therefore, she unmasks her transgressive desire for cultural and literary au-
> thority. But the story of man is not exactly her story; and so her relationship
> to the empowering figure of male selfhood is inevitably problematic. To
> complicate matters further, she must also engage the fictions of selfhood that
> constitute the idea of woman and that specify the parameters of female sub-
> jectivity, including women's problematic relationship to language, desire,
> power, and meaning. Since the ideology of gender makes of woman's life

script a nonstory, a silent space, a gap on the patriarchal culture, the ideal woman is self-effacing rather than self-promoting, and her "natural" story shapes itself not around the public, heroic life but around the fluid, circumstantial, contingent responsiveness to others that, according to patriarchal ideology, characterizes the life of woman but not autobiography.[13]

Smith's observations that "the story of man is not exactly her story" and "the ideology of gender makes of woman's life script a nonstory, a silent space, a gap" echo Jelinek's argument about women's autobiography avoiding "the public, heroic life" in favor of more "circumstantial, contingent" features of her experience. But both Stanton and Smith also raise important issues about the "transgressive" nature of women's desire to develop their own voice and tell their own story. Smith sees the female autobiographer as caught in a double bind: if she elects to say nothing or little, she is silenced; but when she tries speak, to recount her life, she goes up against all the patriarchal assumptions about what an individual self is and how its story should be told.

Smith's way of conceptualizing the issues and problems that female self-writing poses was fresh and insightful and inspired other feminist scholars to pursue these kinds of questions further. Following closely on the heels of these path-breaking works by Jelinek, Stanton, and Smith, there was an outpouring of feminist autobiography criticism. Bella Brodzki and Celeste Schenck, for example, were explicit about the position of their own work when they observed in the introduction to *Life/ Lines: Theorizing Women's Autobiography* (1988) that,

[c]riticism of women's autobiography over the past five years reflects important shifts in feminist argument and commitment. This book was conceived as a complement to Estelle Jelinek's groundbreaking *Women's Autobiography* and Domna Stanton's recently reissued *The Female Autograph*.[14]

Other works followed in rapid succession, ranging from Shari Benstock's *The Private Self: Theory and Practice of Women's Autobiographical Writings* (1988) to Leigh Gilmore's very important study, *Autobiographics: A Feminist Theory of Women's Self-Representation* (1994).[15] The thrust of these studies was both to reveal the existence of many autobiographical texts by female authors that were heretofore unknown and to demonstrate that these and other texts could yield different readings than traditional reading practices might suggest. These scholars argue convincingly that women, as the "Other," are trapped in bodies that define their identity, while males are free to construct themselves as individuals in search of souls, in search of their true, inner, noncorporeal identity. Moreover, they contend that because the canon consists of traditional studies of male texts, the experience of the male subject has been universalized and the assumptions of the patriarchy effortlessly "reproduced" in the "genre" we know as autobiography. The problem is articulated quite succinctly by Judy Long.

> The generic/male subject nests within a masculine canon built upon commentary from male critics. Male experience is foundational. Correlatively, in almost all cases males are selected to typify knowledge, culture, and history. A mutual magnification operates among these elements that acts to naturalize the hegemony of the male subject and the male canon. Female subjects are correspondingly diminished. The same critical processes that elevate the male subject disadvantage the female.[16]

This notion of the male experience as foundational is a central argument for feminist critics because it brings with it the belief that "female subjects are correspondingly diminished." The female autobiographical subject often has to turn to "the story and speaking position of the representative man" for inspiration and direction, instead of to a female figure, which means that she must silence or repress that part of her which is female.[17] This can undoubtedly be a source of tension in the text. The narratives we encounter in this volume are often fragmented and manifest a tension between the goals and plans articulated by the narrator and the social and political reality in which these desires unfold. To draw again upon Long,

> Female autobiography is not autobiography as usual. Women's self-writing is animated by the tension between external control of women and the assertion of female subjectivity, a tension visible in women's personal narratives of whatever form. For the woman autobiographer, the process of self-discovery is accompanied by a sense of contestation and risk. Autobiographical strategies employed by women convey some degree of challenge to the all-male tradition of autobiography and often a feeling of threat. Women subjects anticipate difficulty in being "read" or "heard" by a male audience. And women writing their lives for a public cannot escape the terrors and penalties of trespassing on male turf. Women subjects are at risk because the requirements of autobiography and the requirements of femininity are at odds.[18]

When women assert their own subjectivity through self-writing, when they articulate their desire for political and economic independence, they challenge the system of social and political controls arrayed against them. This is why their enterprise must be characterized by a sense of "contestation and risk." How the autobiographies examined in *Telling Lives* manifest this sense of contestation and risk is the primary question underlying this study; however, it will be useful in the next few pages to review how this topic originally presented itself.

Background: Encountering a "Fierceness with Reality"

I first came to be interested in Japanese female self-writing after I had begun reading autobiographies by radical socialist critics such as Taoka Reiun, Sakai Toshihiko, and Kinoshita Naoe. But once I encountered the memoirs of one of their contemporaries, Fukuda Hideko, I began to ponder whether certain "differences" I was experiencing as a reader were not the result of gender. While the narratives by male authors hovered somewhat naturally around the story of a self's coming to awareness of itself, Fukuda's narrative seemed to be more de-centered and fragmented. Her story was often told from multiple perspectives; doubts and uncertainties were often inscribed at the very core of the narrative. As I resumed my reading of autobiography theory, with special attention to women's self-writing and how it may differ from that of male authors, I found myself at the center of this outpouring of new critical literature on autobiography from the feminist perspective. While reading Fukuda's *My Life at Mid-Point (Warawa no hanseigai)*,[19] I was reminded of a phrase I had encountered very early on in my reading about autobiographical practice, a phrase that appears as an epigraph by Florida Scott-Maxwell in the first chapter of Janet Varner Gunn's study, *Autobiography: Towards a Poetics of Experience*.

> When you truly possess all that you have been and done,
> which may take some time, you are fierce with reality.[20]

This phrase seemed like a profoundly insightful way to characterize the autobiographical act, a way to capture some of the intensity one finds in self-writing. Once narrators go back over the ground of lived experience, they are somehow in a better position to confront their lives. As I began reading Japanese women's autobiographies, I encountered texts in which the authors manifested just such a fierceness with reality, most notably in

Fukuda Hideko's *My Life at Mid-Point* (1904) and Takamure Itsue's *Diary of a Woman from the Land of Fire (Hi no kuni no onna no nikki)* (1964). Fukuda wrote with passion and intensity about being a *magaimono*—a sham, a counterfeit—because she confounded gendered expectations.[21] She also wrote poignantly about the pain involved in telling her life. As she notes in her preface—the first line of which makes reference to the autobiography of Benjamin Franklin—writing her life was a painful process, at times encircling her in a "fortress of pain":

> But I never conceived of this text as a means to forget my pain. On the contrary, the very act of writing itself is a source of pain. With each letter, each word, each line, the pain intensifies.
>
> My agony only grows stronger, but it is not necessarily the case that I wish to forget my past. No, my longings for the past grow stronger with the pain of each word and each line I write. . . . My journey through life has been one failure after another; yet I have always fought on. I have never once wavered. As long as blood flows through my veins, I will continue to struggle. It is my calling, my mission to fight crimes against humanity. The more conscious of my mission I become, the more willing I am to endure these pain filled memories.
>
> There is no cure for the pain of confession but more pain. My mission is to struggle against the crimes of this world and against my own sins. At first, I attacked our oligarchic political structure. Now I know that the real struggle is against monopoly capitalism. I am seeking to aid the poor and miserable people of this world. I will ignore the wild, unfounded criticism against me and try to tell my life story as it happened, as frankly as possible, hiding nothing. But I make no attempt to erase my guilt with confession. Rather, my text is my pledge to renew my struggle with myself and with the world.[22]

The fierceness evident in these lines is rooted in a concern with political oppression and social inequality. Fukuda's text is her pledge to continue her struggle with the forces aligned against her in the world and inside herself. Her trajectory from the popular rights movement to socialism is what gives her text its shape. The power of her language is found not only in the links that she forges between memory, pain, and writing, but in the distortions and tensions, the contradictions and paradoxes, with which she wrestles. The narrative describes Fukuda's attraction to the radical wing of the most progressive political movement of her day, the popular rights movement, and her participation in the Osaka Incident of 1885, an act that resulted in her arrest for trying to smuggle explosives onto a ship bound for Korea. She spent time in prison and had a humiliating affair with a married member of her group, some details of which became public. Then, she married a man for love, over his family's objections, only to have him suffer a mental breakdown and die prematurely. Widowed at age thirty-five with three children, she understood well the difficulties facing women trying to make their way in the world independently.

Fukuda wanted to create opportunities for women to live their lives free of dependence on men, so her aim was to open a school for young women to teach them skills that would enable them to establish economic independence. Hence, the specific conditions surrounding the production of her text come into play and shape the way it must be read. The manifesto for her proposed technical school for women, which constitutes the closing portion of her text, announces her plans to open such a school, and the readers understand that the funds she raises through the sale of her life story will provide the capital needed to open the school. Facing an uncertain future, Fukuda ends her text with these lines:

> Standing at the precipice overlooking life and death, there is but one path to tread: to do everything in my power to bring about truth and justice and then await my destiny.[23]

In this passage, the narrator positions herself both in relation to her text and to the dominant discourse. Although her gaze may be steady, the ground on which she stands is far less stable. Who is speaking at this point in the text is not the "I" of a single, unitary self, but one that has been formed out of multiple discourses and multiple encounters (collisions) with forces ranged against her. Her stance in this passage also operates to bridge the conditions of production and reception of the text. Fukuda is not looking back over a full life as a woman of sixty or seventy; she is only midway through her life, a point that the title of her text reinforces strongly. Yet at the moment she writes, she is facing a most uncertain future. She feels distorted and riven by contradictions. Where should she place her energies? How would she support herself and her children? These kinds of questions brought her face-to-face with her own reality, and the language of her text bristles with this fierceness.

There was a similar kind of fierceness evident in the language of Takamure Itsue's *Hi no kuni no onna no nikki*, a text whose central concern is the narrator's relationship to her spouse and her struggle to preserve her own identity and a space for her to conduct her work within the framework of her marriage.[24] Born in 1894 in Kumamoto Prefecture, Takamure was not particularly politically active, considering herself more of a philosophical anarchist. When young, she had undertaken the Buddhist pilgrimage on the island of Shikoku and written about her journey. But she became extremely interested in feminism and women's issues and wrote prolifically about them throughout her career. In addition, during the 1920s she published several volumes of poetry. She also engaged other feminists like Yamakawa Kikue, Itō Noe, and Yamada Waka in debates on feminist issues in the pages of various journals of the day.[25] In 1930 she was involved in publishing an anarchist journal, *Women's Front (Fujin sensen)*, and also began an independent research project on the marriage system in ancient Japan. In 1936 she published the first volume of *A Women's History of Greater Japan (Dai Nippon joseishi)*, which was titled *Studies on the Matriarchal System in Japan (Bokeisei no kenkyū)*. So it is primarily as Japan's first scholar of women's history that Takamure is remembered today.

But her route to this life of an independent scholar was not an easy one. Although she proclaimed an absolute love for her husband, Hashimoto Kenzō (whom she calls "K" in her narrative), she could not thrive in their marriage as it was constituted. As she notes in the diary she kept at the time,

> K's egoism grew in inverse proportion to my distortion. I had never felt my faults to be so revealed as they were during that period.[26]

In this contest of wills, it was Takamure's identity, her ego, her sense of self, that had to shrink and become distorted as K's ego expanded into the space of their married life. In the process, she felt not only small and distorted, but exposed and vulnerable. It is *her* shortcomings, not his, that are on display. She elaborates:

> I had to engage in self-reflection *(hansei)* on my many shortcomings. I didn't necessarily feel that I was a budding scholar or poet, but there was something there and it made me somewhat of a contemplative woman. This did not bode well for my life as a "service wife." . . . Anyway, needless to say, this absurd, illusory love state that I was in did not fit at all with K's demand for a wife who would take care of him. His hot-temper would flare up and he would beat me violently.
>
> K's violence toward me was the first of any kind I had ever experienced

so I was caught by surprise. Except what worried me most was that K would have a complete nervous breakdown. When he became so enraged, his face would become pale and distorted as he shook his fists uncontrollably—I could hardly stand to look at him. I finally resolved to separate from him.[27]

Takamure's crisis took on new dimensions precipitated by the physical violence against her. She acknowledges that although she did not yet know what she was destined for, something was pulling her toward the "contemplative" life, the life of a writer or an intellectual. This urge was not likely to mesh smoothly with K's need for a "service wife" to cater to his needs. The slow, psychological abuse had taken its toll, but she survived. However, physical abuse was not something she was willing to endure. So she left him the following note and boarded a train to return to her home.

I am afraid of time; I am afraid of space. Hour after hour, I could no longer even imagine what space is. Good-bye. Your little bird is flying away. Please throw out all the belongings I am leaving behind. I am sad. I love you.[28]

Her pain, confusion and disorientation were profound. So, too, was the fear of losing something vital inside herself, of giving up the very core of her identity. Such feelings come through strongly in these passages, as does the depth of her psychological trauma. Her life is riddled by both pain and paradox as she attempts to create as a writer while functioning as a wife. Along with her sense of self, even her sense of space and time are disrupted. As readers, we feel her tottering, about to fall into a frightening abyss. But in the end, she rights herself, at least temporarily, regaining her balance and actually experiencing an "emotional revolution" (kanjō kakumei) that sparked an outpouring of poetry. She states, "Looking back on it, I underwent an emotional revolution, which gave birth for the first time to the poet in me."

Once Takamure became a successful writer, though, the friction with her husband, to whom she had returned, only grew more intense. She was publishing poetry and articles. She had deadlines to meet and was earning manuscript fees. But her husband enjoyed inviting his friends over to drink, and he expected his wife to help with the entertainment chores. Caught in a classic version of the double bind, Takamure resents the demands placed on her time and energies but feels it is wrong for her to protest. She reproduces in her text diary-like entries from 1924 that function as a powerful reminder of the multilayeredness of her text and of the contradictions and tensions at work in it. She records as follows.

Oct. 19

Today's reflection: I am lazy. If I remain idle, the housework piles up. Today I feel languid and sleepy; my brain is addled. I have a stomachache.

Oct. 30

Today's reflection: my mind is twisted, my behavior is wretched. I have become the prisoner of some wicked demon. You wicked demon! Throw me away, I am weak.

I am poised at the summit of my pain.

Nov. 25

Today's reflection: I disturbed my husband. He said we are strangers. He also told me to get out again *(mata ie o dete-ike to mo itta)*. He also hit me again until Kida-san stopped him. I wonder where I can go? Tonight I need to work on my essay, "She Who Gives Birth to Poems," and I should work on my novel but it isn't going well.

Dec. 6

My husband told me to get out. Tolstoy refers to marriage as a vice that women are burdened with. I do not have a single redeeming feature. My existence is a complete minus *(watashi no sonzai wa mainasu da)*. Is it a crime to stay with my husband any longer?

1. I am not lazy but neither am I quick or clever.
2. I cannot fit in with his friends.
3. I am lacking in talent.
4. I can write novels, but they do not sell. I can write essays, but they do not sell either. A spring no longer wells up in my head.
5. I am shy and I hate going out. Therefore, it never works out when I have to run errands for his friends.
6. I am becoming ugly.

Sometime next spring I will leave. Until then, I will put all my energies into looking after my husband and his friends. I am amazed at the strength of the temptation that I might become the kind of person who can successfully take good care of him and have my career too. However, in the end it is the best thing for both of us if I leave.

When all is said and done, my husband needs someone who is not like me for a wife. It's just a repetition of what we went through before, but it is the way I feel.[29]

Takamure clearly experiences the painful paradox of being pulled in too many different directions at once; she must also confront the reality that her subjectivity is the product of multiple, conflicting discourses. The emotions she records in her diary at that time reveal the depth of her pain, as well as the feelings of inadequacy and self-loathing brought on by the double bind in which she finds herself. She portrays herself as twisted, contorted, warped, and divided against herself. And yet she experiences the seductive power of the urge to try and do it all, to take care of K *and* pursue her own writing. We can hear in her words, then, the voice of a woman whose self-esteem is eroding and whose creative powers are waning before her very eyes. She even feels her beauty ebbing. She is on the verge of complete erasure but summons up the courage to contest her fate and confront the oppression she faces at the source. She leaves again and this time refuses to return until her husband agrees to change his ways. He does, and they undergo a virtual role reversal whereby K took care of the house and home while Takamure devoted herself to her research and writing. To depict this kind of struggle openly in her autobiography is undoubtedly to become fierce with reality.

As I continued to read autobiographies by Japanese women, however, I did not always find the same degree of intensity and fierceness that I had discovered in Fukuda's and Takamure's texts. This was puzzling because, by all rights, I knew it should have been there. But, as often as not, autobiographers like Oku Mumeo, Takai Toshio, Nishi Kiyoko, Sata Ineko, and Fukunaga Misao were able to write matter-of-factly, or even obliquely, about events that should have elicited the same kind of passion found in Fukuda's and Takamure's texts. What I have come to appreciate over the years, however, is that while fierceness may actually be present, it is often masked, muted, or buried beneath the surface of the text. Because of autobiographical conventions and cultural paradigms that relegate women writers to the margins of discourse, the language of contemporary Japanese women's autobiographies is self-effacing and reticent. But beneath that placid surface, tensions, anger, and conflicts do exist. No doubt I was expecting Japanese women's autobiographies to embrace feminism more aggressively, or perhaps to rage more openly against the patriarchy. What I encountered, however, were these evenhanded, self-effacing narratives that succeed in driving their points home but not necessarily with the fierceness that I was anticipating.

At this juncture, I found it useful to recall Rita Felski's assertion that when considering feminist texts, it is important "to encompass all those texts that reveal a critical awareness of women's subordinate position and of gender as a problematic category, however this is expressed."[30] If we incorporate in our assessment the degree to which the texts in this study are concerned with women's subordinate position and their willingness to problematize the question of gender, then we can readily appreciate how a certain "fierceness with reality"—subtle and understated though it may be—may indeed be uncovered through careful reading. Felski makes another important argument about female self-writing when she points out that the act of offering up experiences with which women readers can identify helps forge a sense of community among women writers and readers, something she calls a "feminist counter-public sphere." Drawing in part on Habermas' notion of the "bourgeois public sphere," Felski describes "the historical emergence of an influential oppositional ideology which seeks to challenge the existing reality of gender subordination."[31] A principal argument of this book is that the "emergence of an influential oppositional ideology" certainly did occur in Japan during the 1920s. Although it was still in its infancy when Fukuda wrote in 1904, both she, and later Takamure, were present at its birth and helped to shape it. Moreover, they did so fully conscious that their subject positions and their arguments were often conflicted and contradictory. The women whose narratives comprise *Telling Lives* inherited this legacy. Although, as we shall see, their stories are often filled with paradox and contradiction too, it is fair to say that they share with their predecessors the aim of telling their own stories, in their own voices, as directly and as compellingly as possible.

1

Producing Writing Subjects: Women in the Interwar Years

> Primary among the ideological intentions inherent in forms and language, then, is the desire of culture to name and to sustain the difference of man's and woman's subjectivity and, by implication, man's and woman's self-representational possibilities. Thus woman has remained culturally silenced, denied authority, most critically the authority to name herself and her own desires. Woman has remained unrepresented and unrepresentable.
>
> —Sidonie Smith, *The Poetics of Women's Autobiography*

> [E]ven in the narrowest and most ambivalent sense, writing an autobiography can be a political act because it asserts a right to speak rather than be spoken for.
>
> —Leigh Gilmore, *Autobiographics: A Feminist Theory of Women's Self-Representation*

Telling Lives is a study of five Japanese women who wrote and published their autobiographies in the late twentieth century. Although these women were born toward the end of the Meiji period and came of age during the years around World War I, they did not record their lives until the 1980s, after the second wave of Japanese feminism—often referred to as the women's liberation movement—had stimulated a sustained interest in women's narratives. Oku Mumeo, a cofounder of the New Women's Association, was born in 1895; she published *Fires Burning Brightly (Nobi aka aka to)*, her account of her years as an activist in the women's movement, in 1988. Takai Toshio, the common-law widow of Hosoi Wakizō, was born in 1902; she published *My Own Sad History of Female Textile Workers (Watashi no Jokō aishi)*, the story of her relationship with Hosoi and her engagement with the labor movement, in 1982. In the same year, Fukunaga Misao, born in 1907, published *Recollections of a Female Communist (Aru onna no kyōsanshugisha no kaisō)*, her account of her life as a young, female

Marxist in the 1920s. Sata Ineko, the proletarian fiction writer, was born in 1904; she published her *Between the Lines of My Personal Chronology (Nen 'pu no gyōkan)* in 1983, a text that recounts her participation in a small circle of proletarian writers and artists in 1926; her marriage to one of the group members, Kubokawa Tsurujirō; and her emergence as a proletarian novelist. Finally, Nishi Kiyoko, who was born in 1907 and who worked as a journalist for Ishibashi Tanzan's *The Oriental Economist* in the 1930s, published her *Reminiscences (Tsuioku)* in 1988. Very much "new women" in Barbara Sato's sense of the term—that is, women who "transgressed social boundaries and questioned [their] dependence on men" and "started to pose a threat to gender relations"—these women conceived of themselves as feminist subjects and constructed their autobiographical narratives accordingly.[1]

Telling Lives develops four general lines of argument about female self-writing in modern Japan. The first may be stated simply but has profound implications: these narratives illustrate how important a variable gender had become in Japan's historical development and what a disruptive force it could be.[2] In their concern for women's political rights, for economic independence, for women's health and reproductive rights, and in their desire to transcend the narrow limitations of the "good wife, wise mother" morality imposed by the state, these autobiographies support the contention that not only were women being redefined as new gendered subjects during the 1920s and 1930s, but they were also active participants in a wide variety of discourses that, when taken together, constitute a substantive oppositional ideology.

A great deal of insight into the important changes taking place in the everyday lives of Japanese women in the 1920s can be found in Sato's book, *The New Japanese Woman: Modernity, Media and Women in Interwar Japan*. She focuses specifically on the emergence of new women's journals and the appearance of three new types of urban women whose images dominate the era: the modern girl, the housewife, and the professional working woman.[3] But she concludes her book on a somewhat somber note: these new middle-class women, though harbingers of social change, were not able themselves to do much about reforming society. Sato does not necessarily see women from the interwar years as expressing a substantive oppositional ideology. She quotes approvingly from a 1928 article by Yamakawa Kikue, who complained that the "new women" were missing the point. They were exalting the personal over the political and were doing nothing to establish their own economic independence.

Young women today put a high value on love marriages. But they are interested only in personal issues and have no social perspective, never demanding economic independence or trying to become independent beings in their own right. If they attempt to change the traditional relationships that exist between husbands, wives, and families by merely adding the element of romantic love to it, and not reforming the economic structure of society, then the changes that occur will be cosmetic change.[4]

While the women whose narratives make up this volume certainly reinforce Sato's research on the new types of women visible in the interwar period, we do not find in their autobiographies evidence of a reluctance to embrace radical change as Sato contends.[5] While marrying someone of their own choosing was important to them, the women examined in *Telling Lives* did, in fact, join movements and organizations that were seeking to transform society. Moreover, they were willing to fight in order to establish their political and economic independence. They were exposed to feminist critiques of bourgeois marriage, and they may well have read Kuriyagawa Hakuson's theories about love matches *(ren'ai)*. But they wrote very little about their desire to marry for love, nor did they make it a central issue in their narratives.

The second line of argument draws upon Joan W. Scott's contention that feminists and activists are best treated as "sites—historical locations or markers—where crucial political and cultural contests are enacted."[6] In order to fully appreciate the lives and the contributions of feminists, the argument goes, it is not necessary to insist that they were successful in transforming their society in substantial ways. Rather than viewing them as "exemplary heroines," we are better off thinking of them as "sites" or "historical markers" where numerous conflicts and issues intersect. Women like Oku Mumeo, Takai Toshio, Nishi Kiyoko, Sata Ineko, and Fukunaga Misao all recorded experiences in their texts that strongly suggest they were operating in precisely this kind of location where "political and cultural contests" were "enacted."

The third line of argument suggested by this study is that our understanding of how Japanese women began to think and act in new ways during the interwar years—how they developed their own sense of historical agency—can be enhanced by reading Japanese women's autobiographies. Self-reflexive texts intrigue us because they provide powerful insights into how people in different times and places lived their lives and understood the world around them, something that Wilhelm

Dilthey, the grandfather of modern autobiography criticism, clearly recognized.[7] They can also have much to say about historical subjects who
have been silenced, "denied authority," and considered "unrepresent-
able," to use the language of Sidonie Smith's epigraph. But individual life
experiences, even when told in the voices of the people who lived these
experiences, do not necessarily reveal all we may wish to know about historical agency in a given era. As Scott points out, if one is to understand
the emergence of a feminist subject, one must be aware "of the discursive
processes—the epistemologies, institutions and practices—that produce
political subjects, that make agency (in this case, the agency of feminists)
possible even when it is forbidden or denied."[8] To examine women's
lives as recounted in their autobiographies and memoirs is one way to
become informed about the "discursive processes" by which Japanese
women developed both the vocabulary and the consciousness to think
and write about the inequities, the subordination, and the oppression
that they experienced in their lives.[9]

Finally, the fourth line of argument developed by *Telling Lives* is that
female self-writing not only challenges, but often subverts the dominant
discourse. As noted in the introduction, when women write their lives, a
tension seems to arise naturally between their assertion of female subjectivity and the regime of social and political controls that regulate and
define them, which is why there must inevitably be "a sense of contestation and risk" when women embark on the autobiographical project.[10]
When women make their stories—and their "selves"—public, they are
trespassing on a realm traditionally reserved for males, and this entails
significant risk. As Gilmore observes, after quoting from both Virginia
Woolf and Hélène Cixous,

> In the context of these important feminist insights, we could argue that first-
> person, nonfictional narrative offers voice to historically silenced and mar-
> ginalized persons who penetrate the labyrinths of history and language to
> possess, often by stealth, theft, or what they perceive as trespass, the engen-
> dering matrix of textual selfhood: the autobiographical *I*.[11]

She hastens to add that this trespass "does not necessarily denote the liberation of a female speaking subject," but it does require us "to be attentive
to the cultural specificities of self-representational experimentation by
women."[12] Therefore, attending to the "cultural specificities" of Japanese
women's self-representational narratives will be a primary aim of this

book. For example, the tendency for narrators to be oblique and self-effacing when telling their stories may be something culturally specific to Japan. Likewise, the prominence in these texts of tensions, distortions, and
contradictions as the narrators go about the task of recapturing their lived
experiences is something to which readers must be sensitive. In fact, "paradox, contradiction, and ambiguity" may be the dominant impression that
we receive from the life stories of socially and politically active women, so
we would do well to keep this fact in mind as we read the texts excerpted
below.[13]

One may begin an inquiry about women's self-writing with a simple
question: who writes autobiographies and why? "Every life" may indeed
have "a story," but not everyone chooses to *tell* their life story, or to *record*
it for posterity.[14] The women whose autobiographies are examined in
this volume did so, and their motivation for writing their lives was as diverse as the women themselves.[15] Most were engaged in some form of social activism. They were feminists, political activists, labor organizers,
socialists, communists, journalists, and proletarian fiction writers. Therefore, at various points in their lives, all of these women experienced at
least some part of their life being enacted in the public sphere. Of course,
many questions attend to this kind of inquiry. For example, what does it
mean for Japanese women to recount their life stories in a narrative form
that emerged from a European culture that placed great value on individualism, rationalism, and empiricism? Do their stories conform well to
such a narrative form? How do they adapt to a narrative form that was
designed and developed in order to tell men's stories?

Helen Bruss makes an intriguing point when she raises questions
about whether new historicist Stephen Greenblatt's notion of trying "to
speak with the dead"—to hold conversations with people from the past
through "the textual traces" they leave behind—is really such an appropriate place for feminist scholars to launch their inquiries because, as she puts
it, "We hardly know who our dead are: what could they possibly say that
was not conditioned and structured by their place inside the gender system
that silenced them or allowed them to speak only in the limited and oppressive public scripts allowed to women?"[16] Clearly, more work will need
to be done in order to bring the voices and the texts of Japanese women to
light so that we can come to better understand "who the dead are," so to
speak. But it does not necessarily follow that all utterances conditioned by
the existing gender system are of no interest, for they can reveal much
about the assumptions underlying that system as well as illuminate the

ways in which utterances recorded for posterity may challenge the limitations of prevailing ideologies and discourses. Language, after all, does not
consist only of "literal utterances"; it also must be thought of "as a pattern
of meanings that takes an active part in constituting the objects it talks
about and the subjects that embody it."[17]

It is fair to say, in answer to the question "Who writes autobiography
and why?" that certain shared assumptions have prevailed among readers
over the years as to whose life merits telling. It tends to be people who
have done something significant with their lives, made something of
themselves, or otherwise left their mark on the world. In effect, this
means that autobiographies have most frequently been the stories of
men. It was not that women did not *do* things, nor is it the case that they
did not write the stories of their lives. As Valerie Sanders notes in her
study of Victorian women's autobiographies, *Records of Girlhood*, "One of
the paradoxes of nineteenth-century literary history is that whatever was
said publicly about autobiography being inappropriate for women,
women themselves were busy writing it."[18] An important difference was,
however, that their stories did not always circulate widely, and their textual voices were often muted or erased entirely.

Self-writing is always a complex and multifaceted affair, but it is rendered all the more so when the writing subjects are feminists. The texts
examined in *Telling Lives* are capable of revealing much about the
authors' family backgrounds, their education, and their relationship to
their work and to society. They also discuss how the narrator perceives
herself in relation to history and to the world around her as well. But this
does not mean that we always get what we expect from autobiographical
narratives. Just as we might find chaos and contradiction in the place of
order and coherence, in lieu of triumphs and successes we may find accounts of failure and disappointment. This is why Scott cautions us
against placing too much weight on how successful individual women,
or women's groups, may have been in effecting change, for, as she puts it,
"the history of feminism is not the history of available options or the un-
constrained choice of a winning plan."[19] Rather, the history of feminism
may be construed as "the history of women (and some men) grappling
repeatedly with the radical difficulty of resolving the dilemmas they confronted (however successful they were in achieving specific reforms)."[20]
Therefore, readers should appreciate that the underlying issue may not be
whether the efforts of the Japanese women whose stories constitute *Telling Lives* were successful, but whether they demonstrated the courage and

the willingness to accept the risks involved in "grappling" with the important issues of their day.

Since self-representational narratives are bound to embody the dominant social and cultural assumptions about speaking, writing, and acting in the world, inevitably, *Telling Lives* must also be about how autobiography and memoirs have operated as a discourse in twentieth-century Japan. The subject of Japanese autobiography is an intriguing one because some would have it that the whole notion of the self is absent in Japan, while at the same time it is arguable that Japan has a long history of women recording their thoughts and their memories for dissemination. While it is almost a given in Europe and America that when women write their lives they must speak from the margins of discourse, does this hold equally true for Japan, where forms of female self-writing have occupied a privileged position in the canon of classical literature?

This is not an easy question to answer. To be sure, when twentieth-century female autobiographers write their lives, they do not do so in complete isolation from their illustrious foremothers. No educated person in Taishō or Shōwa Japan was unfamiliar with the writings of Michitsuna's mother, Sei Shonagon, or Murasaki Shikibu. Paul Schalow and Janet Walker note in *The Woman's Hand* that "in Japanese women writers' confident ownership of a 'woman's language,' their discursive experience most diverges from that of non-Japanese women writers."[21] No one would question that this legacy was a powerful enabling force in Japanese women's self-writing. But one of the most striking features of Japan's economic and social transformation during the interwar period is the way in which "the new was constantly buffeting against the old," to borrow Harry Harootunian's phrase.[22] Part of what constituted the "new" in this instance was the intrusion of Western conceptions of how to assess and assign meaning to individual life experiences. In the same way that many other manifestations of the "new" in Japanese life during the interwar years did not replace older ways of conducting business or organizing economic activity, Western conceptions of self-writing were at no point adopted wholesale to the exclusion of indigenous ones. But they definitely made their mark.

Beginning with the early Meiji years, readers had been interested in the lives of noteworthy individuals, be it Napoleon, George Washington, Louis Pasteur, or Madame Curie. Since, as Saeki Shōichi argues, autobiography—in the form of diaries by women of the court—preceded biography in Japan, and since these diaries had always been accepted as literature from the very outset, it was biography that became part of the new.[23] So, how a life was narrated in modern autobiography came to be influenced as much by this interest in biographical narrative as it was by such texts as *The Gossamer Years (Kagerō nikki)* and *Lady Murasaki's Diary (Murasaki shikibu nikki)*. Twentieth-century autobiographers did not aim for a timeless, poetic beauty so much as they strived for an accurate, linear portrayal of a life unfolding.

But this is not to say that the spirits of Heian women writers did not hover above the pens and writing brushes of modern women when they wrote. As Lynne Miyake points out, a text like *The Gossamer Years* (in contrast to *The Tosa Diary [Tosa nikki]* authored by a male, Ki-no-Tsurayuki), details an intense personal journey, a private, internal discourse in which the female voice is located at the center of experience.[24] This deeply rooted legacy clearly offers modern Japanese women a kind of permission to explore their lives and their perceptions that must be accounted for. Yet during the long interregnum between the Heian period and modern times—when women's narrative voice was all but silenced—that legacy, and that permission, was very deeply buried. Recently, Terry Kawashima has described how one of the towering Heian literary figures, Ono-no-Komachi—"who stands for female sexuality and literary power"—was systematically marginalized during the early medieval period because, as Kawashima expresses it, her "uncontrollable power to attract was precisely what had to be domesticated in both the Buddhist and patriarchal paradigms."[25] Under the influence of Buddhism and the patriarchal familial system favored by the warrior class, the economic and social position of women gradually deteriorated between 1200 and 1600. After two and a half centuries of Tokugawa rule, during which neo-Confucian orthodoxy limited women's roles to that of wife and mother, women were thoroughly identified with the "interior" *(oku)* of the households to which they were relegated.

The Meiji Restoration ushered in an initial period of political change and wide dissemination of information about conditions in other countries around the world, which, in turn, stimulated a new discourse about the position of women in society. To be sure, women writers in the Meiji era knew all about the legacy of their illustrious predecessors of the tenth and eleventh centuries. But as Rebecca Copeland's study of Meiji women writers reveals, this legacy was not an uncomplicated one. Shimizu Shikin might voice her appeal in 1890, "Where is the Modern Murasaki? Where [is] the Meiji Shōnagon? Eagerly I await your appearance. Nay, even more

than I, our very society longs for your arrival."[26] Yet she and others understood that with the names of these illustrious foremothers came considerable baggage. Copeland elaborates,

> First, when women began to emerge as writers in the modern period after
> "centuries of silence," there was already a concept of what was good and
> proper for writing women. This concept distinguished the critical evaluation
> of their works from that of their male counterparts. And second, this concept
> of women's writing was directly related to characteristics that had distin-
> guished writing by women in earlier centuries. But whereas the women writers
> of the tenth and eleventh centuries were acknowledged as superior writers,
> they were also confined to a tradition that made them inaccessible or inappro-
> priate to a modern literature. Women's writing of the earlier era was limited by
> its elegance. It was too "effeminate"—too interested in its own subjectivity to
> engage the broad concerns of a modern society. Meiji women who wrote "like
> women," therefore, removed themselves from any engagement with issues of
> modernity. They faced a dilemma. If they attempted to move beyond the pa-
> rameters of women's writing, they were rebuked for imitating men. If they
> conformed to those parameters, they were ignored for being feminine and
> thereby insignificant.[27]

If the model of elegant prose from the past was too limiting, too
confining, if it prevented women from engaging the issues associated with
becoming modern, then it is not difficult to see why twentieth-century
women autobiographers in Japan did not evoke the names of Murasaki
and Sei Shōnagon when they wrote their lives. They were more likely, as
Fukuda Hideko did, to invoke the name of Benjamin Franklin. By the
1890s there were a great many issues for women authors to address. There
had been a return to conservative, neo-Confucian values that emphasized
the "good wife, wise mother" (ryōsai-kenbo) philosophy, and women's political and social roles were being increasingly narrowly defined. Moreover,
as we shall see below, the 1920s gave rise to new social and economic conditions that generated a sustained concern with gender issues and
women's rights. How were women to break free from the constraints that
would keep them in little "boxes" and deny them their economic and social independence?[28] This was one of the paramount concerns shaping the
lives (and the autobiographical texts) of women like Oku Mumeo, Takai
Toshio, Sata Ineko, Nishi Kiyoko, and Fukunaga Misao, so it should hardly
come as a surprise that when they conceived of themselves as writing

subjects, they made virtually no reference to their Heian foremothers. True, while in prison, Fukunaga Misao did find herself drawn into the world of the *Tale of Genji (Genji monogatari)* and would eventually publish a book of feminist criticism on the *Genji*. However, she was also equally drawn to the writings of historian Tsuda Sōkichi, a reflection of her more urgent concern to grapple with the problems and the sources of paradox that were confronting her daily in the world in which she lived. In particular, Tsuda's work appealed to Fukunaga because she was a Marxist and he was virtually alone among scholars who confronted directly the historical origins of the emperor system, something with which Fukunaga believed that any Marxist worthy of the appellation needed to come to terms.

The women examined in *Telling Lives* were not blind to their literary heritage, but nor were they willing to be confined by it. Surely they knew that women before them had turned their gaze inward and explored the deepest recesses of their own hearts and minds; but the new times called for a new kind of narrative voice, one that could grapple more effectively with the political and social problems that women were facing. In order to better understand the context for this new narrative voice, and the discursive space in which it was situated, it is important to examine the nature of the interwar years in Japan.

Japan in the 1920s and 1930s

The interwar years were tumultuous times for Japan. World War I had sharply stimulated Japanese economic growth, bringing about Japan's so-called "second industrial revolution." New factories producing chemicals, fertilizer, machine tools, and electrical goods were constructed virtually overnight. They featured the latest technologies and were driven by new sources of power. Prior to World War I, the overwhelming majority of factory workers had been employed in light industry, primarily textiles, and they were predominantly female. After the war, most of the new workers were male and were employed in large steel and machine production factories. The growth in the size and number of factories contributed to a substantial increase in the number of labor unions, as well as an increase in the frequency and duration of incidents of labor unrest. For example, the number of strikes and labor incidents grew from a mere fifty in 1914 to well over two thousand in 1919. Since the wartime gains were unevenly distributed, the militancy of the Japanese labor movement also grew during the 1920s as radical ideologies associated with Marxism-Leninism spread rapidly among union organizers. Andrew Gordon points out how the character of these labor disputes was changing as well.

> In the years after World War I, three previously separate streams of action, which had begun to overlap during the war, converged in the worker's movement. Radical intellectuals inspired by the revolution in Russia, moderate Yūaikai reformers of both working-class and intellectual background, and impatient workplace activists began to work together. The lines between these groups were sometimes blurred, and their alliance was sometimes tense. But their efforts produced one of the most turbulent periods of working-class conflict in Japanese history.[29]

The Yūaikai, once the "friendly society," was reorganized as the Greater Japan Federation of Labor, or Sōdōmei for short, and began to reflect more radical ideologies. In the years after World War I, as Gordon notes, a "dispute culture" emerged among the working classes in the urban areas that at times offered a radical critique not only of working conditions, but of the economy, the society, and the polity as well.[30] As another historian notes,

> As a result of the war and the shift to a new productive register, Japan was transformed into an industrial power equal to most European nations like France, England, and even Germany, according to the leading indices, ahead of societies like Italy and the Soviet Union but trailing the United States.[31]

Historians estimate that between 1913 and 1938 Japan was growing more than twice as fast as Germany, three and a half times as fast as the United States, and five and a half times as fast as the United Kingdom.[32] Urban populations swelled as both men and women left the countryside in search of education and employment opportunities in the cities. World War I had been especially significant in accelerating this rural-urban shift. Both men and women were attracted to the new or better opportunities generated by the wartime economic boom. In the late 1920s, Japan had two major urban concentrations: Tokyo-Yokohama, with a population of over two and a half million, and the Kobe-Osaka-Kyoto complex, with a population of nearly four million.

One of the significant harbingers of modernism in Japan was the Rice Riots of 1918. Reacting to rapidly spiraling rice prices brought on by wartime inflation, a group of housewives in Toyama began a revolt that evolved into a series of urban riots on a scale heretofore unknown in Japan. The central government dispatched over one hundred thousand troops to 140 different locations throughout Japan to quell the riots.[33] One effect of the riots was to convince remaining genrō Yamagata Aritomo that Hara Kei, a party man without ties to the aristocracy or the elder statesmen, was the best choice to form the next cabinet. This move created the impression that the post–World War I period would be the age of democratic politics and routinized party government. With the spread of urbanism, the growth of party government, and, later, the extension of the franchise, the advent of mass politics was a reality. Once strikes, labor agitation, riots, and political violence became a regular part of Japanese life, it is fair to say that "the modern" had arrived in Japan.

As new bourgeois and proletarian cultures emerged in the cities, Japan was experiencing an age of changing tastes and fashions, a time when both women's hair and their skirts were becoming shorter. As Kano Masanao notes, this was an age in which the traditionally sedentary culture for women was becoming a more active one.[34] The rapid spread of modern amenities like the telephone, cinema, radio, private railway lines, department stores, and cafés all spoke to the emergence of a new, urban denizen with increased income to spend on leisure pursuits. Elise Tipton and John Clark note in their introduction to *Being Modern in Japan* that "by the mid-1920s 'modanizumu' became the catchword of the times. 'Modan' this and 'modan' that repeatedly cropped up in the titles of newspaper and magazine articles and advertisements of the period."[35] A new emphasis on "cultural living" *(bunka seikatsu)* also defined the age. Jordan Sand notes how the appearance in 1922 of "Culture village," consisting of fourteen model houses in Ueno Park, marked the beginning of the "culture boom" in the Taishō period.[36] There was a fascination not only with the material and cultural basis of life, but also with how artifacts rooted in Western modernism were making inroads into domestic institutions and practices.

Many of these changes had a significant impact on women's lives. "The marks of this new culture," Harootunian writes, "were Western clothing, cosmetics, and the beauty salon." He continues,

> What the rationalization of household life required, as a concretization of "cultural living," was a change of the position of women in the household political economy. It not only announced the end of the seclusion and isolation women had experienced as virtual prisoners of the household, it had consequences for their status outside of family life, as larger numbers began

pouring into the labor force, especially in those areas like learning, education and sports that had been male preserves. . . . In the process of assuming responsibility for reorganizing everyday life according to new standards of efficiency and economics, women acquired a new sense of subjectivity (when before it had been exceedingly weak) that took them outside of the household to become principal actors in the drama of modernity.[37]

The 1920s, then, were very much the era of the "new woman" as women emerged in multiple locations, busily constructing their own subjectivity. As Yukiko Tanaka emphasizes,

Unlike their European counterparts, Japanese women did not enter the labor market while their boyfriends and husbands were away in the battlefield, but their numbers steadily increased as new jobs and occupations were created. While general economic hardship was the primary reason for the increase in the number of working women, many took employment to gain a sense of independence or to avoid boredom.[38]

Oku Mumeo, one of the autobiographers examined in this volume, wrote, "There can be no question that the number and variety of working women has grown dramatically in recent years. What with teachers, typists, office workers, operators, nurses, a working woman is no longer an unusual sight."[39] They were simply part of the landscape.

There were a number of other forces shaping the era. In E. Taylor Atkins' book on the history of jazz in Japan, the 1920s are portrayed as the era in which American ideas and popular culture replaced European influences: "Syncopated dance music, automobiles, professional sports, and movies from America served as quintessential symbols of modernism, and as the primary conveyers of modernist images and ideals, they shaped Japanese conceptions of modern lifestyles."[40] If, in the West, modernism was the logical outcome of history, what was it in Japan? The new technologies available to Japanese in the 1920s—radio, film, mass circulation print, and other media—ensured that both the ideas and the images associated with modernity would be widely diffused, and there is plenty of evidence that people were reflective about what they were experiencing. Kano points out that much of the spirit of the new age was captured in the title of Yamamoto Sanehiko's new journal, *Kaizō* (Reconstruction), inaugurated in April 1919.[41] Some twenty figures were singled out in the first issue as individuals whose ideas were giving shape to the era. They included, among

others, Marx, Kropotkin, Lenin, H. G. Wells, Edward Carpenter, William
Morris, Ellen Key, Gandhi, and Henri Barbusse. Reconstruction also became the watchword of the day after the horrors of the September 1, 1923,
Great Kantō Earthquake. The rebuilding of the city saw the growth of new
railway hubs like Shinjuku and Shibuya, where department stores, cinemas, cafés, dance halls, bars, and restaurants grew up overnight. The Ginza
truly came into its own at this time, as some dubbed the post-earthquake
years the "Ginza era."[42] This era was also known as the era of *"ero-guro-
nansensu"* (referring to the erotic, the grotesque, and the nonsensical)
when the new, urban middle class pursued its hedonistic pleasures. It was
the era of the *modan boi* (modern boy) and the *modan gāru* (modern girl),
or the *"mobo"* and *"moga,"* respectively. As Atkins notes,

> As icons of the era, the *moga* and *mobo* represented not only the rebellious atti-
> tudes of many well-off urban youth, but also the fears of the guardians of tra-
> ditional culture and morality. The *moga* especially was castigated in the media
> as a "glittering, decadent, middle-class consumer who, through her clothing,
> smoking, and drinking, flaunts tradition in the urban playgrounds of the late
> 1920s."[43]

Flapper styles and provocative behavior were the order of the day.
Sato also finds the bobbed-haired, short-skirted modern girl to be a powerful icon during the interwar period. The "modern girl," she notes,
"made no verbal pronouncements about her position in urban culture.
Hers was a voiceless existence surrounded by ambivalence—the ambivalence of class and occupation, ambivalence presented and represented
through the media."[44] She elaborates,

> What made the modern girl such a powerful symbol was not that she repre-
> sented a small percentage of "real women," but that she represented the possi-
> bilities for what all women could become. She also symbolized consumption
> and mass culture, phenomena identified with women after the Great War.[45]

If the first generation of feminists had sought liberation in the context
of intellectual and literary expression, young women of the 1920s were
simply interested in expressing themselves and experiencing an atmosphere of spontaneous enjoyment of a life not constrained by social conventions and traditional morality.[46] Were the interwar years merely a
period of escapism, when young people turned their back on the world of

political affairs in favor of the pursuit of pleasure and self-expression? The answer might depend on where one looked, because it was also the era of an emerging proletarian arts and culture movement that sought to redefine arts and letters in a way that reflected the concerns of the masses. The *moga* and *mobo* were more about sensual pleasures than they were about social revolution. But that does not alter the fact that they were part of a significant reorientation of cultural values, one that was anathema to cultural conservatives and rightists in general. Most important, they signified a new way of thinking about women. With the increase in journals and other publications targeted at women, the once moderate and largely middle-class "new woman" began to give way to a more radicalized, activist female.

Although the texts examined in this volume were not written and published until the 1980s, their primary focus is these volatile interwar years, and as texts, they bear the imprint of the age in which they are so firmly rooted. We find in the pages of these texts the stories of women who worked in factories, who waitressed in cafés, who engaged in radical politics, and who worked for modern journals. There is another characteristic of these texts worth mentioning in passing: they are all self-identified as autobiographies or memoirs. That is, their titles include such terms as *"jiden," "kaisō," "jijōden,"* or *"jibunshi"*; moreover, they are all first-person narratives with authorial names on the title page that claim to be identical to that of the narrator, something Philippe Lejeune takes to be evidence of an "autobiographical pact."[47] The narratives examined in this volume describe early childhood and education in elementary and later "girls'" schools, followed by departure from home in order to seek employment or further education. Since most of the women whose self-representational narratives are included in this volume dedicated at least some portion of their lives to ending the social, economic, and political subordination of women, when they tell their lives, at least part of the story that unfolds is one of meeting other women, discussing what courses of action should be followed, and creating networks and viable organizations in order to work on behalf of women's issues.

Therefore, the impulse for many of the women to write their lives comes directly out of their engagement with the women's movement or with their professional careers, not from being sequestered away in a private world of domesticity. Many of the narrators, however, do discuss some aspect of their mother's life that they did not wish to see incorporated in their own. One may also find references in these texts to common books that were influential to the narrators, as well as attendance at the same public lectures or political rallies. In some cases, the women actually encountered one another, or had mutual friends. Even if their paths did not cross directly, there are sufficient points of reference in common to argue that they were sharing the same literal as well as discursive space.

I believe that asking a wide range of questions about a set of self-referential texts written by Japanese women is both an interesting and timely exercise. As the works of Saeki, Marilyn Miller, and Livia Monnet have shown, female self-writing has a long, distinguished tradition in Japan.[48] In fact, it may well be that Japanese women invented self-writing during the Heian era only to have the *nikki* form they pioneered appropriated by men, an occurrence that Western feminist critics like Stanton found fascinating.[49] But as noted above, the centuries following the Heian period imposed an increasingly ominous silence on women's voices until the nineteenth century. After the Meiji Restoration, Japanese women had to confront the double burden of Confucian patriarchal notions on the one hand, combined with the externally imposed patriarchy of the Western imperialistic discourse on the other. Under the Meiji Civil Code of 1898, the traditional *ie* system, along with the principle of primogeniture, was installed so that only males could be recognized as legal entities. Moreover, males alone could inherit property, and they were entitled to dispose of women's property freely.[50]

The New Women's Association (Shinfujinkai) was founded in 1920 in order to advocate for women's political rights. But before Japanese women could begin to organize and try to change the system, they needed a discursive framework in which the ideas and the vocabulary necessary to discuss political rights and freedoms could take root. The popular rights movement had taken the first steps to provide such a framework, but it had never allowed for very much participation by women. It took "unruly women" like Kishida Toshiko and Fukuda Hideko to boldly pioneer this discourse; and later on, it was the introduction of socialist and feminist writings from Russia, America, and Europe around the time of World War I that expanded the parameters of this discursive field.

The women whose stories comprise *Telling Lives* were deeply affected by these currents of change. If they were not directly involved in political movements, they experienced the new employment opportunities and the new roles available to women, and these experiences became part of their narratives. But regardless of where the impulse to record their lives originated, it is a fact that a substantial number of Japanese women began to do so in the 1970s and 1980s.[51] This may be taken, I would argue, as a clear indication that Japanese women feel strongly that they have stories to tell and that readers, especially other women, want to read these stories.[52] By carefully examining five of these autobiographical texts and allowing the voices of their narrators to be heard, certain contextual truths about female subjectivity in modern Japan will become apparent. By exploring the process of how female narrating subjects in Japan were initiated into the discourse on feminism and equality and how they constructed and were affected by the discourses in which they participated, *Telling Lives* will do its part to re-present these lives and give meaning to their experiences.

2

Politics Rooted in Everyday Life
Oku Mumeo's *Fires Burning Brightly (Nobi aka aka to)*

Oku Mumeo. Reproduced with permission from Domesu shuppan.

Oku Mumeo was an important activist in the 1920s who was elected to the House of Councilors in 1946, where she remained until she resigned in 1965. In 1948 she established the Japan Housewives Association (Shufu Rengōkai), the capstone of her life's work to forge a connection between politics and the kitchen. Yet her prewar experiences have been overshadowed by those of her more famous colleagues, Hiratsuka Raichō and Ichikawa Fusae. Born in Fukui, the daughter of a blacksmith, Oku entered Japan Women's University (Nihon Joshi Daigaku) in 1912. Active in the New Women's Association (Shinfujin Kyōkai) with Hiratsuka and Ichikawa, Oku later despaired of attempts at legal reform only and sought to reach women where they lived and worked by joining in consumer cooperative movements and eventually establishing women's "settlement houses" in the poorer neighborhoods of Japanese cities.

Most of the women whose autobiographies are examined in Telling Lives *are* not household names in Japan. Oku Mumeo might be the exception. As head of the Japan Housewives Association and member of the House of Councilors for almost twenty years, Oku's name and face were quite familiar in the postwar *period. Yet fewer people are aware that she was a cofounder in 1920 of the New Women's Association along with Hiratsuka Raichō and Ichikawa Fusae. The New Women's Association was inaugurated when Hiratsuka, the founding editor of Seitō, a women's literary journal begun in 1911, recruited Ichikawa, who was working as a reporter for a Nagoya newspaper, and Oku, a fellow graduate of Japan Women's University, to join her in establishing the association. The goals of the movement included revising Article 5 of the Public Peace Police Law—which denied women the right to participate in political activities— establishing a journal for the women's movement, and, eventually, promoting women's suffrage. Although there is not a great deal known about Oku's youth and her other prewar activities, Akiko Tokuza's recently published* The Rise of the Feminist Movement in Japan, *a political biography of Oku, does a great deal to rectify the situation and make the details of Oku's life and career available to English-language readers.*[1] *However, for her account of Oku's life, Tokuza draws most heavily on two of Oku's earlier autobiographical texts,* Dawn to Dusk (Akekure) *(1957) and "My Personal History" ("Wakakushi no rirekisho") (1958), while the excerpts I have translated below come from the more recent* Fires Burning Brightly: The Autobiography of Oku Mumeo *(Nobi aka aka to—Oku Mumeo jiden) (1988).*[2]

Oku Mumeo's story is interesting, in part, because of her centrality to the prewar women's movement. She recounts the early days of the New Women's Association, the campaign to revise Article 5, the last-minute betrayals, and the final accomplishment. But there is much more to her story than this. She also describes the contradictions, the rebelliousness, and the paradoxes that plagued her youth. What sort of educational path should she follow? What should she do after attending a women's college? Should she become a writer, a poet, or a teacher? What about the pull of social and economic issues of her day? What, indeed, of gender issues? More important, what would follow the attainment of the New Women's Association's initial goals? Oku realized that working with middle-class women to effect legislation at the national level held little meaning for the lives of ordinary women. How could she help these women improve the material conditions of their lives?

Oku's narrative reveals an interesting trajectory that propelled her to operate in ever widening and deepening circles of contact with women's lives. Her story is not a record of one successful accomplishment after another; nor should we expect her account to be without its contradictions and paradoxes. For it is precisely within these contradictions and paradoxes that we can discover the insights into women's lives and experiences that are worth knowing.

Blacksmith's Daughter

The house in which I was born was a little outside the Fukui city limits. In the fall, the Echizen plain, which surrounds the city, is a sea of waving, golden rice stalks as far as the eye can see. But in the winter, the homes are buried deeply in snow.

I was born in this environment on Oct. 24 in the 28th year of Meiji (1895). The name on the family register is Wada Umeo but my father did not use Chinese characters, electing to write Mumeo in katakana instead; so I always wrote it that way until I entered Japan Women's University. I changed it to hiragana in later years when I used it as my pen name.

I was the eldest daughter of a third-generation blacksmith. My father's name was Wada Jinzaburō, and my mother's name was Hama. For a blacksmith's family in those days, we were quite well off with a household that included up to three apprentices and a housekeeper. We also had farming implements, a cart and a loom. . . .

Mornings began early in our town. We could hear the sounds of the young women's geta as they trotted hurriedly past our home on the way to the textile factory. Wearing their scruffy cotton kimono and carrying their lunch boxes wrapped in wrapping cloth (furoshiki) by their sides, these young women would always call out "Good morning" to my father as he sat at his desk reading his newspaper. Since he always sat there reading his newspaper at that time of day, he was a familiar face, and he would always return each of their greetings individually.

I once asked my mother, who was in bed sick, "Mama, just what kind of work do these factory girls do who pass by our house every morning on their way to the factory?"

"They weave glossy silk [habutae]," she replied.

"What's weaving?"

"It's putting the silk thread into the looms."

"That sounds like fun! I want to go to the factory and try weaving."

"Absolutely not! That is something poor people do. I never want to hear you say that you want to become a factory girl again! I have never even set eyes on a factory loom."

What an unexpected rebuke from a mother who was usually very gentle. Why would she speak so harshly of the factory girls, I wondered. Why did she dislike weaving so much? These questions lingered deep in my heart for a long time. Later, when I turned my attention toward social problems, these questions always remained at the bottom of my heart. . . .

I also saw many people suffering from tuberculosis. In those days, the medicines that are available today were not around, so tuberculosis was a very frightening illness. People who died from it were quite numerous including my mother, our housekeeper and several women in the neighborhood. It is memories of people like this in my neighborhood who lived in dark, dank houses, breathing in the dust from their looms, and who died because of poor nutrition and a lack of good medicine, that motivated me later to become involved in the rural health movement. (9–12)

Childhood provided Oku with the opportunity to observe working conditions for women in various settings, something that would later shape important life choices that she made. The sharp rebuke by her mother is a disruption in the text, one that replaces a warmer or more natural family conversation. Seeing women die from tuberculosis, including her own mother, motivated her to challenge oppressive regimes that would deny women adequate health care. In the next section, Oku describes how her father was extremely strict with his wife, often causing her to weep inconsolably. He was probably unhappy, the narrator conjectures, because he never wanted to become a blacksmith. He loved reading and learning, and he instilled this love in his daughter.

My Father Disliked Being a Blacksmith

Our father's regret over his own inability to continue his studies was turned in time toward my brothers and sisters and me. Sometimes with a tear in his eye, my father would say to us: "I am going to see that you move forward to the next highest level of schooling, so you had better study hard!" He would tell us that not studying hard was a very serious offense. Pointing to his shelves filled with thick Japanese and Chinese books that he had all labeled and organized like in a library he would often say, "You all must read four or five times the number of books I have read. . . ."

Father was stubborn but he never once told me that I didn't have to study because I was a girl. In fact, he said, "There are women out there like Hani Motoko, Yoshioka Yayoi, and Mori Tsuneko who have made their mark on the world by their own efforts. They are people to be looked up to. In fact, you should learn from them." When the journal *Seitō* first appeared, it was my father who gave me my first copy. He went on to say, "Look, there are women like this in Tokyo who put out their own journal. If you are smart, you could become a writer, or, if you have the looks, you

could become an actress. Mumeo, if you were just a little bit more beautiful, I think you could become an actress." (12–14)

Life with her father, though, was often painful for Oku's mother. A beautiful
woman, much sought after, she had to endure a very circumscribed existence
with her husband. She bore seven children, and this sapped not only her beauty,
but her vitality as well. "How difficult it must have been for a sickly woman like
my mother to give birth seven times," Oku pondered.

It is not at all uncommon in Japanese women's autobiographies to encoun-
ter narrators who perceive their mothers as having sacrificed much and suffered
a great deal. In fact, almost all of the women considered in this study reflected
on the quality of their mothers' experience and decided that it was not sufficient
for them. They also concluded that the subordinate position of women in Japa-
nese society was a critical problem that needed to be addressed. Ever since the
appearance of Seitō *in 1911, there had been much talk of "the new woman" in*
Japan. This influence even penetrated down to the girls' school Oku began at-
tending in Fukui in 1908. Her narrative continues:

New Breath

Compared with primary school, the teachers at the girls' school were very
much in style *(haikaraa)*. For example, although I never took a class from
her, Ueno Nobuko, who was a critic for *Seitō,* had the reputation around
school as typifying the spirit of "the new woman." In class she apparently
would speak on occasion about the lifestyle of the new woman. I heard
that later on she married a military man who would eventually edit a se-
lection of her writings.

Our music teacher was also quite modern. We often sang the latest
western songs. Due to the encouragement of this teacher, for a while I
gave very serious thought to going on to music school. On the whole,
however, the atmosphere at the school was not really all that open as it
persisted in a feudalistic emphasis on a simple and regimented life.

Father was frugal about everything, but books were the one exception.
My brother and I could order all the books we wanted, and at the end of the
month, Father would pay the bill. Of course, we would buy lots of books
that he did not know about, but I think he was secretly pleased anyway.

It was my older brother who first told me about the appearance of the
journal *White Birch (Shirakaba).* We stayed up late at night reading poetry
by Kitahara Hakushū, Saitō Mokukichi, Yosano Akiko, Kuriyagawa Haku-

son, and others.[3] In those days, in our house, we would gather around the foot warmer *(kotatsu)* in winter to read. Beneath an oil lamp, and warmed by the foot warmer, my brother and I would put our heads together and lose ourselves in reading. While feeling the snow steadily piling up outside, we were entranced by the stirrings from a new world that was beginning to unfold.

My Mother's Death

Even though I was the oldest daughter, I virtually have no memories of a healthy mother hard at work. As soon as my youngest sister was born, my mother became bedridden with tuberculosis. . . . Around that time, our mother returned to live with her family. I really missed her and went to visit her there frequently. Her house wasn't far away, so I could go and see her before school. Her home was a large farmhouse with broad fields of golden barley waving in the breeze, and plenty of corn as well. There were also round, white turnips and bright red peppers as well. . . .

In the morning of November 3, 1910, my mother died. She was only thirty-three years old. As with many tubercular patients, she was fully conscious until the end. She called me over to her bedside and said, "Thank you for taking care of me all of this time when I know you wanted to be off playing."

And that was the end. Even though she had spent most of her time in bed, when she died I was suddenly aware of how large her presence had loomed. It was as though a large, gaping hole had opened up in our household.

In Fukui, they say that women with beautiful hair and eyes live unhappy lives. Even though Mother could have had someone marry into her family, she gave in to my father's entreaties and married him. She ended her life as a classic example of a woman rendered unhappy by the feudalistic era. As might be expected, even Father, who always behaved selfishly where my mother was concerned, was crestfallen and dejected after her death.

Refusing Marriage

The death of my mother occurred when I was in my second year at the girls' school. From around that time, I began to get some inquiries about marriage. But my father, who had just lost his wife, said:

You are not strong and you probably won't live that long. So I don't think you should marry. It will only involve a lot of hard work if you were to marry. And if you were to die young and leave children behind, it would be very sad for them. So wouldn't it be better if you did not marry but instead went on to Tokyo and continued your education?

I wondered if my father's repeating these words to me now—the same father who acted in such a tyrannical manner toward my mother but never once said a kind word to her even when he knew he was making her suffer—wasn't some expression of the tragedy of the Meiji man. Within this man, who did not wish to see his daughter tread the same path as her mother, the old and the new seemed to collide violently. (19–24)

The interwar years were defined by the violent clash between the old and the new, and it is very perceptive that Oku could find evidence of this clash within her father's character. This passage also constitutes a concise and cogent indictment of the prewar marriage system, as well as the fundamental nature of the unequal relationship between the genders. It also touches on that force that impelled women of this generation, the women who came of age around the time of World War I, to pour their energies into rectifying the subordinate position of women in society despite the risks to their own personal well-being.

As it turned out, toward the latter half of my term at the girls' school, there was a marriage proposal that my father urged me to consider. But I didn't care for the man one bit. I found him loud and obnoxious. But he would come around and take me out places, ask me to run errands with him and so forth. I even met with several of his friends and could be seen walking around town, talking and laughing with these people.

Finally, when my father found out and scolded me, I said clearly that I wouldn't marry a man like that and he became even angrier. He said: "They are much better off than we are, so they would take care of all the costs of the wedding; but you go around saying impudent things like that! You will pay for that kind of thing." No matter how much he yelled at me, though, I just repeated the same thing over and over again. I would often charge out of the house and go with men to various places that I had never been to before like photography studios and baseball games, which were just beginning to become popular. Unlike the former literary young woman who would spend her time devouring anything she could get her hands on, I was now turning into someone who loved going out and having a good time. My father had just remarried for the second time, so I really didn't have that much to do around the house.

But one day while I was at school, two teachers from school came to pay a visit on my father. They urged my father to "Hurry up and find someone for Mumeo to marry!" He was really angry this time and scolded me with the greatest severity to date. Even though he was crying, I defied him impudently.

Why is it that adults can only think that associating with a man must be interpreted as something strange? I am not going to get married. If schoolteachers are only able to view their students who are studying to become teachers in this manner, then I think it is a mockery. So I am no longer planning to become a teacher. I by no means wish to become something as trivial as a schoolteacher! I rambled on like this without the hint of an apology. My father would get angrier by the day, so frustrated that he couldn't even get a word out sometimes. He was all the more upset because since the school I was attending was the top school for becoming a certified teacher, so he had naturally assumed that this is what I was going to do. (24–25)

It is interesting that at a time before the Taishō period had even begun, Oku was partaking of a lifestyle that would become increasingly popular in the coming years. That is, she was going out to see photography exhibitions, baseball games, and probably to the movies as well—all the new forms of entertainment that were starting to appeal to young, middle-class Japanese. In a way very different from the lifestyles of the previous fifty years, people were trying to find ways to enjoy the new experiences that constituted modern life. But the most important issue being dealt with here is that of marriage and the question of who gets to decide on the timing and the partner. There was a time when this decision was firmly in the hands of the parents, but we can see from several of these autobiographies that young women of the interwar years were beginning to assert themselves on these matters.

My Years at Japan Women's University

Predictably, my father found his rebellious daughter unmanageable. Perhaps he also had the constraint of his third marriage to deal with as well. My older brother had been accepted in the electrical engineering department of Tokyo Imperial University, so I asked if I couldn't go to Tokyo to attend school as well. Perhaps he was impressed that I would even have the courage to ask, but eventually he granted his permission.

I really wanted to attend Meiji Jogakkō from which people whom I

respected like Hani Motoko, Sōma Kokkō, and Yamamuro Keiko had graduated, but my father had his mind set on Japan Women's University. He
said that it was founded by the estimable Professor Naruse Jinzō, so it was
definitely the school for me.[4] I didn't really want to go to a school that advocated the "good wife, wise mother" *(ryōsai-kenbo)* philosophy, but I went
along with my father's wishes and agreed to attend. I asked Father if I at
least could enroll in the English department, but he insisted I enroll in the
home economics *(kaseika)* program. There wasn't much I could do, so I
made arrangements to enroll in the home economics department. (25–26)

In the spring of 1912, my father and I journeyed to Tokyo. Stepping
off the train in my tall geta, carrying my umbrella and luggage, I was as-
tounded to see the incredibly clear skies over Tokyo. Compared to my
hometown of Fukui, which is always cloudy and dreary, what an exciting
vista this was! I can never forget the excitement I felt as I stepped into what
seemed like a completely different world. We went to our inn *(ryokan)* near
Shimbashi, changed our clothes, and set out to see the sights of this bright
and bustling city. Everything seemed so fresh and shiny!

I was in high spirits when I enrolled in school. I was consumed by a
desire to study. Right away I had my interview with Professor Naruse, and
I told him of my desires. But when I said that I especially looked forward to
studying ethics and economics, and he replied that the first order of business would be preparing me to be a "good wife and wise mother," I was
crushed. Moreover, the classes in the department I was in, home economics, consisted of nothing but "good wife, wise mother" so I rapidly became
disillusioned.

Japan Women's University was a world the likes of which I scarcely
could have imagined. Since only the daughters of the wealthy had the privilege of entering this school, of course my classmates were all the daughters
from wealthy households. There was a daughter from the Mitsui household there, and the younger sister of the novelist Kurata Hyakuzō.

Passing My Days at the Library

The year I entered Japan Women's University was the year that the Meiji era
gave way to Taishō. Because of the emperor's death, we had to display signs
of mourning for one year. No sports events were permitted for this year,
something I recall applauding since I didn't really care for sports anyway.

But within the first year, the only thing I could find pleasure in was
reading. I had absolutely no interest in my classes, which I skipped every

day in order to go to the library. Reading randomly whatever I wanted, I took walks through the sunlit campus, stimulated by everything I saw. In my second year, I began to think about reading a bit more systematically and I hit upon the idea of getting a certificate in educational ethics.

One day, when I was discussing this idea with my brother, he pointed out that "if you get this certification, you will be qualified to teach in a girl's school, right? But that would be dull, so give it up. While you are still young, you need to work on constructing your own humanity." He began bringing me books on human nature, art, and literature. He also often took me to art exhibitions. I always secretly admired my brother and his influence on me was decisive I guess you could say.

When my brother was young, he loved to draw, but my father would not allow him to pursue it. Instead, he wanted him to go to Tokyo Imperial University and become an engineer. He married one of my acquaintances from Japan Women's University, and together they built a happy household. But my brother died young, and I was deeply hurt, feeling that I had genuinely lost my guide. Perhaps it was my brother's influence, but I continued to spend my time reading randomly from day to day. At some point, I developed an interest in Buddhism and began to gather all the books I could find on the subject. I read exhaustively in books interpreting the sutras, and I also read biographies of Buddhist priests. . . . As I think back upon it, my life at this time was like a dream. I wasn't giving any thought to what I might do after graduation, or how I might construct a life for myself. But I just kept reading whatever I wanted to, while my school fees were being paid. One day just seemed to flow into another. (26–28)

Toward the Movement for Political Participation by Women

LEARNING ABOUT ZEN

Well, when I graduated from school, I returned home. My father was on his sickbed. I tried cheering him up with talk about goings-on in Tokyo, but steeped as he was in newspapers and books, he was not very excited. After a while, I received a letter from a friend offering me a position in Kamakura as a live-in tutor. I was worried about my father but he said, "You should definitely go." I was delighted to hear these words for even though I had returned home, I still had no interest in getting married. So I began immediately to make preparations to leave home again.

My tutee was a seventeen-year-old beauty who had never been to school but had done all her learning at home. I taught this beloved daughter of a wealthy farmer for one year and they wanted me to write her a certificate of completion based on my status as a graduate of a Japan Women's University. I was given one room at a nearby farmer's house. With a view of the hillside that backed up onto [the Zen temple] Kenchōji, it was a warm, pleasant room. When the breezes blew, the surrounding bamboo bushes rustled. Breakfast and lunch were reverently served me by one of the older maids who would bring me one and then another lavish tray. It was a very plush existence!

I passed my leisure time walking rather than reading books. Visiting the Tsurugaoka Hachiman Shrine and the Kamakura Shrine, I would reflect on all that history; looking up at the statue of the Great Buddha, I recalled the lines from one of Yosano Akiko's poems. Wandering among the temples was very pleasant. I began doing Zen meditation *(zazen)* at Enkakuji during their summer lecture series. . . . I remember thinking when being struck with a staff that this is pretty intense, but it did seem to purify the body and mind. I recall the first *kōan* I was given as well: "Before your father and mother existed your Buddha nature was present." Delivered in a soft but penetrating voice, it left no room for escape and I felt completely trapped.

I also often visited Tokeiji, famous as a nunnery where women went to dissolve their marriages. There was a Zen Roshi there, Reverend Shakumune En who had a wonderful sense of humor and whose lectures I truly enjoyed. . . . My Zen practice never really amounted to much, but I was appreciative of being able to see the Buddhist life up close. Since everything I had come to know about the life of Buddhist priests up until this point had been strictly through books, having the chance to observe one in person opened up a whole new world to me. This turned out to be a period in which I grew up, a period that led me from the conceptual world to the world of praxis. (29–35)

My Father's Death

As promised, after one year I quit tutoring the young woman where I had been employed. . . . I returned home for a while, but when encouraged to do so by my brother, I returned to Tokyo once again. I didn't particularly have designs on any job, but I went to live with a friend from Japan Women's University who was now studying at Tokyo Women's Medical College (Tokyo Joshi-isen, now Tokyo Joshi-idai). I was pretty much doing as I liked: taking care of housework and other things, going to lectures and the library, and so on.

Just at that time I received a telegram: *Father's illness is serious. Return home right away.* I wasted no time and hopped on a train immediately. My brother met me at the station, his face drawn and pale. When I asked him how Father was and whether he had already died, he replied, "He bled profusely after having several teeth pulled and apparently his life is in danger. I don't know if it was because of some backward country dentist who didn't know what he was doing. . . ." His voice was choked with emotion and he looked like he was about to cry. That past New Year's, neither of us had the money to travel, so we hadn't come home. Now we wondered if he hadn't been terribly lonely and very upset with us, and we were filled with regret.

In the end, he died very shortly after I returned. On his face, there was no trace left of the stubbornness that had driven my late mother to cry incessantly. It seemed like his face and his whole body had shrunk to one size smaller. The same father who had poured the new ideas of the era into us and pushed us into the stream of new experiences also caused our mother a lot of pain. This was the father who was now dead. It was the middle of February, 1918, with the snow still deep all around us. Father was forty-two years old. (33–36)

It is interesting to note that the passage about her father's death precedes a section of her autobiography called "The Road to Social Revolution." Perhaps the passing of this patriarchal figure liberated Oku to pursue a path she was drawn to but not willing to battle her father over. Her father, we may recall, had been described earlier as one in whom the new and the old seemed to collide. Indeed, if someone wanted to characterize what the social fabric in Japan was like after World War I, after the Rice Riots, certainly the word "collision" would come to mind, for many more constituents in society were being placed on collision courses with one another than had been the case during the previous fifty years.

The Road to Social Revolution

It seems that around that time there were more meetings linking Buddhism and social problems than there are these days. Labor issues were also being noisily debated, and there were numerous lecture and discussion meetings where various mixtures of Marxism, Anarchism, and Syndicalism were being discussed. Whenever I was free, I attended these meetings and was learning the rudiments of the labor problem. I made appearances at a number of the research group meetings that I was invited to and got to know a number of the well-known teachers who would also attend.

For example, I became quite familiar with the members of Ōsugi Sakae's anarchist group. Ōsugi was a very brusque, unaffected, but pleasant man. He was very sharp and seemed to enjoy teasing those around him. He would even make fun of the policeman who was assigned to follow him everywhere, so the people around him were concerned about that. But he didn't care a thing about it. I recall how he would explain difficult theories in his slow, halting way to young workers whose eyes would shine as they became increasingly engaged by what he was saying.

I guess I bore some resemblance to Itō Noe because he seemed to like me, always telling me that he felt like I was Itō's younger sister. Later on, after I got married and had a son, he sent me an old, used, black baby carriage that had originally come from France. Just at that time, I was busy with the New Women's Association, so I would fasten my son to my back and use the pram to carry around copies of our journal, *Women's League (Josei dōmei)*. I trust that Ōsugi would have understood.

At this time, I also had friends who were interested in the philosophy of [Henri] Bergson, [Rudolf] Eucken, and [Friedrich] Nietzsche, as well as friends who were interested in literature. After staying up late at night arguing about human nature, we would stop for some yakitori, *oden*, or even a milkshake on the way home. . . . There was some kind of Dadaist group, too, and I believe that people like Tsui Jun and Soeda Azenbō were working hard trying to create something. Around this time, I also received a marriage proposal from the writer Nakazoto Kaizan. I was even arrested one time for being in violation of Article 5 of the Police Security Regulations because I attended a political meeting at a time when women were not allowed to do so. A strike occurred in one of the spinning mills around this time, and many of my friends were busily engaging in support activities for the strikers. I even went down to the factory just when the shift was ending and stood atop a rickshaw waving a large banner and yelling as loud as I could: "There will be a meeting tonight at such-and-such a place. Everybody please come!" That night I made the rounds of the places where most workers lived.

In addition, the first International Labor Conference was being held and questions about Japanese female labor and about dumping were being taken up, so we avidly followed the newspaper reports every day. Since I had grown up amidst the plight of female factory workers who worked in the mills of Fukui, I wasn't likely to think of this issue as somebody else's problem. I felt that the question of female labor was a serious social problem. But all of a sudden, it seemed, the idea of sending me as a delegate to represent female workers at this international conference came up. The government had already selected Tanaka Takako as the official delegate, but just at this time, people in the labor movement realized that they wanted to send somebody of their own. Yamauchi Mina from the Yūaikai was an excellent candidate, I thought, but due to some circumstances internal to the Yūaikai, she had stepped down. At that time, I was working as a reporter for *Labor World (Rōdō sekai)*, which was owned by Hashimoto Teppa and edited by Katō Kanjū. In that connection, I had occasion to speak about the problem of women at labor meetings. I had learned much from Tanaka Takako's husband, Tanaka Odō, and it was probably because of this connection that my name was being brought up in this context.[5] But, however one wishes to think about it, I was still a young person who was just beginning to learn something about labor issues, so I didn't feel it appropriate that I should go. Accordingly, I declined and did not attend the conference.

The narrator assumes a very self-effacing stance here, but once again she has made it clear to her readers the nature of the influences to which she was being exposed. Bergson, Eucken, and Nietzsche are her philosophical inspiration, while she looks to contemporary progressive thinkers such as Tanaka Odō, Katō Kanjū, and Ōsugi Sakae for her understanding of the implications of industrialization and modernism for Japan. She is in a position to be regarded as one of Japan's leading spokespersons for issues having to do with women in the workplace. So, clearly, she is moving toward becoming an activist and advocate for working women's rights. Her first step in this direction is to directly observe working conditions for female textile workers.

A Record of My Experiences as a Female Worker

THROWING AWAY THE BOOKS

At this juncture, I reached a spiritual turning point in my life. It had been more than two and a half years since I had begun wandering back and forth between philosophy, ethics, and religious texts trying to discover my inner self. Instead, I succeeded only in becoming caught up in the sense of frustration that all my book reading was distancing me from something really essential in life. Not knowing what I should be doing, I was running back and forth like a spoiled child, and this only deepened my frustration.

If I wanted to cry, there was no one to hold onto and this made me wonder if this was the time to begin exploring relations with the opposite sex. But the only upshot of this was that I enhanced my feelings of self-loathing.

Tsui Jun observed that if I could just get down into writing what I was feeling, I would have the makings of truthful novel. But I didn't believe that I had the literary talent to write a novel, so I wound up just staying in my room passing day after gloomy day, counting the knotholes in my ceiling over and over again.

Then one day, it just hit me. I had been reading too many books. I had succeeded at becoming a bookworm, but, in the end, I was losing anything I might have gained from reading all those books. The truth is within ourselves, and it is found in practice. This is the conclusion I reached. But it was hardly the result of some organized thought process. It was just that after all that mental wandering, it just struck me all of a sudden: I was no longer going to read any books so I went and sold off almost all the books I owned.

To the Spinning Mill

That's it! I'll become a factory worker! I'll go to work at a spinning mill and share all the joys and hardships with my sisters. Once I had decided this, I could scarcely contain myself, so I rushed straight out in search of hand-bills recruiting female workers. As soon as I found out that the Fuji Gas Spinning Mill in Honjo was hiring female workers, I immediately sent for a copy of a relative's daughter's family registration, and using a false name and academic record, I succeeded in getting myself in the door at the mill.

At that time, the Fuji Spinning Mill, which later was destroyed in the Great Kantō Earthquake, was housed in an old building. Watching the faces of the young women who worked the night shift as they exited the factory gates, they appeared so pale and exhausted that they looked as though they had come straight out of hell. When I had come the day before for my physical exam, I entered via the handsome granite gate. But once I was an employee, I left by the rear gate with its heavy, steel door. Carrying a *furoshiki* bound with a broad, red muslin cord from college days that contained some copies of sutras, and the one book I couldn't bear to part with, [Tomonaga Sanjūrō's] *A History of the Growth of an Awareness of Self in the Medieval Period (Kinsei ni okeru ga no jikakushi)*, I pushed open that steel gate.[6]

Life in the factory was far worse than I had imagined. Sanitary conditions in the dormitories were horrible. There were bedbugs, fleas, lice, and other vermin. They kept a candle burning all through the night to kill mosquitoes. If you got bitten by one of the bedbugs, it was like being gouged with a claw! It goes without saying that the rooms and the cafeteria were filthy, but the bathroom and toilet were so bad that I automatically walked on tiptoes.

I considered myself accustomed to eating a fairly simple diet, but even I could hardly manage to swallow the black millet mixture they served. There would be just the tiniest amount of vegetables. Occasionally there might be a piece of salted salmon, but somehow, with a great deal of skill, they managed to serve just the skin and bone with all the fish that should've been in-between gone! There was nothing to do but suck on what there was, which was less than two bites. Since all the thirteen hundred women who lived in the dorms got the same fare, one wondered where all that flesh on their bones that was melting away was going.

All the outgoing and incoming mail was censored. Since most girls had been advanced funds of between thirty and fifty yen at the most, they were not allowed to leave the mill at all. If they couldn't take the heat and humidity and needed a drink of water, they would have to go to the wooden fence by the rear gate and try to call out to some passerby. How pathetic and absurd. The attitude with which the supervisors treated the workers was as though they were slaves. And the wages they received ranged from only a low of twenty-five to forty sen per day to a high of one yen and forty to fifty sen. But despite these conditions, we didn't let our frustrations show. We just worked, slept, and laughed. Deceived by the smooth talking recruiters, these were simple girls who had left home in order to reduce the number of mouths that had to be fed at home. I became friends with many of these girls and I heard many of their stories. I recall feeling that the horror stories they had to tell of their miserable lives in the countryside were heartbreaking.

My progress at work was slow. I wanted to learn my job and become an independent worker as soon as possible, so I poured all my energy into this task. But I felt as though I was being pursued by the ghosts from all those books I had resolved to quit reading. If my mind went off on its own course, then the thread would break or get tangled. It was as if the line of thread could see right into my mind. It seemed I spent endless days in frustration. However, we normally worked the night shift, in which case we would return to the dormitory, close the shutters (amado), and fall into a deep sleep.

Driven from the Mill

Although I tried to tough it out, I kept being plagued by doubts. A little voice kept insisting that this was enough, that it was too difficult, and finally, I could no longer bear it. I went to the dorm supervisor and told him and said I wanted to meet with the head of the mill.

Management was visibly shaken. As far as they were concerned, a major incident had occurred. "Sending someone like you into our mill was a huge mistake for your side," they exclaimed, but I had no idea what they were talking about. It was not much of a conversation. They claimed, "You were here for ten days so you must have a very clear picture of conditions in this mill." All I wanted to do was get out of there gracefully. . . . It was early June 1919 and I was twenty-three years old. My days of getting out into the world and learning about labor problems firsthand had begun. I was invited to speak at many meetings and rallies, so I became accustomed to mounting the podium and speaking. . . .

Marriage

I enjoyed learning about labor problems, but I was more than a bit embarrassed the public seemed to make such a big deal out of someone like myself who wasn't even a worker. I began to have serious doubts about continuing to go out into the world and my old feelings of self-loathing began to resurface. I wound up passing my days in a depressed state. It was at a time like this that I decided to get married.

The man's name was Oku Eiichi. A poet whose works didn't sell, he was employed in the translation department of Sakai Toshihiko's *Baibunsha*. Oku came from Shingū in Wakayama Prefecture, from the same town as Sato Haruo, with whom he was quite good friends. They had been in middle school together and ultimately both left school to come up to Tokyo where they lived at a gathering spot for young, unpublished writers.

Oku was also close friends with Tsuji Jun and Ikuta Shungetsu. Tsuji-san used to come over quite regularly after we got married. Sometimes he would appear in the garb of a Zen flute player. Shungetsu was as thin as a rail, and when he committed suicide by drowning, Oku wept inconsolably. His widow, Hanayo, had been a close friend of mine for years. (37–45)

It seems rather astounding that out of the blue comes this sudden and brief description of Oku's marriage. All we can gather is that he was a progressive thinker, working for the Marxist Sakai Toshihiko, and was also a literary type. How did they meet? Did they fall in love? What was their married life like? Supposedly, women's autobiographies gravitate to the personal and the domestic as opposed to the public, but here Oku provides amazingly little information about something so personal and so significant. Details are never lacking, however, about the public dimensions of her life experience.

Toward the New Women's Association

A VISIT FROM RAICHŌ

It was late 1919 when, out of the blue, I received a visit from Hiratsuka Raichō. I had great respect for her as someone who had preceded me at Japan Women's University, and since the inauguration of *Seitō* had been active as a pioneer for the "new woman." I had once accompanied Tsuji-san on a visit to Raichō, so it was not as though we had never met. Still, I was surprised by this sudden visit. Raichō was about to launch a new organization, the New Women's Association, and she wanted my help. I was well aware of this impending new organization, as the preparations for its formation had been reported fervently in the press. Its purpose was to improve the position of women and help them attain basic political rights. But at the time I was three or four months pregnant and really did not have the desire to get back out in the world and work, and I didn't feel that my condition would allow it. I declined the offer emphatically, saying that I had slipped completely into the "good wife, wise mother" mode. But Raichō just pushed all that much harder to gain my cooperation. She tried hard to persuade me, saying, "Eiichi said you were the type of woman who could keep her silence. We need people like you in the women's movement."

After Raichō left, my husband and I began to argue. But when I said, "I have gone so far as to become a stay-at-home housewife because I did not want to go out and work," he countered with the idea that "If it's Raichō we're talking about, she's a wonderful leader. Helping her would be a great learning experience for you. Besides, you wouldn't be working a set number of hours. She said she wants you to help her by editing the organization's official publication, so you would have some freedom. And if you find you can't do it, you could always quit." So he made a strong case.

In the end, I gave in to their arguments and agreed to throw myself wholeheartedly into the organization. Ever since that day, for the next nearly seventy years, I have consistently worked hard for the women's movement. From time to time, I have wondered what path my life might have taken had this opportunity not come along when it did. Thinking back on it now, it seems that all the actions I have taken in my life that were the direct result of my own will—things that I decided to do on my own, including my decision to marry, to launch the household economics movement, and to construct the housewives center *(shufu kaikan)*—all were to a greater or lesser degree influenced by external factors. However, this kind of work in a social movement is not the kind of thing you can easily neglect or turn away from. I was born in the north, so I know about patience. No matter how painful or difficult the work became, I was able to endure the many years of pain and frustration. The starting point for all my social work was this New Women's Association, so, I guess you could say that Raichō and my husband helped shape the direction my life would take.

Although her husband figures very minimally in the narrative, here Oku gives him credit, along with Hiratsuka Raichō, for one of the most momentous decisions of her life. She says other things, including her marriage, were influenced by external factors, but is silent on what these factors might have been.

The Start of the New Women's Association

At the time I joined the organization, Raichō and Ichikawa Fusae had already issued a proclamation which declared that the organization would launch two petition drives directed at the soon to be inaugurated 42nd Diet. The first would be to reform Article 5 of the Police Safety Regulations, and the second would be to pass a law to prevent men with venereal disease from marrying. The Public Peace Police Law had been passed in 1900. Article 5 proclaimed that women, like soldiers, priests, and people not yet of age, were forbidden from joining political parties and from giving speeches at political meetings, and even from listening to such speeches.

A campaign to strike the words "and women" from Article 5 had previously been launched by Iwano Kiyoko in the late Meiji era, and it had succeeded in passing a bill through the Lower House. Now, we wanted to revive that movement and establish the principle that women have the right to participate in political meetings. We saw this as the first step toward firmly establishing women's political rights. It was just at that time that the Universal Suffrage Movement was taking off, and we were learning about women obtaining the right to vote in one Western society after another.

The other thing we were adamant about was the tragedy of women's lives being ruined by marriage to men who had contracted venereal disease. We wanted to see some limitations placed on the right of men with such diseases to get married. (45–48)

A Declaration from the New Women's Association and the Hiroshima Incident

At the opening ceremony, the following declaration for the New Women's Association was decided upon, raising the curtain on a new chapter in the women's movement. And the general principle of supporting equal opportunity for men and women and the attainment of rights for women and children was declared.

> **Declaration of Principles, New Women's Association (abbreviated)**
> The time has come to unite in order to pursue the legitimate rights and duties for all women. Not only should each woman pursue her own individual education and self-development, but the time has also come for us to unite as a group and work together to improve the social position of women, and to participate in a practical movement alongside men to attain our rights as women and mothers in this postwar (World War I) era. If we do not stand up at this time, then our future society will be no different than the present patriarchal society, which excludes women. And we believe that this would be an utter calamity for one half of humanity.

After this declaration was agreed upon, there was an election of officers, and three of us, Raichō, Ichikawa, and myself, were elected as directors. In addition, ten others, including Yamada Waka, Sakamoto Makoto, Tanaka Takako, Tanaka Yoshiko, Katō Sakiko, Kishida Kiyoko, and Yabe Hatsuko, who worked with me in the movement for years and years, were also selected.

On the way home from the ceremony, while thinking about the faces burning with desire of all the women who had gathered at the meeting, I could not escape the impression that this was a powerful new beginning. For the first time, an organization was being born, one in which women, by their own efforts, were standing up for their own rights and making the improvement of women's position a primary objective. We saw the organization flutter its wings, and slowly begin to rise under its own power. And my body trembled to think of embarking on that long, difficult road that would carry us into the future. . . . (50–52)

There was quite a response to our inaugural issue. Letters arrived from throughout the country expressing joy and giving us encouragement, and there was a steady stream of well wishers stopping by our headquarters incessantly to express their support. It was heartwarming to realize that we had so many supporters who felt exactly as we did. We could truly feel the passion of women from all across Japan who had been waiting for a movement like ours to awaken them.

We wanted to increase our membership, so we appealed to female teachers all across Japan to join our organization. The response was swift, and within a very short period, we had branches of our organization established in various places throughout the country. Nagoya, Osaka, Kobe, Fukuyama, Mihara, and Hiroshima—in all these places the flames of enthusiasm were fanned. When Raichō heard that we had formed branches in all these places, she was very excited. Moved by the passionate stirrings from all these locations, first Raichō and then all of us at headquarters began to feel buoyed that our movement would soon flourish.

However, before long, an incident that dashed cold water on our activities occurred. We soon learned that the Mihara and Fukuyama branches in Hiroshima Prefecture were subjected to pressure from the police, prefectural authorities, and school principals who urged dissolution of these branches. Sasaki Nobu at the Mihara branch and Sasaki Mitsu at the Fukuyama branch did their best to stand up to the pressure and resist, and at headquarters, we received inquiries from a variety of sources including the Home Ministry and the Ministry of Education, which provoked complaints in the press. Even the high-handed prefectural officials and school principals who would not change their position, perhaps because they saw the disadvantageous position they were in, finally softened their stance and agreed to recognize participation in the New Women's Association, which could in no way be construed as a political organization, and the right to engage in the petition movement against venereal disease was recognized as well. But they would not allow participation in political activities such as trying to get Article 5 altered and urging electoral reforms. For many, this was a difficult conclusion to accept, but at least we had survived the first major crisis that we had faced since forming the organization. (55–56)

Rejection of the Revision of Article 5

On December 25, 1920, when we learned of the opening of the session of the Lower House of the Diet, we filled the few seats that were available for female spectators (in those days, seats for men and women in the gallery were separated by a wire screen). The revision of the Public Peace Police Law into which we had poured so much of our lifeblood was being presented on the floor. We came to see what would become of it. As we assumed, the version sponsored by the Seiyūkai and supported by the government, which only permitted women to attend political speeches and to be involved in their promotion, passed unanimously. It was sent on the House of Peers. Just one more step! We hugged each other in anticipation.

On March 26 of the next year, we held our breath as the bill came to the floor of the Upper House. After a number of other bills had been debated, finally discussion of the Public Peace Police Law was begun. Famous hard-liners like Representative Shimizu Shiji upset us with his strange remarks about having to supply face powder or ashes from the stove for people to paint their faces if women were allowed to attend political meetings. But supporters like Kamada Eikichi explained the significance of passing the law and introduced a supporting statement from a Home Ministry official.

At last, the final stage. Just at the moment when we all felt certain that the bill would pass, Baron Fujimura Yoshirō slowly arose, and when he received permission from the chairman of the Fairness Committee to speak, he argued: "Women's natural place is in the home. History shows us that if women participate in political activities, unfortunate results will follow. If this body were to give permission for such activities at this time, I believe it would interfere with our nation's national polity (*kokutai*). Therefore, I oppose this bill unqualifiedly." Immediately thereafter, the vote was called for and our bill was defeated.

It happened so fast that we were in a state a shock. Once we returned to our senses, an anger and frustration welled up that we could not suppress. All of our efforts up to this point had gone down the drain just because of a few words by some stubborn old man! The fact that all the efforts in our Diet campaign could end in vain in this way stuck in my craw and my whole body felt as though it would burst. (55–58)

The Debate with Yamakawa Kikue

In April of the same year, the socialist Yamakawa Kikue established the first socialist women's group. Called the Red Wave Society (Sekirankai), it had women like Sakai's daughter Magara, Kutsumi Fusako, and Nakasone Sadayo at its core and made quite a splash when the majority of its members were arrested at the second May Day demonstration.[7] We were delighted to welcome the birth of Japan's first socialist women's group and by no means wished to antagonize them.

However, in the July issue of *The Sun (Taiyō)*, Yamakawa Kikue wrote a short piece titled "The Shinfujinkyōkai and the Sekirankai," in which she attacked our organization. In terms of content, it was an extensive criticism of Raichō individually, and our organization as a whole. According to Yamakawa, "Only the XX [the word "destruction" had been censored] of capitalism can genuinely benefit the female worker," so she criticized our movement for concentrating on the Diet and on "improving working conditions." I respected Yamakawa Kikue as a pioneer in the women's movement, but I was terribly disappointed in her denunciations of Raichō as "aristocratic, self-indulgent and self-righteous."

However, as regards her viewpoint on the women's movement, I felt that I wanted to make our position clear, so I presented a counter-argument in the August issue of the same magazine. In my article called "Our Position and Viewpoint," I argued that just making many women aware of Article 5 of the Public Peace Police Law, and illustrating the evils of its provisions, was extremely significant in and of itself, and that in order to further raise women's consciousness, bourgeois and anti-bourgeois advocates ought to join hands in a common effort.

After the appearance of my article, Yamakawa published her response in the October issue. She argued that calling for women to ignore class differences and join hands was the typical response of bourgeois women toward the proletarian class they aimed to control. It's the same thing as asking the wolf to guard the sheep.

At that time, I had no doubts that socialism had a great deal of meaning and power to offer. However, I was not persuaded by the self-satisfied sense of superiority that was so evident in Yamakawa's writings.

There is no doubt that in the larger picture, anarchism, syndicalism, and all the other "-isms" had much about them to respect, and we took many suggestions from them. Of this there can be no question. However, no matter what the -ism, it cannot penetrate into real life and actually change the way of life and the mode of thinking that people have developed—for better or for worse—over a long period of time. I felt that it was just a little too simple to believe that a theory could have that kind of impact. This has been my basic belief since then, right down until the present. So while I had connections to various different "-isms," I never fully adopted the viewpoint of a single "-ism."

How much time has been expended over the years arguing over theories that are supposed to apply to people's actual lives? I believe that Raichō also agreed with me that women ought to transcend their class affiliations and unite in a common effort. Most of the women in the New Women's Association also supported what I had written. (58–61)

Few critics were more articulate or hard-nosed than Yamakawa Kikue. It was her belief that women should dedicate themselves to the socialist revolution if they were serious about attaining equality. Influenced by August Bebel's Women and Socialism, *Yamakawa considered the New Women's Association to be bourgeois and naive.[8] The debates in which these two important women's groups engaged attracted a great deal of attention from readers across the country. But meanwhile, disputes arose within the organization that were less beneficial to the advancement of women's issues.*

Disputes

Exactly when was it that people inside the organization began to become irritated with and attack one another? It seemed that suddenly that bright, fresh atmosphere, which visibly seethed with passion, was extinguished and all people could see was each other's flaws and shortcomings. Especially, the criticisms from those around Ichikawa that were directed at Raichō began to grow stronger by the day. No doubt, this was in part because Raichō tended to write slowly and her opinions diverged from most of the others. However, more than anything else, I believe people were just displacing their frustrations over the lack of funds, the incessant pressure, and the physical and spiritual exhaustion of working for the movement, and taking it out unnecessarily on one individual.

I often went to see Raichō at her Tabata residence. Whenever I went, it would make her little boy Kyōshi cry. This is because he thought that when I showed up it meant that his mother was probably going off someplace. Of course, I always took my child with me. But the pain Raichō went through leaving her son was considerable, I know. And then when she would go out, to have to put up with all the slander directed at her by members of the organization, it must have been difficult for her to bear. But she never said a word to anyone; she just endured it all in silence.

I can recall us getting together on the second floor of a *soba* restaurant for a meal and a fortifying bottle of sake and noticing how worn out she looked. Tsuji Jun would come along to encourage her and console her and offer his insights on things. My sympathy for Raichō was unqualified, and I was in a position to see how she was feeling up close. But I never said a single word to her, nor to anyone else in the organization, about the denunciations against her. To just continue doing the work that I was asked to do without saying a word—that was my position with regards to these internal disputes within the organization. At some point, I began to hear of a litany of complaints about me as well. I was inclined to say that enough is enough, but I had to remind myself that working for the women's movement was never easy.

But then, before I knew it, Ichikawa announced suddenly that she was going to America. She resigned her position as director and also withdrew from the staff of the Women's League (Josei Dōmei). I was surprised to say the least, but since I was not familiar with the sequence of events that led her to that decision, I respected her decision. . . .

Then, like a thunderbolt out of the blue, Raichō up and moved to the foot of Mt. Akagi [in Gumma Prefecture]. The reason was that up until the time she left she had been overworked, suffering from exhaustion and illness, and needed someplace quiet and tranquil to rest. But we had not met with her, nor did we have any communication with her at all. We were shocked and overwhelmed. Since I had always been supportive of Raichō, I wanted to sympathize with whatever was going on in her mind, but it really was a difficult time for us as an organization.

Those of us who remained had to get together and talk over what we should do from here on out. Thinking about it very dispassionately, we concluded that this was not the time to abandon the movement, which we had brought this far; it was agreed that we would rally the troops into some new battle formation organized around me. We were already in our third year of existence, and many well-informed people, as well as newspapers and magazines, had given us their support. Several political parties had even agreed to endorse our proposal to reform the Police Safety Regulations, so this was not the time to give up. We resolved instead that for the sake of the liberation of later generations of women, we needed to see it through until the end. (61–63)

Times were difficult not only for the fledgling women's movement, but for Oku and her family as well. As she describes it,

Naturally, our personal finances were not in any better condition. My husband used to say, "If you were just teaching at a girls' school you could get by without being so poor." But I replied that it was precisely because we were so poor that I felt I had to take part in a social movement. At that time, my brother's salary—he had graduated from University of Tokyo—was forty-five yen per month, while a teacher who graduated from a women's university made about thirty-five yen. I was not ashamed that we made so little money. Being committed and poor, this is what being in the movement was all about. "We are not lazy. The fact that we are poor is not because there is something wrong with us. There is something wrong with the structure of the social system *(yo no naka no shikumi ga warui)*. So I just poured more of my energy into the movement. (64–65)

Finally Reform of the Public Peace Police Law

Thinking back on it, it has been twenty-two years since the Public Peace Police Law was passed in the thirty-third year of Meiji (1900) and women were prohibited from joining political associations, as well as being prohibited from sponsoring political speeches, or even attending them. Then, at the end of Meiji, Iwano Kiyoko launched the Public Peace Police Law reform movement, and in 1920, Raichō followed this up with the formation of the New Women's Association. For the next two years, we continued to work tirelessly and selflessly. Finally, with all our energies and resources spent, we made our final stand. At last, on March 25, 1922, on the last day of the 45th Diet, we succeeded in getting our reform of Article 5 passed. It was publicly proclaimed on April 20th, and on May 10th it was implemented. It was the day for which we had been waiting so long. We thanked one another for all the years of hard work, and we rejoiced. . . .

Once the reform of the Public Peace Police Law went into effect on May 10, the first women-sponsored women's political speech assembly was held. The Kobe branch of the New Women's Association sponsored a huge gathering to celebrate the reform of Article 5 of the Public Peace Police Law at the Kobe Christian Youth Hall. Over fifteen hundred people attended, filling the large hall to standing room only capacity.

Thereafter, similar celebratory assemblies were held in Nagoya, Osaka, and Tokyo, all filled to capacity with people overflowing with happiness. Women across the country were starting to think in terms of attaining the right to join political associations and to participate directly in politics. As for myself, I was sent around to places throughout Japan as a featured speaker at political assemblies as though I was a star.

Unpleasant Memories

At the end of August, I delivered a son prematurely. However, his nutrition in the womb had been inadequate, and one week after he was born, my son died. Oku was deeply saddened by his death and he gave him the name Asatsuyu (Morning Dew). It was difficult for me to separate from his burial urn, so I kept it near me for a long time. I had been laid up in bed since early August, and after the death of my son, my physical condition became worse. Plagued by thoughts of my deceased son, I felt as if I were dangling. I was overwhelmed by feelings of irritation and sadness. In the meantime, the very success we had had getting the Public Peace Police Law reform through seemed to crystallize doubts about the whole parliamentary strategy that had been smoldering beneath the surface.

Speaking earnestly, during the four years we had worked so steadfastly to improve the political status of women, we had set foot in the Diet one hundred times, and repeatedly made the rounds to call on Diet members. But even though as a result we had achieved an epochal liberalization of the political status of women, it did not seem to have much of an impact on the everyday lives of ordinary women, which pretty much continued as they had before. Even though women could now go out and make political speeches, and the assembly halls were filled with spectators, there were not that many women who attended.

Most women seemed virtually unconcerned and hardly even expressed much delight in what had transpired. For whom, indeed, had we worked so hard and persevered in this movement even when it brought misery to our own children? Was it for my own individual interest or to attain fame? No! Definitely not! In my own mind, I had been working for the benefit of all women, trying to open up these new avenues. But our movement was not meeting the needs of the masses of women.

What a lonely and unsatisfactory experience the parliamentary movement had been. While we had raised our voices in protest in order to bring about some basic political rights for women, we were never taken seriously by the men who governed the political world. Even though we had tried our best on behalf of women, they appeared to be uninterested. . . . I became depressed. I lost interest in the movement to obtain the right of political participation for women. At the very least, as long as I had to persist in my own poverty, it was a mistake to pursue these rights for women that wouldn't amount to anything. So, after this kind of reflection, I thought that the thing to do was to go out and live among the ordinary masses of women. Then I thought I could go on to create the basis for a life in which women, tired of being subjugated by poverty and forced into silence, would want to have political rights and would want to attend these political rallies.

I recall how at just this point, the Seiyūkai and the Kokumintō, in a bid for popularity, usurped our whole position on the Public Peace Police Law reform program. It was after this point that it was firmly etched in my mind that it was a mistake to ask the established political parties for any kind of assistance.

At the end of 1922, we received a message from Raichō that she wanted to dissolve the New Women's Association. On December 8, we held a final meeting of the Special Steering Committee at Ms. Kodama's house and agreed to form a new organization. On December 17, the Women's League (Fujin Renmei) was established.

The directors were Kodama Shinkō and Shūki Yasuko. I was also asked to add my name to the list, so I did. But I was soon to lose my desire to work for women's political rights, so I resigned shortly thereafter.

Thus, I decided to part company with the movement for women's political rights and proceed to the movement that I felt I needed to embark upon. Throughout the period that I dedicated myself to the New Women's Association, I had always wanted to raise the consciousness of the female masses, so now this was the direction into which I naturally wanted to go. (68–72)

So far, the narrator has given a fairly detailed account of the operation of Japan's most important prewar women's organization, the New Women's Association. What comes through clearly here is the disappointment that after all the hard work lobbying Diet members, enduring the frustration of a last-minute defeat when they were unsuccessful at reforming the Public Peace Police Law, then finally seeing those reforms realized, it was clear that the lives of ordinary women were not being affected. Ordinary women were busy either working or taking care of the home, and they were often oblivious to goings-on in the Diet or in Tokyo. Below, the narrator wrestles with what to do with herself next. Part of her wants to stay home and give her family the attention they merited, but this turned out not to be in her nature.

Sixteen Lectures on Women's Issues

I wrote a letter to my colleagues in the New Women's Association announcing my retirement and wanted to just rest at home for a while before my health collapsed entirely. I no longer wanted to attend lecture meetings or meet with people. I thought, perhaps, I could recover from the exhaustion that had been plaguing me. But, of course, our impoverished status hadn't changed at all. Thinking that once I caught my breath I needed to do something to rebuild our family finances, I started to look over manuscripts that I had written over the past several years. Next, I realized that I needed to look at some relevant documents connected with what I had written. So, seeing the need to systematically pull some material together, I started going to libraries and government offices in order to do some research.

At this point, I began to develop a rough overview of women's issues and began to put my energies into writing something that should have the effect of assisting in raising women's awareness. As I recall, the book sold for two yen and fifty sen and did quite a bit to raise interest in women's issues while managing to sell quite a few copies along the way.

As a result, I was able to alleviate our family's financial straits for a while. I genuinely thought that I was through going out and working, that I would become someone who worked in their study, a woman who would be a good mother while she studied women's problems. So I got a cat for my children, spent my time at home repairing our torn shoji and caring for plants.

However, in the end, it was not to be. I was not a stay-at-home person. Believing as I did that politics was not something we could separate from our everyday life, I knew I had to plunge myself into the world of impoverished mothers, of housewives busy managing their households, and of the working women who were strapped for time. (73–74)

It is at this point that the trajectory of Oku Mumeo's life and work take an interesting turn.

As the Rear Guard of the Women's Movement

ESTABLISHING THE WORKING WOMEN'S ASSOCIATION (SHOKUGYŌFUJINSHA) AND LAUNCHING *WORKING WOMEN* (*SHOKUGYŌ FUJIN*)

Around springtime in 1923, I kept running into Shimononaka Yasasaburō, head of Heibonsha Publishing House, at a certain lecture series. On the way back from one of these lectures, I accepted his invitation and for the first time in quite a while we went out for some stewed chicken *(torinabe)*, just the two of us. We talked about a number of things, but gradually moved on to the topic of women's issues, and after I had stated how I felt, Shimononaka, who listened intently, suddenly said: "Well then how about if you establish an organization for working women? It is something you could definitely do, definitely! The first thing you should do is publish a magazine for working women. I'll do whatever I can to help you."

Needless to say, even without Mr. Shimononaka bringing the topic up, the problem of working women was one that was continuing to grow and attract my attention, so I was quite taken with his proposal. Ever since leaving the movement for women's right to participate in the political process, I had been experiencing some degree of dissatisfaction; therefore I found his idea very intriguing. So I replied, "If I could be of some help to working women, then I couldn't be happier."

In this way, I turned my attention to young working women and embarked on a new movement. Accordingly, on April 20, 1923, I established the Shokugyō Fujinsha, or Working Women's Association. On June 1, we published the first issue of *Working Women (Shokugyō fujin)*.

My young associates were Murakami Hideko, Yoshinaga Fumiko, and Chiba Chie, as well as my friend from the old days at the New Women's Association, Yabe Hatsuko, who served as my editor and publisher. For our office, we used the lodgings of one of our cohorts in the Jimbochō area of Kanda, not far from Heibonsha. For funds, we relied initially on my advance from *Sixteen Lectures on Women's Issues (Fujin mondai jūrokkō)* as well as some support from Mr. Shimononaka. Later on, we developed a list of supporting members. Among these supporters were Mr. Shimononaka himself, Akutagawa Ryūnosuke, Kikuchi Kan, Shimanaka Yūsaku, Katayama Tetsu, and about 200 other people. To these people we owe a tremendous debt of gratitude.

In the inaugural issue of *Working Women*, I contributed an article called "My Position." In this piece, I called for a place where working women who shared the same desires and pride—women who, no matter how hard they worked, still remained mired in poverty—could join hands and support and encourage one another without interference.

The women who joined our association held a wide range of positions; they were telephone operators, postal workers, typists, teachers, and bank clerks. But they all shared the anger at the low esteem with which they were regarded by the world at large, so they had considerable expectations for our journal. So, beginning with the inaugural issue, we carried the stories of the joys and sorrows, the frustrations and the irritations that they experienced as working women, and appealed to our readers for support.

Also in the inaugural issue was an article by Sano Manabu, a leader of the social movement and a professor at Waseda University titled "Women and Society."[9] The thrust of his article was that without the destruction of capitalism, there could be no real liberation of women. Given the period, when there was still a great deal of excitement over the success of the Russian Revolution, to get a manuscript from one of the top spokesmen for that wing of the movement was, especially for the younger women in our association, a real triumph, something to be very excited about. Sano, himself, seemed to like our publication, as he contributed articles frequently, and there were a number of people on our editorial staff who were deeply involved in his movement. In fact, they would say to me from time to time, "Mr. Sano says he is willing to help pay for our printing costs, so we could put out this magazine without having to be so poor. Won't you at least meet with him once?"

Sakai Toshihiko, who was always too good to me, summoned me and suggested that if I would just agree to it, we could put out an official magazine for socialist women and I wouldn't always have to have such a hard time with money. At least give it some thought, he pleaded. But I had to tell him frankly that due to my own lack of study, I didn't really understand socialism that well, and I felt it would be wrong to use funds from the movement just because we were in financial straits. . . .

Social movements were thriving and our magazine received a lot of support from the reading public, and sales were strong. Readers stretched from north to south and encompassed a wide range of people. However, when they began arresting Communist Party members one after another, I was surprised to see that among the women who were arrested, nearly 90 percent appeared on the roster of our readership. It was shocking to see that women whom I had never met but who had written to us as working women, as farm wives, or students, were being arrested one by one. (75–78)

Returned to Ashes and Dust by the Great Kantō Earthquake

As we rode the wave of enthusiasm for *Working Women* and were taking good care of the publication, we were suddenly assaulted by the Great Kantō Earthquake on September 1. After shaking us so hard we thought the world might be turning upside down, fires broke out everywhere, turning Tokyo in a single day into a burnt field. An enormous number of people lost their lives and their homes were thrown into a terrible state of confusion. On the morning of the next day, September 2, I went walking amid the burnt-out ruins of Kanda in search of our editorial offices. I will never forget my feelings when I stumbled upon them. In one single night, all our work and dreams had been turned into ashes.

It was at this same time that Ōsugi and Itō [Noe] were murdered. (79)

On Receiving Takamure Itsue

It was a little bit after [I had returned to Shingū and given birth to my daughter] when I had an unforgettable experience at Shingū. It was September of the year following my daughter's birth; we were on the way home from my mother-in-law's funeral. I was notified by the Shingū police that there was a woman who needed protection and could I come get her. Her name was Takamure Itsue and apparently I was being appointed her guarantor. Without being able to absorb all the details of the situation, I immediately ran down to the police station.

I knew Ms. Takamure quite well through her husband, Hashimoto Kenzō. Since I was fairly close to Hashimoto, I had corresponded with Takamure frequently and solicited manuscripts for our magazine from her. Takamure had grown weary of living with Hashimoto and had left him, fleeing all the way to Shingū, where the local police had picked her up for her own protection. Fearful that she might commit suicide, Hashimoto had asked the police to keep an eye out for her.

Not having seen her for a while, I was struck by how tired Takamure looked. We spent one evening together talking, noting how the current family system did not do much to sustain a woman's life (Takamure wrote more extensively about her feelings on this matter in her article "Women and the Family: Why I left Home" ["Onna to katei—Watashi no iede ni tsuite"] in The Women's Movement (Fujin undō), combined Oct.–Nov. issue, 1925). The next day, Hashimoto came to get Takamure.[10]

Thereafter, Takamure and Hashimoto became a couple who were the envy of everyone. With her husband's devoted cooperation, Takamure laid the foundations for women's history in Japan. I was impressed with how these efforts were so typical of the kind of work of which she was capable.

Changing the Name to *Women and Labor (Fujin to rōdō)*

So the magazine did see the light of day once again. We decided to change the name of the magazine to *Women and Labor* and resolved to try to make it a movement with working women at the core. This was April 1, 1924. Not wanting to have a repetition of what had happened before, we poured a lot of energy into stabilizing our finances. We reduced the amount of money we would pay for poetry, and conscientiously went out and called on our supporters to collect their contributions every month. We also put forth some effort to increase advertising revenue. . . .

We somehow managed to put out *Women and Labor* every month as intended. Many kind people like Yamakawa Kikue, Hirayabashi Hatsunosuke, and Abe Isō willingly contributed manuscripts. Also, friends of mine like Takano Tsugi, Hirata Nobu, and Ikuta Hanayo were active contributors on a regular basis. Perhaps more importantly, many people with no name recognition at all, the many working women, the women in the factories, and the impoverished housewives at home, submitted their contributions.

I had written [this appeal]:

Let us discover together our own existence amongst the many trials and sorrows, and all the pain and frustration that well up in our lives everyday. To this end, let us not allow unknown people to be buried and isolated by themselves. Let us raise our voices and join our hands together!

The Problem Is Our Lifestyles Today

There can be no question that the number and variety of working women has grown dramatically in recent years. What with teachers, typists, office workers, operators, nurses, a working woman is no longer an unusual sight. Every year, around the time of graduation, all the women's magazines target the working woman. They invite young girls to dream by displaying extensive photographs of working women clad in the uniforms, smiling and laughing. As a result, naive young women flock to Tokyo wanting to become working women, but that doesn't mean their days of poverty are over.

It's really no joke. Their irresponsibility infuriates me. Do these women's magazines that deceive women with their glossy photographs offer the slightest hint of the difficulties of trying to get a job in Tokyo, or of the poverty and loneliness that may await them there? Will they offer up one single job to these young women who can't wait to leave their homes and set foot in Tokyo? It is hardly the norm that these earnest but poor young women from the country are going to possess the skills to fend for themselves in the middle of a big city like Tokyo. I found myself frequently placing a statement in our journal to this effect: "Please beware of leaving home and coming to the city unprepared!" ...

We also published in our magazine many stories incorporating the tragic experiences of many of the young women who came to Tokyo in search of jobs. And even if they do succeed in landing a job, the wages scarcely amount to anything at all, and when they get home, they have housework and child-care duties waiting for them. We also ran letters from women who were in tears because of unwanted sexual remarks and advances from their supervisors, but knew they couldn't afford to quit their jobs. All the frustration and sadness that attends these women working two or even three jobs, but still, their existence is still mired in poverty. This is the reality of the working world for the majority of women. It is precisely this reality that we must improve.

Since it was my belief that it is movements arising from social realities that are the most significant movements, I had naturally distanced myself from those movements that want to continually go back to the established parties in search of support extending the franchise to women. Moreover, I had gradually grown apart from that type of woman who never has to worry about her own "pocket money." I spent my time running around with my daughter strapped to my back taking care of editorial duties, selling advertising, and helping young women find decent jobs. (80–85)

It was difficult to keep Working Women *going after the earthquake and while Oku took time off to have another child. In order to appeal to a wider audience of working women, the name was changed to* Women and Labor, *and they would change the name again in 1925.*

Changing Names to *The Women's Movement (Fujin undō)*

As of the September issue, 1925, we changed the name again, this time from *Women and Labor* to *The Women's Movement* ... and we moved our home and the offices to Shimo Uratachō. This was a reflection of our attempt to broaden the range of our readership—and the object of our concern—from just working women to incorporate proletarian women. At this time, the proletarian movement was gaining momentum, so there was influence from this direction. But it was also because I wanted to bring together women with various backgrounds and experiences—women from all over Japan, be they proletarians, farmers, factory workers, office workers, housewives, students—women who could speak from schools, kitchens, offices, and factories and create a movement that could actually "recover women's authentic position" *(hontō no onnajishin no chii ni tachikaeru undō)*. If this was to be regarded as a proletarian women's movement, then I wanted to see *The Women's Movement* as its foundation.

At one of my lectures, I raised the following argument:

Should women really be rejoicing because women's occupations have been on the rise? Why has the scope of occupations in which women can work expanded so much? Is it because women are economical and easy to employ? Is it because they don't tend to organize and voice their complaints? At any rate, it is hardly because society is equipped to understand what the working life of women is actually about.

Finally, people are learning a little bit about how difficult is the life that proletarian women must lead. Whether they get married or not, they are going to have to work if they want to survive. These women who have long endured their situation without raising their voices are finally starting to open their mouths. But how come these women do not vent their various frustrations and anger, but only bow their heads and complain softly? Don't they realize that it's not their fault that no matter how hard they may work, they never escape poverty? Society continues to work. I felt strongly that it is up to us, with our own hands, to develop and spread a proletarian women's movement. (86–88)

Toward the Consumer Union Movement

ABOUT THE WESTERN REGIONAL CONSUMER COOPERATIVE SOCIETY (SEIKŌ KYŌDŌSHA)

One day, Nii Itaru, a social critic with whom I was familiar, visited me at my home, urging me to move to Nakano to assist with the Nakano Consumer Union Movement, which had been growing at a substantial rate. He said that he had located a good rental and could arrange a loan for the deposit.

Given that I was already quite interested in consumer union movements as an outgrowth of my interest in the housewives movement, I responded positively to Mr. Nii's kind offer and decided to move to Nakano right away. My house was a very convenient five-minute walk from Nakano Station. At the same location as my new house were the offices of the Seikō Consumer Union Cooperative Association. It was the fall of Taishō 15 [1926], just after the foundation of the Seikō Cooperative Association.

The cooperative was established as a branch of the League of Kantō Consumer Unions, which was based on the concept of consumer unions for workers as a result of a proposal by Okamoto Rikichi. It was centered around a group of proletarian intellectuals. . . . Mr. Nii lent me book after book on the consumer movement, and I had the chance to study up on the idea. I became completely immersed in the movement, and my enthusiasm welled up strongly. I began to visit houses in the neighborhood, pledging to myself that I would add two new members to the union membership rolls each day.

In November of 1927, the women in the union movement founded a new "Association of Households" (Kateikai). It was based on the realization that the position of housewives was extremely important to the unions, and without them, the unions could not prosper. Since I felt that housewives were the primary actors in the whole consumption process, and that the consumer union movement should be led by mothers and housewives, I was delighted by the creation of the Association of Households and planned to work hard for their development. . . . (89–91)

Forming the Cooperative Women's Consumer Union

It is not really possible for the ordinary housewife to separate her life from the life of the family, so it is really through the act of consuming that she comes to understand the workings of society. Therefore, it seemed to me that this is where meaning resided for housewives' participation in the consumer union movement. In fact, the consumer union movement was the movement best suited to housewives.

Since I hoped to see mothers with their infants on their back, or taking their young child by the hand and participating in the consumer union movement, I put out a call to women who shared the same vision to form a consumer union by and for women. I decided to call it the "Women's Consumer Cooperative Society" (Fujin Shōhikumiai Kyōkai). I was the chairwoman, but I was assisted by Akamatsu Junko, Maruoka Hideko, Hirata Nobu, and Murayama Fumiko. First we needed to come up with a slogan to attract members, and we came up with "All women [should join] the Women's Consumer Cooperative Society" (fujin wa subete shōhikumiai *kyōkai e)*. Our offices were located at the outset in the same place as the Working Women's Association in the Ichigaya area of Tokyo.

As consumers, women were interested first in things like price increases and the marketing of poor-quality products, but also in child welfare, motherhood, school reform, tax reform, the increase in social welfare facilities, and the like. These were the areas to which we needed to lend our voices, and when we weren't busy doing that, we would pursue things like getting agricultural products directly from the producer to the consumer, gathering price data, inspecting the quality of everyday goods, and calling for the increased availability of instructional classes. . . .

At the outset, the Women's Consumer Cooperative Society sponsored a series of lectures on "Women and the Economy" featuring speakers like Okamoto Rikichi, Kagawa Toshihiko, and specialists in the field of consumer unions. In terms of a bulletin, we put out a monthly newsletter, *Women and the Household*, to disseminate this information. Membership fees were fifty sen per person. Up until that time, the women's movement had really neglected the everyday problems confronted by housewives, but now the Women's Consumer Cooperative Society would be taking each one up carefully. So we grew steadily, and by 1930 we were able to host our second nationwide conference with representatives from all over Japan. At this conference, there was an outpouring of lively discussion on such issues as enacting a mother-child assistance law, establishing public birth control information centers, abolishing the sales tax, and so on. Moreover, the year before, during the Tokyo City Council elections, we had issued a declaration of support for the proletarian party candidates, indicating the breadth and variety of our concerns.

However, in the end, we were forced to dissolve the Women's Consumer Cooperative Society. This was in large measure because many of the working women who constituted the core of our union were dismayed by the dissolution of the proletarian parties, and this resulted in a splintering of their efforts. I was extremely disappointed. I had genuinely believed that a union made by and for women was an ideal worth pursuing, and this conviction continued to run through the depths of my being so that in the postwar period, it would translate directly into the creation of the Shufu Rengōkai, or Japan Housewives Association. . . . (91–94)

Oku had begun a trajectory that would take her from a powerful organization of women who pressured the legislature to change the laws regarding women's participation in politics to an organization dedicated to meeting the needs of ordi-

nary working women. But the very definition of working women was changing in post–World War I Japan so that after launching this second organization, Oku realized she was attracting urban office workers and the like but was still leaving thousands of poor women unaffected. Her next step, then, was to try and reach what she called the proletarian women by direct appeal and by working through the proletarian political parties that appeared after the Universal Manhood Suffrage Bill was passed in 1925. As she explains below, she considered her activity as a "rear guard" action, or her way of supporting revolutionary ideals without belonging to any specific political party, legal or otherwise.

Why a "Rear Guard" Action?

THE COLLAPSE OF THE PROLETARIAN WOMEN'S MOVEMENT

In 1927, as a backdrop to the formation of the proletarian parties, efforts to form independent proletarian women's organizations were begun. Of course, since women lacked fundamental rights of political participation, not to mention the right to form political parties, the tendency was there to establish a nationwide organization, a Fujin Dōmei, or Women's League. This should have constituted a substantial political movement capable of mounting a significant push for issues important to women such as the right of women to form political associations, the abolition of gender inequality in law, the abolition of wage differentiation between male and female employees, equality in education, the abolition of prostitution, prohibiting women from doing night work and working in mines, protecting mothers and children, and so on. . . .

The Women's League at first claimed that its class base would be proletarian women, so I had high expectations for the organization. However, as I pushed for my ideal of practical, realistic movement grounded in the everyday life of the masses of women, it became apparent that this was an unrealizable ideal. I continually had conflicts with the left-wing proletarian men who operated behind the scenes or through some of the left-wing women. They were happy to see our women's organization turned into something they could control as their puppet. I couldn't help seeing the women who fronted for these men as somehow lifeless.

Anyhow, I could not accept the idea that we should abandon the issues that mattered most to women and call instead for an all-out class war. Besides, the people in this camp had their share of complications that normally arise in human society between men and women, such as unexpected pregnancies, and, in the end, it was always the women who had to take care of these sorts of things. I knew a number of young women in the movement who had these kinds of distressing encounters, and it just reinforced a sense in me that women had to stand on their own and quickly establish their own base. . . .

Oppose the Dissolution of the Proletarian Parties

The first general election held after the enactment of universal manhood suffrage was held in February 1928. . . . I did not actually belong to a proletarian party, but many asked for my support. So I would head out almost every day and encourage women by declaring that "All women should support the proletarian parties!"

These proletarian parties, who also represented people who had been oppressed for a long time, adopted a class position that called for the liberation of women who had likewise endured oppression. The proletarian parties who advocated that women's issues were identical with those of the proletarian class appealed to women to join hands with them and strive for liberation. This was not the same as the established political parties like the Seiyūkai and Minseitō supporting the idea of recognizing women's rights just because it may work to their advantage. Rather, I was calling for each individual woman from her place in the kitchen, the office, the classroom, or the factory to support the proletarian parties.

However, later these very proletarian parties betrayed our passionate support of them by repeatedly fragmenting in a way that was completely disheartening. Prior to the general election of 1930, I expressed my deep anger and disappointment, as well as my hopes for the future, in the January issue of *The Women's Movement.* I wrote,

> The established political parties are mired in a bog and struggling. We should take advantage of this opportunity to promote the causes of our proletarian parties. But most of them are in disarray, engaging in mutual name calling and spreading distrust. Oppose the fragmentation of proletarian parties! We women need to avoid getting caught up in the maelstrom and work to preserve our proletarian parties.

I had various friends in these parties that were fragmenting, and they were good people, people whom we could trust. But, no matter how excellent they were as individual people, when it came to accusing each other and becoming entangled with each other's affairs, it was truly sad. The proletarian parties should not have been fragmenting in this manner. My own attitudes were criticized as being "opportunistic," but that didn't change the way I felt. Remember, at the time I wrote these words, the established parties were defining citizenship in very conservative terms, wanting to place limitations on women's rights by arguing that "Women's civic rights should be restricted to city, town, and village. Women elected to honorary positions ought to have their husbands' permission." So I recall being extremely frustrated amid circumstances like these. (94–98)

The general election in 1928 was the first time the expanded electorate created by the Universal Manhood Suffrage Bill of 1925 was able to participate. A number of small "proletarian" parties had crystallized on the left and attacked the "established" parties like the Seiyūkai and Kenseikai (later Minseitō). Oku was grappling to find her own way to realize her goals and aims for Japanese women. While the expansion of the electorate was a welcome development, nothing had been done at that time to incorporate women into the electorate. Although Oku was undecided exactly what form her movement should take, she understood that women needed to establish the grounds of their own being, to constitute their subjectivity themselves. Advocacy for women's rights at the parliamentary level had hardly scratched the surface of women's lives, and when it came to reaching out to working women and impoverished proletarian women, care had to be taken that they were not prevented from defining their own subjectivity, from determining the basis of their citizenship. She was willing to work with and through Marxists and proletarian political organizations, but she was not willing to have her autonomy and identity erased by them. In the following section she continues her quest to understand what is involved in awakening women politically and discovers that the answer might lie in the ordinary, mundane activities in which women engage.

What does it mean to politically awaken women? When I think about this, a small number of women who leave their homes and their children, give up their jobs and throw themselves into politics, comes to mind. But can we call this a real political movement? What I think of as a genuine political movement occurs when ordinary women discover politics that is rooted in their everyday lives and they make their path a source of light, a road to a bright future. We tend to make such a big deal out of elections and the Diet these days, but there are many mundane, ordinary tasks that pile up in our everyday lives. So my idea of what a women's movement should be is one in which housewives, mothers, and working women all dig down into the root of their very existences, organize on that basis, and participate in politics. I had reached this conclusion previously when the New Women's Association had ended up becoming a movement aimed at gaining adherents in the Diet. . . . In 1931, when the Lower House passed women's civic law but the House of Councilors rejected it, I wrote the following.

> The right of women to participate in politics is an important part of world trends right now just like radio, talkies, and airplanes. It is not, therefore, something that women should have benevolently bestowed upon them piece by piece by the established parties like the Minseitō and Seiyūkai. It is something women must obtain for themselves just as they decide where they might live or what they might eat.
>
> Women, step forward and seize [it]. Advocate! Join hands and don't take a single step backward. Stand on your own two feet and grasp your civic and political rights in just the same way that men do. In the end, it will be in anticipation of that day when we will rise up and use political participation as our weapon! (*The Women's Movement*, February 1931). (98–100)

The Meaning of "Rear Guard"

I was often told by radical Marxists,

> People like you are frightening reactionaries. Instead of implanting basic revolutionary thoughts in the minds of these women whose social consciousness is still limited, you get them all involved in consumer economics, rationalizing their lives, and participating in a cooperative lifestyle. But that just increases their interests in those sorts of activities, and necessarily postpones the arrival of the revolution.

In such instances I would stiffen my spine and reply,

> Our job is to pursue the second and third lines of the social movement. In other words, we are doing the work of the rear guard. To the fighters of the vanguard, just to have the revolution is enough. Love, children, the consumer economy, the cooperativization of life—these are merely unimportant details. However, for the ordinary proletarian housewife who lives in poverty, the main problems, the ones that press upon them every day, come from their children and from the household economy. The price of a diaper

or a serving of tofu—these are what count. The fact is, even on the eve of the revolution, women will be giving birth to babies and raising children. To put roots down in the midst of their everyday life, and to cut out a path to social revolution—this is our job!

Our standpoint is that we will always be with the rear guard, we will always be part of the actual, the real *(jissai)* movement. Doubtless, there will arise among us fighters who, time after time, will choose the first line, and with close connections to their comrades, they will light the signal fires and prepare to do battle. But we have to continue to soak our babies with milk, cut the grass in our fields, and, while stained with factory dust, look to advance the social revolutionary movement as people who are enmeshed in the problems of everyday life.

As long as time and health permit, I am resolved to pour all I have into the cause of those women who must suffer everyday in agony. I am not passing judgment on the role of any of the women who might throw themselves into the proletarian movement, or immerse themselves in the suffrage movement, or take part in the first line of activity. In fact, I have learned much from these people, and I have been assisted by them, while, in turn, I have helped them as well. But, for myself, until the end, I want to walk alongside the ordinary masses of women; I continue to believe that I want to be solidly grounded in the rear guard of the movement. (101–102)

Starting Women's Settlements

In 1930, I took up a new task: the Women's Settlement Movement in Honjo. Up to this point, settlements had been something that members of the privileged classes did for the underprivileged; that is, they taught them, offered them guidance, and assisted them. But was this really the true way a settlement should operate? Shouldn't there be a martial arts training facility *(dōjō)* or a social school *(shakai gakkō)* where people could help each other, learn together, and forge a common bond? I had watched a number of settlements cropping up here and there, and it was my thought that there could be just such a place. . . . (118–119)

Women's Freedom to Choose

Whenever I think about birth control, I remember my own mother who died so young. Memories of her experiences—giving birth to babies one after another, falling ill every time she gave birth, then, finally, dying—

taught me well about the tragedy of multiple births. There is not only the tragedy of the young mother who must leave behind her beloved children, but there are also the children who must get along without their mother. People are fond of saying, "The poor always have lots of kids," and no doubt this is true. But there are many instances when parents have lost their own health because of so many children. Whenever I see these weak and sickly mothers in the cities, the mountain villages, and the fishing villages, I always see visions of my mother's face.

For women, birth should be something sacred, a source of great joy. Unfortunately, however, aren't there really only a privileged few for whom birth brings such happiness, and who actually have the wherewithal to sufficiently nurture and raise their child in a good environment? For the poor, knowledge of birth control is essential. The entire basis for my advocacy of birth control is simply that women must have the right to decide this most basic issue that affects their happiness: whether or not to give birth.

Finally, with the tragic rise of mother-child suicides in the wake of the Shōwa Panic, the necessity of birth control gained some social recognition. This was coupled with the visit to Japan by Margaret Sanger and the development of the birth control movement by Umajima Hiroshi. Finally, we could see the possibility of averting the tragedy for women of these multiple births. In January of 1931, the League for Birth Control in Japan was established, which I joined and offered my ideas as effectively as I could.

In actuality, though, even though birth control was ostensibly being addressed, it was largely in the hands of profit-driven doctors and businessmen, a kind of sham movement, restricted by officialdom to "only when the physical health of the mother is affected." So there really were not many instances when birth control was spoken about in terms of the health of motherhood, as a social problem, or as a woman's right. Consequently, there were cases under the rubric of "pregnancy termination" in which unsanitary implements were used and women's health was impaired.

Whenever I gave a speech or wrote an article about birth control, I would always get tons of letters asking for advice. Later, many women actually came to me directly for consultations. They were all poor, uneducated, good women who just believed that if they had one more child, they would have no choice but to let it starve to death. Among the letters, there were ones from mothers who seemed to be bedridden, dictating to a friend who would write in an unsteady hand, asking if they couldn't get some information on birth control. I couldn't help but feel a pain deep in my heart that there were so many women out there in need of accurate birth control information. . . . (128–129)

Everyone into Settlements! Let's Have Settlements Everywhere!

"People with talent, give talent. People with money, give money. People with time, give of their labor." I liked to think of women's settlements as a school for society. Here, women learn as they continue to work, and as they learn, they begin to function in a larger social context. In the settlement, there is no such thing as a single isolated individual; there are an unlimited number of friends to help you out, to teach you and share your joys and sorrows. We don't want to turn our lives over to an entrepreneur. We want to have all our needs met by the settlement so that our children's clothing, food, health care, hobbies, amusements are all taken care of by women working cooperatively. In order for this to happen, it is necessary to have a cooperative system to join all women. That is why I went around calling upon all women to contribute their learning, their talent, their energy, and any extra money to the settlement. This will definitely provide each of you with a broader social vision and should leave you with something very special. (135) . . . I was able to continue the settlement movement with the help of many children, fathers, mothers, employees, and countless other famous and completely unknown people who cooperated with us. From the vantage point of the whole country, it was just a tiny little movement, but it was our "settlement for women, by women, and belonging to women." There were definitely hard times, but the settlements were also the source of our sense of ownership.

However, I poured so much time and energy into the settlement that I neglected *The Women's Movement*. Readership fell by two-thirds. People said to me, "Others can do the settlement work, but you need to do the work that others can't do." Ultimately, though, I was unable to abandon the settlement movement. Both were necessary to me: *The Women's Movement* for theory, women's settlement for practice. (137–138)

The Working Women's Houses *(Hatarakufujin no Ie)*

All these working women, cooperating together on their own initiative to improve their lives, mutually helping one another, and by being helped, joining their hearts as one, together building and sustaining a social enterprise—this is what the ideal of the "Working Women's House" was all about. And we could say that the fact that all of the groups of working women in Tokyo, Osaka, Fukui, Nagoya, and Kyoto soon gave birth to their own "Houses," one after the other, is testimony to the resonance that this ideal of young working women generated in the hearts of so many women. (147)

Toward a Workplace with Flowers *(Hana aru shokuba e)*

At this time, Japan began embarking on a straight line toward war. In July of 1937, the Marco Polo Bridge Incident occurred, which launched the Sino-Japanese War. In 1939 there was the Nomonhan Incident, followed by the outbreak of the Pacific War in 1941. So, it was like a snowball effect as Japan expanded its war effort, which continued until 1945 and Japan's defeat.

After 1933, when the Osaka Working Women's House was completed, followed by Tokyo's version in 1935, the war raged more fiercely every day. This meant that the number of soldiers being shipped out was also growing by the day, so the importance of working women grew accordingly. Unlike the men who were being shipped out by the government, women were being told to work, work, work! Women who were already working were now expected to make up for the lack of manpower due to the war and were asked to work even harder. Many began to experience physical hardships as a result. I think it was around August of 1939 at our own Sunflower Dormitory at the Osaka Working Women's House that women began collapsing from overwork one after another, and women with anemia and low-grade fevers grew steadily. A doctor dubbed these symptoms as constituting "the sunflower disease." . . . (154)

So the ideals I had cherished for so many years were being distorted by the wartime experience. My vision of constructing bottom-up cooperative associations had been realized over time in the form of the settlements and Working Women's Houses. Organizations like the women's consumer unions arose out of the desire to pursue the ideals of cooperativizing and socializing our lives. Through the rationalization and collectivization of life, women should have become more liberated.

The women's settlements and Working Women's Houses, too, brought with them the conveniences of modern civilization that had heretofore been restricted to use by the wealthy. Lessons in things like cooking and ikebana, which had previously only been available to women with leisure time on their hands, were now made accessible to many more women. It demonstrated what women could do if instead of acting alone, they joined hands and cooperated with one another. I appealed to these women to join hands and, at their own initiative, earnestly walk along the path to collaboration *(kyōdōka)*.

Then the war came along. Under wartime pressures, women's lives became even busier; they became poorer and more harried. If people wanted to think about ways to make women's lives a little more comfortable or give them a little sense of pride, I always urged people to make housework and the rest of their lives more cooperative as well.

Of course, rationalizing life, socializing it, meant that there would have to be a revolution in men's consciousness. Along with giving working women more recognition and recognizing the power that working women possess, I explained that women in the workplace would have to be given jobs commensurate with their abilities, while men would have to start doing their share of housework. During the wartime emergency, if women of leisure didn't have to work, then that would be unfair. If women who had not had to work up until now helped working women with their housework, or else took on their own fair share of work, then working women could reduce their hours by up to two hours per day. There should also be more days off. I felt that the inescapable burdens and sacrifices required by the war ought to be shared equally by everybody.

My dream of women autonomously socializing and cooperativizing their lives was embarked on a path to realization by the war, but in a distorted form. In villages, for example, the 210 union-based collective cooking facilities of 1938 became 18,364 in number by 1941, while collective nurseries numbered 30,949, an increase of over ten times what it had been before. In the cities, neighborhood groups had been organized in 1940 that pushed for the rationalization and collectivization of life. But it was all for one single purpose: "to win the war." (156–158)

Analysis

> [M]emory leaves only a trace of an earlier experience that we adjust into story; experience itself is mediated by the ways we describe and interpret it to others and ourselves. . . . Even more fundamentally, the language we use to "capture" memory and experience can never "fix" the "real" experience, but only approximate it, yielding up its own surplus of meaning or revealing its own artificial closures.[11]

The story that Oku Mumeo seeks to impart about her life is the story of a

*dedicated feminist in search of the most effective ways to enhance women's politi-
cal and economic power. To this end, she uses language to the best of her ability
in order "capture" and "fix" real experience and insert it into the historical record.
Her aim is to depict the rise and fall of the New Women's Association and her
subsequent involvement with organizations that sought to connect with women in
the workplace or on the home front, and to do so in as factual a manner as possible. But this is not say that her autobiography is lacking in depth and subtlety.
The narrator explores a range of intellectual, religious, and philosophical positions
that she wrestled with before settling on the course that she chose to pursue. But
often the path chosen would prove unsatisfactory, and she would have to discover
another one. In this sense, Oku epitomizes Scott's notion of a socially active
woman as a historical "site," a location "where crucial political and cultural contests are enacted."[12] In her experimentation with different personal philosophies
and ideologies and her employment of a range of strategies to achieve her ends,
Oku was grappling with real problems that she found before her and contesting
the political and economic conditions in which women labored.*

*She begins her account, interestingly, with something very basic: women
and work. She entered a spinning mill under an assumed name to gather information about working conditions in the industry that employed the most women
throughout the country. But soon she joined forces with the leading feminists of
her day to form a political organization dedicated to obtaining basic political
rights for women. In the end, these efforts were disappointing because, aimed as
they were at elites, they did little to engage or connect with ordinary Japanese
women. So what comes through clearly in Oku's text is the centrality of numerous contested positions and the narrator's quest for some way to engage women
at the point where their everyday lives were lived.*

*Oku had begun her activism by working through the media and the New
Women's Association, petitioning the Diet, and trying to change the laws. Although she and her comrades were modestly successful in their endeavors, it did
not seem as though ordinary women's lives were being very significantly affected. As she would write in her text, "What I think of as a genuine political
movement occurs when ordinary women discover politics rooted in their everyday lives and they make their path a source of light, a road to a bright future.
. . . [M]y idea of what a women's movement should be is one in which housewives, mothers, and working women all dig down into the root of their very existences, organize on that basis, and participate in politics." This led Oku to try
and address women's issues through a working women's association and ultimately through consumer cooperative associations, and, finally, through the development of women's settlements. All of these efforts were successful to some*

degree, but especially after Japan moved to a wartime footing, their liberal, feminist sympathies and the emphasis on birth control became unwelcome.

Oku's text suggests that although she never formally embraced socialism or became a Marxist, her sympathies were with ordinary people and with the proletarian parties. But as her remarks in response to Yamakawa Kikue's critique of the New Women's Association suggest, she was always more interested in practical results than in ideology or "-isms," as the put it. Therefore, her story is not about the triumph of a particular ideology or even a specific strategy; nor is it the story of an individual woman who sacrifices everything in order to remain true to her principles. Rather, it is very much the story of a woman who was willing to do whatever was required to help women make any kind of progress under an increasingly repressive state. Although it is downplayed somewhat in Fires Burning Brightly, *Oku was more than willing to compromise and embrace the wartime program of "communalization" as long as it advanced the cause of working women. As Narita Ryūichi notes,*

In sum, Oku Mumeo's activities under the wartime system supported and contributed to that system, sought official recognition, and were directed towards modernization of the working class and especially the home environment of working women. . . . Oku aimed to transform women into active subjects solely as the bearers of domestic labor and the possessors of motherhood. Because the social situation itself changed between the 1920s and the wartime era, in the sense that private entities of all kinds were converted into public ones, Oku's own logic reflected that change. But throughout, she consistently adhered to the objective of modernizing the life circumstances of working women.[13]

This is why, in the postwar years, Oku was able to resume her work seamlessly, standing for election to the House of Councilors in 1946 and establishing the Japan Housewives Association in 1948, the symbol of which was the rice ladle (shamoji). *If she was consistent, though, she was also often paradoxical. She embraced almost all the prominent left-wing causes but declined to actually join any Marxist parties or organizations. Although her non-ideological brand of social activism could, at times, be quite radical—such as when she campaigned actively on behalf of the proletarian parties in the late 1920s—it was always governed by a practical bent. Oku was a woman interested in helping women and getting results. Moreover, the driving force behind her social activism was a fierce commitment to gender equality. Her recollections of her youth centered on her father's willingness to hold up women writers and social activists as examples to emulate, and on the difficulties her mother faced as a typical Japanese housewife. Bullied by a tyrannical husband and forced to bear seven children, Oku's mother's life was over by the time she was thirty-three. Despite the fact that her father manifested a liberal and enlightened outlook to his daughter, Oku never forgot what her mother had to suffer through, and she dedicated her life to improving conditions for working women and housewives. If her text is, like others, "a medium for resistance and counter discourse, the legitimate space for producing" a narrative that undermines the very essence of patriarchal hegemony, then surely it is because of this underlying awareness rooted in her own family.*

But, of course, family is only a part of the story. Education and the sociopolitical environment in which the narrator grew to maturity are also important variables. As we shall see in chapter 6, when Fukunaga Misao entered Tokyo Women's University in 1924, she found an active leftist student movement in which to immerse herself. Oku, attending Japan Women's University twelve years earlier, entered a much more conservative institution in an era before World War I had sparked a fascination with liberal politics and socialist ideals. Therefore, Oku was completely bored and spent her time reading in the library. She read eclectically and found herself drawn to theories of art, religion, and philosophy. It is no coincidence that after graduation she went to work as a tutor for a wealthy family in Kamakura, a center for Zen Buddhism, and realized after trying to practice Zen that neither intellectual nor religious pursuits were what inspired her. She wanted to throw herself into the world and see what she could accomplish in the realm of social activism.

By this time, World War I was over and left-wing study groups were fairly ubiquitous. Oku was familiar with all the leading Marxists and feminists of her day and had read a wide variety of economic and political literature by them. Inspired by her contact with Ōsugi Sakae and his anarchist followers, Oku was drawn to the labor movement. In a quest for praxis, she entered the Fuji Gas Spinning Mill under false pretenses in 1918 in order to see firsthand what working conditions were like for women. From that point forward, her life was dedicated to trying to improve the quality of women's lives by whatever means seemed the most effective. It was a journey that took her through political work, publishing, and finally efforts to bring politics into the workplace and the kitchen, where women's lives were centered. This is where women faced problems of power, gender, and sexuality. Oku became a passionate advocate of birth control and wanted to make sure that basic information about birth control be disseminated to poor women in both the city and the countryside. As she wrote, "To put roots down in the midst of their everyday life, and to cut out a path to social revolution—this is our job!" Through her Settlement Houses, Oku hoped to disseminate information about women's bodies and birth control, but the onset of the Pacific War and the official government policy of increasing the population all but negated her efforts.

Perhaps more than anything else, Fires Burning Brightly *is written to set the record straight, to provide a detailed account of what prewar feminists tried to do on behalf of women. Inevitably, it is a narrative that incorporates all the pain, the contradictions, and the frustrations that accompany the experimentation with different political orientations, and the groping for the correct path to follow in life. Writing in the late 1980s, there was every reason to fear that the stories of such people as Oku Mumeo would be completely unknown to young Japanese women. Wanting to create an accurate record and leave behind an account for future generations to read, Oku decided to write her life and to try and capture in her text not only the sense of risk and contestation that she constantly faced, but some of the passion and commitment that "burned so brightly" in her life as well.*

3

Changing Consciousness
Takai Toshio's *My Own Sad History of Female Textile Workers (Watashi no jokō aishi)*

Hori (Takai) Toshio was born on October 26, 1902, in a remote mountain village on the Ibi River in Gifu Prefecture. Her father, the third son of a farming family, was a charcoal maker, and her early childhood memories were mostly of poverty and hardship. Conscious of becoming an economic burden on her family and desirous of being financially independent as early as possible, young Toshio was excited when recruiters from the textile mills came to her village. She began her career as a mill worker when she was barely twelve years old. In the years just after World War I she became exposed to the union movement and strikes for better working conditions. Through her involvement in the labor movement she met Hosoi Wakizō, the pioneering researcher on working conditions for female textile workers. They lived together while he was immersed in completing the research for his manuscript, but he died shortly after his book appeared. Takai was devastated by his death. She tried to resume her career as a mill worker, but her association with Wakizō compromised her ability to obtain and keep a job in the mills. In the meantime, she met a carpenter and labor activist named Takai Shintarō. Eventually they would marry and have children, but harassment by the police and the hardships of World War II took a toll on their family life. Her autobiography tells the story of the varieties of hardship she encountered in her life with both Hosoi and Takai.

Many Japanese women who chose to leave a record of their lives were social activists in the 1920s and 1930s, dedicated to such causes as the expansion of women's political rights and the organization of female workers in the emerging industrial economy. For them, it was important to leave an account of their struggles, their triumphs, and their defeats. It is as though writing is their way of reordering their lives—lives that were shaped by momentous social and his-

torical events. Of course, as we have seen, most feminist scholars agree that just the act of writing their lives is an act of assertion that is significant in terms of reversing women's status from object in a male-dominated discourse to an assertive, speaking subject. But women were also writing in order to supplement the public record and leave a clear account of how they struggled to achieve greater gender equality in their society.

In her study, Lives of Their Own, *Martha Watson identifies an important force motivating women who elect to write their lives as "the desire of a person who had worked actively for a cause to demonstrate that her efforts and the cause she espoused were meaningful and important."*[1] *There can be little doubt that when Takai Toshio wrote the story of her life, she was writing in order to document and to justify her years as an activist in the labor movement. She was also seeking to establish the legitimacy of her claim to the legacy of Hosoi Wakizō (1897–1925), the man who wrote the powerful and compelling book about female textile workers,* The Sad History of Female Textile Workers (Jokō aishi). *The title of her own narrative,* My Own Sad History of Female Textile Workers (Watashi no jokō aishi) *echoes Hosoi's original and reflects the fact that she was his spouse at the time he researched and wrote his famous book. Watson goes on to observe that*

> [i]n writing their life stories, these women were expressing the possibility of a new kind of womanhood for others; in recording their life stories, these women were redefining womanhood and personhood for their contemporaries. To borrow and adapt Domna Stanton's terminology, they were constituting a new female subject.[2]

Expressing the possibility of a new kind of womanhood was very much on the minds of a significant number of autobiographies by Japanese women that appeared in the 1970s and 1980s. Having come of age in the 1920s and 1930s, these women desired to let younger women know what their foremothers had experienced in the prewar years. Witnesses to the rise of both the labor movement and the women's movement, these women have much to teach the younger generation, a point Takai makes explicit in the poem that appears at the end of her autobiography. Moreover, there can be no question that the varieties of self-representation found in texts like Takai's and others found in this volume offer a model for readers to measure their own lives and experiences against.

Although quite a few women had participated in the popular rights movement during the 1870s and 1880s, including Kishida Toshiko (1863–1901), whose fiery speeches inspired women like Fukuda Hideko to become politically engaged, it was after thousands of young women began entering the textile mills that the labor disputes and strikes began to involve women in broader social movements. As we have seen, the interwar years were transformative for Japan. There was a new emphasis on urban living, leisure, nightlife, and entertainment. Women were becoming serious consumers. They haunted the new department stores and experimented with new fashions. They dressed like flappers and adorned themselves with new cosmetics. They smoked, danced, and behaved promiscuously. But this modern flapper girl was only one of the new varieties of Japanese women. There were also women who were seeking to transform their lives in new varieties of employment. Moreover, there were also educated and discriminating housewives who were always in the market for tips on cooking, cleaning, and marital relations.³ These new women were sufficiently numerous to generate a bevy of new magazines that were aimed specifically at them, such as Women's World (Fujin sekai), Women's Club (Fujin kurabu), *and* Housewives' Companion (Shufu no tomo).

In addition to these developments in the new, urban, bourgeois culture, there was also a proletarian arts movement that was spreading among writers, artists, and filmmakers during the 1920s. Frequenting the less ostentatious cafés and dance halls, these young bohemians listened to jazz, spoke of revolution, and explored new forms of artistic expression. Meanwhile, in factories and textile mills, young men and women were organizing, reading left-wing tracts, and engaging management in labor disputes. When Hosoi Wakizō published his classic study of working conditions in the textile mills in 1925, it captured the attention and imagination of many readers. Published by Kaizōsha (which also published a monthly progressive journal, Kaizō [Reconstruction]), it was an impressive piece of investigative journalism that somehow seemed to be in tune with the times. Exhaustively researched and richly detailed, The Sad History of Female Textile Workers *was an exposé of working conditions in the mills, and as such it touched on a wide range of topics ranging from food and dormitory life to sexual harassment by predatory male supervisors. The book was something of an instant sensation. It sold extremely well and was widely read and cited.⁴ Unfortunately, the young author died within a month of his book's appearance. The immediate cause of death was acute peritonitis, but he had suffered numerous ailments throughout his life, for as an impoverished and often unemployed mill hand, he had never been able to afford adequate health care. In 1980, Hosoi's common-law wife, Takai (née Hori) Toshio, published her own autobiography in order to clarify the record about the early 1920s, her relationship with Hosoi, and her contributions to his work.*

Like Fukuda Hideko and Takamure Itsue, Takai Toshio's name was associ-

ated with a certain incident in her life that brought her notoriety, namely her relationship with Hosoi and the attitude taken toward her by the press and the publisher of Hosoi's work after his death. Her text is her opportunity to offer her version of events. But it is also an account of how a young twelve-year-old girl began a career working in the textile mills of Japan and where that first step of her journey would take her.

Hosoi Wakizō first met the young Hori Toshio in 1921, and they began living together shortly thereafter. Although Hosoi himself had worked extensively in the mills, for a great deal of his information on conditions in the workplace he relied on Toshio, who was working in the mills to support him while he completed his manuscript. Nearly every day he would ask her questions about working conditions and would often ask her to gather specific information for him. She was, in effect, his eyes and ears inside the textile mills, for once it was known that Hosoi was working on this book, he was denied access to the mills by management. When Toshio could not find work in the mills, she worked as a café waitress to support him and his work. After his death, Toshio received royalties from his work for a time, but later the publisher, Kaizōsha, upset with her lifestyle and her relationship with a man, refused to recognize their common-law marriage as legitimate and ceased forwarding any funds to her. The following is her account of her early life, her years with Hosoi, and some of the years that followed.

Early Life

Takai Toshio's life was not an easy one. The family moved frequently and usually lived in impoverished circumstances quite far from the nearest school. Therefore, although quite intelligent and academically adept, young Takai did not like school, where she felt the sting of teasing from other children to whom she was nothing more than the poor charcoal maker's daughter. She contrived to stay home from school whenever she could, but when present, she was the best student in her class at reading, writing, and mathematics. To the other children, however, she was just "the little monkey girl from the mountains," someone to ridicule and ostracize. But it was probably the deaths of two siblings that most marred Takai's childhood years.

Both My Younger Sister and Younger Brother Die

The next year, my little brother was born and I became a lot busier taking care of children. Then one summer's eve Shizue, my little sister whom I adored, became suddenly ill, and the next morning, when I awoke, she was already dead. It was the first time for me to experience the sadness of being separated from another human being by death. Worried about my poor younger sister being buried in the village cemetery, I bolted out of the house in the middle of the night to go see her. When my parents realized that I was gone and had not come back by morning, they were very worried. I came home just when they were about to go out and look for me, and I got scolded. My kind grandfather felt sorry for me and built a little shack for me just behind Shizue's grave. Mother took some of Shizue's hair—which she had cut off when they put her in her casket—from the *butsudan* [Buddhist altar] where it was kept and made a little grave out of pebbles that she gathered and placed the hair inside. So, every morning when I would wake up I would go right to her little "grave" and say, "Good morning, Shizu. I bet you are lonely today." I would put out flowers for her or, in the fall, beautiful autumn leaves, or chestnuts or grapes. I was seven and Shizue was just three years old.

My younger brother, who was born before Shizue's death, was given the name Shigeyuki. It was my father's first son, so he loved him a great deal. . . . But Shigeyuki died from burns he received on January 19th of his fourth year.

This happened a short while after Shizue died. . . . My mother had given birth to another little girl, and she was resting in bed. I was in the kitchen preparing dinner. Suddenly, I heard Shigeyuki scream, and when I ran out of our cottage, I saw him running toward me, covered in flames. I was completely stunned. I yelled, "Mother! Shigeyuki is on fire. Come quickly!" and ran after him with a cup of water, which I threw on him, but this was not a fire that just a little water could put out. My mother came running out and threw Shigeyuki right in the water jar. But it was too late. Shigeyuki was burned all over his body. My mother's hands were both burned as well.

My father and grandfather, who were cutting wood at the foot of the mountain, could hear the terrible wailing of my mother and her two children and they came running. My father burst into our cottage with his sandals still on, screaming, "What is it? What is wrong?" When he saw my mother holding Shigeyuki and crying, his face hardened and he did not say a word. Shigeyuki's body was burned all over from the tip of his toes to the bottom half of his face. The other men from the village gathered swiftly and helped out making a stretcher to carry Shigeyuki to the hospital in town, but he died on the way. The doctor and resident examined him, and three days later he was buried in the village cemetery. It was so cold that my

brother had made a fire, and his kimono went up in flames. After that, my
father never said another word about it either to me or to my mother.

My mother was prostrate with grief and illness and my father wouldn't
say anything. My grandfather would sit before our little *butsudan* each
morning and night and offer up a sutra. I was so beset with grief that I
could barely stand it. . . . After school, I would take a roundabout way
home, stopping at the cemetery where my brother was buried and make an
offering of flowers I had picked along the mountain roads, or yellow
mountain strawberries wrapped in a butterbur leaf. It made for a pleasant
daily commute. (8–10)

*Her description of a pleasant commute belies the deep pain she must have felt
over the loss of both her sister and her younger brother, the male child so beloved
by his parents. She does not address any feelings of responsibility she may have
felt for Shigeyuki's tragic death, but she recounts the incident in an open and
forthright manner without attempting to absolve herself. She goes on to talk
about her own painful affliction, an infection in her leg that became very serious. When her leg became swollen and infected, her parents finally took her to a
doctor.*

My Leg Becomes Crooked

Soon, we arrived at the doctor's house, and when he examined me, he exclaimed, "How come this was allowed to get this bad? If we don't operate,
I won't be able to help her." So he gave me a shot and performed the sur-
gery. There were no rooms to stay in at his place, so I was placed in lodgings from that day forth. Everyday, my father would carry me on his back
to the doctor's house, and even when I had to urinate, he would hold me
and help me. In order to keep my spirits up, he would sing to me, tell me
interesting stories, and buy me picture books. So I felt in my heart that my
father was really a good person and that I should hurry up and get well so
that I could be a filial daughter to him. (11–13) *male dom.*

*As we have seen, the narrator's early life was one of grinding poverty and uncer-
tainty. Two of her siblings died prematurely. Although she does not say so directly, she probably felt some responsibility for her younger brother's death,
something that was no doubt very difficult to bear. We also learn that she was
physically very small of stature and had one bad leg. Certainly not the ideal beginning for a young woman's life, but this part of the narrative allows the reader*

to see the narrator as a person of considerable strength and determination. But from it all emerges the narrator's resolve to go out and start working as early as she could in order to support herself and not be a burden to her family. We have also seen the narrator as someone who will speak her mind and stand up for what she believes in. The following descriptions of her life as a young factory worker around the time of World War I are an important addition to the other memoirs and accounts of this life and the hardships it entailed.

I guess I was around twelve, though really, I was only eleven and five months. The year was 1913. In March, a recruiter for female textile workers came to our village. He stopped by our house and said, "How about it? Wouldn't you like to send your daughter to work for the Ogaki Company? We have dormitories, the work is easy and pleasant. There's silk-reeling and weaving, and you get paid thirteen sen per day. We feed them and clothe them, so it's really a help to the parents." Once I heard all this, I made up my mind.

If I were getting paid thirteen sen a day, that means I would earn three yen in a month. Counting my chickens before they were hatched, I reckoned that with that kind of money I could buy my mother and sister something, so I said, "I will do it. Please, mister, I'll work." My father, seated nearby, made a worried face so I said, "Come on, Dad, won't it be great if I go? If I go anywhere I will work very hard." When I said this, my father said, "But I would worry about you by yourself. If your older sister could go too, I would feel better about it. Hide can't go on being an apprentice forever, that would be too much." He turned to the recruiter and said, "How about it? I have one more daughter. Her name is Hide. She's this child's older sister and she's been a seamstress at a dressmaker's in Ibi." The recruiter replied, "That's no problem. The company would prefer to have two girls rather than just one, so I will ask to get them placed in the same dormitory." So I went and got my sister, and the next day we left the village with about ten others for Ogaki's Tokyo Woolen Goods, Inc. (Tōkyō Keori Kabushikikaisha). . . .

So, for the first time in my life I was heading for a place where I could earn the money I had been longing for. I took the physical, and though they said I was a little small, it was all right because I had my sister and cousin to look out for me. I was elated, but what we heard and the actual conditions were two quite different things. What we had heard was paradise; the reality turned out to be hell. The thirteen sen we were supposed to earn per day was before deductions were made for food (nine sen), and for the soap and toilet paper and straw sandals we had to buy each month (three sen), so we were left with less than one sen. In effect, then, all we were left with was our fatigue. At that time, Kaō soap was nine sen for a bar, and toilet paper was three sen for a bundle.

In the dormitories, they put twenty people in a twelve-mat room. When we rolled out our futon to sleep at night, we had to sleep in two rows separated by not more than three centimeters. . . . The dining hall was filthy, dark, and gloomy; there were virtually no side dishes with meals. All we got everyday was miso soup and pickles, but even the pickled radishes were old and smelled bad, and there was nothing of real substance in the soup, though occasionally a fly or a cockroach might float to the surface. . . . (19–21)

So small of stature was Takai that the only assignment they had for her was to pick up the scraps from the weaving machines.

All I got to do was clean up waste pieces of thread. For twelve hours a day, from 6:00 A.M. to 6:00 P.M.—with thirty minutes for lunch and fifteen-minute breaks at 9:00 A.M. and 3:00 P.M.—I was standing or walking and collecting leftover pieces of thread. No matter how much I collected, there was always more that would fall from the machines. My legs became stiff, my feet were swollen, and I would be stumbling around. Nevertheless, sitting or resting during work hours was not permitted, so I was constantly in tears, just trying to hang on. And for the whole year, I was ridiculed as nothing but a kid. So that whole year was filled with painful and embarrassing moments. (21)

Causing Losses to the Company

I did not want to continue picking up scraps indefinitely, so I was thinking that if I could actually work on my own, I might have a chance to earn a little more money than I currently was earning. So I went to speak to Mr. Akimoto, the supervisor, and said, "Listen, I have worked picking up scraps for one year now and I would like you to let me work at a loom." To which he replied, "Well, it doesn't seem to make a difference how long you work, you can't do anything useful, so I don't know what to do with you. But if you want to work on a loom, I will see what I can do." By Monday of the following week, I was working in the weaving section. I figured the situation was desperate because if I couldn't work in spinning, and if I was not successful in the weaving section, then there would be no place for me to go. So I poured everything I had into learning how the loom worked—how to reel the thread—I ran from the front of the machine to the back trying to study everything. After about a month, I finally got my own machine, and I worked as hard as if my life depended on it.

Then I began to think that this was not a company I wanted to stay with. I had worked for a year picking up scraps, but from beginning to end my daily salary never changed: thirteen sen. All the while they were on my case, calling me stupid and a runt. Now I had transferred to the weaving section and the work was a lot more important, but still my salary did not go up at all. I thought I had better get away from a company like this.

Ever since I was little, I had a competitive spirit, but I also tended to be a daydreamer. I felt that if I dwelled on the sad and embarrassing moments of my life, I would only want to die, so I always tried to focus on other things. . . . The supervisor and the section boss would scold me almost every day, sneering, "This little brat is lazy. I don't even like to look at her face." The situation became all the more desperate as I got lazier and just wouldn't listen to what my elders were saying. Then one night, during working hours, I received a serious injury to my wrist.

The machine that reeled the mill-spun thread was long and narrow—about twenty meters long—and right in the middle was the gear mechanism with lots of small and large teeth that twisted and coiled the threads. One time, a piece of scrap got coiled up in the large gear teeth, and before I even realized it, my right hand was pulled into the teeth of the gears. I pulled my hand out with all my might, but I lost a chunk of flesh from my wrist the size of a small coin. You could see right down to the bone.

The machine boss and the supervisor came running over, saying, "You stupid idiot! All the threads are cut. If your hand hurts, it serves you right. You weren't paying any attention. You've really created a substantial loss for the company. There's no excuse for that." They scolded me severely, and no one offered me any treatment at all. So I went to the gatekeeper by myself and when I said, "I'm going to see a doctor," he replied "What? You have an injury? I'll put a little medicine on it. If you go to see the doctor without any money, he won't see you anyway." He slapped a little phenol on my wound and bandaged it, so I returned to the mill only to be accosted with "Where the hell did you go during work hours? You really are a lazy one!" I thought to myself, "You sons of bitches—are you even human? I'll get even with you, you better believe it!" (25–27)

Quitting the Company

So, in the spring of my fourteenth year, I left Ogaki's Tokyo Woolen Mill and entered a cotton-spinning mill in Yamato Kōriyama, in Nara Prefecture. I don't remember the precise circumstances, but there was a man, Mr. Matsushita, from the personnel office at Ogaki who was taking about 30 female workers to this company in Kōriyama. I couldn't get them to take me at that time, but I thought that if I just followed this Mr. Matsushita and his group of women to the company, something might work out. So I just left the dormitory. . . .

I finally arrived at the gates of the Yamato Kōriyama Spinning Mill and asked the man at the gate to let me see Mr. Matsushita, and when the red-faced, portly Matsushita came out to the gate he said, "So, it's you. What do you want?" When I said, "Mr. Matsushita, please let me work at this company, too, because I am never going back to Ogaki," he replied, "I can't if you continue to work like you have been. Can't you work harder so that I don't completely lose face?" I entreated with him, "I will work hard, so please use me." They showed me into the dormitory. . . .

The next day I took my physical and went straight to the mill floor, where they were weaving a double width of cotton. In the end, the wages were low, the food lousy, and I was disappointed that this is what I had gone to all the trouble to run away from Ogaki for.

At that time, the company employed a lot of Korean workers. They came as families, so there were lots of mother-and-daughter pairs, the daughters being around twelve years old. Even though they were working at the same company as Japanese women and doing the identical work, they were always being ridiculed and called "Chōsenjin, Chōsenjin." Of course, they couldn't really speak Japanese, so it must have been quite difficult for them. I felt sorry for them. I not only sympathized with them, but I felt angry. Thinking that I wanted to befriend them, I went to their room in the evenings just to visit. Although we had no common language, sincerity can be communicated effectively, and I wanted to learn some Korean and teach them some Japanese anyway. Not long after I had been visiting them every night, I began to get along very well with the young girls who were about my age.

The girls used to like to braid their hair in three strands and tie it with pretty red and pink ribbons. I even had them braid my hair in the same way, but when I returned to my own room, the other girls laughed at me: "What are you doing copying the Koreans?" I wanted to do something for the mothers as well, so I would massage their shoulders and they would say in their halting Japanese, "You really are a nice girl. Are you sure you are a Japanese?" Somehow, this made me sad, and when the tears started flowing, they wiped my cheeks with a towel and combed my hair with a comb. I couldn't help feeling that the people who were discriminating against such kind folks were the disgusting ones. Ever since I was a little girl, I hated people who bullied others and discriminated against those weaker than them. I wasn't yet familiar with the word discrimination (sabetsu), but my own internal sense of what was right and wrong was deeply offended by the contradictions I perceived in the world around me. . . .

I was always presumptuous, fond of talking, and interested in the latest things, so my father used to scold me: "Be quiet! Women should be silent. You shouldn't read so many books. If you are not gentle and quiet, no one will want you for a bride." I wondered who had given birth to a daughter like me? Did it have to be in this poor household? Couldn't I have been born into a rich or noble house? When we went to live in the mountains, my father doted on me, bought me books, and flattered me by telling me I was his little treasure. He had me look after my younger brother and sisters. But now that he was working for a company, he began to put on airs. (31–36)

Young women in Japan in the early twentieth century did not always have a lot of options. In the scene above, the father seeks to silence the daughter, to teach her to be gentle and quiet so that she can be properly married. Even her mother could not be her ally, for she has inexplicably declined to bond with her daughter. The narrator considers extricating herself from the situation by finding a suitable partner on her own and just running away from it all. In the meantime, things in her family take a turn in another direction. Her father seemed to be spending less and less time at home. It turned out that he was seeing another woman. After her mother gave birth to another daughter, she bled profusely and had a difficult time recovering. Takai describes the events that followed.

Then, in September, Mother died. . . . As soon as the thirty-five days passed after my mother's death, Father moved back in with his lover and formally made her his wife. I was rather surprised. Part of the problem was that his second wife was really too young, and the house was very crowded as my father was not working and just sat around the house all the time. My stepmother was twenty-two years old and I was seventeen. My father had been fired from the company so we had very little income.

My stepmother had also worked at the same company—she had been a nurse in the infirmary—and since company romances were forbidden, they were both fired.

After thinking it over, I decided it was time for me to leave home. Because I had been on leave ever since my mother had given birth, I had taken on a lot of the household work, but two young women beneath the same roof is one too many. Even though I didn't have any money, they were newlyweds and I was in the way. . . . So within the day I had packed my bags and set off for Nagoya. It was the fall of 1919. (36–38)

Takai soon found herself working in yet another mill, this time directly experiencing labor unrest for the first time.

A Single Pamphlet

One April day, as winter gave way to spring, I arrived at work, but even when it was past our starting time, the whistle never blew, and everyone remained seated in front of her loom. When I asked, "Aren't you able to work today?" I was told by one of the girls, "Today is a strike. You can't work, so you might as well enjoy yourself." I thought to myself, "That's a waste," but I just relaxed and did as they said. At that time, a white-collar worker came by wearing a suit, a dress shirt, and a tie—it was the first time in my life I ever laid eyes on such a person. He handed over a single poster and said, "Everybody, please read this carefully—it's got some good information." He gave me one too, and since I loved to read, I read it from top to bottom, and front to back. This one poster changed my whole approach to the way I was living my life.

That evening, I read over the flyer I had received at the factory once again. It was an essay by Yoshino Sakuzō that filled two columns called "The Discovery of Individuality" ("Kosei no hakken"). I can still remember the gist of what it said.

> All human beings are equal no matter who they may be. Each individual selects his own schooling and work according to his individuality, and tries for his own sake and for that of society to live a happier life than before. He must make himself a priority. And, he must respect others. Workers can improve their lives by talking with one another, learning together, and by joining together. Scholars, doctors, politicians—all have to make efforts to discover their individuality. Workers, unite. Awaken to your own value.

Anyway, that was the gist of it. I mean, it was more than sixty years ago, so my memory has probably failed me, but this essay by Yoshino Sakuzō breathed life into my soul. It became the inspiration for the rest of my life. Later on, whenever I was faced with hard times, whenever I was down and out, or whenever I felt like quitting, I carried in my heart this call to action by Yoshino Sakuzō.[5] After I read this flyer that I received at the strike, I found that I could not contain myself. That night, I sold off all my belongings and used the money to take a train up to Tokyo. I felt bad for my friends and nice people like Mr. Muronaga because I had lied to them, telling them that my mother was ill. As a result, they bought things from me more expensively than they needed to, and even gave me farewell presents. When I put the money together with what I had, it totaled up to thirty-six yen. I caught the last night train up to Tokyo in order to begin my new life to which I had just given birth. (38–40)

After arriving in Tokyo and checking into an inn, the narrator began walking around Tokyo to look for places to work. As she explains,

[E]veryday I would go out and walk around, trying to get the lay of the land while I did some sight-seeing, trying to get a fix on where I might find work. I went to Shimbashi, Ginza, Nihonbashi, Ueno, and Asakusa, but I didn't see any likely places of employment. Since I wanted to get oriented to the geography of Tokyo, I didn't take the trains; instead, [I] walked everywhere, from one end of Tokyo to the other, so I would actually know where things were located. . . . Anyway, I walked and walked, from Fukugawa to Honjo, from Yanagishima to Kameido.

There was a little river flowing through Kameido, but it was completely black. I remember being surprised at the rivers in Tokyo, how different they were from the countryside. If you walked upstream, there would be a whole bunch of factories lined up on the left side of the river. The first was Tōyō Muslin, the next was Kaō Soap, then there was Tokyo Muslin.[6] On the right-hand side of the river you could see the Mizuno Rubber Factory. Since I didn't know one from another, I figured it didn't matter much where I worked, so I just picked Tokyo Muslin and walked up to its gates.

However, she was not able to talk her way past the guard.

That night, I had no money, no place to sleep, so I walked the streets of Kameido until I came upon a temple. Its name, Hagidera—Bush Clover

Temple—was written on the outside, and since I loved bush clover, I figured that I could sleep somewhere on the grounds for one night. So I slept outdoors at the rear of the cemetery that night. (41–44)

The Kameido area that Takai mentions was one of the central working-class districts of Tokyo and a place where labor activities were the most intense. Home of the Nankatsu Labor Union (Nankatsu Rōdō Kumiai), one of the most radical unions of the early 1920s, Kameido was the site of frequent clashes between labor and the police. The Nankatsu Labor Union had been formed in 1922 and was led by Watanabe Masanosuke, a member of the Japan Communist Party. On the occasion of the confusion following the Great Kantō Earthquake on September 1, 1923, the police brutally murdered a number of labor activists in what came to be known as the Kameido Incident.[7] Between September 2–4, over seven hundred labor activists were detained, and at least ten were murdered by police, though nothing appeared in the newspapers about it until a month later. As labor historian Stephen Large notes, "A virtual reign of terror existed in the Kameido industrial area where many communists in the Nankatsu Labor Union were killed by police."[8] Clearly, the narrator's experience living and working in this area shaped her consciousness and radicalized her politics. It was through her contacts here that she would be introduced to Hosoi Wakizō. Hosoi, who had partaken of the "spirit of Nankatsu," particularly loved the Kameido area and wanted to return there while he was putting the finishing touches on his manuscript.[9]

A Model Textile Worker

My job was to take fine threads of cotton and weave them into double-width pieces of muslin. Holding true to Dr. Yoshino's teachings, the first step toward becoming a worker second to none was to work with a newly instilled attitude, so I woke up before anyone else, and while others were washing up, I would clean our room. I listened carefully and paid attention to what other people said, and people responded favorably, calling me by my name and seeming to take an interest in me. . . . (44)

Salary in those days for one person working four machines in the loom area was between forty and fifty yen per month, take home. With the year-end bonus wrapped in, I had some months in which I would make 105 yen. Of course, that was just a one-time thing. But unlike others, I did not send money home. So, with the exception of the company savings program and the deductions for food, I received everything in take-home wages. I spent my own money on books, which I loved, nice kimono, and obi, and, at the end of the year, I bought a nice Swiss gold watch at Tenshodō on the Ginza. . . .[10]

I wanted to study and begin to live like a human being. I was wondering just what freedom was. Even though we are all human beings, why should some people be unable to marry because they are of a different social status? Or why should I be disparaged because I am a poor textile worker? Even now, people in the towns look down on textile workers, call us pigs *(buta)*, and discriminate against us. Somebody, somewhere has to spin the thread and weave the fabric on a loom so that people can stay warm in the winter and live comfortably. But somehow people feel that textile workers are doing something wrong and are angry with them. As a result, we have to scrape by and barely make a living. What I came to understand, a little at a time, from reading Dr. Yoshino's essay, is that if you want to right the wrongs of the world and correct injustices, you have to study on your own and get the workers to join together in struggle. Unlike before, I now had made some friends. I knew that if I worked hard, I would be fine. But I did not understand how I was supposed to struggle, so every Sunday, I went to the library and read books and then took home as many as I thought I could read in a week.

In the area of literature, I read Japanese translations of works by Tolstoy, Ibsen, Zola, and Turgenev and greatly admired them. Even now, a work that continues to smolder deep in my heart is Ibsen's *A Doll's House,* which taught me that before one is a wife or a mother, one must be a human being. In those days, Japanese women, whether they were wives or mothers, were just attachments to men, like kitchen implements. The daughters of poor people were cotton textile workers, or sold into sexual slavery by their impoverished parents, so where were they supposed to discover their humanity? It seemed that there were no happy people around me. Even though I thought this was terribly sad, there was nothing to do but endure the hardships.[11]

Strike

On May 2, 1920, I attended the first ever May Day demonstration in Ueno Park. No one in particular had invited me, but I just went on my own. I wasn't so much thinking that I would be participating in May Day activities; I just followed a boisterous crowd, and as soon as we came to some woods, I was amazed to see a huge crowd of people waving lots of red flags.

Sometime afterward, I forget the exact month and day, but I believe it was during the summer, we had a strike at Tokyo Muslin and even a Revolutionary Action Committee (Kekkishukai).[12] It was located in one of the large rooms inside the dormitory, the lecture hall where we studied tea ceremony and flower arranging, and we got to hear speeches by famous people. Interestingly, there were some men who did not live in the dorms but commuted, and some important people from the All Japan Federation of Labor (Nihon Rōdōsōdōmei Yuaikai) whom I had never met before. Everyone was gathered there to listen to remarks from these officials. We sat there listening with vacant looks on our faces while speakers raised complicated issues such as how Japan's labor movement was among the least developed in the world, and that in other countries workers had rights of freedom, the 8-hour day, wage increases, and so forth.

I wanted to speak up so badly that before I realized what was happening, I stood up and mounted the podium. But then my legs began to shake, I didn't know what to say, as I couldn't even remember what it was I originally had in mind. My face was burning red with embarrassment. I was trembling all over and couldn't even get my voice to work, so I just stood there dumbfounded. The secretary, Mr. Fujiyama, said, "Miss Hori, did you get up there just to tremble? If you have something you want to say, get it out!" All of a sudden I remembered that when I was young, I was considered a pretty accomplished orator, so I thought to myself that I am not going to blow this opportunity. So I said something like this:

Listen, everyone. We are all Japanese. Don't we all want to eat the same domestic rice that our mothers and fathers are fixing in the countryside? Wouldn't you like to eat one sardine, or one measly sliver of salmon? The townsfolk call us pigs, but why is that? It's because they feed us worse than pigs, and when we walk around town on a Sunday half asleep after working all night, we look like a bunch of pigs! But we are the young daughters of Japanese people. We want to eat food that is fit for humans, and we want to become more human, to be like young Japanese women. So let's demand improvement in our food!

This is more or less what I said. There was a loud applause from the entire audience and I felt myself getting light-headed. But, in response to those demands, the next day we had *inari-zushi* [fried tofu stuffed with vinegared rice], and the following day, they cooked some sardines for us.

Occasionally, we got *katsudon* [breaded pork cutlet served over rice] and curry rice, and thus, the strike was over.

Of course, it still remained to get the 8-hour day and to abolish the late-night work shifts, but Secretary Fujiyama laughed and said, "Only Miss Hori is smiling." I had learned that whatever you might say as an individual, you are weak, but when you join together, you may, at least, get one of your demands met. So, my very first step in the labor movement was taken at the time of this Tokyo Muslin strike, and I was really happy that some of our demands were met. The name of our labor union at Tokyo Muslin at that time was the Labor and Politics Association (Rōseikai). We didn't actually call it a labor union, but Mr. Fukui was our chairman, and Mr. Fujiyama was the secretary. Those are the only two names I really remember. I suppose that because of political pressure, it was best not to reveal the names of the executive committee members and the officers of the union. (44–50)

Driven out of the Company

The next misfortune was to be the object of oppression from both the company and the police. As long as I was a model worker, a young vagabond who had shown up at the company doorstep without a guarantor so that the gatekeeper had to vouch for me, the company was delighted. But once I elected to speak up during the strike, had bought myself a gold watch, and was agitating among the otherwise docile female workers, I was apparently anathema to the company. All of a sudden, I was being harassed from all sides, and it was clear they were trying to get rid of me.

First, it started with our room monitor, Aoki. I don't know whether she was bribed or threatened by the company, but all day long she would say things to me like, "All you do is read books. You're impudent," and "Even though you are from the country, you're impertinent." . . .

After that, I was working happily until early one morning the cops showed up suddenly. "Is Hori here? We've got a few questions we'd like to ask you, so come down to the station with us." For no real reason, then, they took me down there. From that moment, my battles began and now I had to fight alone. "You seem to live pretty well for a textile worker. Looks like you've gotten yourself a nice kimono and obi. You have a nice, new gold watch. So where did you really get them from?" It seemed they thought I was a thief. Even though I told them that they were purchased with my own money for which I had worked hard, and gave them the names of the stores with whom they could check, they ignored what I said and detained me for a week. During that time, they hit me, kicked me, and tortured me. Since I was alone and they were going to torture me no matter what I said or didn't say, I decided to say nothing and to refuse to eat. Since I assumed that torture was more a part of the old Tokugawa regime and not part of this new, enlightened Japanese state, I was more angry than afraid. I considered it beneath me to say anything to people like that, so for one whole week, all I did was drink water and refuse to say a word.

Finally, on the seventh day, the detective who had picked me up at the company said, "Okay, you can go back now. You must be hungry, so here, have something to eat." There was sushi, *udon*, and various cakes all laid out on a table for me, but I didn't feel that I could trust anything these men said, so I didn't make a sound.

"You are really a stubborn one, aren't you! You really are free to go today and if you don't eat something, I doubt you will be able to walk very far."

But my reply was, "I won't eat a thing. When I leave, I will buy something with my own money. You brought me here, so now please take me back to where you picked me up."

"Don't be ridiculous," they retorted. "You think police officers are going to be seen escorting a female textile worker back to work? Get the hell back there by yourself!"

"Oh, I guess it didn't look so bad when you brought me in here?" was my rejoinder.

"You are really a smooth talker, aren't you," they said, but they called a car for me and took me back, though they got the company to pay for it. I had my own money, but my theory was that the company and the cops were in cahoots on this, so I wasn't going to come up with a single penny of my own money. (50–54)

When Takai returned to her dormitory, she found her things had been packed up and moved to a rooming house. The company didn't fire her, but they wanted to make her commute. She had a room of her own over a bookstore, so there were some compensations. Around this time, she met Hosoi Wakizō for the first time.

My Encounter with Hosoi Wakizō

It was May of 1921 when Mr. Fukui introduced me to Hosoi. According to Mr. Fukui, "Mr. Hosoi is one of our union activists. He was fired from his job year before last. It seems now that he is ill and having a hard time of it.

He would be happy if you visited him, so why don't you drop by? He is a smart, interesting young man." So one Sunday afternoon, I went to see him. It was my first time to meet him, and I was paying a courtesy call on someone who was ill, though I didn't know with what, so I thought I should bring along some flowers. So I got a hold of some kind of potato flower and went to see Hosoi in his little rented room above a charcoal seller on the back streets in Kameido. He was very happy to see me.

"So, you're Miss Hori then? Very interesting flowers! They are Western flowers, aren't they? You are not very typical of a female textile worker. You are more of a middle-class lady," he said. To thank me, he gave me a copy of Bebel's feminist writings and urged me to read them. It turned out his illness was an anal fistula, "A disease with absolutely no sex appeal," he said. "It apparently often follows tuberculosis and lung disease. I don't think I will be living a very long time, so, somehow, I just want to finish what I am working on now." When I asked him what it was he was working on, he replied, "I want to put out a book that depicts the spinning mills and the miserable lives of the female workers they exploit. Since I am not healthy, I really can't do any other kind of work, and I have been blacklisted by all the capitalists who invest in the textile business. So even if it means I have to nibble on stones, I want ordinary people out in the world to understand something about the conditions in these mills." So I said, "I don't know what I might be able to do, but if I could help, I would be glad to."

It was our first meeting, but we continued to talk until late afternoon. Even though he was a young man, I felt like I had known him a long time. He was someone with whom I felt very much at home.

This man Hosoi didn't have any of the masculine qualities that my father or Kado, my first love, had. He was a kind person, like a teacher. He told me that his father, who had married into his mother's family, had returned to his original family before Wakizō was even born. His mother, who was also a textile worker in a crepe factory, had drowned herself in a mountain pond at the age of only twenty-seven. So Wakizō was really raised by his grandmother, who died when he was barely twelve years old. He was deeply saddened by this and was virtually on his own thereafter. He got on as an errand boy at the factory where his mother worked and had been on his own right up until the present. Being sickly, he was fired from his job, so he was presently in financial straits, and I felt sorry for him. I wanted to do whatever I could to help him out.

As I think about it now, since we were able to speak so openly with one another on our very first meeting, perhaps we were destined to be together. So, I continued to visit with him, telling him about my jobs, life in the dormitories, and how female textile workers think about things. When I told him the story of the strike, his eyes glistened and he clapped his hands and said, "Way to go! I wish I could have heard that speech!" As we spent time together reading Bebel's feminist theories, or listening to his stories about the labor movement, I realized that Hosoi was the only person to treat me as another human being, every bit his equal. My father was one to have the attitude that "Women ought to shut up. If they aren't quiet, no one will want to marry them," and even Mr. Kado was kind, but he had made remarks about me hurrying up and quitting work as a textile worker so I could take some preparatory classes for married life. With Hosoi, we would get together sometimes to exchange books and talk, or eat together, but I never thought of him as a man very much.

Our friendship continued like this for a year, and then we decided that we should marry as friends. He said that he was thankful that the world was made of men and women, and he believed that they should be completely equal, and he wanted our marriage to demonstrate this. We lived together for three years and we never really quarreled once. While I would go to work each day, he would take care of the laundry and prepare dinner. And he was really good at it! He appreciated cleanliness, so our rooms were always very tidy. When I would come stumbling home from a long, twelve-hour night shift, he would have the futon warmed up for me if it was wintertime, while in the summer he opened the window and fanned me, apologizing all the while he was doing it. So, we may have been poor, but our days were peaceful and happy. (54–56)

The Great Kantō Earthquake

It was September 1, 1923. I had worked a twelve-hour night shift that day without sleeping. It was too hot to sleep, so I was just trying to relax around the apartment. Wakizō had said, "When it's this hot, I don't even feel like eating, so I'll go out and get something cold" and had bought us a couple of ice creams. We had just started to eat them when all of a sudden, everything began shaking. I thought I might bolt for the door and get out, but when I tried to stand up and walk, I couldn't. I rolled down the stairs, and when I finally made it outside, all the old houses next to us had collapsed in a row. Although we could hear voices from beneath the rubble calling out for help, before we could do anything, the aftershocks began in earnest, so there was nothing we could do. The building we lived in was a two-story building of recent construction, and, not only did it not collapse, but amazingly, it did not catch fire, so we were fortunate.

Flames became immediately visible from just beyond a little river toward the direction of Honjo. I thought that if we didn't get somewhere where there were not a lot of houses, we would be done for, so we took off in the direction of the rear of the muslin factory. It seemed like it took a long time just to go the usual five-minute walk to the front of the factory. I had no watch and fled with just what I had on, but when we finally arrived at the lotus pond behind the factory, we could see Tokyo across the river, and it was a sea of flames. Just then, the aftershocks were severe. It was impossible to stand, and I started to feel as though I were seasick. Just at that moment, I remembered something my grandmother had said. Even houses that did not collapse when the first big quake hit may collapse when the aftershocks arrive so that one cannot be careless about entering houses. . . . But by evening, Hosoi reasoned, "My pen and my manuscript are my life, so I am going back to get the manuscript I am working on." So he went back to our place and picked up a little money, some towels, and his pen.

On the evening of the 2nd, we went back to our apartment, and since we had a little rice left, we cooked it up, salted it, and made some *onigiri* [rice balls]. That evening we went back to the lotus pond and spent the night there. From around the 3rd and 4th, I saw them starting to round up Koreans and take them to the Komatsu River. I heard people saying that Koreans had put poison in the wells. At the time, I didn't really know whether it was army reservists, right-wing nationalists, or police who did this. But I saw them take as many as twenty to thirty Koreans, tie them to one another in rows, and, while beating them with wooden staffs and bamboo swords, force them to the Komatsu River. I saw some Koreans jump into the lotus pond and hide beneath the large lotus leaves. It was so sad I couldn't say anything. After a while, I couldn't stand it any longer, so I offered them some of our rice balls and water. They pressed their palms together in a gesture of gratitude and thanked us. It was horrible.

Around about the 5th, Hosoi and I went to Honjo to see the aftermath of the destruction. Since it was a catastrophe on such a scale that we were not likely to see again in our lifetimes, we were curious to have a look. But what we saw was pure hell on earth. There were burnt-out military vehicles, dead horses, and corpses littering the roadsides. There was even the body of a young woman with a baby protruding from her abdomen. Severely wounded people were calling out for water in their thin, raspy voices. The bridge from Honjo to Asakusa had burned and collapsed, and the Sumida River was laden with corpses. It was an endless panorama of horrors as far as the eye could see. Yet, interestingly, there were no signs of any rescue squads or public relief officials on the scene.

By around the 7th it seemed that the aftershocks had subsided for a while, so we thought we might return to our apartment. But we ran into Yamamoto Chūhei, a poet friend of Hosoi's who had shaved his head and had a rope headband with a blue seal tied around it. He said, "What are you two doing here. Get out as quickly as you can. They'll kill you! They have killed all of the officers of the Nampa Labor Union. I'm getting out of here. I'm heading for the countryside. You had better get out of here quick. They'll grab you if you try and go back to your apartment." He said his piece and then left.

Our Honeymoon Trip

So we started walking with just the clothes on our backs, went to Ueno Station, took the train to Naoetsu, where we wanted to pick up the Shin Etsu line for Nagoya, but the train was extremely overcrowded. Even the roofs of the cars were packed. Several young people who were inside the train finally gave up and pulled me on board after I had cried when they repeatedly tried to push me off. Hosoi somehow managed to squeeze on top of the roof. With people so crammed in against one another that they looked like they were about to break, the train finally began to slowly and agonizingly pull out of the station and leave Tokyo behind. At the stations where we stopped along the way, farmers passed baked sweet potatoes and rice balls they had through the windows for us. It was as though we were in hell but had encountered a Buddha. Since Hosoi was on the roof, it seems he pretty much had to go hungry.

Then, at Karuizawa Station, I heard some of the most hateful words I have ever heard in my life, and I will never forget them. Right in front of me, there were two women with their children. In talking with each other, they uttered some really horrible things that should never be repeated. One said, "Oh, I am so glad to see that you are safe," and the other replied, "Oh, yes, and it's great that everyone in your household is fine." "Yes, thank you. We are all safe. We did lose our maid, however. She died." "Is that right? But at least it was just a maid. There are plenty of others to be had." When I heard that, I thought my blood would start running backward! Every day of our lives, we depend on the rice and the vegetables that the farming families supply to us. And even just now, wasn't it the farmers who came to the station to pass us food through the train windows and to give us encouragement? The maid who was burned to death in her bed was the daughter of one of these farming families. Yet these people don't even think of them as human beings on the same level as themselves. It made me so furious that I gritted my teeth and couldn't help balling my hand into a fist.

The farmers, with their large, bony hands, had filled their large straw baskets with sweet potatoes and handed them through the windows to us. I am not sure where my strength came from, but I somehow managed to push people out of the way and lift the basket from his hands and pass it around to people who were not sitting near the window. Then, these two women I was describing spoke up and said, "Please pass it over here, too. We have children who are hungry." But I said, "No way! We are not giving you any. These potatoes were made by farmers who are just like the parents of the maid who died in the fire. You have forfeited the right to eat their food!"

After that, at each of the stations at which we stopped, when farmers brought food to hand into the train, I absolutely did not allow any food to be passed to them. I said in a loud voice, "Your children are Japanese children too. How sad do you think the parents of that maid would feel if they were to hear you? What do you feel when you see a child who has no food or water? Perhaps you need to experience a little hunger once in your life, and experience the fact that there may be one or two people in the world who do not think they way you do!" So, I kept a vigil at the window, and the fact that no one else on the train said anything was probably because they were immersed in their own concerns over what they might do next, now that they had escaped with their lives. On the train, there were people whose homes had been burned, who were separated from their families, whose family had perished, who were half crazed. So, perhaps they didn't blame me for my behavior, or else they might have thought that I was completely insane.

Finally, after a very long time, we arrived at Nagoya Station. At a Red Cross Relief Center outside of the station, a doctor gave me a shot and put some medicine on the back of my legs. Then we headed on to Gifu Station. When we finally arrived at my older sister's house in Gifu, it was evening of the second day after we had left Ueno Station. We rested for about three days at my sister's, and then we left for my grandparents' house in Tsu-kumi. Since we had both left with just the clothes on our backs, I borrowed a *yukata* and obi from my sister, but Wakizō just had the one shirt, so he got a blue-on-white *kasuri* kimono with a black waistband from my great aunt and uncle, and he got some kimono undergarments as well as something for him to sleep in. Our various relatives in the village hosted us for short periods and we stayed about a week walking among the mountains and rivers.

When I recall what Wakizō said during that time, it still brings tears to my eyes: "This is great! The mountains and rivers in the countryside are beautiful, and everyone here is steeped in human kindness. You must be very happy. If I were to go home, there really would be no home, no blood relatives, so there is really nothing to return to. I am truly a child without parents." He seemed very sad. As he spoke, we were on a mountain road beside a mulberry field, looking out at the foot of a nearby mountain. I was very moved by what he said, and, typically, optimist that I am, I said, "Well, you are no longer alone. From here on out, until we die, let's stick together." As I spoke, I gave his hand a squeeze. At that moment, his eyes were brimming with tears and he looked beautiful. I remember that his lips almost looked like he was wearing lipstick. Although we had been lovers for one year, and had been married for some time, we had never been alone like this together, taking walks and relaxing. It's odd, but the earthquake forced us to return home, and that trip was like our honeymoon. (56–62)

The juxtaposition of the joy of a moment of intimacy with the horrors that Takai witnessed is striking. The horror she witnessed was twofold: the one unleashed by the Great Kantō Earthquake, with all the destruction and human suffering it caused, and the human behavior that left so much to be desired. In the first place, there were the actions of the police, the military, and the emerging right-wing nationalists in Japan. At first they were directed primarily against the Koreans—thousands were senselessly murdered—but it was soon directed against social activists and labor organizers as well. Finally, there was the callous selfishness displayed by the upper middle-class women on the train whom Takai denounced. The emerging class differences in Japan of the 1920s entered Takai's narrative at this point, injecting a tension in the narrative. We should note also the fact that many poignant, touching recollections of days and weeks spent with Hosoi—how he looked so beautiful as his eyes filled with tears of happiness—are juxtaposed against rather horrific events in the world around them. It is another way of reminding the reader of the multiple forces at work on the text and the narrator's subjectivity. After finding jobs at the same mill in Inagawa and working there for a while, Toshi and Hosoi returned to Tokyo. Since so many of the factories had been destroyed in the earthquake, it was difficult to find a position. Takai had to consider other alternatives.

Wanderings and the Life of a Waitress

On February 23 of the next year, 1924, we bid farewell to Inagawa, where we had gotten to know people, and to the friends we had made at the mill over the past six months, and headed for Tokyo. . . . I went to a café in Midorimachi, Honjo, called the Midori and started working as a waitress. So it was there that I began my miserable career as a waitress.[13]

Because I was so small of stature, people assumed I was single, so none of the customers had any idea that I was married to someone. They would always say things like, "Toshi-chan, are you about eighteen? You're not exactly beautiful, but you are really cute!" They seemed to like my childlike looks and would give me pocket money and buy me drinks. Late at night, after midnight, when there were no trams or taxis and I didn't have any money anyway, I would have to walk all the way home. Walking alone late one December night, a strange man started following me. I felt very uncomfortable, so as we got near to our house, I took off running, and he started running after me. When I told Wakizō about it, he got worried and from the next night, he came all the way to the café to meet me and walk me home. Three days later, the owner said that he didn't like the fact that a man was coming to the café and hanging around outside until I got off work, so he told me to quit. So once again, I got fired.

After that, I worked at different places around Tokyo as a waitress or a maid, two days here, three days there, just to make ends meet, while Wakizō worked frantically on his manuscript. As a waitress or a maid in these small restaurants, I had to drink my share of bitter sake, and it seems that among Wakizō's friends there was one who thought I wasn't a very respectable person. But at that point, short of becoming a thief, I didn't really have another means of earning a livelihood, so I didn't have a lot of room to worry about what others may think of me. (64–66)

After a couple of different jobs as a waitress, Takai went to work for Hoshi Pharmaceuticals, a well-run company that treated its workers very well. She got along well with everyone and was happy there.

Even though the salary wasn't that much different from working in a spinning mill, I was always happy when we got paid at the end of the month. I would go to Gotanda and buy some meat and the latest magazines, and I would make some Western recipes that I recalled from my waitress days. That time was probably the period in our married life when we lived most like ordinary human beings *(ano tōji ga watashitachi fūfu no ichiban ningenrashii mainichi datta to omoimasu)*. (66–68)

Wakizō's Death

Soon, Wakizō said he wanted to return to his old haunts in the Kameido area. So, while I was working, he went back to Kameido and rented my old second-floor apartment above the bookstore. I was surprised, and when I asked him what was going on, he replied, "Kameido really suits my character better. I can't live in a bourgeois place like this." I remember thinking at the time that men can really say some selfish things, but in those days, I believed that it was the wife's duty to follow her husband, so I didn't argue with him and just joined him there. Once again, to make ends meet, I had to go back to being a waitress.

After a short while, I became pregnant. By summer, I was starting to show quite a bit, and since I didn't like going to work at the café, I went to work in a small restaurant in the Suginami area where I could live in. Customers would say, "Hey, are you gaining weight? Your stomach is starting to stick out a little." And the owner would say, "Are you going to have this baby and raise him by yourself? Did you get dumped by somebody? What kind of guy was it? I'll have a talk with him if you want." I tended to be embarrassed and worried and was about to burst into tears when a telegram arrived, saying, "Hosoi is critically ill. Return immediately." So I rushed home right away. When I got there, Wakizō looked at me and said, "Get me to a hospital. I don't want to die." I asked Kawada for help, and we got him into the Kameido Charity Hospital. Kawada, who had come with us from the Inagawa mill, was working for Tokyo Muslin. Wakizō loved him like a younger brother.

I asked Kawada to stay with him while I ran out to try and raise some money. I finally got about thirty yen, but when I got back to the hospital, they said he had acute peritonitis and that it was too late. He died that evening at 6:00 P.M. It was the 18th of August, 1925. It was actually the evening of the third day since the onset of his illness. It was as though he died of exhaustion after pouring all his heart and soul into his book, *The Sad History of Female Textile Workers*, which finally was published by Kaizōsha in July of that year.

I will never forget his dying words:
It's too bad. I still have work left to do. Please take care of our child for me.
After he spoke these words, there was a sound like a rubber balloon popping, and he vomited up red and black blood. He appeared to be in pain as his arms and legs convulsed violently. After about a minute, he didn't move any more. When I heard the doctor pronounce, "It's over," I couldn't help it, my tears began to flow. Then I heard a voice above me say, "You can't cry. If you do, he won't be able to become a Buddha." When I looked up, I saw that it was Mr. Yamamoto [Sanehiko], the head of Kaizōsha.[14] A number of Wakizō's friends, and people like Professor Fujimori Seikichi, came to pay their respects. But there were many people I didn't know, and I was dazed and had no idea what I should or shouldn't be doing. Thankfully, Kawada, Mr. Yamamoto Nobuhiro, and Mr. Tsurumaki helped me take Hosoi's body back to our second-floor apartment, and many friends came by that evening for the wake.

Yamamoto Chūhei came up with his posthumous Buddhist name for Hosoi: Nanmu Musan Daikyōshi. [There is some playful irony here: the word *"musan,"* which means "property-less," was used to refer to the masses or the proletariat.] We did not actually summon a priest for, as Yamamoto Chūhei pointed out, "Hosoi hated priests and temples, so I'll perform the 'address to the departed soul' *(indo)."* That was fine with me, as I really didn't believe in Shintō gods or Buddhist deities, and I didn't have the money anyway. The landlord was a bit disgusted with us and had to turn away, but we really didn't notice. In the end, it was a rather shabby send-off, and I feel ashamed about it.

The funeral was the following day. We all rode in the hearse to give "Musan Daikyoshi" his proper send-off, but, appropriately, we had no ride back. Of course, no one was dressed in formal kimono, and folks from the neighborhood carried his coffin out of the hearse. The crematorium was at the Komatsu River, so the hearse was trying to go underneath the Tōbu trainline tracks, but the clearance was very low, and the roof of the hearse hit the concrete ceiling of the underpass and Professor Fujimori was hurt. The driver had to change his route, and when finally we arrived at the crematorium, it was evening and the western sky was a deep red as the sun was just about to set. Kawada took my hand and gave it a squeeze, saying, "It looks like Hosoi really didn't want to leave his wife behind. That's why the hearse couldn't pass under the bridge and we had to go out of our way. He just didn't want to die. It's very touching."

That evening, after everyone had left, I cried and cried from grief and loneliness. But while crying, I was thinking: I really don't have the time to be crying. I have the responsibility of a child on the way, a child whom I will have to raise by myself. As if responding to my thoughts, I felt the baby move inside me. The next day, when Kawada dropped by to see me after work, he said, "At any rate, you shouldn't be alone. You are going to have the baby any day now, so why don't you go stay at my house." So on the seventh day after Wakizō's passing, I packed up our meager belongings and moved to Kawada's house. Kawada was staying in Tokyo Muslin's company housing at the Kameido plant. He was married to a beautiful young textile worker from Akita Prefecture, and they were both very kind to me. There was a Keiō University student named Inoguchi who had read *The Sad History of Female Textile Workers* and was so moved by it that he talked it over with his friends and decided to hold a fund-raiser to help me out. They raised a total of twenty-seven yen and sixty sen.

As I think back upon my three years with Hosoi, we virtually never quarreled. He said, "You are working and supporting us, so I will take over the wife's role. If I don't, I won't get enough exercise." So, he took care of the chores, and in the afternoon, when it was quiet, he worked on his manuscript. He never talked a lot. When he was eating, he was always deep in thought. Suddenly he would think of something, put down his chopsticks, and jump up from the table to get his manuscript. "Here, this is something I wrote today. What do you think? Are there any mistakes here? Do you think it's all right?" It appeared that all he could think about for those four to six hours was his manuscript.

Also, we often went together to hear lectures. It cost about two yen at that time, I believe. We usually went to the lecture series for auditors at Waseda's Department of Literature. We also attended sessions at the Labor School. They had excellent speakers at those talks such as Abe Isō, Yoshino Sakuzō, and Yamamoto Senji. There were a lot of young people who turned out to hear Yamamoto Senji's lecture on biology, because he was speaking on sex education.[15] Abe Isō's talk on economics was also very informative.

As a result of being with Hosoi, I learned a great deal about many things. After the war, when I became a day laborer and worked on form- ing a union, what I had learned in my youth came in very handy as a base on which to build. Hosoi died much too young, but I would never have traded our time together for money. I don't care what people may say, or how I may be regarded, but I believe that I have carried on a legacy from Hosoi to which no one else could lay claim. (68–72)

Because of events that follow, this claim to Hosoi's legacy stands as one of the most important passages of Takai's text. In the pages above, she gives the reader a glimpse of the life she shared with Hosoi and the sacrifices she made in order for him to be able to devote himself to his project. Many autobiographers in Japan, as elsewhere, write their lives in order to address some central event or question about their lives that has already been made public. Both Fukuda Hideko and Takamure Itsue were known for particular acts of transgression that their texts felt obligated to address. In Fukuda's case, she dared to transgress politically by engaging in terrorism and socially by taking up with fellow radical Ōi Kentarō and then later a socialist disciple of her husband who was more than ten years her junior. Takamure transgressed by challenging the definition of a wife's role in a bourgeois marriage and the capacity for a woman to establish herself as an independent scholar conducting research on women's history. Takai Toshio dared to engage in labor actions against the textile companies and in defiance of the police. She also worked alongside an influential radical social critic and activist, enabling his research to be completed. Finally, after she became a widow and started to see other men, she was rebuked in the press for being disloyal to Hosoi. But, here, she wants to emphasize how Hosoi mentored her, introducing her to radical ideas about feminism and social change. The Waseda lecture series to which she refers is highlighted by political reformers (Yoshino), socialists (Abe), and experts on sexuality (Yamamoto), indicating how many new worlds were being opened up to her. As we will see below, she would later be denounced, and her claim to be Hosoi Wakizō's legitimate heir would be attacked. Here, in this passage, she makes her claim to that legacy clearly and forcefully. Her text continues with an account of some of the horrors that occurred in the wake of Hosoi's death.

Two Urns

Beginning on September 1, I moved in with the Koderas in Shitameguro. Mr. Kodera was a distant relative of mine from the same part of Japan. . . . Perhaps because I was finally able to relax and feel secure, on the seventh night after I arrived in Meguro, my labor began. I had moved twice already in the two weeks since Wakizō had died, so it was probably because of exhaustion and anxiety, but my baby was born one month prematurely. Both the baby and I were weak, so by the third day after labor started, I still hadn't given birth, and we began to get concerned that we needed help. We got three more yen to add to the money we received from Inoguchi and called a doctor. Finally, two hours later, a little boy was born. He didn't make a sound, perhaps because he was tired, I thought. It was 11:00 A.M. on the 9th of September. I named him Akatsuki (Morning Twilight). In naming him, I was mindful of a dark side to his past, how he was the second generation of fatherless sons, and I was hoping for a bright new dawn to appear soon, so that his future could brighten along with Japan's. But his voice was very weak, he lacked the strength to nurse sufficiently, so he grew smaller by the day. I even expressed milk by hand and tried pouring it in his mouth, but by the seventh day after his birth, his brief life was over. (72–73)

Since Mr. Kodera drank and could not be easily awakened, the next morning they arrived late at the cemetery to bury the newborn baby. The gravediggers charged the young widow double, rendering this miserable day all the more painful for her.

What I felt at that time was less sadness—there were no tears to shed— than a sense of being sucked down into the bottom of the earth. The loneliness I experienced was like that of being the only person left on this whole wide earth. Even when I think of it today, it is a deep, penetrating sadness that is difficult to bear.

I began to grow desperate at this point. My postpartum recovery was slow, but I didn't feel that I could remain indefinitely as a guest in Mr. Kodera's house. So, at the beginning of October, I rented a little place above a printer's shop nearby and moved out. I was worried that if they saw a young woman moving in with just a little bit of furniture and these two urns, one large and one small, that the landlord might not want to rent to me. So I hid them inside my futon and went ahead with the move. Even afterward, as I moved frequently within Tokyo and walked the streets looking for a job, I always carried these urns with me. Why I did not give them to a temple to look after for me, I cannot explain to this day. (73–74)

Desperation

For about the first seventy days after Wakizō's death and later the death of our son—while I was conducting the baby's funeral, and moving into my own place—I was using money that came from a variety of sources, including Kaizōsha, the funds the students raised, and contributions from various people. But, after a while, the money was gradually used up, yet my health was still not fully recovered. I began to feel as though I should just die. It was a difficult time because folks like Kawada, the Koderas, and Mrs. Noro had been so kind and helpful to me that I felt it would be rude to them if I did try to kill myself.

Around the end of October, Kaizōsha put out Wakizō's second volume, *Factory (Kōjō)*, and the royalties from that were about three hundred yen, as I recall. Subsequently, in November and December, I received an additional two hundred and three hundred yen, respectively. Then, Kaizōsha began to publish one of Wakizō's works after another, *Slave (Dorei)* and *The Endless Bell (Mugen no kane)*, so that at times I received as much as six hundred yen from them. Unfortunately, I took no pleasure in the receipt of this money. I was feeling so desperate that rather than thinking about what to do with the money, all I could think about was how to get rid of it. Somehow, having money had no meaning for me.

Takai Shintarō

Then, in December, I believe it was on the 13th, there was a report in a Kawasaki newspaper about a strike at Fuji Spinning. Having grown weary of the bourgeois lifestyle, I realized that I wanted to see the faces of some workers engaged in a struggle, so I took off immediately for Kawasaki to see if there wasn't something I could do to help. When I arrived, there was no smoke spewing from the factory smokestacks, and all around the factory it was eerily quiet. By god, there really was a strike taking place! My heart was pounding and I felt that I, too, wanted to join the strikers, so I walked around to strike headquarters. I said nothing about being Hosoi's widow, author of *The Sad History of Female Textile Workers*, but instead just told them that I was a textile worker too, and they took me in immediately. For the first time in a long time, I sat with a group of my fellow workers eating a dinner of rice balls, dried plums, and salted mackerel—and having a great time! The food never tasted better.

The next morning I awoke at 4:00 A.M. and was in the first wave of the picket line closest to the main gate by 5:00 A.M. Since it was December and dawn came late, a few male workers were straggling through the gray darkness on their way to work. These men tended to be around forty years of age, all thin and their faces pale. Very few got through to where I was standing, as most were persuaded to give up and go home; but a few with deep loyalty to the company, or workers who loved their jobs, did try to cross our final line. But I tried to stop them to the cheers and support of many of the strikers who thought me a precocious young worker. There were some employees who went ahead into the factory without saying a word, and others who gave up and went home. . . . Afterward, we proceeded to march in a demonstration. It was the first time I had ever participated in such a demonstration.

In the newspaper the following day, there was a picture of me right in the front ranks of the marchers. That evening, we met again at strike headquarters, such as it was—just a run down, vacant house—where we held a lively discussion. The following day, those of us in the support group decided to return home for the time being. Though I had come alone, I left with about six friends, all of them male. Among the young men who left with me were some who worked at a factory somewhere in Gotanda and labor activists who had been fired from their jobs. One of them was Takai Shintarō. He was an unemployed carpenter who had been fired from Mitsukoshi's furniture manufacturing plant for his labor union activities. While working there, he had formed a union. He was twenty-eight years old at the time. He was born in Tokyo but had lived with his parents in Yokohama from ages thirteen to twenty-one. While he was an apprentice, he did not get paid, and he had to do things like baby-sitting and running errands. At twenty-eight, he was a typical Tokyoite carpenter, a smooth talker who had studied at the Sōdōmei labor school; he was a very fit and handsome young man.

He came to see me the next day at Meguro and invited me to see a storytelling *(rakugo)* performance at the Suzuki Hontei, a vaudeville hall *(yose)* in Ueno. It was the first time I had ever seen *rakugo* and for the first time in a long while—a really long while—I forgot about everything else and just laughed. Takai said to me, "You are still young. You have to stop crying and enjoy your youth a little. If you're willing, I volunteer to be your partner any time." So the two of us went out for sushi in Asakusa, then he took me home. After that, he came around to see me often, taking me out to listen to music or to watch a Chaplin film. Takai lived in Oimachi with his parents and his younger sister. As an only son, he was rather spoiled, and even though he was unemployed, his lifestyle did not seem to be very crimped. He was always dressed in nice suits. He was twenty-eight and I was twenty-three, so he was like a brother who was five years older than I. He was always kind to me, and since I was not without feelings, I began to care for him. (75–79)

Common-Law Wife

The year finally ended and it was around the beginning of April of 1926, as I recall, that my picture appeared on the third page of the morning edition of the *Hōchi shinbun*. When I read the headline, I was shocked: "The

Profligate Ways of Hosoi Wakizō's Widow." The gist of the article was that every day I was out running around with a certain man, spending money recklessly, hardly a model for proper conduct. It is incomprehensible to me, but as I think back upon it, since the three largest newspapers always try to print some big story on page three—and perhaps there hadn't been any legitimate news stories that came in that day—it must have been at somebody's instigation that they ran this picture of me, which, by the way, I have no idea how they obtained it. In fact, I cannot help thinking that it was probably the authorities who wanted to bury *The Sad History of Female Textile Workers* who did this because the book had had such an impact not only domestically, but internationally as well.

Then, three days later, Mr. Yamamoto, the head of Kaizōsha, said to me, "Since you were not actually Hosoi's legal wife, we cannot send you any more royalties." When I said, "What do you mean I wasn't his wife?" he replied, "A common-law wife does not have legal rights of inheritance." I had never thought that much about the law before, but these words were as cold as a steel sword blade, and I did not know what to say. But not knowing my rights was no way to leave matters in a case like this, so I went to see Katayama Tetsu at his law offices in Shimbashi.

Mr. Katayama said pretty much the same thing as Mr. Yamamoto: that common-law wives do hot have inheritance rights under the law. When I asked him where the royalties would go, he said, "To the government." I said, "Are you telling me that after all the long years of poverty and sacrifice that we endured in order to write *The Sad History of Female Textile Workers* and *Factory*, the proceeds are going to be taken away by this bourgeois government? I can't accept anything as insane as that! Isn't there something you can do?" When I blurted this out, Mr. Katayama said, "I suppose that if we wanted to honor the deceased's intentions and use his money to good purpose, we could create a fund for implementing Hosoi's Wakizō's wishes and that way the government wouldn't get it." The next day, I went to Fujimori Seikichi's house and told him all about what Mr. Yamamoto and the attorney Mr. Katayama had said. Although I did not think that much about it at the time, the reason people at the places I used to go had distanced themselves from me and were treating me coolly was because of the article on page three of the newspaper three days ago. As one who had never finished elementary school and was a naive, sheltered textile worker, I was not experienced at questioning people's motives; moreover, I never dreamed that the laws of the country would so blatantly deny women their rights.

After that, times were difficult. Mr. Yamamoto was as good as his word. After April, even though the books continued to sell, I did not receive a single sen of royalties, so I had no income. Since I am the kind of person who will just go out and find a job if I don't have any money, I wasn't too worried. When I told Takai about it, he was surprised. "Why didn't you tell me about all this lunacy sooner? Working the night shift at spinning mills, putting up with being a waitress—why did you go through all that? Of course if Hosoi dies, those rights belong to you! If you just leave it to others, what will happen to your own livelihood? Japan is a capitalist country. The legal and political systems are set up to ensure that no matter how hard you work, you will remain impoverished. But what I like most about you is that you care about other people. But I don't know what would happen to someone like you if you were alone. Let me say it clearly: let's get married. Then we will go speak to both Kaizōsha and to Mr. Fujimori." So we soon went to see them both. (79–81)

But it was to no avail. Takai was quite prepared to support herself, but it was not that simple.

I was twenty-three years old, with no money, but I was happy to work. My husband and child were both dead, but I believed that I could get by on my own if I needed to, although that may have been a woman's superficial thinking on my part.

When the money was about to run out and I went out to various companies in order to look for a job, I kept being turned down as people would say, "Oh, you were Hosoi's wife. If we hired someone like you, people would have bad things to say about the company and that would be problematic." As I began to get desperate for food money, I went back to the café, but they also said no: "Oh, you're that writer's widow whose picture was in the paper. Sorry, no go." Gradually, I grew weary of being in Tokyo; I was afraid of having any relationship with a man, and I was ready to give up on marrying Takai. So I thought it best if I got out of Tokyo. All I had left at that point was one ten-yen note.

The first thing I had to take care of was disposing of the remains of my husband and son. I couldn't carry them with me, and I didn't know any temples I could prevail upon, so, although I knew it an unreasonable request, I went to ask Mr. Shigehiro at his residence in Hibiya if he would take care of the urns for me. I told him that as soon as I found a job, I would come retrieve them, but three months passed, then half a year, and

I still wasn't settled. Then even more time passed and, before I knew it, the Fund for Hosoi's Last Wishes purchased a plot in Aoyama Cemetery.

The Sad History of Female Textile Workers was bought and paid for as a manuscript, but it had sold many more copies than anyone had anticipated, and, to his credit, Mr. Yamamoto arranged to have royalties passed on to the fund whenever there was a new edition published. Some of these funds had gone for establishing and maintaining his grave. Today, this grave is the site of the tomb of the Unknown Soldier in the liberation movement. . . .

Kaizōsha collapsed after the war, and now *The Sad History of Female Textile Workers* is published by Iwanami Shoten; but even though I always show up for the graveside ceremonies, and they know my address, I have never heard a word from either Fujimori nor the fund. I learned of the Iwanami edition only after it had appeared. Perhaps, since Professor Fujimori opposed my presence at these ceremonies anyway, Iwanami Shoten may not have told him anything.

So why do I even bring up this kind of subject here? The younger people of today may not understand this at all, but under the old legal system, you could not legally register a marriage if the head of the household did not give his permission. There was absolutely no way that my father, as head of our household, was going to give me permission to marry an unemployed, unpublished, left-wing writer at work on a manuscript. Yet Hosoi and I felt the same: that if we loved each other, and both believed in the importance of getting the facts about working conditions for female textile workers out to the public, then we were going to unite our efforts toward a single goal. So we did not pay a whole lot of attention to this business about a common-law marriage.

However, because I was a common-law wife, I had no legal grounds on which to inherit the authorial rights, and I couldn't even be considered legally his wife. Because I did not understand that wives were subject to this kind of denial of rights, I am a good example of what can happen when a woman entrusts her rights to someone else. So I have had to swallow my pride and tell my story just as it happened. (81–83)

Although this part of her story is not easy to tell, it is the core of her narrative. She recounts her "transgressions" such as they were: spending time with poet Takai Shintarō, enjoying films and nightlife. But once her picture appeared in a tabloid, she became anathema. The former friends of her husband turned away from her. But postwar readers would have little appreciation for what women went through in the 1920s and 1930s, and the narrator is certain that younger readers do not realize how the prewar legal system operated to deny women their basic rights. The narrator believed in a cause, she worked hand-in-hand with her husband to help him realize his dream to expose working conditions in the mills, but the laws and the patriarchs conspired to deny what she stood for and to erase her from the picture. But her legacy as Hosoi's widow followed her everywhere she went. So although she could not be formally recognized as his spouse, her relationship with him could be used as a basis for discriminating against her in terms of employment. She continues her story.

As the Widow of *The Sad History of Female Textile Workers*

Anyway, on the next day after I entrusted my urns to Mr. Shigehiro, I fled Tokyo without even leaving word for Takai. I paid up my rent to the printer for my place in Meguro, put my belongings in a little wicker trunk that I asked them to hold for me, and told them they could use my futon and left. At that point, Takai was down in Kyūshū supporting a coal miner's strike. He had done a lot for me, and I did care about him deeply, but I had become concerned about all the public attention surrounding me, and my relationships with men. I just wanted to be on my own. I knew that I was most at peace when I was working alongside other female textile workers, struggling with them in order to try and improve our lives. No matter how much I liked someone, I did not want to be dependent on anyone but myself. I resolved to make a clean break and start over again. So I left Tokyo Station by myself and slowly plodded down to Osaka, where I arrived at 7:00 P.M. that evening. (83–84)

Through a broker, Takai found a job in an Osaka mill, the Sano Spinning Mill. Her narrative continues.

Anyway, I passed my physical and was accepted into the company, and I thought everything was fine. But then the man from the employment agency said, "Well, that worked out well. It was a good thing I came all the way out here with you. But there was last night's dinner, and your use of my futon, so I'll have it taken out of your pay at the end of the month. So, work hard, now!" Then I was taken to my dormitory, and that evening, when I met my twenty roommates, I was delighted. I felt like I was coming back to life again!

Starting the next day, I was standing in front of my machine, working very hard, but thoroughly enjoying it. At the end of the first month, after they deducted for meals and for the employment agency, I hardly had anything left, but still, for the first time in a long while, I went out and bought daily-use items with my own money, and on Sunday, I went sight-seeing at Yoshimi-no-ri Beach. Even though I had been there less than a month, I already had made some friends. At the beach, I got some wonderfully fresh fish from a fisherman's wife. It was great just to experience the solidarity and warmth that existed among working people.

Then, about a week later, I was suddenly called into the personnel office. I wondered if they might have a background check, and when I went in, I was fired. "Miss Hori, after today, please leave this company. I am sure it won't cause you any financial difficulties." I was stunned; it was a lightning bolt out of the blue. When I asked, "I have been working hard, so why are you firing me?" they replied, "Don't try to deceive us, Mrs. Hosoi. You are the widow of Hosoi Wakizō, author of *The Sad History of Female Textile Workers*. We can't let you work at this company. The company makes arrangements for coworkers to meet and be friendly too." I responded with, "Hosoi is dead. I am just a single female textile worker trying to get on with my life who wants to enjoy working every day. So there's no reason to have me quit. For openers, I have no place to go, no place to live. I have no other means of survival, so please don't fire me." But we could not come to an agreement that day.

The next day, we both repeated the same words we had uttered the day before. When they said, "Even if you really don't want to quit, there is the company to think of," I replied, "I have myself to think of as well. I also have an idea. I will send a letter to the newspaper and then hang myself in the dormitory." Predictably, this caused the personnel manager some concern. "So you won't quit under any circumstances?" I replied, "I haven't done anything wrong or made any mistakes on the job, so I won't quit. If I have to quit, it will be the same as dying. This is the first time in my life I have worked for such a good company in such a nice location where I enjoy working every day. I love this company!" The manager said, "You certainly know how to talk sweetly. I'll tell you what, I'll give you some money, so please resign." I said, "I don't care about money. Please let me work here." We went around and around for days like this. Finally, after a week, they said they would give me thirty-yen severance pay, and if that wasn't good enough, they were prepared to throw me out forcefully. I was finally ready to throw in the towel, so the next day, I collected my severance pay plus an additional six yen and fifty sen to cover train fare back to

Tokyo, and, with deep regrets, made my exit from Yoshimi-no-ri [where the Sano Spinning Mill was located]. (84–85)

She soon found another position in another Osaka mill, but the results were the same.

However, after about a month, I was fired from there as well. Wherever I tried to go, they would find out I was Hosoi's widow and I would be fired. So, there I was with my belongings wrapped in a little wrapping cloth *(furoshiki)*, walking the streets of Osaka. I felt that, in the end, it was the photograph and story run by the big newspaper that had robbed me of my access to a job. I didn't feel that it was especially sad or disappointing, because I still had faith that I was a young worker, and I could find a job. . . . There are good people out there in the world, and when I needed it, there was always someone to say that if I without a roof over my head, I could stay with them for the night. So it was actually kind of a fun period in my life. Genuine humanity can be found in the hearts of the working people.

Remarriage

One evening, I was walking in front of the Osaka Nakanoshima Public Hall when suddenly I noticed a huge, white banner hanging down from the window above reading, "A Million Souls Saved." I thought to myself, "That is certainly someone with a lot to say!" So this is how I first heard Kagawa Toyohiko speak.[16] Later, he and his wife extended a lot of kindness to me. Even though I entered the hall as an unemployed member of the lumpen proletariat with no particular place to stay that night, I was relaxed and casual. Mr. Kagawa was around forty years old at that time and gave the impression of a man in the prime of his life who could speak for hours in a strong voice. After his speech was over, there was a huge applause, and they passed the hat around to raise funds, but I didn't have any money, so I couldn't contribute. Looking puzzled, the person next to me said, "Go ahead and give whatever you can. Even a little bit is helpful." I didn't know what to do. Then a young man spoke up and said, "It's also all right if you can't give any," and he took the hat from me. I thought I recognized the voice, and when I looked to see the person, sure enough, it was Takai Shintarō.

Takai's face drained of color and he took my hand and said, "Come on outside with me. I need to talk to you," and he whisked me away without another word. We sat on a bench in the park and he told me, "It's good to see that you are still alive. After you disappeared three months ago, I have been walking about looking all over for you: Nagoya, Gifu, Kyoto, Osaka. I've become a lumpen proletarian! That was cruel of you to leave without saying anything." As he looked into my face I could see that his eyes were brimming with tears. I explained, "Wherever I went in Tokyo, I was getting fired because I am Hosoi's widow. I didn't want to die of starvation by myself, so I thought I would go to Osaka and get a fresh start. I didn't want to involve you in my troubles, and I wanted to try living on my own. No, not really on my own, but with other female textile workers in the mills. Those of bourgeois and intellectual backgrounds don't understand my feelings nor my motives, but the other women at the spinning mills understand me. So I want to speak up for eliminating the long night shift, improving the quality of food, and getting rid of tuberculosis."

When I told him he should "Hurry up and go back to Tokyo and relieve your parents' anxiety," he replied, "When you say something like that to me, it makes me want to die." I retorted somewhat spitefully, "I don't care for a man who whines and whimpers like this. If you want to die, go ahead and kill yourself." Thinking about his parents who were worrying back in Tokyo, I felt that even if he were to marry me, he would no doubt have a difficult time. He said, "Just say we'll be friends as we have been up till now. If you'll do this, I will work my whole life for the labor movement. Sometimes we can meet and talk. I want you to listen to some of what I have to say." So that evening we walked around Osaka talking until dawn. (84–89)

Eventually, Toshio decided to marry Takai, and their married life began auspiciously.

Takai enjoyed the relaxed married lifestyle for about a year, then he resumed his activities in the labor movement. Along with the director of the Amagasaki branch of the Greater Japan Federation of Labor, Fujioka Bunroku, and his associates, they began to organize workers at Hanshin. In 1929, our second daughter, Nobuko, was born. . . . In the spring of my thirtieth year, February 1932, my oldest son was born. My husband was delighted and named him Masanobu. Although it was highly unusual, he took care of the children at home. To celebrate his first week of life, he cooked *sekihan* [rice sweetened with sweet red beans], and just as we were prepared to celebrate his seventh night of life, two men from the Amagasaki Special Higher Police (Tokkō) came and said, "It's nothing major, but please come with us for a while," and they took Takai away and incarcerated him for three months. When three days passed, and then seven days, and he still had not returned, I went down to the police station with my three children. It was exactly thirty days after my son's birth. When I had met with the local branch chief of the Greater Japan Federation of Labor, Mr. Fujioka, and asked him what was going on, he explained that there had been a strike at the Mukawa Rubber Factory and that some workers, angered over some capitalists' extremely insensitive remarks, had thrown sulfuric acid at the company president at the railroad station, and he had been badly burned. They believed that Takai was one of the agitators, so they arrested him.

When I arrived at the police station they said, "Oh, so you are Takai's wife? We are really sorry, but he is no longer at Amagasaki." I asked, "Where is he? As you see, I have brought his newborn with me even though he is just barely one month old and cannot really hold his head up by himself. After this child was born, Takai never set foot out of the house for the next ten days, so don't you think you are being unreasonable? I can't work with three children to care for, so we are in financial straits. Please hurry up and return these children's father who is very important to them." But they just replied, "You can say whatever you want, but there isn't anything we can do about someone who is not here. He is in Nishinomiya." So, I put the infant on my back, took my two daughters by the hand, and boarded a Hanshin train for the Nishinomiya police station. They told me he wasn't there either, so I had to go to the Ashiya police station. We finally got to see him, but the two girls were frightened by the sight of their father with his scraggly beard and they began to cry, and soon the baby joined them. I was completely exhausted. No matter how hard I tried to explain the situation to the police, they wouldn't listen. We finally returned home in the evening, and Nobuko was crying, saying that her legs hurt, and we were all hungry. It was one of the worst days I can ever recall.

The next day, when I brought Takai some underwear and some cold medicine because he had caught a cold, I was addressed bluntly, "Are you back again? If he's such an important husband, you should take better care of him and keep him out of the labor movement. This isn't a hospital or a rooming house. Don't try bringing him these luxuries like fresh clothes and medicine. Just get on back home!" I blurted out, "Are you jerks even human? He is not convicted of any crime, so why are you already treating him like a criminal? You just remember, when these kids grow up they are

going to change the Japanese political system and your heads are most as-
suredly going to roll!" But the day ended in a standoff as their reply was,
"Oh, how frightening! So the devil's wife is a devil in her own right! If you
didn't have your kids with you, I would throw your ass in jail too. But I
hate to deal with kids!" Next, I went to see a Mr. Kawakami at his office in
Kobe and explained our situation to him. Finally, after another seven days,
thanks to Mr. Kawakami's tireless efforts, we got Takai released. (89–91)

*Throughout the 1930s, things only became more difficult for progressives. As
her narrative continues,*

Japan was becoming a wartime society, and times were getting increasingly difficult. In 1936 there was the February 26 Incident (the attempted
coup d'état by infantry officers and troops), and I think it was around that
time that the Special Higher Police showed up at 6:00 A.M. with their typical summons for my husband. It was still cold and dark at that time of the
morning in February, and they gave him no opportunity to eat or make
any preparations; they just whisked him off to Nishinomiya. He didn't return for a full month. When I went to see him, they wouldn't allow me to
visit, but he sent out the overcoat he was wearing when they took him
away with a message to get something for the kids with it. So, on the way
home, we stopped at a pawnshop and I borrowed five yen. We already
owed the rice distributor, so after paying him off, there really wasn't much
left. Consequently, I don't recall buying anything much that day. . . . In
1942, our second oldest boy, Yoshihide, died suddenly of acute appendicitis. It was around the end of June. He was operated on in the neighborhood clinic, but the results were bad, and he came down with peritonitis
and died in a great deal of pain. Three days previously, he had said he
wanted some dark candy, so we looked all over Nishinomiya for some,
but could not find one single piece of candy. Then, on the morning of the
day he died, he requested some sushi (*norimaki;* rice and seaweed). We
had just three pieces of Asakusa seaweed that we were carefully safeguard-
ing, so I bought a little bit of bonito and made three pieces of rolled sushi
for him. He said it was delicious, but he just ate one-fourth of it, saying,
"Give the rest to Kanji (his younger brother) and Miyoko (his younger sister) and my two older sisters. It wouldn't be right if I ate it all. And Mom,
I am sorry for all the times I talked back to you. Once I get better, I'll go
anywhere you want me to on errands. I'll even take good care of Kanji and
play with him." As he spoke, he looked straight into my eyes and he

looked beautiful. Even today, as I write these words, I cannot hold back the tears as I think back upon the days when I could not find him that one piece of candy he wanted.

He died that evening at 6:00 P.M. If it hadn't been for the war, he would be a forty-four-year-old man today. Yoshihide—he was smart and manly. I think that those people who survived the war owe it those who suffered much harsher deaths than Yoshihide, to make sure that we do not have another war. Yoshihide was ten years old when he died.

Our oldest boy, Masanobu, had died earlier in July of 1933 at the Katsurō Hospital in Nishinomiya. We were told that the name of his illness he died from was an intestinal catarrh. That summer in Nishinomiya, this intestinal catarrh had afflicted many infants in the neighborhood, and quite a few had died. When our second son died, I wanted to die myself. But when I thought about the surviving children, I went ahead with the funeral.

Portrait of Hell

On August 6, 1945, at around midnight, the air raid siren wailed, and as I went to wake up the sleeping children, I could hear the echo of explosions from the B-29s. Incendiary bombs were falling on the city like fireworks. I was the first to leave. I put Katsuko on my back, and then I took Kanji by his hand, draped his summer bedding over his head, and set out to escape from the sea of burning houses that was our street. Later, I heard that our second daughter, Nobuko, grabbed a bag with some rice and our first-aid supplies and ran out by herself, while lastly, my husband and our oldest daughter, Aiko, got out with a trunk of clothing between them. When we finally arrived, bedraggled, at a large grassy field outside of town, it was filled with people who had fled for their lives.

Thinking that this field would not be safe enough, we moved on from there and went almost all the way to the beach; but it seemed dangerous there as well, so we went back to where we had come from, and by accident, we came upon a well in the midst of a square. Three of us hid in that well. A young man came walking by just as we were getting in, and he said, "Ma'am, please use this briefcase as a cover for the well. There's no way I can take it along with me anyway." So he gave us a large-sized suitcase and we used it to cover the well. I am not sure how long we were in there, but after a while, it became very quiet all around us, and we could not hear any airplanes. When we peeked outside the well, everyone seemed to be lying around sleeping. Everything seemed eerily quiet, but when I looked more carefully, I could see that they were all dead. Three bombs had landed right in the square, and all the people aboveground were killed by the blast.

What first hit my eyes was the sight of a young boy, about four years old, who had been carried on his mother's back. But his head was blown in two and his brains had spilled out all over his mother's shoulders. They looked like spoiled tofu. The mother was still alive, but a bomb fragment was lodged in her shoulder. I immediately tried to reach for the boy, but his face was completely lifeless as his eyes dangled from their sockets, and his skull had been virtually emptied out. I had never seen anything so horrible—it was beyond pitiful, it was ghastly. Without thinking, I quickly dropped the child's hand. I just took our one bedding set out and draped it over child and said to his mother, "You must not look at your child" as I wiped her face gently with a towel. Just then, soldiers appeared with a stretcher, and when I said, "This person is wounded. Please help her quickly," they put her on a stretcher and took her away. Although her son's corpse was covered with a blanket, I can remember the mother's face as she looked back at her son's body as they were carrying her away.

Bodies with no heads, arms and legs scattered everywhere, human heads lolling about in the fields like watermelon—the sight was so frightening, it was all I could do not to throw up.

Gradually, the nighttime gave way to dawn, and I thought it best if we departed from this horror-filled square. Heading for the Imazu Elementary School, which was a designated shelter area, we had to be careful where we walked so that we didn't tread on the corpses that littered the ground like fish in an open-air fish market. I was holding my son's hand and we were just about to exit the plaza when I saw the family of the dentist in our neighborhood sitting peacefully with their belongings piled neatly around them. I thought it a bit odd that they seemed so quiet and relaxed sitting there, but I figured that dentists were ultimately different than we were . . . but then I knew something was wrong. I said, "Doctor, you and your wife, please come on, let's go to the elementary school. It is just too sad to stay here," but there was no response. I said to his wife, "Come on now, your baby is crying," but when I touched her shoulder, I was startled. It was cold to the touch, so I went up to each one and touched them, calling, "Doctor! Hey, young man! Miss!" But they were all dead. Only the infant was alive, clinging to her mother's arms, crying. I sat down, quite shaken.

Just then, their second oldest daughter came stumbling out from somewhere and said, "Mrs. Takai, Auntie, what am I going to do? My father, mother, my sisters, my younger brother—they are all dead. The baby and I are the only ones to survive. What can we do, what can I do?" She threw herself down and cried; I felt so forlorn for her—she had nobody. It made my blood run cold. Although I was crying too, I nursed the little baby for a bit. He was a sad little case too, as his backside was injured and he was bleeding. It was a boy who was just a little over two months old. I wonder where they are today? His older sister was about the same age as our second daughter.

Through all of this, my own children had not cried, and eight-year-old Kanji was carrying a bag with all our important papers in it, stuff we had completely forgotten as we were in such a hurry to get out with our lives. He handed them to me, saying, "Here, Mom. These are for you." Inside were cash, insurance policies, and our savings passbook. So at least half a year's assets had been entrusted to our little eight-year-old boy as we ran to escape disaster. As we headed for the exit, our second daughter was there holding her bag; so she had escaped to the square as well. The dentist's family had called out to her to join them, but fearing it would be too dangerous if a bomb fell, I got her to seek another well in which to hide. Thankfully, we were both thinking alike on this so that she survived with us too.

As we went to walk the path along the Arakawa River, we found my husband and oldest daughter waiting at the bridge. They had gotten out last, and many people around them had collapsed and fallen, overcome with smoke. But we had two gas masks in the house, so they put those on, and keeping themselves wet with water from a fire hydrant, they finally managed to escape the sea of flames. My daughter's leg and my husband's hands were burned, however.

While we were delighted to find that we were all safe, when we went back to look at the house, there was nothing left. It was burned right down to the ground. All that was left was the skeletal remains of a large acacia tree that had been in our yard.

When we arrived at the relief shelter at the Imazu Elementary School, parents, children, and old people were all over the place, crying, looking at corpses. Someone apparently had gotten a hold of a cart from somewhere, and you could hear the sound as he piled the dead bodies on it. Just then another man came up with a cart with the charred bodies of a woman and five children on it, saying, "I am in charge of the civil defense around here, so I was out, but when I got back home, this is what I found. My wife had just given birth seven days ago. How could this happen to someone so innocent." He was crying, so we got up to see, and it was horrible. The corpses were a mother and five children, but you couldn't tell who was who. They were all on one straw mat, but they had all become hardened into a single lump of charcoal. With all the shocks the night had brought, most people were just stupefied as they sat there, staring off into space with empty looks on their faces, not even aware of their hunger. (98–102)

Two days later, on August 8th, in the morning, we went to the Nishi-nomiya Municipal School, where my oldest daughter was working as a substitute teacher. We were going through burnt-out rubble, gathering melted zinc, and sleeping out in the open. But my husband was burned, could not work, and our second daughter pointed out, "Father is not going to get better if we remain sleeping out of doors, and it is tough on the little children, so I will go look for a house." She took a little money and went to see a close friend from school.

Within the day, she and her friend had scouted out a place in North Amagasaki on the Hankyū line at a place called Tsukaguchi. They found this place just a little bit off a residential street not far from the station that was vacant because of evacuations. They signed the contract on it right away.

However, we heard rumors that some "Death Ray" had been visited upon Hiroshima, and there were still reports of bombing raids here and there, so I thought it might be safer to still sleep outside among the ruins for a little longer. Fortunately, since it was summer, we were still able to do that.

On August 15, the day the war ended, we listened to the emperor's broadcast and concluded that it would now be safe to proceed to the house Nobuko had rented. Takai was finally able to walk, so we took off, children in tow, and arrived late in the evening of that day. The verdant freshness of the hedge surrounding the house was in stark contrast to the burnt earth around Nishinomiya, imparting to us the feeling that somehow things might come back to life one day.

That night, we slept deeply on tatami mats for the first time in a long while, but mosquitoes catching the human scent seemed to return with a vengeance, so it was impossible to sleep through the night. My daughters and I gathered some mugwort from the back garden and made a mos-quito-repelling smoke fire, which we then took turns watching so that the baby could sleep. We passed the night this way until dawn.

The next day, neighbors brought us plates, teacups, and futon, so we finally began to feel like we were returning to normal. We had no firewood and nothing to cook, so we were still facing some problems, but Mrs. Fujita from across the way brought us over a box of dried corn and that was a big help. We cooked it up right away, and it was fairly tender, so we got some squash from the back garden that the previous tenant had been raising, steamed it with salt, and ate it. Our son said it was delicious and was delighted. "Pumpkins taste great, Mom. Please make some again!" For some reason, I just couldn't help it, and I started to cry. I couldn't say anything. I just felt so angry and frustrated at Japan's militarists and capitalists who had brought on this war that would deprive innocent children of food. My son noticed the expression on my face—I was gritting my teeth uncontrollably—and he said, "I am sorry, Mom. I won't say anything else bad." This just made me cry more. I went to give my poor little son a hug. . . .

My husband was bedridden, we had no food, and all our reserves had been burned up in the bombings, and we watched helplessly as our minuscule savings shrunk day by day with the postwar inflation. By the end of December, we had virtually nothing. Since we would be starving to death if we continued along as we were, on the morning of January 5, 1946, I went to speak with an old colleague of my husband's from the labor movement in Nishinomiya. Right off, he said, "Here, go sell these black-market *manjū,*" and he gave me a bunch of these steamed buns to take with me. So I had my daughter take them to the black-market area near the Tsukaguchi Station and sell them.

Suddenly, my husband gasped for air noisily and died in his bed. When Nobuko came running in, delighted with herself that she had sold all the buns, her father was dead. Only our second daughter did not know of her father's death. Takai had been bedridden for the past five months since he had been burned in the bombing raid. At first, it was just the back of his right hand that was affected, but with poor nutrition and no medicine, it soon got much worse. The skin ruptured, his flesh began to fester, and soon the infection spread throughout his whole body. He became blistery all over and finally he died.

The day before he died, I had managed to buy two *daifuku mochi* [rice cakes stuffed with bean paste] at the black market, which I hid from the children and slipped inside his bed. He was delighted and devoured them with relish. He said, "This is really hard on you. I am not much of a father. I haven't been able to do anything for the family for a long time. The war is over, so as soon as I can get better, I want to start working again and take the burden off of you." I said, "Look, I am not trying to bribe you with two rice cakes. You have to stay with the path you have chosen for yourself. I will somehow manage to work and raise our children to be outstanding Japanese adults." It seemed like we were recapturing some of the intimate thoughtfulness that characterized our early married life for the first time in a long while. My husband said, "Our children are really kind and reliable children, aren't they? I really don't want to die an leave them behind." He buried his face in the covers and wept. I said, "Watch what you are saying! If you die now, it will be like giving up. Live! You've got to survive!" But the next day at 2:00 P.M., he breathed his last. He was forty-nine years old. (102–106)

The remainder of My Own Sad History of Female Textile Workers *is episodic and made up of diary entries from the early postwar years when Takai sold goods on the black market in order to survive. But she does write of the periodic ceremonies to commemorate the life and work of her first husband. On the occasion of the fiftieth anniversary of Hosoi Wakizō's death and the publication of* The Sad History of Female Textile Workers *she wrote the following poem:*

Fifty Years since *Jokō aishi!*
Aa, Hosoi. Fifty years have passed since you died
I've become a seventy-two-year-old grandmother
I think that I have lived well
When you died, they vilified me as a bad wife
I drank sake, I ran around with men,
Under the old constitution, I had no inheritance rights
But I have inherited much from you!
Your beliefs, your determination
The incredible poverty you suffered—
I certainly inherited all of these!
And now, at seventy-two years of age,
I am poor and happy.
I speak with young people
I study with them—
I have become a *"hen na obaasan"* [strange old lady]
After you died and I became part of Takai's family
I wanted people who had nothing to do with your family to remember you
Assets are not just property and money
They are the way you think, the way you live
The real person who carries on the legacy
Is the one who will protect these ideas and way of life at all costs
This is what I want people to know
The Wakizō who had no parents, no children, no brothers and sisters
Who lived in the depths of poverty
Had nothing to leave behind

But along with *Jokō aishi*, your heart, and your perseverance will live forever
I have received all of these things
And I will pass them along to the younger generation
Even though I am seventy-two years old,
I have many young friends
And with *Jokō aishi* as our text,
We study together, learn together
Poverty is no big thing
This is all that one poor, happy old lady has to say (October 1974) (213–
   215)

Although this last line may seem dismissive and self-effacing, it belies a defiantly assertive stance. In a clear voice, Takai Toshio asserts her claim to Hosoi Wakizō's legacy. It is she who has continued to struggle and live in poverty; it is she who is truly carrying on the work that Wakizō began, not the powerful men of the publishing establishment. A person's legacy, she reminds us, does not consist only of money and property. It includes the ideas and the values around which their life was centered. This is what she has "received," and she will pass it along to others, especially to the next generation.

Analysis

Clearly, Takai's text is permeated with the kind of "awareness of women's subordinate position and of gender as a problematic category" to which Felski refers.[17] That is, as the narrator invites the reader to see the world from the perspective of this small, embattled, working woman, she is underscoring what a subordinated position female textile workers found themselves in the 1920s and 1930s. Moreover, Felski also observes that feminist confessional writing tends to concentrate on communicating individual experience as well as finding the representative elements of women's experience with which other women may identify.[18] Takai makes every effort to do this when she focuses her reader's attention on the discrimination and hardship women experienced in the workplace and in Japanese society as a whole. The story of her years with Hosoi Wakizō and of later being stripped of any financial claims to his estate is an account of a woman being denied her rights because of her gender. After all, even marriage offered no respite, for, as she notes, "In those days, Japanese women, whether they were wives or mothers, were just attachments to men, like kitchen implements." In her narrative, she exposes the way in which the prewar legal code denied women their fundamental rights as citizens. In fact, her very identity as the common-law wife and companion of Hosoi was effectively denied.
    Long notes in Telling Women's Lives *that*

[a] major theme of women's self-referential writing is the desire to be known, which springs form many sources. A woman's desire to write her life may be inspired by the desire to document her life, to "make sense" of it, to celebrate it, to assert her unique subjectivity. . . . It may express solidarity with other women and serve the function of resistance.[19]

No doubt, Takai wanted to "make sense" of her life and to assert her subjectivity. It is obvious she also desired to express solidarity with workers as well as other women and to encourage a politics of resistance. Her appeal to younger readers seems especially directed at transforming the world around her so that other women will not be subjected to the injustices she was. As Judith Fetterley points out, "Feminist criticism is a political act whose aim is not simply to interpret the world but to change it by changing the consciousness of those who read and their relation to what they read."[20] Surely Takai—who writes of her commitment to working with young people and maintaining her ties to the movement—expects her readers not just to see the world as she encountered it, but to alter their way of thinking about it. Takai attempts this not only by relating what had happened to her concerning Hosoi and her right as a widow to go out and support herself, but also in her depiction of the end of the Pacific War. She incorporates in the text her memories of the horrors of the U.S. bombing raids in order to denounce prewar militarism and to encourage young people to be staunchly antiwar.

Takai's narrative is a tale of discrimination, suffering, and incredible resilience. Ill equipped to deal with the world around her because she was so small of stature, so poorly educated, and hobbled by one bad leg, she was repeatedly humiliated and discriminated against because of her gender. But she persevered, overcoming the loss of two husbands and four children and enduring the constant harassment of male authority figures, be they the wealthy publishers, the factory owners, or the police. Denied access to a livelihood, driven from her abode, and forced to wander and sleep in the open air, it seems that the narrator survived an unimaginable ordeal. The stories of poverty, death, and violence constitute a narrative strategy that interrupts the larger, chronological unfolding of her life story and disrupts it with accounts of fracture and discontinuity. Of course, there is paradox imbedded in the narrative as well. The young woman who assisted one of the labor movement's true heroes was reviled in the press, and her reputation was tarnished, because of her liaison with a man she would eventually marry. In the eyes of the patriarchy, she was somehow being disloyal to or dishonoring Hosoi's memory.

Nevertheless, the narrator does manage to survive her ordeal, and in choos-

ing to tell her story, to write her life—even though many portions of her narrative summon up memories that can only be painful to revisit—she creates a voice in which she can assert herself as a subject. Unlike Fukuda Hideko, however, Takai Toshio does not dwell on the question of the pain that remembering or writing may bring. Rather, her desire is to set the record straight and to tell her own story. But even in her own telling, there are interruptions and disruptions—her struggles, her wanderings, the deaths of husbands and children—all of which disturb the otherwise placid surface and linear structure of the narrative. As Gilmore elaborates on her notion of "autobiographics,"

> Even in their surface presentation of unity and linear development, autobiographics pull together such a variety of kinds of writing (history, memoir, confession, even parody) that the "unifying" I at their "center" is already fractured by its place in varying discourses (political, philosophical, psychological, aesthetic), and what frequently fractures such totalizing theories of identity is gender.[21]

Takai, too, draws upon various types of writing: she offers the reader glimpses of history, snippets of confession, and an abundance of personal memories and, of course, a poem. In so doing, she draws upon a variety of discourses, including politics, literature, and social history, and the result is a text that is filled with a sense of contestation. But when Takai speaks in the text, giving voice to her own subjectivity, she inhabits a discursive space usually left to males. For this, she pays a price; the patriarchs, in the form of the publishers and former supporters of Hosoi, banish her claims to his legacy. The more we learn about the life of someone like Takai Toshio—about what she has learned in her life and where and how she learned it—the more we come to appreciate just how "complex and multiple" the tapestry of prewar Japanese women's historical subjectivity is.

4

Her Mother's Voice
Nishi Kiyoko's *Reminiscences (Tsuioku)*

Autobiography demonstrates that we can never recover the past, only represent it; yet, it encodes the possibility of recovery as desire and the possibility of representation as its mode of production.
> —Leigh Gilmore, *Autobiographics: A Feminist Theory of Women's Self-Representation*

Nishi (née Ishihara) Kiyoko was born in 1907 in Kobe to a traditional Osaka merchant family. Determined to become a financially independent woman capable of resisting the tyranny of a traditional family, she attended a commercial college in Kobe and then went on to study at Waseda University in Tokyo. After graduation, she joined Ishibashi Tanzan's journal, The Oriental Economist *(Tōyō keizai shimpōsha), during the war years. In the postwar period, she joined the staff of the* Yomiuri shinbun *and was a witness to some of the infamous postwar labor disputes there.*

My Phantom Mother

WHAT REMAINS IN MY MEMORIES

Among my childhood memories, the most prominent are memories of my mother. In reality, though, it boils down to a single memory. Beyond that, there is virtually nothing else to recall. Yet, remaining within these memories are various mysteries that continually resurface from the deepest recesses of my mind. It all has to do with the happenings on a summer day when I was about seven years old. . . .

My mother was an only child, so my father had married into the family and adopted their name. Since he would not be inheriting the rice business my grandfather managed, my parents lived separately in Osaka.

My father worked in a Mitsubishi warehouse for Osaka Harbor Construction, supervising longshoreman. How my father, who was the third son of a farmer from Tokushima Prefecture, came to marry my mother is a story I never really heard. My recollections about my father are that he was called "Pop" (Oyaji-san), and he was known to enjoy the good life.

Anyway, suddenly, my mother was called back to her family home in Kobe. It was a hot summer day. Since my grandparents doted on me, I do not recall particularly longing for my mother's affection, but I did miss her. Seen through the eyes of a child, she was a beautiful woman. She was pale skinned, slim, but able to carry herself with dignity. Even today she reminds me of a woman in one of Takehisa Yumeji's illustrations.

Evening meals were usually late in merchant families, but that day, after eating surprisingly early, my mother said to me, "Would you like to enjoy the cool of the evening and take a little walk?" Grabbing on to the sleeve of my mother's *yukata*, we set off. I cannot recall a thing about the pattern on her *yukata*, but I remember distinctly that she was wearing Japanese-style clothing. Our house was on Kobe's Nakayamate Dōri, but instead of heading downtown, she proceeded upward toward the mountains. Even though the summer days were long, the light was fading, and darkness was beginning to surround us. Getting a little nervous, I suggested that we start heading back, but my mother said, "Wait here a minute," and left me alone while she started up a mountain path. It came to me that this was a place we often came to play as children, the entrance to a path up to Mt. Futatabi. After a bit, my mother returned, saying, "I thought I could see some lights so I went to investigate, but it was just a water wheel. Oh well, let's go home." She took my hand and we started walking on the road home as though nothing had happened.

When I woke up the next morning, though, my mother was nowhere to be found. I thought that maybe she had gone back to Osaka, but it turned out that she had vanished before my eyes forever.

The next memory I have is of sometime after my mother disappeared. I am swaying to and fro in a rickshaw that was being pulled alongside a river somewhere. My grandfather is in the rickshaw with me. He was straddling me with his legs and I was holding on to a red blanket with both hands, so it must have been early autumn. As I think back on it, it must have been Kobe's Minato River that we were running along. I do not recall being told where we were going or why. I just remember that both my grandfather and I were wearing our best kimono.

Our destination was a temple. Inside the chilly main hall of the temple, my grandfather handed the chief priest a small package. From inside the package, one corner of a flat, wooden object—I can't remember if it was black or white—was protruding. I have no recollection of the nature of any conversation my grandfather might have had with the chief priest. I only learned seven or eight years later that the object was my mother's mortuary tablet. By that time, I was already attending a girls' middle school. I don't really recall the context, but the only clue that I had as to what was going on came from overhearing my grandmother say that "Yoshino (my mother) had really done something pitiful."

Why Did She Choose Death?

My mother committed suicide. That summer evening, when she had ventured up the path of Mt. Futatabi, she was conducting preliminary surveillance. At the top of the path she found a lake at a place called Shūhōgahara, which is where she threw herself in. It is not as though the mountain was very high or anything. But a young woman running up a little-known mountain path, racing toward her own death—what could she have been brooding so intensely about? I must say that even to this day, the truth eludes me.

Both my grandfather and father died without uttering a single word about it. All my grandmother could say was that it was "very pitiful." Whenever I tried to pursue the matter, somehow all my friends and relatives just kept silent.

According to things I heard about my mother, she was an extremely gifted seamstress. Whenever she would make an Edo-style skirt for someone, it was a real work of art. So why would a mother like that cut short her life?

Perhaps I was reading too many romance novels for young women at the time, but I began to believe that when she had suddenly disappeared from her family's house in Kobe it was because she had run away from some situation at home and was secretly living somewhere in the city. So whenever I saw someone who looked like her on a street corner, or at the public bath, I would run to get a closer look. I never did ask anyone straight out, but I just persisted in this daydream by myself. It sounds odd, I know, but I thought I might be able to penetrate the veil that surrounded my mother's whereabouts by continuing to pursue her with my questions and my hopes.

When I eventually learned what really had happened, I remained extraordinarily calm and collected. Since no one would tell me the whole story, I came up with the following plausible scenario:

Caught between her father and her husband, she ultimately felt cornered, with no way out. I had always heard that my father was weak and that he liked to speculate. But even based on what I recall, it was unlikely that someone like my father, who tried his hand speculating on commodity futures and lost and that whenever he did get ahead speculating on stocks he would spend everything on a good time in the pleasure quarters of Osaka, would ever be able to get along well with my grandfather, who was, by personality, a stereotypical Osaka merchant type. He may not have done anything on a grand scale, but he did insist on protecting his own authority as head of a small merchant family, and though my father may have been a clever and interesting man, as the adopted son-in-law of the family, he was subject to my grandfather's authority. Since my mother had been required to marry my father so that the family line could be preserved, her fate was really determined by the prevailing family system.

Originally, my grandfather had been born the second son of a small landholder in Okayama Prefecture. . . . My father's academic record was nothing special, but in addition to enjoying a lively, exciting life, he did have a strong affinity for learning. He always liked to read the difficult intellectual journals like *Reconstruction (Kaizō)* and *The Sun (Taiyō)* and enjoyed talking about politics. So, although I have no idea about the particulars of what went on between them, it seems reasonable that, in the end, my mother felt hopelessly trapped by the tension and discord that must have characterized the relationship between her father and her husband.

Of course, there might well have been some tension occurring between my mother and my father as well. My own little imaginings are really that and nothing more—I don't know a single fact about what actually went on between them. However, given the little bit of reason that I do possess, I cannot accept the notion that the behavior of this mother of mine who elected to commit suicide was impulsive. I have to see what she did as some form of resistance.

By the way, my mother's bizarre behavior was not so much of a shock to me, nor did it affect me emotionally so much. I just had to live with some nagging, unanswered questions about why her will to live couldn't have been stronger, and why such an expert seamstress as herself didn't think she could find some way to live out her life.

In the end, there never were any materials to shed light on my mother's death, but I was determined that I would never succumb to the same fate as she did. Why? Well I, too, am an only daughter. I knew that it might be impossible to ever feel free if I had to marry someone who was being adopted into the family to preserve the ancestral line. This was not something I would ever be able to bear.

It was around that time that I began to feel the seeds of my own being start to sprout and take root. I came of age as a young woman during those years after World War I when the influence of the Bolshevik Revolution was in the air, and everyone was talking about democracy. Western books and customs were entering Japan and exerting quite an influence on us. Moreover, my development as a young woman took place in the unique atmosphere of the city of Kobe, which also shaped the pattern of my development. (9–15)

This opening passage is a moving account by a narrator who still longs to have a conversation with her mother in order to understand why she would take her own life. The question that she may want to ask but cannot quite put into words is, What made your life so unbearable that you were willing to abandon me? A number of feminist scholars, most recently Kristi Siegal (Women's Autobiographies, Culture, Feminism) *and Jo Malin* (The Voice of the Mother), *have made the argument that women's autobiographies contain an embedded intertext that constitutes a dialogue or conversation between mother and daughter. Here, the narrator clearly yearns to hear her mother's voice, to come to some kind of understanding of why her mother did what she did. This desire will shape her entire narrative, one that may be read as an account of how she ordered her life around avoiding the fate that befell her mother. How was she to accomplish this?*

She makes three observations about her mother's situation that seem crucial.

- "Her fate was really determined by the prevailing family system."
- "Caught between her father and her husband, she ultimately felt cornered, with no way out."
- "I cannot accept the notion that the behavior of this mother of mine who elected to commit suicide was impulsive. I have to see what she did as some form of resistance."

Cornered by the family system, she had no recourse but to take her own life. That, in turn, became her act of resistance. If the narrator is to avoid her mother's fate, it is up to her to resist any efforts of her family to make her marry an adopted son-in-law in order to prop up the family system. In order for her to resist, then, the narrator must structure her life (and her narrative) around the principle of establishing her freedom and independence from the patriarchal family system. She must never be caught between a father (or a grandfather) and a husband.

If it is true that gender is a pivotal element in women's attempts at self-representation, and if disruptions and rhetorical violence are frequently found in female self-representational texts, then it is interesting to ponder the things that Nishi Kiyoko singles out in her opening chapter as powerful forces that have shaped her narrative. At the head of the list, of course, is this wrenching story of her mother's suicide, the story within her story that she must confront. Gender is clearly a force at work in this story: the young mother had been caught in the middle of a dilemma created by the patriarchy. Although she cannot prove conclusively that her mother's suicide was an act of resistance, it is her feeling based on credible circumstantial evidence: the attitudes and values prevailing in an Osaka merchant family, the incompatibility of her father's carefree nature with the rigidity of this value system, and the need of a patriarch to "protect his own authority."

But these internal circumstances, in turn, were juxtaposed against another set of powerful external forces that operate on the narrator, namely the brave new world into which the narrator was coming of age. The years before and after World War I brought about so much rapid urbanization and social change that, in many ways, Japan was a very different country than it had been in the early 1900s. One of the most salient features of the 1920s was the emergence of new mass-circulation magazines, many of them targeted to women readers. Women's Review (Fujin kōron, *1916*), Housewife's Friend (Shufu no Tomo, *1917*), and Woman's Club (Fujin kurabu, *1920*) were among the leading periodicals with substantial readerships aimed at women. With educational and employment opportunities expanding for women, there was a new literate readership for these magazines. As Sato points out, this was an age of "massification" and "consumerism," an age in which the latter was incarnated in "the media, popular music and jazz. It was symbolized by the neon lights, the cafés and dance halls, Western fashions, and the bobbed hair of the modern girl."[1] It was an age in which stories traveled far and fast in the media, and the magazines and newspapers of the day carried advertisements for consumer goods, many of them aimed at female readers. Moreover, this was the era of the department store, with their ubiquitous mannequins, and the "modern girl" even came to be referred to as a "mannequin girl."[2] This was also the era in which cinema became popular in Japan; when you add to this the neon lights, the cafés, the dance halls, radio, trolley cars, trains, and even baseball parks, you get a sense of how the pace and nature of Japanese daily life was changing.*

In terms of the accelerating pace of life, Harootunian has noted recently that "speed, shock, sensation and spectacle" were the "constituent elements" of the modern experience.[3] Nishi often observes how she was caught up in a vortex of rapid social and economic change. In particular, she singles out the advent of the post–World War I democratic movement, with its rhetoric about freedom and revolution, the introduction of Marxism into Japan, and the emergence of mass politics in the form of the Rice Riots. World War I had pulled Japan into the larger global community, and since it was a boost to Japan's economic development and rate of industrialization, it meant that Japan was more enmeshed in the process of becoming modern than ever before. The labor force more than doubled from the time of the Russo-Japanese War, and, along with the emergence of a modern, bourgeois culture, there were ample signs of the appearance of a proletarian culture as well. Before 1919, annual labor disputes numbered in the hundreds. Beginning in 1919, such disputes numbered in the thousands. The very large strike by shipyard workers in the Kobe-Osaka area, to which Nishi refers below, involved over thirty thousand strikers and lasted for over one month.

The rise of labor militancy was but one dimension of the new Japan that was emerging in the post–World War I era. New forms of media—print, radio, and cinema—appeared, and new leisure activities became more available to all urbanites. New social classes and new social actors were even beginning to appear as well. New industrial workers, middle-class salaried employees—"salarymen"—sales clerks, telephone operators, typists, café waitresses, what Nishi calls the new bourgeoisie, were now a part of the everyday landscape of Japan. One of the signal events of the new postwar era was the Rice Riots, an alarming series of uprisings and urban riots that disrupted life and affected people all across Japan. Already mass media, mass culture, and consumerism were figuring in the lives of urban Japanese. Now, Japanese were witnessing mass politics on a scale they never had before. The Rice Riots are the focus of considerable attention in the next section of Nishi's text as the narrator describes their "impingement" on her family's life.

My Family, the Rice Riots, and the Shipbuilders' Strike

The household in which I was raised by my grandparents, along with two young apprentices, was a strict household located amid small and medium-sized homes in the Nakayamate District of Kobe. It was just a little corner of a not very distinguished neighborhood. There were no particularly large homes, just the usual array of small shops: confections,

groceries, a liquor store, and a public bath. Our house was just around
the corner from Yōkōmachi, one of the small side streets, and catty-corner
from us was an obstetrics clinic. On cloudy days, the scent of disinfectant
would waft up from the sewer. The assistant director of the clinic was a
woman who lived by herself just opposite our home. I can remember
watching her rushing in and out of the clinic dressed in her long, pleated
skirt *(hakama)* as I followed her with my eyes somewhat longingly.

Most everyone else in the neighborhood around us were "salaryman"
families. I can remember the smell of toast and coffee emanating from
their kitchens. There was also a sailor's home in the neighborhood, too. I
remember getting a snack of toast from his house and responding enthusi-
astically with surprise that there existed such a tasty treat in this world.
When it came to snacks, we had braised beans, sliced rice cakes, or, occasionally, some biscuits. So you can imagine how envious I was.

It wasn't only their food of which I was envious. Compared with the
busy life of a merchant household, the sense of harmony and the atmosphere in the salaryman homes was also very enviable. No matter how
good a report card I brought home, it would always get just a cursory examination and never a word of praise. Not only were my grandparents
busy, but also they were strict disciplinarians. (15–17)

*The lifestyle of these new middle-class, "salaryman" families, stands in contrast
to her own, tradition-bound merchant family. Somehow in the houses of the
new bourgeoisie, people were living more relaxed, more modern lives. In her
family, expectations were high, affection withheld, and discipline strictly en-
forced. But if her family lacked some of the warmth and harmony that she
imagined one could find in the homes of the salarymen, it did promise stability.
Until the Rice Riots profoundly disrupted that stability.*

The Rice Riots Impinge

Except for my mother's disappearance, life in our household was rather
calm and peaceful until one day, out of the blue, a major incident intruded
into our lives. It was the Rice Riots. . . . I recall feeling in those days that
there was some sense of unease evident in the talk around the shop. What
I remember most clearly was that the price of rice was rising daily. . . . It
just felt like something was about to happen. Then, housewives in a small
fishing village in Tōyama Prefecture attacked a rice dealer, launching what
came to be known as the Rice Riots. In Kobe, anxiety had become a way of

life. In the evening on August 12, 1918, the Suzuki *shōten* was burned to the ground. . . .

From atop my father's shoulders, I stared incessantly and in utter fascination out of the second-floor window at the flames from the burning Suzuki store as they leapt into the night sky and bathed it in red. Before long, a loud cry went up from the corner where a throng of people was pushing its way toward us from the downtown area. They all carried sticks in their hands and held banners aloft proclaiming their grievances. They began knocking down street lamps and screaming. In the neighboring area, people had closed their shutters and were waiting quietly.

Suddenly, one of the young people who worked in our shop said, "All those people, they are from Ujigawa." Ujigawa was an area inhabited mainly by the *buraku*, the outcastes. As I peered fearfully out of the window, I could see lots of adults, both men and women, but also some young girls my own age. I thought, "That might be so-and-so from my school." There were many outcaste girls in my class. When I thought about this, I suddenly became quite sad for some reason, and tears began rolling down my cheeks. I didn't really know why. Perhaps it was just the shock of seeing someone whose face I saw everyday in the classroom and feeling that even she was against us, too.

Then, somebody shouted, "We'll be back tomorrow!" The next morning, my grandmother and I were sent off to a nearby park. When we returned around noon, all the rice, barley, soybeans, and red beans had been looted. My grandfather just responded philosophically to the attack, saying, "Well, they took everything they wanted and they didn't even need any money." Of course, as a child, I had no way of understanding how serious the loss may have been. . . .

The Rice Riots in Kobe were put down abruptly when military troops from the Himeji division were called out and martial law was declared. Many people were arrested, but probably the outcastes were in the majority. It is always people like that who become the victims.

World War I ended just three months after the Rice Riots, and rather suddenly, the world fell on economic hard times. In Kobe during this time, unemployment increased and strikes began to occur here and there. In the case of our own business, there were numerous defaults on debts, and I recall my grandfather sitting at his desk every evening until late working on his calculations. My grandfather was very fair-minded and his character would never permit him to be greedy, so he continued to deliver rice to families who were facing hard times, saying, "There are times when you just cannot demand payment." Perhaps because he continued to do this too often, a few years later even this small little shop of ours had to close its doors.

Sympathy for the Shipbuilding Strike

Around this time, the number of labor strikes and demonstrations in our area increased steadily. Once again, it was an incident that occurred on a hot summer's day. My grandmother and some of the neighborhood ladies took a table and some tea makings out into the street and set them up. When a group of demonstrators came from the same direction that the rioters had come during the Rice Riots, the ladies hailed them, calling out, "Hey, are you thirsty? Come on, have something to drink," offering them cold barley tea and shaved ice drinks. The men, clad in their overalls, thanked the ladies and slaked their thirst. When asked, they said they were strikers from the Kawasaki Shipbuilding Yard. But I wondered why, since there were no Kawasaki workers among our relatives or neighbors.

So why were they striking? I heard someone say that these men were just going to visit a local shrine, so I asked, "Why are these young strikers going to visit a shrine?" Having just started school, there was still quite a bit I didn't understand!

Anyway, this scene remained fixed in my mind as a riddle for a long time, even until I became an adult. Or, I kept wondering if there wasn't something I had misunderstood about the situation because it just didn't add up. Then all of a sudden one day I jumped up with a start. It was 1985.

Actually, it was one day when I received from the Japan Federation of Labor (Nihon Rōdō Kumiai Sōdōmei) a very thick book by Suzuki Bunji called *Twenty Years of the Labor Movement (Rōdō undō nijūnen)*. Needless to say, Mr. Suzuki was the founder of the Yūaikai, the predecessor to the Japan Federation of Labor, a man who left a huge impression on the history of the labor movement in Japan. When I opened the book and looked straightaway at the section on "Labor Disputes in Kobe," I found the following comments on the page dealing with strikes against the Kawasaki and Mitsubishi shipbuilders:

On August 6th, the funeral was held for young Mr. Tsunemine who had died tragically when a policeman's saber sliced him from his back through to his lungs two days earlier. His dying words were encouragement to his comrades to go forth and complete the task they had begun. Over twenty thousand of his cohorts turned out for the public funeral and the citizens of Kobe, in a show of support, expressed their heartfelt sympathy by offering the strikers tea and water.

So that's what it had been about! I felt as though I had finally stumbled upon something for which I had been searching for a long time! It had been a funeral demonstration after all! Suzuki's book provides the details on how union members from both Kawasaki and Mitsubishi had visited seven different shrines, renewing their pledge to triumph in their dispute with the companies. The strikers flocking to shrines, citizens pouring out [of their homes] to offer their support—what a simple but touching scene of social turmoil.

But even so, what about my grandmother's conduct? In Kobe in those days there were many workers from the shipbuilding industry as well as other factories living in the neighborhoods. So it seems likely that she felt not only a sense of familiarity with them, but was concerned about issues of fairness and frustrated by the onset of economic hard times as well.

By the way, this big strike against Mitsubishi and Kawasaki, which demanded wage increases and an end to worker dismissals, ended in a crushing defeat for the workers. The strike began in June of 1921 and ended on August 11th after much suffering. (16–25)

Two additional events from the world outside the narrator's family that impinged on her have been added to the list of forces shaping her youth: the intrusion of the Rice Riots and the shipyard strikes that occurred when she was a child. Certainly, the Rice Riots were the more traumatic of the two, with the burning and looting that eventually led to her family losing their business. Hundreds of thousands of people participated, and, as Nishi points out, troops were called out to restore order in some areas. Over twenty-five thousand people were arrested and over eight thousand eventually prosecuted. Nishi's recollections of the shipyard strikes and her subsequent research on what she might have witnessed as a child indicate that the advent of mass politics, strikes, and labor disputes was part and parcel of the world of her childhood. Obviously, these events left a lasting impression on her. The remaining element in her narrative that configures for the reader how her subjectivity was constituted was the education she received at a women's school in Kobe and later at the university.

I was born in Kobe and raised there until the age of seventeen. So, naturally, upon hearing that, most people assume that for college I went to

Kobe Women's College (Kobe Jogakuin), right? I guess people thought I looked like I went to such a school, but whenever I would reply, "Heavens no! I am not the fancy Kobe Women's college type. I went to Kobe Women's School of Commerce," people would look dubious. . . .

As for classes, in addition to the standard business curriculum consisting of classes on the abacus *(soroban)*, bookkeeping, business English, and typing, there were various specialized courses. What stands out in my memory is that we were given very little of the "good wife, wise mother" *(ryōsai-kenbo)* sort of education there.

Given this kind of curriculum, we students developed into strong young women with a healthy curiosity and a feeling of confidence that we could be entrusted with responsibilities. Even in the midst of economic depression, in 1917 we were affected by the news of the Russian Revolution, and words like freedom, independence, and free love crept into our vocabulary. Somehow, books like Kuriyagawa Hakuson's *The Modern Idea of Love (Kindai no ren'aikan)* and Bebel's *Women and Socialism [Shakaishugi to fujin]* were showing up in our classes.

A Number of Celebrity Love Affairs Occur

The years I was a student at the Women's School of Commerce were from 1920–1924. During that time, out in the real world, there were a number of sensational romantic incidents reported in the newspapers, and I can recall that we felt emotionally caught up in them. In order to confirm my recollections, I consulted a book from the Chūō Kōron Publishing House called *Fifty Years of* Fujin kōron *(Fujin kōron no gojūnen)* and there were a number or prominent incidents recorded. For example, in the year 1921 alone there was the case of Hamada Eiko, daughter of the chief of the Hamada Hospital who committed suicide when her parents refused to allow her to marry the man with whom she was in love. This was followed by the liaison between the scientist Dr. Ishihara Jun, who had a wife and child, and the *tanka* poet Hara Asao. Moreover, the so-called queen of Tsukushi at that time, the distinguished lady and poet Yanagihara Teruko [Byakuren], left coal baron Itō Denyūzaemon, the man she had been forced to marry in an arranged political match in order to aid her father, and ran off with a younger man, Miyazaki Ryūsuke, who was her lover. Next, in June of 1923, the novelist Arishima Takeo and Hatano Akiko, a reporter for *Women's Review*, committed suicide at the Arishima family's vacation home, Jōgetsuan, in Karuizawa.

And before this incident—when I was still in grade school—there had been the Countess Yoshikawa Kamako, who committed suicide with her beloved driver, as well as Matsui Sumako's suicide following on the heels of that of her lover, Shimamura. But we had not really comprehended such things [at our age]. However, in the 1920s, when we were older, there was no way that these events involving such well-known people would not have an impact on us. I remember a girl in our class who was skilled at *tanka* poetry and who would always come in carrying a newspaper article, very excited, and would gather us around and say, "Wow, that was great! Especially for Yanagihara Byakuren—what a wonderful person she must be!" And we secretly admired her. And she would murmur things like, "This is really something—it's truly the age of free love!" I began to really feel strongly that as the daughter of a woman who had had to marry an adopted son-in-law for the family without any regard for what she may have wanted, I wanted to smash that kind of destiny, and I wanted strongly to marry someone I loved.[4]

Three months after the Arishima Takeo incident, on September 1 of 1923, the Great Kantō Earthquake struck. Those of us living in Kobe were mobilized to help. Having just moved into our new school, we gathered a huge amount of cloth to make *yukata* for the earthquake victims. We also went to Kobe Station and Sanmiya Station and took refugees by the hand and led them to their destinations. I remember my impression of the scale of that earthquake when I noticed that our own clock at home had stopped. Although we could not fully understand what we read in the newspapers about what was happening in Tokyo, such as the murder of Ōsugi Sakae and the mass murders of the Koreans, I can recall that we at least felt that it was very frightening.

We had our own earthquake of sorts in our family as well. The year following the Kantō Earthquake, I am not sure of the surrounding circumstances, but perhaps it was due to the continued economic disruptions following the war and the big earthquake, our small family business folded. My grandfather remained to conduct final negotiations with some warehouses in Kobe, but my grandmother and I left for Osaka to join my father, who was living there with his new wife and my younger sister. . . .

Upon graduation, most of my classmates became typists or office workers in trading companies or shipbuilding outfits, except for those who went into their own businesses. They were the vanguard of working women. I was always envious of my friends who did this. I also thought it would be wonderful to be out on one's own, working, earning a salary, and living by one's own free will. But, since our Kobe store was closing, I went with my grand-mother to my father's house in Osaka and had to say good-bye to the city of Kobe that held so many precious memories for me. (27–34)

Two things seem noteworthy about the narrator's reconstruction of her educa-tional experience. For the second time, she underscores the significance of the impact of "the Russian Revolution and words like freedom, independence, and free love" for her generation. While still in high school, her father had intro-duced her to the mass-circulation journals like Reconstruction (Kaizō) *and* The Sun (Taiyō), *where considerable discussion of and debates about social is-sues occurred. Now she notes that even students at a women's commercial col-lege were reading books on socialism, feminism and modern theories of free love, and so on. The other observation she makes relates to the penetration of mass culture into the cities and even the outlying areas of Japan in the 1920s. By 1920, nearly a fifth of Japan's population was living in urban areas, where leisure pursuits were growing to accommodate the new urban denizens.[5] A new mass culture featuring print media, cafés, amusement parks, department stores, radio, and cinema was in evidence in the cities. Perhaps as many as half a mil-lion households owned radios by the late 1920s, and specialized magazines aimed, for example, at young women, were common. When Nishi and her classmates became fascinated with the lives and affairs of the celebrities of the day, it was indicative of the penetration of this new culture into the lives of schoolgirls. What Nishi was determined to gain in this new age, though, was her own economic independence and autonomy. She refers to this as her "struggle for independence."*

The Struggle for Independence

When my father became an adopted son-in-law, this was not uncommon for the second and third sons in farming households. But this was the age of industrialization, so opportunities for males other than the oldest son were starting to open up. In the meantime, there were no signs that my grandfather's stubborn clinging to family bloodlines, and his fear as head of the family that the family line might die out, were in any danger of crumbling. My father was not in a position to freely express his own opin-ions. It seems as though ghosts of the archaic family system lingered on in our family, caught in a vicious circle but unable to find a way out. I was the one for whom it was really unbearable. There had to be something I could do. . . .

As a result of thinking things out, if I were the one who had to find a way to break out of this vicious circle, I would have to have the will to develop my own lifestyle unfettered by convention.

However, living freely might result in my being cut off entirely from my family. That being the case, as long as I was dependent on my parents for my basic livelihood, I would be prevented from saying anything. So I really had no choice but to first establish my economic independence, and then let my free will express itself. Obviously, it would not be possible for me to realize both of these goals overnight. However, from this point on, it was this desire that set the course for my life's direction. (35–38)

Clearly articulating the "desire that set the course for my life's direction," the narrator identifies what is at stake for her. She needs to go to work, to establish her own independence, if she wishes to avoid her mother's fate and become a victim of the tyranny of an old-fashioned merchant family. She was painfully aware that "ghosts of the archaic family system lingered on in our family" and that she was "caught in a vicious circle but unable to find a way out." Since this language echoes the experience of her mother, it would be up to her to exercise her will if she wanted to discover her own way out. But it would be a delicate operation unless she was willing to be completely cut off from her family. For the time being, then, education would have to be the source of her liberation.

Furuya Women's English Academy and Osaka High School

At that time, I was registered for classes at the Furuya Women's English Academy (Furuya Joshi Eigaku Juku), a small-scale private English school. I had really wanted to go to Tokyo and study at the Women's English School, which was later to be known as Tsuda Women's Academy, but, in the end, I was not able to realize this dream. But I just wanted to study at this point, regardless of my gender *(musei ni)*. It wasn't that I was particularly fond of English, but I guess I was stimulated by the notion that if you were studying something foreign, then somehow you were in touch with what was new. . . . (38–39)

I came to understand much later that in 1925, with the passage of the Universal Manhood Suffrage Bill and, at the same time, the Peace Preservation Law, our freedom of speech was being seriously suppressed. In response to this, the first thing to occur was that students organized protests against military training on the various campuses, and scholars affiliated with the student movement *(gakusei rengōkai)*, such as Kawakami Hajime from Kyoto University, Kawano Takashi from Dōshisha University, and Kawakami Buntarō from Kansai Gakuin, were arrested along with about thirty or so students. . . . Afterward, in 1928, there were the mass arrests of Japan Communist Party members, the so-called March 15 Incident. At that time, many campuses had organizations known as Social Science Research Associations, and many coeds at Tokyo University were arrested. I can recall them being referred to as "Marx Girls. . . ." (41–45)

With My Uncle's Help I Go to Tokyo

At that point in time, my father was working at a newly opened emporium, and I was seated in one corner of the establishment, selling tobacco. So I had become a cigarette girl. My uncle, my father's younger brother, had just returned from studying abroad in America, which he had left his job to do. It was not the era of airplanes, so we all went down to the dock in Kobe to welcome him home. Then, we gathered around the table in our Osaka home and celebrated his return. . . .

My uncle occasionally wrote me letters from America telling me how free and liberated American women were and how they not only took jobs in society, but were also active in a number of realms. I don't recall ever speaking to my uncle in any depth about women's lifestyles, but my uncle may have been able to catch a glimpse of the gloom I felt in my heart.

Actually, it was because of my uncle's help that my life took a momentous change. When, shortly after his return, my uncle inquired about my plans and I reported to him that I was trying to figure out how to get a job with a newspaper, he said, "In order for a woman to get a job and establish her independence, the first order of business is to get some more education. So you should come to Tokyo where I'll take responsibility for you." Moreover, he was able to put it to my father in a positive manner and persuade him to go along with the idea. Alas, as to be expected in our family, some trouble did arise. Perhaps because of my grandfather's reservations, my father got angry and accused my uncle of instigating the whole thing. My grandfather looked dumbfounded, and, to make matters worse, my father's older brother came running, and we had to have this whole family meeting. In the meantime, I secretly packed up a few of my belongings and hid them in a closet. Depending on the outcome of the meeting, I was prepared to take off without permission if I had to. My father finally gave in and granted permission when, with all the stubbornness I could muster, I made it crystal clear that I wanted no part of marrying an adopted son-in-

law just to continue the family's name. Instead, I said I wanted to take responsibility for my own life. Even so, my father maintained until the end
that I wasn't being allowed to study so that I could go out and become a
working woman. Perhaps he needed to save face. Finally, on the day of my
departure, he told me to make my farewells in front of the Buddhist altar,
and he took me to Umeda Station and made arrangements for my bags.
. . . It was March of 1928 and I was twenty-one years old. (45–47)

*Nishi's narrative places her struggle for social and economic independence at its
core. Because of the lessons learned from her mother's suicide, it was extremely important to her to establish her independence from her family by supporting herself
and by determining her own marriage partner if she chose to marry at all. In the
passage above, the narrator negotiates a route to attaining her own independence
by conferring with the family, but she makes it clear that she was prepared to bolt
and go out on her own had it become necessary. Once again, the narrator
specifically alludes to the radical student movement, which was instrumental in
diffusing Marxist ideas among young people and was an important source of Communist Party membership. The next passage deals with her experiences with
higher education and some of the people and student organizations she encountered there. She also makes it a point to underscore her "first encounter with gender discrimination" at the university where she was not permitted to be a regular
matriculating student because she was a woman. In discussing Waseda University, she goes to considerable lengths to describe the Waseda Oratorical Society—
another radical student organization—and the impact that this organization, and
other progressive students and intellectuals, had on her. It would seem that she is
eager for the reader to be aware that she was exposed to Marxism and the Japan
Communist Party during these years and was quite familiar with its activities.*

As an Auditor at Waseda University

MY FIRST ENCOUNTER WITH GENDER DISCRIMINATION

My reason for choosing Waseda was, in part, due to my uncle's advice,
but also because I had somehow learned that Waseda had a Department of
Newspaper Studies, so I had hoped to enter that program. However, it
turned out that the department had been abolished, so I wound up in the
Department of Politics and Economics. Of course, they had a literature department as well, but I took a certain degree of self-satisfaction as a woman
in entering the politics and economics program because I believed it
would help me establish my independence.

However, what was frustrating was the way I was treated as an auditor as opposed to a regular student. I tried raising the issue [of my treatment] with various offices on campus, but I pretty much got told the same thing everywhere: "I'm sorry but this is university policy." . . .

Of course, I had not had to pass a rigorous entrance exam, just a simple oral interview.

At that time, the universities that had opened their doors to women were Tōhoku Imperial University (1913), Tokaidō Imperial University (1918), and Kyūshū Imperial University (1922), while private schools such as Dōshisha University in Kyoto admitted women also from 1922. As for female auditors, Kyūshū, Tōhoku, and Waseda began accepting women in 1921 (see *Fifty Years of* Fujin kōron). So, if I wanted to select an all-male school in Tokyo, Waseda was virtually my only choice.

Nevertheless, what I had trouble understanding was why I had to pay the identical fees and had to take the same end-of-term exams as the regular (male) students. Moreover, when the men graduated, they were called *"gakushi,"* or bachelors of arts, but we women were still just auditors. That is exactly what is written on our graduation certificates. It was the first time for me to directly experience gender discrimination. (48–49)

Other Women at Waseda at That Time

Among the other auditors at that time were Sampa Takako, who was in my same department, [and] Kanda Asano, who was studying Russian in the literature department. . . . Miss Sampa had a scholarly disposition and later earned a reputation as an economic critic. Her major work, *A History of the Japanese Cotton Industry (Nihon mengyōshi)* drew high praise from critics. I understand that she was the daughter of a well-to-do family from Fukushima Prefecture, but she spoke rather ponderously in her thick Tōhoku accent, and that may have given the impression that she was a rather quiet person. However, I found in her eyes a powerful light that somehow shone brightly. I am not certain what fate might have befallen her, but I heard that she died alone in an old person's home in the postwar period.

Miss Kanda Asano had apparently been interested in the Japan Communist Party since she was a student, and she was implicated in one of those mass roundups of party members in the late 1920s. Also from a rich family who managed a paper manufacturing plant in Tsūyama City in Okayama Prefecture, I can recall getting some help from them during the war on several occasions when I was reduced to having pretty much nothing. She was well bred and had a calm, quiet personality, but I would sometimes have a hard time following her when she spoke rapidly and passionately about things, throwing out difficult concepts of Marxist-Leninist theory in rapid-fire fashion. Although she may have been quiet by nature, there were many times when she would lose me.

I was fairly close with Miss Kanda as a friend, but I really was not in the same ideological camp as she was. However, she was fairly close with the novelist Miyamoto Yuriko, and I recall that at my request, she went out of her way to arrange a meeting with her for me. I remember that it was no simple matter to do this and we had to be extremely careful. Not only was she a well-known figure, but she was also a member of the Japan Communist Party and had to be cautious about trusting me. Actually, at that time I greatly admired Miyamoto Yuriko and Yamakawa Kikue. This dated from my Osaka days, when I worked in my father's store selling cigarettes. My main consolation was that I got to read a lot of books. Around that time I got my father's permission to go hear both Yamakawa and Miyamoto read from their works as part of a monthly forum sponsored by *Women's Review*. In those days, I was inclined to prefer social criticism that directly addressed the questions of human nature [over] literature per se. I felt I could understand criticism better. So I said to myself that I would really like to meet these people! (49–51)

In the above passage, the narrator's expressed admiration for two of Japan's most prominent Marxists-feminists is another clear indication of the kind of progressive views to which she was drawn. Of course, in the same passage she claims to not be in the same "ideological camp" as her friend Kanda Asano, who was active in the underground Communist Party. But her sympathies are clearly with women like Yamakawa and Miyamoto. The next passage introduces the reader to a radical student organization at Waseda, the Oratorical Society, which was just in the process of being disbanded.

The Waseda Oratorical Society

One day, after I had been at Waseda for about a year, I stumbled for the first time upon a mass meeting of the student body. One day, when I had come to school just like I did every day, in one of the school plazas—I think it was in front of Ōkuma Shigenobu's statue—a whole bunch of students had gathered and were shouting things at one another. At a central podium, speaker after speaker took turns addressing the student body. Just when I thought things were going to continue like this, there was a big commotion below the speaker's podium and people began to shout. There was the sound of some object being thrown, and someone else yelled. I watched from a distance, spellbound as an undulating crowd of students surrounded the administrator's quarters. What was going on was a confrontation with the Sumō Club, which was determined to halt the student assembly. As soon as the confrontation ended, the assembly was over and I ran off to class, but classes were canceled for the rest of the day.

I was to learn later that this was an assembly to defy the order to dissolve the Waseda University Student's Oratorical Society meeting. According to the records, this occurred on May 15, 1929. . . .

Recently, I have learned what a lengthy and distinguished history Waseda's Oratorical Society possesses. According to *A Comprehensive Record of Student Movements (Sōdai gakuseiundō no kiroku)*, it was founded in December 1901 at the time of the Ashio Mine Incident.

The Ashio Mine Incident was a serious social problem that occurred in the town of Ashio, Tochigi Prefecture, where the Furukawa Copper Mine's smelting process was releasing sulfuric acid in the form of both gas and smoke, which resulted in damaging the lives and livelihood of the surrounding farmers, fishermen, and residents. Beginning in 1891, Diet member Tanaka Shōzō, elected from this district, continually called for an end to the mine pollution and halting of the mining company's activities, but without effect. Meanwhile, every time it flooded, pollution victims marched on Tokyo and repeatedly had confrontations with the police. Finally, in 1901, Tanaka resigned his seat in the Diet, and when the emperor was to appear at the opening ceremonies for the new Diet, he tried to approach the emperor directly with a petition. He was arrested immediately. These are the main facts of the Ashio Incident.

In the midst of these events, students at Waseda launched a program to aid the pollution victims. On December 30, 1901, the students founded a group [called] Aid Mine Pollution Victims, which later evolved into the Youth Cultivation Society (Seinen Shūyōkai), and, on December 8, 1902, became the Waseda University Oratorical Society (Waseda Daigaku Yūbenkai). (From *A Record of the Waseda University Student Movement [Sōdaigakuseiundō no kiroku]*.)

So the protest against the dissolution of the Oratorical Society that I had witnessed had occurred some twenty-eight years after this organization had been founded, and it underscored the end of a long and glorious tradition. More than glory, over the years this organization produced a great deal of human talent.

For example, from the Meiji era there was Nagai Ryūtarō, Nakano Seigō; in the Taishō period there was Asanuma Inejirō, Sugiyama Motojirō, Toganō Takeshi, and Miyake Seiichi, just to name a few people of whom I have a direct recollection. So that among these politicians, labor leaders, farmers, and journalists, including many who were elected to the Diet as LDP [Liberal Democratic Party] representatives, the number who had been members of the Oratorical Society was substantial. At the time, the reason this tradition-rich Oratorical Society was being pressured to disband was because of its strong left-wing tendencies. The year before, in 1927, there had been the Ōyama Ikuo Incident at Waseda in which a liberal faculty member, Professor Ōyama Ikuo, became an active member of the recently established Farmer-Labor Party and was advised by the administration that he ought to resign his academic appointment.[6] Students from the Oratorical Society and from the Social Science Research Society stood up and organized a protest against this attempted dismissal of a faculty member.

In the end, the faculty member did resign and a number of students were disciplined. Before entering Waseda, I had read all about this incident in the newspaper and was genuinely hoping to take a class from Professor Ōyama, but it was not to be. In the meantime, in society at large, the Japan Communist Party was facing mass arrests of its members in the March 15 and later the April 16 roundups, so that, along with the flap over the Oratorical Society, both on the campus and off, the world was being shaken by these incidents that so affected intellectuals.

One also should not forget that during this time, within Marxism, Fukumotoism was taking the world by storm. I had not yet entered Waseda, but Fukumoto Kazuo had demonstrated that he had a charismatic appeal not only for males, but for females at Tokyo Women's College as well.[7] Eventually, Fukumotoism was regarded as erroneous and was rejected by the JCP [Japan Communist Party]. In the March 15th arrests, not only Fukumoto himself, but also a number of students, male and female, were arrested.

Like someone possessed, I still continued to advocate for my own personal autonomy and financial independence from my family. Though I may have been small, I was prepared to dig in and defend myself. And it was amid these kinds of turbulent social conditions that my eyes were forced open to the world around me. The shock of witnessing the conflict over the Oratorical Society had no small impact on me. (54–58)

Again, the narrator seems intent on displaying her familiarity with key personalities and issues that were being debated among prominent left-wing figures in the late 1920s. She is positing a connection between her own advocacy for—indeed, her obsession with—her "personal autonomy and financial independence" and the progressive ideologies that were swirling around her on campus and elsewhere. To bring up Tanaka Shōzō, the Ashio Mine Incident, and the mass arrests of communists on March 15 and April 16, 1928, and to connect these historic events with the popularity of figures like Ōyama Ikuo and Fukumoto Kazuo is to clearly situate herself in relation to one of the most progressive streams in Japanese intellectual history. But she is also saying clearly that the suppression she witnessed of organizations like the Oratorical Society delivered a message to her about the risks involved in embracing left-wing ideologies. This connection is explored further in the section below on becoming a "Marx-Engels Girl."

A "Marx-Engels" Girl

So one day, and I don't remember by whom or how I may have been invited, I showed up at a study-group meeting of the people from the Oratorical Society. The society itself had already been disbanded, but the same students had just founded a new student newspaper. Of course, most of the students had been expelled or suspended from school, so the meeting was not held on campus under faculty supervision, but on the second floor above the Takadabokusha Coffee Shop.

There, we would just read books, underline passages, provide tutoring, and lead discussions on books. They were all difficult books like *From Imagination to Science, The State and Revolution, The Theory of Imperialism,* and *On Historical Materialism,* so I can't even recall how much we might have really understood. However, I was in complete agreement with the Marxist idea that capitalism possessed numerous contradictions and that workers and farmers were, on the whole, its victims. I also believed that in order to rectify the situation, a social revolution, with workers and farmers as the primary agents, was a necessity *(rōdōsha, nōmin o shutai to suru shakai-kakumei ga hitsuyō de aru).*

At that time, Japan was in the grip of a severe depression brought about by the 1929 stock market crash in America. Wages were not being paid, small and medium-sized enterprises were failing, workers were being thrown out of their jobs in large numbers, and the countryside was feeling the burden of many of the losses being shifted onto the primary sector. The newspapers at the time were reporting the appearance in the

cities of young peasant women, sold into prostitution, their bodies
bloodied from the struggles of rural life, their legs battered by the wind
and cold. In these circumstances, my sense of indignation was stirred
mightily, and I came to believe in Marxism.

However, other than hanging around with the activists, participating
in study groups, and helping facilitate some of the actual agitators, I was
not really deeply involved with the movement. Which is to say that I did
not have direct contact with [that side of the] movement. After the March
15th and April 16th roundups, the JCP's official activities were proscribed.
The movement henceforth was completely illegal—it had to go underground—and any contact with such people was prohibited. But I am sure
that some of the men in the study group had some kind of connection
with groups outside the campus.

Actually, once, quite a bit later, I was asked if I wouldn't join the organization of the Tokyo Transportation Workers. It was so sudden and I
thought it might have been a trap, so I refused. In the first place, I didn't
really have the courage, the passion, nor the confidence to pose as a con-
ductress in order to do organizing work. I had not been conditioned to be
that kind of a hardened Marxist.

If I had told the more committed activists, they may have pronounced
me a *"puchi-buru"*—a member of the petit bourgeoisie—nothing more, in
the end, than a little "Marx-Engels" Girl. I guess I wouldn't disagree. It was
just the way things were.

So, while I continued to be enthused about Marxism conceptually,
since I was still focused on my heartfelt goal of becoming employed as
soon as possible and establishing my independence, I was an unlikely candidate to become a full-blown activist.

But, at study group sessions during this period, I can recall the writer
Hirabayashi Taiko showing up, and we would talk about Kolontai's *Three
Generations of Love*, and we read *From Imagination to Science* together and just
enjoyed chatting very familiarly with one another. Also, beyond Waseda's
campus there was the Kantō Oratorical League, which often held lecture series on women's issues, inviting people like Hirabayashi, Oku Mumeo, and
Kora Tomi, pioneers in the women's movement. I participated actively in
these events, expanding my range of activities and my contacts with my fellow women students. But, that was all there was to it. (58–62)

*Two things about Nishi's education stand out. One, even though she attended
the same classes and did the same work as her fellow students, her degree would*

indicate that she was just an auditor, not a regular matriculating student. This was due primarily to her gender. The other thing that stands out is her exposure to Marxism, social activism, feminism, and the labor-organizing activities of the Communist Party and her appreciation of the risks that these positions entailed. The narrator denies that she was ever "deeply involved with the movement," and yet she is certainly familiar with a lot of the specifics. Moreover, she clearly subscribes to the ideal of social revolution and states unqualifiedly that capitalism deserved to be overthrown by workers and farmers. She also read a number of socialist and feminist works during her student days; this helped shape her view of the world. True, she would have us believe that her connection to activism was weak, that she remained unapologetically "petit-bourgeois." Once the party became an underground organization, she understood the risks and disavowed further involvement with the organization. But the fact remains that as a student she was a member of left-wing student groups, read a number of critical texts, and claimed sympathy for the progressive ideals of Marxism and socialism.

Because she needed a job, she sought a position with a favored women's journal, Women's Review, *but the interview was not successful. She then went to interview with Ishibashi Tanzan (1884–1973), a liberal economist and publisher of* The Oriental Economist. *She noted in passing the contrasting atmosphere at the new, upscale Maru Building, symbol of the new capitalist age, which housed* Women's Review, *and the older, more quaint building in which Ishibashi oversaw his journal.*

About Ishibashi Tanzan

Well, with my hopes of becoming a reporter for *Women's Review* dashed, I was at a loss for what to do when Mr. Ebizaki of the student affairs section suggested that I take a look at *The Oriental Economist*. I hardly had the luxury of being choosy, so I got a recommendation letter from the school and set out for the Yarai neighborhood in Koshigome. Yarai was fairly close to Waseda, a place where there were a lot of publishing houses and newspapers, and writers tended to live nearby. In the prewar era, especially around the Kagurazaka area, this was a kind of gathering place for literary types. Unlike a highly modern neighborhood . . . the atmosphere around Yarai had an older feel with lots of wooden buildings.

The Oriental Economist occupied a corner location. But even so, to be frank, I was a little surprised. As I entered this dark, old, wooden building and climbed the stairs to the second floor, where I was to wait for Mr. Ishibashi, I was enveloped in gloom. I couldn't help feeling miserable as I thought to myself, "Am I going to have to work in a dirty place like this?" I may have some tendencies toward vanity, but just one look at the Maru Building and I felt it was too much. But, in the end, it turned out that the office was going to move to Ishimachi in Nihonbashi any day, so when I heard that, I was quite relieved.

After Mr. Ishibashi asked me a few simple questions, I accepted the offer of a job, although it was a little bit of a letdown. However, once again, the specter of gender discrimination raised its ugly head. As Mr. Ishibashi said about how I was to be treated, "I am really sorry, but I have to limit your salary to forty-five yen per month. In fact, your academic record is very strong and you passed your interview with me. Therefore, I would like to pay you the same as I would a male, but there are some commonly accepted social ideas at work here, and I would like you to just be patient with the situation for a while." At that time, the monthly salary for males was fifty yen per month, meaning that there was a difference of five yen per month. I didn't have a strong counterargument to make, so although I wasn't persuaded, I had little choice but to go along with it.

Of course, one thing was that these were hard times and at least I had landed a job. There was no way I was going to turn it down! The second issue was his use of the term "commonly accepted social ideas." There was no way around it: this was a barrier put up against women. So why wasn't Mr. Ishibashi willing to try and break this barrier down? He had a concern for women and colonized subjects, and he advocated for their liberation and the improvement of their status. And, starting with me, he had opened up the workplace to women and Korean minorities, so he was a progressive individual. Why, then, did he allow the atmosphere within the company to remain underdeveloped? Or, to put a more negative spin on it, when it came to management, did he just consider that separable from his beliefs? In later years, after I got to know him well, I mentioned this to Mr. Ishibashi, but he just chuckled and said, "You may be right about that." Basically, his policy of maintaining a wage differential never really changed right up until the end.

Anyhow, when I went to report to Sakai Toshihiko[8] that I had gotten the job, he said, "That's great! I can agree with your choice!" (67–72)

Writing about Ishibashi Tanzan, one of the staunchest liberals of the prewar years, is a delicate matter for the narrator. She does not want to castigate him, but she has made clear to the reader that though he embraced many progressive ideas, in the workplace that he supervised, he upheld the status quo. In this sense, her critique is pointed. Once again, gender is placed front and center as an issue. We also see how important it was to the narrator to establish herself and be financially independent of her family. Gender and identity formation are closely linked, then, as the narrator has to steadfastly adhere to her plan to gain her independence without creating an unnecessary rupture with her family.

Another part of the text that stands out to the reader is how she situates herself and her experiences squarely in the context of the history of the era in which she came of age. Her student days were during the high tide of prewar Japanese liberalism, and indeed, she went to work for one of the more outstanding liberal products of that age, Ishibashi Tanzan. Ishibashi was educated at Waseda University, where he was under the wing of Tanaka Ōdō. A Keynesian economist, Ishibashi supported such socially progressive ideas as the promotion of unionism and the establishment of factory councils. But Nishi's working life commenced with the onset of the dark days of prewar history, when, due to the depression, the rise of right-wing nationalism, and Japan's eventual embrace of military expansionism, liberalism was in scarce supply. In the following section, the narrator describes some of the events from this tumultuous period.

The Assassination of Dan Takanuma Nearby

My days and nights as a fledgling reporter passed as though I were in a dream, but meanwhile, the outside world was as unstable as always. The economy was recovering, and there emerged an unhealthy trend in popular culture known as "Ero, guro, nansensu" [Eroticism, grotesqueness, and nonsense], which seemed to suggest social degeneration. In the midst of this trend, the Manchurian Incident took place, just about six months after I started working. The Manchurian Incident occurred when Japanese troops clashed with Chinese soldiers after there was an explosion on the Manchurian Railway. Later, there were rumors that this was purely a plot fabricated by the Japanese, but since it was something taking place in faraway Manchuria, even though it felt wrong, no one in their wildest dreams imagined that this was the incident that would plunge Japan into a fifteen-year war. . . .

Afterward, one extreme incident occurred after another, experiences the like of which Japan had never before encountered. I worked at *The Oriental Economist* from 1931 to 1939, and these are the main events that occurred while I was there:

September 18, 1931   The Manchurian Incident
January 28, 1932   The Shanghai Incident

March 1, 1932	Founding of Manchukuo
February 9, 1932	Murder of former Finance Minister Inoue
March 5, 1932	Murder of Dan Takanuma, head of Mitsui
May 15, 1932	Assassination of Prime Minister Inukai, as well as attacks on other high officials by army and navy cadets
March 27, 1933	Japan withdraws from League of Nations
February 26, 1936	Attempted military coup d'etat by young army officers calling for the national reconstruction of Japan
July 7, 1937	War with China begins

So, from the Manchurian Incident to the beginning of the Sino-Japanese War, I was employed at the journal. But it wasn't as though each single incident had a direct impact on my daily life. Of course, at the magazine we were exceptionally busy, and tensions tended to run high. One that I recall well, if I am not mistaken, was the morning of Baron Dan Takanuma's assassination. I went to work that day as usual. The office was quite noisy and excited. Most of the male reporters weren't there yet, so people were milling about the corridors. When I asked what was going on, they said that Dan Takanuma had been assassinated outside the Mitsui Building. I can remember turning pale. So, that was it. A month earlier on the same day, former Finance Minister Inoue Junnosuke had been assassinated. I stepped outside, and I could see that people were crowding around the Mitsui Building in ever growing numbers. . . . At that time, *The Oriental Economist* had something called the "Economics Club," where financial leaders could exchange information and hold meetings. So Dan Takanuma's assassination may have been especially shocking to our staff. . . .

These terrorist incidents continued with the assassination of Prime Minister Inukai in the May 15 Incident. Next, I was shocked to learn the following year of Japan's withdrawal from the League of Nations because of the issue of recognition for the state of Manchukuo. Public opinion was supportive, but it was deeply troubling to me because I was concerned about Japan's isolation from the rest of the world. And then there followed the February 26 Incident.

What I remember about this incident was that on that morning, there was a deep snowfall, and over the radio came the announcer's excited voice announcing that martial law had been declared and that there was a possibility of shells being fired. Unable to go to work, I recall cowering behind my chest of drawers *(tansu)*. I was chagrined by the reality that if I were a male, I might have leapt in a car and gone into work anyway. . . .

What was the February 26 Incident anyway? It wasn't likely that an ordinary person like myself could grasp it very clearly. Moreover, it seems that people are still arguing today whether it was grew out of a conflict between two military factions, the Imperial Way Faction (Kōdōha) and the Control Faction (Tōseiha), or whether it might not have been contrived by the upper echelon of the military taking advantage of the young officer movement in the Imperial Way Faction.

Whatever its origins, the attempted coup d'état failed, and the Control Faction was able to carry out a purge and effectively seize control of the military and basically place Japan on the road to greater militarism, giving the military a greater voice in political affairs. Ultimately, the country was moved increasingly toward a wartime footing.

Thereafter, the term "emergency" was used with increasing frequency. (75–79)

One of the most important, if wholly unexpected, outcomes of working for the liberal Oriental Economist *was the opportunity to become engaged directly with the women's movement. Although the narrator was clearly exposed to radical social and political ideas as a student and labeled herself a "Marx-Engels Girl," she had never become directly engaged with feminists or the women's movement. This would change when she was asked to facilitate a women's study group that wanted to focus on economic issues and how they affected women. She explains below.*

Meeting Ichikawa Fusae: The Seminar of Women and Economics (Fujin Keizai Kenkyūkai) as Backdrop

While working at *The Oriental Economist*, I reaped one totally unexpected benefit. This was the opportunity to meet Ichikawa Fusae. Not only did I get to meet her, but it was the occasion of my first real contact with the Japanese women's movement.

One day, I was called in to see Mr. Ishibashi, who said to me, "I am told that there is a Miss Ichikawa Fusae who wants to study economics with us. Since we will be hosting her, I want you to see to her needs." Since work had become fairly well routinized by that time, I was eager to comply.

As far as pioneers in the women's movement, I had met Hirabayashi Taiko and Miyamoto Yuriko, but I really hadn't run across any of the principal activists in the movement yet. I really hadn't had the opportunity to meet such folks, but also, at that time I believed wholeheartedly in an orthodox Marxist position to the effect that "Without liberation from social class, women's liberation is impossible. The movement for women's rights of political participation is just bourgeois democracy." But rather than rejecting the position of movement leaders like Ichikawa, I was curious to see what kind of people became activists in the women's movement.

As for why she wanted to study economics at this time, Miss Ichikawa has written in her own autobiography as follows:

While very busy, I take up the study of economics

In recent days I have become painfully aware that I personally, and the whole executive staff of the women's movement, are weak in the area of economics, and since I wanted to volunteer my time to learn something more about it, I consulted with Mr. Ishibashi Tanzan of [The Oriental Economist]. I had heard him lecture and he spoke in a way which was very easy to follow, and considering the fact that his journal, [The Oriental Economist], deals with real, everyday economic problems, I decided to approach him. Mr. Ishibashi acceded warmly to my request, and he agreed to supply a meeting space, lecturers, and office space, all at no charge, so, as I recall, we started right away that September (1934—Showa 9). We called it Seminar of Women and Economics (Fujin Keizai Kenkyūkai) and once a month we would meet on the fourth floor of the [The Oriental Economist], probably in their materials room; Ishibashi and then members of his staff would come in and teach us about economics. We continued until almost the end of the war. As far as making arrangements and sending out notices and such, two employees there at the time, first, Kanda Asano and then Ishihara Kiyoko took care of everything for us.

Ichikawa Fusae jiden

Actually, her recollection was faulty in one respect: it was the other way around. Kanda Asano followed Ishihara Kiyoko. Ishihara, of course, was my maiden name. . . . (80–82)

The Seminar of Women and Economics began meeting that September of 1934. . . . Also participating in the study group were some key members I recall like Kaneko Shigeri, Oku Mumeo, Kawasaki Natsu, and Kondō Magara. They were all lively and energetic and seemed to be quite busy. Sometimes, after a session, we might get together somewhere, but for me, it was my first contact with this whole world. (80–84)

Writing a Column for the *Yomiuri* Newspaper

While doing these various things, I began to find these issues much more interesting than regular work, so suddenly, I found myself developing a strong interest in the women's movement. So I began to read as many articles as possible that had appeared in newspapers and magazines about the women's movement, and I purchased a copy of Oku Mumeo's book, *Twelve Lectures on Women's Issues (Fujinmondai jūnikō)*. I also took the trouble to walk in the company of Ichikawa, Kaneko Shigeri, and Oku Mumeo so I could talk with them while we walked. At Miss Ichikawa's Yotsuya office were always a number of people there, with piles and piles of books, newspapers, and magazines all around them, buzzing with activity as they sought to publish a journal, set up the schedule of activities, concentrate on the campaign to win women the right of political participation, and so on, and I found all the energy stimulating. Ichikawa and Kaneko were often arguing a point with one another.

I think I probably had met Oku Mumeo sometime at her Fukugawa Settlements, but she was also involved at that time with the "Working Women's Club," and I was generously included in these activities. I can recall staying up until all hours at night speaking with Oku and her followers. I really cannot recall either the names or the faces of the other folks involved.

Anyway, as I was becoming so absorbed in this world for the first time, I was suddenly struck by something. What came through clearly to me was just how realistic the women's movement was. If you think about it, this is an extremely ordinary observation, but for someone like myself who had come to accept the conceptual, theoretical Marxist position that without liberation from social classes women's liberation was impossible, it was a rather startling discovery. And, I came to appreciate the fact that precisely because it was so realistic, the movement had to publicly confront some serious issues, and this required a great deal of courage, confidence, and resolve. The themes such as women's suffrage and other topics of interest to the movement may not have been about class warfare, but they were definitely about expanding women's political rights. If you want to appreciate how difficult it was to put forth such issues, you have only to recall the strength of the right wing at that time and the type of pressure that the police authorities were able to apply to the women's movement. I could hardly find any evidence of the mild, agreeable image associated with so-called bourgeois democracy in the conduct of Miss

Ichikawa. Rather, she provoked more the image of a fighter imbued with faith in her principles. It really opened my eyes to the practical side of women's issues and the women's movement.

By the way, to the best of my recollection, the following individuals were members of the Seminar of Women and Economics:

Ichikawa Fusae	Kaneko Shigeri	Oku Mumeo
Kawasaki Natsu	Maruoka Hideko	Tatewaki Sadayo
Kondo Magara	Katsume Teru	Hirata Nobu
Imai Kuniko	Hirai Toshi	Kamichika Ichiko
Senbonki Michiko	Kato Taka	Ōshikawa Mika
Maejima Fuku	Takenaka Shige	Takeuchi Shigeyo
Otake Sei		

I was particularly indebted to the unforgettable support extended to me by one of the members, Kamichika Ichiko. At that time, Kamichika was putting out a journal called *Women's Art (Fujin bungei)*, and I used to show up and work on the journal sometimes. Perhaps, because of this connection, one day I received the following postcard from Miss Ichikawa:

> I have recommended you to the *Yomiuri Shinbun* as a writer to write a regular column on women for their newspaper, so I trust you will do it. Do your best and don't let any of the veteran reporters outdo you!

It was at the Yomiuri *that Nishi first met Baba Tsunego, who later became editor of the* Yomiuri *during the turbulent postwar strike years.*

The chief of the women's department was a Mr. Hirano, who was a very understanding person who took wonderful care of me. It was he who invited me to the Hoshigaoka Tea Garden in Akasaka and introduced me to the feminist Baba Tsunego. In the postwar period, when I joined the staff of the *Yomiuri*, Mr. Baba had become the publisher, and he was very kind to me. It is strange the way connections can work sometimes. (84–87)

In the following chapter, Nishi describes her travels in 1937, between early April and early May, to Korea, Manchukuo, and China. Although she had to take a month's leave from The Oriental Economist, *Ishibashi had asked her to collect some data on the Japanese cotton mills in China. Her motivation to travel was, in part, to simply keep pace with many of the male reporters who were getting overseas assignments. She would have preferred, she writes, to visit*

America and learn more about the lifestyles of American women, but she was determined to make the best of the opportunity she was given. If her Marxist inclinations made it problematic for her to journey to these areas under Japanese colonial control, she avoided exploring this in any depth in her text. But we do find a passage like the following, which is extremely interesting.

What was really startling for me was when the person showing me around the new capital of Manchukuo said one evening, "It may shock you, but there is someplace I would like to show you." He took me down a small side street to a dark building. We came through a gate and came upon the entrance to a long tenement-style building. I gasped as I could see inside around ten crude beds lined up, separated only by grungy curtains. From two or three of the beds, I could hear the voices of men and women having sex. The light in the room was so bad I couldn't make out any facial features. It was a so-called "comfort zone." According to my guide, these women lay about in these cots all day while any number of soldiers came to be serviced by them. The women were mainly brought here forcibly from Korea. That scene remains indelibly imprinted on my consciousness. (97–98)

Of course, the issue of the comfort women was something that Japanese society had to confront in the 1990s, and the issues of compensation and acceptance of responsibility remain unresolved today. From this passage, we learn that a professional journalist was clearly a witness to one of these institutions of sexual slavery and wrote about it forthrightly in 1988. And yet, left open is the question of why she never wrote about what she saw any earlier. Was there no sense of outrage? She is also the kind of observer who could be moved to tears at the sight of the Japanese flag on the roof of the consular office in Harbin (100). Is the reader to assume that even a liberal journalist with considerable exposure to radical politics was not immune to the appeal of chauvinism?

She had another shocking revelation in Peking. Another reporter from the Yomiuri, Murakami Noriyuki, was showing her around when the following occurred.

One day, he suggested we visit someplace that wouldn't ordinarily be seen, and he took me to a dark, dilapidated building. I don't recall exactly where it was, but there was one big room on the first floor, while you could gaze down on this space from all sides from the second story. Both upstairs and down, men were just lying around, apparently sleeping.

They were all smoking something like tobacco out of pipes. Holding on to their pipes, they seemed to be intoxicated into some dreamlike state. Needless to say, they were using opium.

"Won't you try a puff," said Murakami, "it will be all right." With his encouragement, I screwed up my courage and took a puff off the pipe that was being offered me. It had a pleasant odor like roasted black beans. When I asked a frank question, "Cannot this kind of thing be controlled even in the heart of Peking?" I was told by Murakami-san, "Actually, if you were caught on the streets with this stuff, you would be sent to a drug rehabilitation facility, so you would never want to do it in public. But most of the people who run these places where you can smoke opium are Japanese or Korean."

What was going on if the Chinese government was trying to control this problem while the "black hand" of Japan was undermining their efforts and conniving to undo their programs? . . . (104)

Japan was now on a wartime footing, but what events transpired between 1940, shortly after my return to Tokyo, and when I left three years later? In a nutshell, here is what had been occurring:

First, domestically, the general mobilization law had been passed, along with the national conscription law, the Imperial Rule Assistance Association was formed, as was the Industrial League to Protect Japan, while internationally, Germany had invaded Poland, England and France declared war on Germany. World War II was declared, and Germany, Italy, and Japan joined in the Axis alliance, while in Nanking, Japan's puppet government of Wang Chingwei was established.

I actually cannot recall how I, personally, might have reacted to each one of these developments. I guess there was still some distance between these events and everyday life. However, I remember that we were told not to hoard goods, and we were urged to exercise self-restraint and not get permanents for our hair. I was on my way to work one day and a couple of boys nudged my hair with their sticks and said, "Come on, let's get rid of these perms!"

As Japan proceeded in this fashion to get ever more deeply embroiled in war, organizations like the League for Women's Suffrage, the Proletarian Political Parties, and the labor unions were all disbanded (as of September 1941).

I, myself, wasn't actually a member of the League for Women's Suffrage, but since around 1936, when the journal *Women's Suffrage (Fusen)* was changed to *Women's Perspective (Josei tembō)*, I had been acting as the chair of the magazine's discussion forum, and I became director in 1938 of the Research Association for Women's Situation and helped out in various ways. (122–124)

In the following chapters, the narrator discusses a love affair she had with a married professor and its end when he returned to his family because his daughters were beginning to grow up. Then the text goes on to describe the narrator's sudden marriage to Nishi Masanori, a widower with three children. He is perhaps best known as the translator of Engel's The Origins of the Family, Private Property and the State. *His first wife was Kaibara Taiko, a student at Tokyo Women's College (Tōkyō Joshi Daigaku) who had been a follower of Yamakawa Kikue. She had also joined the Sekirankai with Sakai Magara and the others and had met Nishi when she was a student of Yamakawa Hitoshi. Active in the underground Communist Party movement, she suffered many hardships and died young from a cerebral hemorrhage. There was an older son from a previous marriage who was already a teacher, but it was the two younger daughters, Yuri and Mari, with whom Kiyoko would live. After marrying Nishi, they moved to Shanghai as Nishi had rejected his earlier Marxist beliefs and went to work for the South Manchurian Railway Company. Shortly after the Sorge Spy Ring affair, Nishi Masanori was arrested by the Japanese secret police (Kempeitai), and he died in prison a year and a half later in March 1944. Not counting this year and a half, the star-crossed couple lived together for only two years. Kiyoko felt very much as though he died before she ever really got to know him well. Why had he turned his back on Marxism? Did he really support Japanese imperialism? It seemed so unlikely. What was the whole South Manchurian Railway Incident [Mantetsu Jiken] all about? Since he was a taciturn man not given much to conversing with his wife, these questions remained unanswered. (130–165)*

Until the Day the War Ended

LIVING WITH THE AERIAL BOMBARDMENTS

Naturally, there was some discussion about what to do with the two children who had lost both of their parents, but I was resolved to raise them myself. Clever little Yuri, perhaps sensing the nature of our discussions, alertly remained steadfastly at my side.

One evening, when we were alone, she started to cry. When I asked her, "What's wrong? Are you lonely because your father is no longer here?" She replied, clinging to me, "No, it's not that! I'm afraid that you're going to return to your own home now that Daddy's gone, and I don't want that!"

I suddenly remembered a time when we were living in Shanghai and I was on my way home from work. It had started to rain, and even though I didn't call home or anything, I can still recall the image of little Yuri waiting for me at the bus stop with an umbrella.

"It's all right," I assured Yuri, patting her little head with its bobbed hair.

My own father understood what I was doing, and we all agreed we would help out with the tasks ahead. But I didn't know what I would do next to make a life for myself. (166–167)

Eventually, Nishi moved to Kurashiki in Okayama Prefecture in order to escape the bombing raids on major Japanese cities.

But the bombing raids even extended to peaceful-looking Okayama Prefecture. On the evening of June 29, 1945, just after dinner, when I was talking with the children, suddenly the air raid warning siren screamed. We quickly extinguished the lights and ran out back to a makeshift bomb shelter. Directly east, beyond Tsurugata Mountain, I could see three of four enemy planes circling, mercilessly dropping their black clods, not unlike birds dropping their feces. Then, plumes of red smoke exploded upward from the ground and spread outward.

It was Okayama. Once we were certain the airplanes weren't coming our way, we stood for a while in the field staring in amazement. The next day, people were saying that the street that runs along the Asahi River was heavily damaged and that 1,750 people were killed. Later on, it was recorded that over 25,000 homes were destroyed. I began to think about the Mizushima factory area in Kurashiki and began to think about sending the children to some relatives who lived deep in the mountainous area of Hyōgo Prefecture. This was where Nishi Masanori's elder sister worked.

Train tickets were difficult to come by, but I managed to get a hold of some and would travel over five hours by train, then take a bus in order to bring them some fish and oil. As soon as they saw me trudging up the hill after getting off the bus, they came running to greet me. Living in a home without other small children Yuri and Mari were very well cared for, but they were always anxiously awaiting me whenever I came.

Then, one hot day in early August, everyone in Kurashiki was excited. Some never before used bomb had been dropped on Hiroshima, and

many people had died. An old man in the neighborhood said he had relatives there and wanted to go and check on them. He grabbed some rice
balls and took the train as far as it would go and figured he would walk the
rest of the way.

We knew it was some new type of bomb, but no one could explain exactly what it was. It was the August 6, 1945, tragedy that was Hiroshima.
Not long after, on August 9, another new bomb was dropped on Nagasaki.

I felt that it was time for me to get out and join the children. So I went
to the relocation section of the city office, but, surprisingly, this office,
which was always busy, was mysteriously silent. The eyes of the young
woman behind the counter at the relocation center were red and she was
biting her lower lip. When I inquired, "What in the world is going on?" she
burst into tears and said, "We have lost! Japan has lost the war!"

I was at a loss for words. I stood in amazement for a while, and when
I returned to my senses, I couldn't suppress a laugh that welled up inside
me. I really felt relieved—yes! We were saved! It was August 15, 1945, the
day the war ended. (170–173)

*Documentary film footage of the day of the emperor's special radio broadcast
announcing the end of the war always shows people, especially women, prostrate
and weeping. As viewers, we cannot be sure if people are weeping from despair
or relief. Perhaps it is some mixture of the two. In this text, the narrator gives us
a view of two extreme reactions: one a woman who cannot hold back her tears,
and the other, the narrator, who rejoices in the fact that she and her children
have survived. But, of course, as readers, all we have is her recollections of this
moment, and we have no way of knowing how accurate or truthful they may be.*

*As it turns out, the narrator's next appointment with history was to be an
employee at the* Yomiuri *at a turning point in the postwar labor and social history of Japan. With the military and the right wing discredited, Japan's prewar
leftists had been released from prison and encouraged to organize labor unions.
The number of labor unions increased dramatically, and many felt that the very
nature of labor-management relations in Japan was on the verge of being radi-
cally transformed. Between Japan's surrender in August 1945 and General
MacArthur's outlawing of the planned General Strike in February 1947, there
was an unprecedented period of flux and social transformation as working-class
radicalism asserted itself, seemingly with the blessings of SCAP. The Yomiuri
strike had particular significance because this newspaper had become the most
politically progressive in its tone among the big three newspapers, and its workers were threatening to take over the newspaper in the name of "production*

control," *which would involve the workers directly controlling the editing, print-*
ing, and shipping of the newspaper. As Joe Moore notes in Japanese Workers
and the Struggle for Power 1945–1947,

> Under production control the *Yomiuri* took a progressive stance editorially
> and overnight became the most left-leaning and outspoken of Japan's major
> newspapers. The new policy gained public approval, and circulation rose
> sharply. Many outside organizations rallied to the side of the Yomiuri work-
> ers, such as the other newspaper unions, the JSP (Japan Socialist Party) and
> the JCP (Japan Communist Party).[9]

The seizure of production control by the Yomiuri *editorial staff and workers*
served as a model for other businesses throughout Japan, many of which came to
Yomiuri *headquarters to observe and learn.*[10] *Eventually, in the second* Yomiuri *strike, even though the struggle committee was willing to defy management*
(now in the hands of Baba Tsunego, who had replaced Shōriki Matsutarō when
the latter was indicted as a war criminal), police were summoned in force, in-
cluding American M.P.'s, and workers were forcibly ousted from their offices.
Finally, Major Daniel C. Imoden, chief of the press division of the Civil Infor-
mation and Education Section of SCAP, was brought in to lecture the strikers on
the rights of the legal owners or their delegates to run the newspaper. In the face
of this kind of show of force, the union conceded on most points and the strike
ended in defeat. Below are Nishi's recollections of those days, though she claims
to have not been very centrally involved in the labor dispute.

Labor Disputes at the *Yomiuri*

In February of 1946, clad in my pantaloons *(monpe)*, I returned to a Tokyo,
where the odor of scorched earth still lingered. I returned in order to join
the staff of the *Yomiuri* Newspaper. One of my bosses from when I worked
at *The Oriental Economist*, Miyake Haruteru, provided an introduction to
the now head of the *Yomiuri*, Baba Tsunego. Perhaps because it was just
after the war, I was able to land a job pretty easily.

I could have stayed where I was in Kurashiki. Someone I knew even
said I could get a job as a middle-school teacher, but I wanted to get back
to Tokyo as soon as possible. The reason I was interested in the *Yomiuri*
dates back to that meeting I had had with Mr. Baba in the prewar period,
and the impression he made on me that he was a fine person with a good
understanding of people and things. I also knew him to be a staunch lib-

eral, and I figured that if he was heading up the paper, then it would be a good place to work. . . .

Meanwhile, there were some troubles going on at the heart of the newspaper. I didn't really follow what was going on, but I would see these banners and posters with big letters proclaiming "democracy" and "struggle" in the name of the union. From time to time, there would be mass meetings in the workplace that I would attend, but all the union leaders were men, and they were strong orators.

I really don't recall the specifics of what they were talking about. But my own consciousness as a member of the union was heightened when I participated in the first May Day celebration to be held in ten years. The first postwar May Day was celebrated outside the Imperial Palace. Way back in my Waseda days, I recall being captivated by the long lines of people marching out from Shiba Park on May Day, and hopping on a streetcar to follow them. Sandwiched between the ever-present police units, if any of the demonstrators became the slightest bit rambunctious, the cops would mercilessly yank them out of their row and arrest them.

On this 1946 May Day, the weather was bad, but everyone's spirits were irrepressibly high. . . . For the first time ever, I sang May Day songs and the Internationale, and after going forward with the group for a while, I eventually peeled off with Tsurumi Kazuko and headed back to the newspaper office. We rushed to a bathhouse together in the basement of the *Yomiuri* building and got warm. We joined the young women who distribute the type to the typesetters and we washed each other's backs. It was the only time I had done something like that, but I had a genuine feeling of fulfillment.

I guess it was from around this time that I was encouraged to become the head of the women's department of the union. I don't think I agreed to do it right away because I said I didn't know anything about what to do, but I remember going to two or three meetings then. Really, far from having any policy on women, the union was simply holding discussions on complex problems like establishing editorial rights and following the press code issued by GHQ [Civil Information and Education Service]. At the union offices, people like Mr. Akinami from the *Asahi* and Hirabayashi Taiko's husband Kobori Shinji would often show up. I felt very let down once when Kobori said to me, "You graduated from the politics department at Waseda, didn't you? Boy, that's really strange, isn't it—a woman studying something like that." Whether he was just trying to say that I was unique or whether he was putting me down, this recollection I have of Hirabayashi's husband is a disappointing one.

Stage Two of the Labor Disputes

Well, not long after May Day was over, the *Yomiuri* fell into a complete up-
roar. Mr. Baba announced the resignation of the head of the editorial section, Suzuki Tōmin, and five of his staff members. Although I had joined
the company only in the postwar period and didn't know anything about
prior history there, I was shocked. So I went down to the union offices to
see what was going on. I recognized Hishiyama Shin'ichi and was about to
go over to ask him something, when all of a sudden a Mr. I rushed over and
pulled me out into the corridor by the arm and said to me in an agitated
voice, "I know you are on good terms with Mr. Baba, but I think my situation has been seriously misunderstood. I hope you can intervene with him
on my behalf."

I was totally shocked. Perhaps I did get on at the *Yomiuri* through my
connection to Mr. Baba, but that didn't make him someone I could drop in
on and chat with anytime I wanted. This was a really difficult situation. I
really could do no more than reply, "Hey, that is not something I am in a
position to do." This Mr. I was apparently one of the six on the dismissal
list.

As a result of this move, the *Yomiuri* faced its second major labor dispute of the postwar era. I really have nothing to say about the events of the
ninety-day strike that occurred previously because the very moment that
the union and the newspaper squared off for their confrontation, I was
summoned by Miyake Haruteru: "Don't go off half-cocked and do anything rash or foolish. You need to be circumspect." And, he told me had a
message from Mr. Baba, which was, "Think quietly at home for a few days."

Actually, it was very dangerous at the newspaper at that time. The
union and management were waging a poster war, and it was difficult to
get to work trying to go through the union picket lines and the company
police. Since I personally felt that I lacked the background of what went
on before and during the war, I just wasn't able to throw my lot in with
the union at this point. But I wasn't prepared to side with the company
either, so for two or three days, I stayed away from work.

But then, concerned, I went down to the newspaper offices and there,
on the balcony overlooking the front entrance, was Suzuki Tōmin deliver-
ing a passionate speech to the representatives from other unions who had
come to support the *Yomiuri* union members. This was my first time to
really see him in action. My impression was that he was more concerned
with activities outside the company than what was going on within.

A few days later, having heard the news that the company had forcibly removed the strikers from the composing room they were occupying and driven them to the Yaki Building in Yurakuchō where they were currently holed up, I went back to the office. I found that both sides were still jostling with each other in front of the entryway, and I was immediately pulled inside by someone on the company side.

Concerning the plan to recapture the composing room, I would later read the following in Mark Gayn's *Japan Diary:*

> Anyway, Baba hired some *gorotsuki,* or professional toughs, and waited for trouble. . . . Baba has formed a company union, and yesterday ordered its members to drive the strikers out. Spearheaded by professional toughs, the small army forced its way into the composing room and threw the strikers out.[11]

Mark Gayn also wrote that after the first *Yomiuri* strike, when Baba replaced Shōriki [Matsutarō] as editor, "Tsunego Baba, a tall, cadaverous-looking essayist regarded as a liberal, was nominated by Shōriki as publisher" (23). Now I am fond of Mark Gayn's work as a journalist, but I did not really care for the way he described Baba Tsunego above. Also worth noting, there is the following account of the recapture of the composing room in the *History of the Development of the* Yomiuri *Newspaper* (Yomiuri *shinbun hattenshi*):

> On the morning of July 16th, the Conference Committee moved to implement their plan to remove the strikers from the composing room. The chief of the editorial section Mr. Yasuda, and head of administrative affairs Mr. Muto, Mr. Takeuchi, head of the society section and other managers set out from the floor above with about 300 other employees to assault the composing room on the second floor. They came down the narrow stairways on both sides of the building to enter the composing room from two separate doorways at once. They removed all the desks and chairs which were piled up against the doors, and this reformed Conference Committee used their power to oust the strike faction from the company. They proceeded, then, to retake the union offices and the machine shop in the main building. The composing room was in disarray, but the cases of letters were unharmed. The employees who participated believed strongly in their hearts that "the strikers loved the newspaper too."

I have to feel that this version is a little more objective than Mark Gayn's subjective diary. . . .

The strike finally was resolved on October 16, 1946. Suzuki Tōmin and five others were asked to resign while the other thirty-one fired employees were offered reinstatement, but they resigned of their own accord. On October 18 there was a reinstatement ceremony for the three hundred-plus strikers. My own work on behalf of the neutrality faction was considered by the company to be sectarianism, so I was given a salary reduction as a punishment.

By the way, I learned only later on that a man whom I would eventually marry, Komiyama Chiaki, was among those reinstated strikers.

The Background of the Strike

The *Yomiuri* strike has been chronicled in detail in both the *History of the Development of the* Yomiuri *Newspaper* and *A Comprehensive History of the* Yomiuri (Yomiuri *sōgōshi*), and according to these sources, on just the eleventh day after the end of the war, fifty staff members, including seven editorial staffers, called for a democratization of the paper. They wanted publisher Shōriki to resign and for several of the editors who bore responsibility for the wartime jingoism of the paper to be fired. They also called for improvement of working conditions as well.

Next, they began negotiations to form a "Society for the Study of Democracy" (Minshūshugi Kenkyūkai) while Shōriki countered by firing anyone who supported this idea, including the group's leader, Suzuki Tōmin.

In response to this, the employees formed a union and made public Shōriki's wartime activities, which became the jumping-off place for the first *Yomiuri* strike. But, before long, when Shōriki was arrested as a suspected war criminal and sent to Sugamo Prison and also had to sell his 30 percent interest in the *Yomiuri*, he named Baba Tsunego as his successor. Suzuki Tōmin became editor-in-chief.

This formed the backdrop for the second strike at *Yomiuri*, as under Suzuki's leadership, the newspaper had taken a distinct turn toward the left. In response to this, GHQ, which had been an ally during the first strike, now used the pretext of the press code to start interfering [with editorial policy]. There was a strong reaction within the paper, and Baba lit the fire when he demanded the resignation of Suzuki and six others.

All of the above is based on the records, as I was not aware of most of it at the time.

But, anyway, what was the *Yomiuri* strike all about? I am not really one to try and comment, but nevertheless, I feel that the *Yomiuri* staffers were genuinely trying to move Japan forward from the old system to the new. Against the backdrop of the emerging postwar democratic movement, these people were among the first leaders who tried to play the role of pioneers in moving Japan forward. In this sense, they were right on.

However, on the company side, among those who opposed Suzuki, it is not hard to appreciate that these men were trying with all their might to preserve the life of the newspaper. Because they knew that the presses had been stopped, and if pressure from GHQ mounted, the *Yomiuri* could be destroyed. . . . In the end, I can't help but conclude that the *Yomiuri* strike was a bitter incident occurring amid the confusion of the postwar era in which we were tossed about on the cresting wave of postwar democracy.

The *Yomiuri* Employees Union was officially formed, and a labor agreement established, just one week before the strike was resolved, on October 8, 1946. Watanabe Buntarō was nominated as head of the union. Within the agreement we developed I was able to add two provisions:

1. Women are eligible for two days of paid leave for their periods.
2. Women are eligible for pre- and postpartum paid leave of up to one hundred days.

When this part of the agreement was announced, I jumped up on a table and expressed my delight to the female union members. From the perspective of the prewar period, this was a revolutionary accomplishment! Anyway, on the matter of paid leave for menstruation, we took the lead, and I was so happy that the *Yomiuri* labor agreement had addressed this issue.

Later on, under the Red Purge of 1950, one man from our Yearbook Team was forced into retirement, a cause for some bitterness on my part. (174–183)

Nishi's account of the Yomiuri *strike differs somewhat from the picture presented by* Chicago Sun *reporter Mark Gayn and by Joe Moore's study. Despite her Marxist sympathies as a youth, her affiliation with "old liberals" like her mentor Ishibashi Tanzan—who was himself associated with pro-business postwar economic reforms—and Baba Tsunego prevented her from depicting Suzuki Tōmin or the striking workers in a very sympathetic light. She is willing to write the strike off as a "bitter incident occurring amid the confusion of the postwar era" and leave it at that. Gayn, by contrast, records in detail, in his* Japan Diary, *under the July 11, 1946, entry, just how extensive the SCAP influence on the strike was.*

Once again the *Yomiuri*, Japan's largest daily, has become a testing ground of our labor policies. This noon, after weeks of jockeying, 750 of its employees went out on strike.

Spread over the strike lies the shadow of Major Daniel Imoden, chief of the Press Division. A few days ago, representatives of Baba, publisher of the *Yomiuri*, called on Imoden and discussed the impending strike with him. Whatever it was Imoden said, Baba immediately summoned members of his staff, one by one, and told them Imoden was behind him, and asked them to sign a statement supporting his stand against the union. (263)

And on July 17, 1946,

The *Yomiuri* strike is over, with the union defeated.

There really never was a fight. While the *Yomiuri* was on strike, other units of the Newspaper Union merely watched the show. So did the other unions. And on the *Yomiuri* itself, more than half the workers stayed out on strike. What sympathy they might have had for the strikers, shrank with each reminder by Baba, the publisher, that Headquarters was behind them. (265)

And again, on October 4, 1946,

The *Yomiuri* is back in the news.

After four months of desperate maneuvering, Kikunami's Newspaper and Radio Workers Union went on strike today. Ostensibly it is seeking to force Baba, the publisher, to comply with the order of the Labor Arbitration Board to rehire the thirty-one men he fired in July. But no simple explanations ever apply to the *Yomiuri*. The union wants more than justice for thirty-one men. It is fighting for its own life.

With the help of General Baker and Major Imoden, the Japanese publishers are gradually destroying the union. Baba has set up a company union on his paper. Imoden has helped to break up the union on a daily in Japan's north. Now he is moving in on the two great newspaper chains, the *Asahi* and the *Mainichi*. The union knows that it will be crippled if Imoden succeeds. (328)

Of course, succeed he did. As Joe Moore notes,

The dramatic events at the *Yomiuri* alerted workers in other sectors of the economy to the fact that the balance of power within Japan was beginning to change against the labor movement. . . . (208)

A working-class democratization of postwar Japan was not to be. Too much was against it—the early surrender, the retention of power of the old guard, the divisions on the left, the presence of SCAP. The fight for a new Japan during the early occupation must be seen, nevertheless, as one of the peaks in the history of the Japanese working class. (243)

It's not as though Nishi's assessment diverges that sharply from either Gayn's observations or Moore's analysis. But there is a distinct difference in tone. To Gayn and Moore, it was an opportunity lost, an opportunity for the spread of genuine democracy and worker participation in the corporate workplace. Nishi seems vague about what she believed was at stake in the strike. As a participant herself, however much on the fringes, she looks in retrospect primarily at the positive gains she was able to point to for female workers. She may lament the forced resignation of a colleague in the "Red Purge" of the 1950s, but she does not see it as something that was prefigured in the way the strike of 1946 was resolved.

Nishi resumes her narrative with an account of her travels to the United States.

A Member of an America Observation Team

In the fall of the following year, I was unexpectedly recommended by the Labor Ministry to travel to America. As part of the Occupation policy, there was an exchange of persons program so that people could observe working conditions in America. I was included not as a union representative, but just as an individual. For three months we were to visit factories, mills, the phone company, iron and steel plants, and department stores and talk to union representatives and women executives in various places throughout the country.

Before departing, I called upon editor-in-chief Yasuda, and he suggested that I be given status as a foreign correspondent, but since I knew that it came from GHQ (the Civil Information and Education Service), I politely declined but requested, instead, that I be assigned to the editorial staff when I returned.

Once before, Mr. Yasuda had invited me to join the political department. I assumed it was because in the postwar period there had been a number of women elected to the Diet, but when I asked a colleague he suggested that I would probably just be answering phones over there, so I was not able to break new ground at that time. The reason I wanted to be on the editorial staff was that whenever there was a story for the *Women's Weekly (Fujin shūkan)* or on women's labor problems, some man from the editorial staff would come to talk to me about the editorial. So I felt that I might as well be writing these pieces myself.

In America, I was surprised to see the depth and extent of racial prejudice, and how deeply held, even in the unions, was a fear of the Soviet threat. As regards the racial prejudice issue, in Atlanta I was deeply impressed when a black leader said to me, "I know that the United States is thought of as an exporter of democracy, but I hope that you will not return to your country without having seen at least one feature of this democracy which you won't want to incorporate."

On the matter of anti-Soviet feeling, I was startled to see one labor pamphlet screaming out the headlines: "This is the Soviet Union!" and to see a picture of a man affecting the see no evil, hear no evil, speak no evil posture while a barbed-wire fence is being put up around him. But everywhere we went, we heard the words "Union, union," and it felt like this was how a democratic society looked. . . . Around that time, I decided to marry a member of the political department, Komiyama Chiaki, so after thinking everything over carefully, I decided at that time to quit the *Yomiuri*. So, the next year, in the spring of 1952, I left the paper. It was just as the Occupation ended. (174–185)

Becoming Free

Nishi goes on to talk about her work for NHK on a radio program called the "Women's Hour," which dealt with women's rights and duties in a democracy. Various strategies to improve women's position in society were discussed. She also became involved with various government-sponsored initiatives to address women's issues and helped conduct Japan's first nationwide survey of women's issues. She also discusses her marriage to her husband, Komiyama Chiaki, and his difficult battle with cancer. She came through this experience convinced that patients have the right to know when they are terminally ill (186–215).

The final chapter in her autobiography concerns the death of her stepdaughter, Yuri.

Yuri's Death

On September 1, 1958, Yuri died suddenly. She took an overdose of sleeping pills. She was only twenty-two years old.

The reason for her suicide was her enduring feelings for a man, Mr. F, but, unfortunately, the relationship was not a successful one. Even during the relationship she had confided in me quite honestly, but I guess she must have brooded over things too deeply.

I can still hear what turned out to be the last words she ever said to me: "My confidence has just gone!" The other side of this outwardly vivacious, spirited, and smart woman was a daughter who was still too dependent on her mother. Her younger sister Mari was more relaxed, spoke in slow motion compared with Yuri, and, perhaps because she had so much common sense, she could feel at home with almost anyone she might meet. But, from the point of view of personality, Yuri was a much more difficult child. She, alone, had accompanied me back to Tokyo after the war, and had experienced the change in environment accompanying my second marriage, so she was inclined to find just one man to be with. It was a tendency I was uneasy about.

At that time, long after my remarriage, she had been living with the Yamada Hideo family. Although Yuri, Mari, and I all lived apart, we were like three legs of a triangle and always kept in touch by letter, phone, and frequent meetings. One of those times, Yuri wrote me the following:

> Mother, you have done so much for us, even though we were the children of your former husband. But we are still counting on you to look out for us.

Even though she was not under my direct supervision, Yuri seemed to be blossoming into a terrific person. Thanks to wonderful things that the Yamada family did for her, she was magnificent beyond my wildest dreams. I was just so thankful she seemed to adjust so well to her environment and seemed to be working so hard to live a good life.

At the time, she was working as a stenographer. She had become a mature person with a responsible job. I felt as though she had been successfully launched. She often went on business trips to various parts of Japan and was a well-regarded employee. But she still could not let go of her dependence on me. That day when I returned from China, she came out to Haneda Airport to greet me. I saw the excitement on her face as she came running through the crowd and said to me impatiently, "After the plane landed I was calling out to you 'Mom, Mom' as loud as I could, but everyone around me was yelling too and my voice somehow just couldn't reach you." Just a half a year before she died, she had her appendix removed, and while she lay in her hospital bed, she looked deeply into my face and said,

"You know, I have been thinking about it while lying here. In this whole world, you have been my best friend; you have always been the person I can talk with. So, I am begging you, Mother, please have a long life!"

My face crumpled and there was nothing really I could say. But I was so happy! I held her to me, that body which had overnight become such a dazzling and beautiful woman's body.

I have so many memories of Yuri. Yet she left this world without saying a word to me. Why was it that whenever I saw her I felt so much love for her? I guess that somehow all that love I felt for her from a distance, and all the goodwill there was around her, was not enough to combat her loneliness. In fact, just three days before she died, because her spirits were so low, I had arranged for just the two of us to spend the night in an inn *(ryōkan)* at Atami. I was hoping that a night of lying down next to each other and talking things out might help her feel better. But this wish of mine was in vain, for Yuri chose death instead. She left not a single word for anybody.

But, unexpectedly, the autopsy revealed that Yuri was clearly suffering from a brain tumor. In fact, she had complained of headaches and insomnia, so perhaps she took the sleeping pills to get away from her pain. Yet I know that as far as Yuri was concerned, more than any illness, it was the pain of disappointment that she was trying to overcome. No one noticed the sleeping pills at the Yamada household. But what could I say. I can only reproach myself for what happened.

If there were anyone in my life so far that I would want to apologize to, it would have to be Yuri. But I can imagine she would just give that odd little smile and say, "Don't worry about it. Just let it go." But she might also be the one to say, her voice steeped in regret, "Oh, why did I decide to kill myself anyway?" She was that kind of daughter.

The memory of sitting with the box, holding her still warm bones on my lap, is really much too harsh. Today, Yuri's remains are resting in eternal sleep on the top of a hill near a mountain village in Okayama, adjacent to the graves of her parents. Her younger sister Mari pledged, "I will have to live my sister's share of life, too."

Mari lives an ordinary life: she is happily married but continues to work. Her daughter has gotten married and has even given her a grandchild. They call me "Mom" and "Grandma" respectively, and our relationships are natural and healthy. I guess I should say I am happy.

Yet, with all this, there are many times when I wonder what life would be like if Yuri had been willing to live. It seems that as the years pass, these kinds of thoughts only deepen. (216–219)

In effect, Nishi's narrative is framed by two suicides, her mother's and her step-
daughter's. If it is true, as some feminist critics believe, that the mother-daughter
relationship configures many women's autobiographies, then Nishi's text is in-
teresting for its presentation of both sides of the relationship. Of course, her
mother's suicide remained for her a mystery. It is the desire, the yearning for the
missing answers that gives the text its shape. Her mother's death, and the ensu-
ing silence about it, results in the mother looming as a "phantom" figure (gen-
ei) or an illusion that haunts the margins of her text. Although Yuri left no
suicide note, there is at least one fact to console the narrator: she was suffering
from a brain tumor. Nevertheless, her stepdaughter's death is shrouded in mys-
tery and silence as well. Both of these deaths haunt her deeply, and it makes her
self-reflexive as she brings her narrative to its conclusion.

Overlooking the End of Life

It just hit me that having been born in 1907, this year I have completed a
full eighty-one years of life! I guess I did live a long life after all. The average
life span of a Japanese woman is eighty years now, so living more than that
means that I have had no shortage of years in my life.

But still, as I look back over my life, I realize that I have experienced
quite a lot. Society has also been through tremendous changes as well, but
so have I as an individual. In particular, prewar society, unlike this tranquil,
peaceful world we know today, was unimaginably tumultuous, dark, and
painful. Amid all the violent upheaval I have been through, I nevertheless
managed to survive my youth, become an adult, go to work, and take my
place in society. In much the same way as the society itself, I often felt as
though I were running in a dream, trying desperately to escape something.

And the fact that I have lived to see this new postwar period—with
all the changes that have happened to it—well, I would have to say that I
feel a deep happiness. . . . After a half a century of working, now that the
U.N.'s Decade of Women is coming to an end, I have distanced myself
from activism. I have heard lots of other people who have also withdrawn from activities say, "After so many years of pulling out all the stops
and working hard, it's difficult to know what to do with oneself!"

I guess everyone feels the same when all of a sudden you are just staring at a big blank. But, surely, everyone must go through these things—
slowing down and pulling back. . . .

Fortunately for me, even though we may not be related by blood, I
have a daughter, grandchildren, and great-grandchildren who look out for

me now and again. Furthermore, there are young people who come to check up on me at my home: friends, relatives of my deceased husband, and so forth. I also have my own friends, and the neighborhood people are terrific. So I am not lonely by any stretch of the imagination. But even so, it is a fact that living alone can make you uneasy; it can be frightening and lonely in the end. And yet, living alone allows you a kind of freedom you cannot otherwise obtain. You don't have to worry about time or about getting along with somebody else. Except for the stress that may come from loneliness, one is free from all the stress that comes with worry. This is something desirable and it is good for one's health. One can reflect on things.

How much longer will I live? That is something only God knows. I don't have any notions of putting all my energies into experiencing a brilliant close to my life in my twilight years, but if I can be around to turn a few more pages on the calendar, that will be great.

In the end, it is up to each and every one of us to keep our health and spirits up, and to keep our relationships alive. Getting old, in the final analysis, is each individual's problem. . . .

Finally, I want to say how grateful I am for the peace and the democratic social order with which we are blessed. As one who lived through the violent upheavals of the prewar period, these feelings represent a very deep stratum of my being. No matter how old I may become, I will always place great value on these freedoms and I will cling stubbornly to my unwavering refusal of ever returning to that kind of past.

Afterword

I had always felt the urge to write down something about my life, but I worried that calling it an autobiography *(jiden)* might sound impudent. It's not that I have lived my life in such a remarkable way, but that the time period through which I have lived has been a full and tumultuous one. And, by coincidence, there were a few times when I stood up as an individual against this swirling tide. Moreover, people have been asking me increasingly of late if I wouldn't record my recollections and my experiences for posterity's sake.

With all this in mind, I sat down at my desk in January of this year (1988) and wrote straight through until the end of April. I made use of various resource materials, so at times it became quite an undertaking. Moreover, at times I had to leave myself exposed, and this necessitated some resolve on my part, while at other times I was too timid. However, my aim from the outset was to try and look at the period through which I lived head on, and to layer my own personal history over its surface. My desire to go back and confront this dark past, during which those in power controlled us from above, is rooted in my rejection of this abominable past, and in my most cherished belief that we must value highly the peace and freedom that we have in society today. (220–226)

Analysis

Self-representational narratives take shape in a variety of ways. The narrator of Reminiscences *informs us about her methodology: she sat and wrote straight for four months, consulting outside resources on occasion to shore up her recollections. Her text is a retrospective narrative, and it is evident from her conclusion and her afterword that she was able to stand back and review her life in its entirety to see the shapes and contours of the terrain her life had traversed. She has also probed her experiences in an effort to "make sense" of the choices she made in her life. As Gilmore points out,*

> Autobiography describes the textual space wherein the culturally constructed and historically changing epistemology of the self finds particular expression. Pressured all around by textuality, the autobiographical self owes its existence to the system of representation in which it finds expression. . . . Autobiography provides a stage where women writers, born again in the act of writing, may experiment with restructuring the various discourses—of representation, of ideology—in which their subjectivity has been formed. Thus, the subject of autobiography is not a single entity but a network of differences within which the subject is inscribed.[12]

Nishi Kiyoko, "born again in the act of writing," negotiates her way through the "network of differences" amid which her identity was constructed. Her text, Reminiscences, *is permeated with references to the multiple discourses out of which her subjectivity was constituted: her family, the values of a traditional Osaka merchant household, World War I, democracy, the Rice Riots, shipyard strikes, Marxism, feminism, World War II, postwar democracy, marriage, and parenting, just to name a few.*

Her text retains much of the shape of a "traditional" (male) autobiography: it follows a trajectory from birth and early life, through education, work experiences, marriage, family and, finally, old age. But there are markers throughout

*that suggest both tensions with the form she must adopt in order to write her life
and the centrality of the issue of gender to the reconstruction of her life. Clearly,
the issues surrounding the two deaths by suicide that frame her narrative are
telling; they underline the contradictions and the paradoxes that shaped the
lives of all three women. Her mother was a victim of the traditional, patriarchal
family structure, the clash between an autocratic family head (the grandfather)
and the adopted son-in-law (her father). We must recall what she writes at the
beginning of her narrative.*

> I cannot accept the notion that the behavior of this mother of mine who
> elected to commit suicide was impulsive. I have to see what she did as some
> form of resistance. (13–14)

*And, indeed, the act of writing her own story must be seen as her own act of re-
sistance. Like her mother, she, too, is an only daughter, and the thought of having to endure a fate like her mother's—being forced to marry someone adopted
into the family to preserve the family name—was so anathema to her that her
retelling of her life story was dedicated to constructing an account of how she attained and preserved her independence on the terms that mattered most to her.
"Like someone possessed," she writes, "I still continued to advocate for my own
personal autonomy and financial independence from my family." It is as though
nothing mattered more to her.*

    *It is interesting to note in passing that the deaths of her grandfather and
father do not even find a place in her narrative. They are striking by their absence. This is not to say that her text is completely given over to a denunciation
of the prewar family system. It is more subtle than that. It is clear that the attainment of financial and personal independence is one of the most important
threads in her text. Although she preferred to do so with her family's blessing,
she pursued education and avoided an arranged marriage because her personal
goal was independence. Therefore she writes about her "struggle for independence" (jiritsu e no agaki) as she pursues college and later postgraduate work
at Waseda University. Her primary goal was to be able to support herself and be
independent. Attracted to the ideals of socialism and Marxism, she refrained
from committing herself to the movement because any such involvement would
have to be subordinate to her need for financial independence. At the end of her
life, she writes about finally feeling free and about how precious postwar freedoms are to her, having lived through the dark days of Japan's militarism and
expansionism.*

    Although the narrator would have the reader understand that she was never a full-fledged Marxist radical nor a doctrinaire feminist, it is also apparent that she was influenced by the principles of both of these ideologies. She goes to great lengths to make clear to the reader how well read and informed she was on Marxist and feminist ideology, something that adds a strong undercurrent of contestation to a surface narrative that tries hard to appear non-ideological. Her account of breaking into journalism by working not for the feminist women's journal she had hoped to but for a liberal economics publication is essentially the story of finding a job in difficult times, keeping her position, and avoiding the arrests and detention by the prewar secret police that plagued so many other social activists. Her position with The Oriental Economist *also brought her into contact with the leading feminists of the day and led to her continued involvement with women's issues for the rest of her career. Finally, her account of the* Yomiuri *strike, although moderate in tone, occupies a significant position in her text. Her subject position in relation to this very pivotal strike was not that of a radical, but the fact that she chose to situate the event in such a significant position in her text is noteworthy. Taken together with the other parts of her narrative, it underscores the portrayal of Nishi Kiyoko as a progressive woman concerned with issues of social and economic justice, a woman who firmly embraced an oppositional ideology but who was also determined, above all, to establish and preserve her own independence.*

Gender obviously plays a central role in this narrative. Framing the text are complex and painful relationships between mothers and daughters. Weaving their way throughout the narrative are the threads of a woman's multiple stories—stories about learning, working, living, marrying, parenting, and surviving. Whether passages are about growing up in a traditional family structure, studying at a women's school, entering a top university as a female graduate-student auditor, or entering the male bastion of the workplace and experiencing wage discrimination—all these experiential accounts have everything to do with gender. Long discusses narrative strategies available to women who choose to transgress and write their lives in terms of three possibilities: 1) "telling it slant," (drawing on allusion and indirection, pronouncing disclaimers, denying being affected by certain things, avoiding confrontations with the dominant discourse, or even writing fiction); 2) "telling it messy," (dirt, diapers, blood, disruptions, interruptions, lack of control, lack of closure, process with no product); and 3) "telling it straight," or correcting the biases and distortions of the female experience by setting the record straight. [13] *Evidence for all three narrative strategies can be found in* Reminiscences. *When she alludes to the problems inherent in the family structure as the cause of her mother's suicide, she "tells it slant," because she tells the tale without a frontal assault. Everything comes down to a "plausible scenario" that she must construct. When she writes about the Allied bombings of Japan and about Yuri's suicide, she "writes it messy." But it may be argued that the prevailing narrative strategy she adopts is "telling it straight." Is there anything more important to Nishi than letting the reader wander the landscape of her personal narrative in order to discover for herself the kinds of paths that were encountered and that she had the courage to walk down? "My aim from the outset was to try and look at the period through which I lived head on, and to layer my own personal history over its surface" she tells us, because her "desire to go back and confront this dark past, during which those in power controlled us from above, is rooted in my rejection of this abominable past and in my most cherished belief that we must value highly the peace and freedom that we enjoy in society today."*

Nishi wants to tell it straight so that her readers will understand what was "abominable" about the past and what needs to be corrected in order to ensure that Japan's postwar freedoms are preserved. Few in postwar Japan benefited more by the adoption of the revised constitution in 1946 than women whose rights were specifically guaranteed. Reminiscences *is one of the many narratives that reminds its readers of the pain, the contradictions, and the paradoxes that constituted family life, education, employment, marriage, and political life in Japan before these reforms were implemented. As Scott reminds us,*

> Reading for paradox requires a different kind of reading than historians are used to. We are used to reading for the clash of opposing positions (feminists versus liberal politicians, for example), but not for internal tensions and incompatibilities (within feminism, within liberal individualism, within concepts such as liberty, or separate spheres or the individual) of which these clashes are both symptom and cause.[14]

As readers, we may want the lines in Nishi's text to be drawn more clearly, to see her situated squarely on the side of the left and the Marxist critique of capitalism and against the entrenched conservative elites in both prewar and postwar Japan. Her story, though, is one of ambiguities, contradictions, and compromises, all in the name of achieving her most cherished goal: personal and economic independence. But, as Scott argues, "to ignore the unsettledness that paradox, contradiction, and ambiguity imply is to lose sight of the subversive potential of feminism and the agency of feminists."[15] The power of Nishi's text may not necessarily be where we expect it to be, but it is there, inscribed on the surface and embedded in the layers of its reminiscences.

5

Re-presenting the Self
Sata Ineko's *Between the Lines of My Personal Chronology* (*Nen'pu no gyōkan*)

Sata Ineko. Reproduced with permission from Chūō kōron shinsha and Kubokawa Kenzō.

Sata Ineko (1904–1998) was born in Nagasaki, the daughter of a fifteen-year-old mother and an eighteen-year-old father. Her mother died of tuberculosis, and when Sata was only eleven years old, she went to work in a Tokyo caramel factory at her father's urging. After a brief marriage to a wealthy student, she worked at various jobs, including as a clerk at Maruzen Bookstore and as a café waitress. It was while working in this latter capacity that she met Nakano Shigeharu (1902–1979) and others associated with the Proletarian Literature Movement in 1926. At their urging, she began to write fiction, publishing From the Caramel Factory (Kyarameru kōjō kara) *in 1928 in the journal* Proletarian Arts (Puroretaria geijutsu). *She remained active in the proletarian literature movement and in 1932 joined the Japan Communist Party.*

Sata Ineko is the only literary figure to appear in this study of female self-writing. This is not because women writers do not write their lives. But the majority of women included in this study were social or political activists. In a sense, this is the case with Sata as well, for she first gained recognition in the literary world

as a proletarian writer, the author of From the Caramel Factory, *a novel about a young girl working in a candy factory. While working as a waitress in one of the many cafés to appear in Tokyo during the 1920s, she met a group of young, politically radical poets and writers who were members of the Proletarian Arts League. She joined them and began to write fiction that aimed at realistically depicting the experience of the working class.*

This chance encounter between Sata and the proletarian writers occurred in 1926, in the midst of a decade in which labor unrest increased almost tenfold as the number of factories in both heavy and light industry increased more than fivefold. The cities grew as rural folk migrated in order to find jobs in the new factories, and soon, all kinds of new leisure opportunities presented themselves in the urban areas: radio, film, newspapers, and journals were the media while bars, nightclubs, cafés, exhibition and dance halls, parks, zoos, and museums constituted the new sites where urban denizens could recreate. Japanese cities in the 1920s were energetic and alive. Wages had risen to over 300 percent of what they had been in 1914, and when the price of rice rose so high and so rapidly in 1918 that the Rice Riots broke out, it was an expression of this new kind of urban energy and a new willingness for labor to confront management. In this sense, Japan was simply mirroring global trends—witnessing the emergence of mass production, mass consumption, and mass politics.

The proletarian literary movement with which Sata came into contact had roots going back as early as February 1921, when a small group of people from Akita Prefecture in northern Japan published a magazine called The Sower (Tane-maku hito). *Writers in this magazine argued that the time was ripe to construct a theory of art rooted in historical materialism, and they focused their readers' attention on the works of Marx, Engels, Henri Barbusse, and others. The following year, a new successor journal, or* Literary Arts Front (Bungei sensen), *appeared. Then, over one hundred interested literary figures associated with this journal joined together on December 6, 1925, in order to found the Japan Proletarian Literary Arts League (Nihon Puroretaria Bungei Renmei) and make* Literary Arts Front *their flagship magazine. In January 1928, the Japan Proletarian Literary Arts League merged with other groups to form the All Japan Federation of Proletarian Arts (Zennnihon Musansha Geijutsu Renmei), known also as NAPF, which published* Battle Flag (Senki) *as their official organ. But it was a smaller, more informal literary journal of the period published in Tokyo called* Donkey (Roba) *that Sata happened upon. As she got to know the young men who published this journal around 1926, they urged her to join with them and even encouraged her to publish her first attempt at proletarian fiction.*

Some of the leading figures in the proletarian literature movement were the poet and Marxist critic Nakano Shigeharu (1902–1979), Kubokawa Tsurujirō (1903–1974), Kurahara Korehito (1902–1999), Hori Tatsuo (1904–1953), Sata Ineko, Hirabayashi Taiko (1905–1972), and Kobayashi Takiji (1903–1933). It is perhaps Kobayashi's work, especially his novel The Factory Ship (Kani kōsen), that is the most well known of the proletarian literature movement. A story about the harsh labor conditions and a valiant strike effort on a crab processing vessel in the Okhotsk Sea, it dramatically depicts men being awakened to the importance of solidarity even in the face of intervention by sailors of the Imperial Navy who were dispatched to board the ship and arrest the strike leaders. Seemingly the strikers have been defeated, but the story ends with the workers pledging "One more time!" as they learn that solidarity is their key to victory.

If Kobayashi's novel is one of the most well-known works from the proletarian literature movement, Nakano Shigeharu must stand as its most respected author. As Silverberg points out in her study of Nakano, his involvement with the Donkey group signaled a move away from the lyrical style of poetry he had been writing to poetry and criticism that explored the connections between "art and social structures" and came to the inescapable conclusion that "politics and culture were mutually informing and reinforcing.[1] Nakano believed that art has the capacity "to make revolution through the alternation of consciousness."[2]

The term "proletarian literature" does not resonate very positively with American readers. The term generally summons up images of hack writers in the 1930s who were active in left-wing socialist and communist circles and whose fiction aimed "to bring the worker to class-consciousness, steel him for the coming revolution, [and] prepar[e] him for the role he would play in the next stage of history."[3] While some of this radical literature of the 1930s remains viable today, proletarian literature as a whole has not been taken very seriously by critics. As Constance Coiner notes, "[W]orking-class literature has been generally considered crudely tendentious and aesthetically inferior to bourgeois literature."[4] Or, as Chester Eisenger claims, "[T]he novel written in the Marxist ambience . . . fails to give the imaginative satisfactions we can legitimately expect from fiction."[5] In fact, though, the proletarian literary movement enjoyed greater respect and commanded a more enthusiastic following in other countries where it commenced earlier and played a more significant historical role.

As noted previously, there was a substantial proletarian literature and arts movement under way in Japan by the early 1920s. The success of the Bolshevik Revolution in 1917 and the socioeconomic changes fueled by World War I were responsible for inciting a strong interest in socialism in Japan and in a literature *that would speak to conditions among the working class. Sata tells us that she learned to think about what literature is, what it could be, and what it should be from the young proletarian writers led by Nakano.* She chronicled those years in her autobiography, Between the Lines of My Personal Chronology, *a text that offers some valuable insights into the activities of these proletarian writers and what it was like to be present in the early stages of the movement.*

Her path to the cafés of Tokyo, and ultimately to the literary world, was not necessarily a smooth one. Her mother died very young, her father remarried two more times, and her formal education had to end prematurely when her father sent her off to work in a caramel factory. Sata's own first marriage nearly ended in a double suicide, and her second marriage not only required a great deal of work, but posed wrenching issues about her identity. Toward the end of her text, the narrator struggles with the issue of how her identity as a writer could conflict with expectations about what it means to be a wife. Her discussion of these issues culminates with reflections on how and why she changed her name—the way in which the world sees and identifies her—from her spouse's name, Kubokawa, to Sata, the name of a favorite uncle, Sata Hidezane, who would also die prematurely. Her uncle symbolized for her the world of literary pursuits; also, his name was neither her father's nor her husband's, so it was something she could identify as her own. Sata begins her text with some reflections on her girlhood in Nagasaki.

My Youth in Nagasaki

Whenever the name Nagasaki comes up, the image that comes to mind is of a landscape drenched in sunlight. It is not so much a transparent light as a thick, yellow brightness heavy with humidity.

And if one were to say something particular about my birth, it would be that my parents were so young, caught up in all the heat and passion of first love. And then I was born.

My father, Tajima Masafumi, was eighteen years old, in his fifth year at Saga Middle School. My mother, Takayanagi Yuki, was fifteen years old, a second-year student at the Saga Prefectural Girls' High School. There is a photograph of my mother that remains from those days. She looks like a typical female student of her day. She is wearing a pleated skirt *(hakama)*, which she fastened with a belt bearing the insignia of her prefectural girl's school.

I guess I was actually present for that photo in the sense that I was there, growing inside of her, hidden beneath her pleated skirt. . . . Indeed, because I was in there, she had to abandon school, which is why she had this commemorative photo taken. It is heartrending to think about it. Her face still had an innocent, childlike quality to it. After all, she really was still just a child. (7)

This is an extraordinary beginning for a self-representational text. The primary vehicle for discussion is a photo of a fifteen-year-old girl, the narrator's mother, who is pregnant with the narrator. The narrator gazes at the photograph and situates herself in the photograph and in relation to what her mother must sacrifice and undergo in order to bear her.

"Be a Good Wife"—My Mother's Parting Words

Along with the two newlyweds, my grandmother and my aunt, my father's younger sister, lived with our family. My younger brother Masahito was born in November of Meiji 39 (1906), at which point my parents formally registered their marriage. I was listed as the foster child of my mother and father.

At that time, our household was rather strapped financially, so there was a need [for my mother] to get out and earn money. She took a job at a Nagasaki factory that manufactured tin cans. . . . Perhaps the stress of giving birth, along with working at the can factory and setting up a new household were too much for my mother, for she contracted tuberculosis and collapsed. It's only a vague memory, but I seem to recall a Sunday when Father was home and we decided to have an outing to Tateyama. On the way, my mother's condition suddenly became worse, and she was upset that we had to return home early. I remember feeling sad. I think I recall my mother coughing up blood on that occasion. It was very difficult to deal with . . . especially for my poor mother. In those days, tuberculosis was a terminal disease. Therefore, my mother returned to her own home in Saga to "recuperate." . . .

My mother may have been wondering whether or not she would recover. It had to be very sad for her to think about leaving her two small children and returning to her home to die.

In August of 1911, the year my mother had entered me in Nagasaki's Katsuyama Elementary School, she died at the age of twenty-two.

At the time my mother died, I don't really remember clutching her and crying. As I thought about the fact that amid all the comings and goings of the adults my mother had just passed away, I would feel sad. I would get away by myself, to the empty space near the well out back, and cry. I can remember the sadness of a very touching scene as twilight descended and everything seemed to be bathed in a golden light. . . . (10–12)

Just before my mother died, she sent me a letter to assist me in learning *katakana*, as I had just entered the first grade. It was a half page written in pencil and included the following:

> Study hard so that you can become a good wife.

I believe that she knew she would die soon when she wrote those words, because she did not write "Be a good girl," but instead wrote "Become a good wife." She knew she would not live to see me grow up and become a bride. She took great pains [to write] clearly and legibly, ensuring that a first grader like me could read her words. But this gave her letters a very childlike appearance.

These heartfelt words, written in such clear *katakana* characters, transmitted a powerful message from my mother. What remained in my heart as a memory of my mother was not her face, her voice, or the warmth of her body, but rather a letter written in those clearly printed *katakana* characters.

Given what had happened, I was never again to be hugged or carried on my mother's back. Even after her death, I was too busy trying to live my life fully to spend much time missing her or crying over her death. In fact, when I would think of my mother, I felt more pity then I did a yearning for her.

Later, when my own child was around ten years old, at the time I was writing *A Gray Afternoon (Haiiro no gogo)* and things in my marriage were extremely difficult, the word "Mother!" *(Okaasan)* just gushed out, and I cried. Up until this point, there had been nothing I really needed from my mother, but it was as though these feelings had just been wrung out of me. It wasn't as though I was calling out "Mommy" as a little child might, but I was calling "Mother." Why I would say something like that at that time was a mystery to me as well, but it was as though things were just too tough and I needed someone to hold on to. Suddenly, I just uttered the word.

Perhaps it was not so much about my mother the actual person, but about someone who fit into the category of mother. I suppose it was a sad longing for someone to cling to, someone like a mother who could provide unconditional love. I never thought of myself as spoiled, and I really did not have the capacity to spoil others, so I surprised even myself when I uttered those words. Human emotions are indeed interesting! (13–14)

Human emotions are indeed interesting, and the narrator alludes to a number of them in this passage: the feelings of loss, abandonment, and loneliness that a young girl of six feels when she loses her mother. There is something poignant about her noting how she missed being held by her mother or being carried on her mother's back when she went out shopping or on errands. This was the close physical relationship to her mother that she was denied while growing up. Although she claims not to have felt terribly deprived at the time, later, when she herself becomes a mother, she cannot hold back her tears and finds herself calling out for her mother. As Jo Malin notes in her recent book, "Every woman autobiographer is a daughter who writes and establishes her identity through her autobiographical narrative. Many twentieth-century autobiographical texts by women contain an intertext, an embedded narrative, which is a biography of the writer/daughter's mother."[6] Almost all of the texts in this study contain some such embedded intertext, and several, like Sata's, contain as well empty spaces where that narrative belongs but is absent because the mother's life was so short. Instead of the mother's voice having a strong presence in the text, there are questions, hopes, and desires that cannot be fully articulated. Here, it is doubly poignant when the narrator reveals that her mother's last words were written, delivered to her as part of a school lesson, and in the form of an admonition.

Although the narrator does not comment directly on her mother's admonition that she should strive to become a good wife, it speaks volumes. It says something about the limitations upon the vision that a young mother, stricken with tuberculosis, could have for her daughter in 1911. "Become a good wife"; this is simply what women did. But it turned out that it wasn't necessarily something that was easy for Sata to do. So already, in the first few pages of this text, gender issues are introduced in such a way as to frame the narrative. What happens when a fifteen-year-old schoolgirl becomes pregnant? What becomes of her educational opportunities? What will become of the life script for the daughter, born out of wedlock, entered into another family member's household registry and then registered in her own as a foster child? How does she make her way in life when her mother dies so young?

As we shall see below, Sata's subjectivity is constituted out of a number of social and political discourses. But here, very early on, an important discourse about gender-based expectations for young women in the early 1900s is presented. Not only was she to be a "good girl," but she was expected to grow up and become a "good wife" as well. As the narrative unfolds, however, we learn that the narrator struggled with two different marriages and had to raise a daughter on her own. How much of this was because her own mother did not live long enough to accomplish this herself? What role does family instability play in the way the narrator situates herself in relation to her own text?

Finally, consider the closing scene of this opening section, the scene where the narrator jumps ahead to when her own daughter is ten years old and she is a writer struggling to preserve her own marriage. When the word "Mother" surfaces suddenly, she weeps openly and utters a cry for her own mother. She is still a daughter yearning for her mother; but she is also a mother thinking about her own daughter. It is as though the light bulb above her head has gone on, and instantly she understands her own longing and what is missing in her life. Her response goes beyond the verbal and comes out as raw emotion. She is no longer a child crying for her mother but an adult, a mother herself, who needs to invoke the name of her own mother. It is a significant moment in the text that reminds the reader how important the imposed silence has been for Sata, how the things that she has missed, the things that have been absent in her life since her mother died, remain as empty spaces within her. Meanwhile, as the narrator returns to the chronology of her upbringing, she tells us that her father remarried very shortly after her mother's death, only to have this marriage end in divorce. Soon after moving the family to Tokyo, Sata's father was having a difficult time getting along with his third wife. The narrative resumes.

At the Caramel Factory

MY UNCLE SATA HIDEZANE

When we left Nagasaki to go to Tokyo, my father's first wife had died, he had divorced his second wife, and was currently not getting along with his third wife. So we had encountered a number of obstacles on our life's journey. Even though he was still young, I am sure that my father had grown weary of working for Mitsubishi. He was only about twenty-eight years old. This is something I have reflected on literally only after I became a writer, but I think that when he resigned from Mitsubishi, he probably experienced a sensation of liberation. . . .

THE CARAMEL FACTORY

In retrospect, coming to Tokyo with the idea that somehow things would work out was completely reckless, and to put it in literary terms, it was an extension of my father's romanticism—and I was made a victim of it. In the very same way, my father was being completely unrealistic when he sent me out to work in a caramel factory. In terms of the cost of living in Tokyo those days, if there had been such a job in the immediate vicinity, it might have contributed something to the household income. But to have to ride the train to work every day meant that there was no way for it to work financially. My father apparently thought it would be good for a child to work in a caramel factory, but he had not thought through the economics of it at all. Whatever I earned in a day was eaten up by the train fare. . . . (34–35)

The finished caramels came down to us in a large metal container made of tin or something, and all of us female employees were standing at this work table where we were to wrap the individuals pieces in paper. So our job was to wrap the individual pieces of candy and then place the wrapped caramels in five- or ten-sen boxes, which we then packed into a larger box. So, in a day, we would each pack up several of these large boxes. The workers who were really fast might do seven or eight boxes, but I usually would get only two or two and a half boxes done in a day.

I described the following incident in [my novel] *From the Caramel Factory*, but in order to encourage and admonish the female workers, the factory would post the names of the workers who filled the most boxes and the number they filled, as well as those who completed the fewest. In other words, they would post the highest number and the names of the female workers who packed them. I was always the one with the worst record. I think I was also the youngest employee, but whenever I read my name on the list for having the lowest totals, I was taken aback. In school, I was used to seeing my name at the top of the list of students with the best records; now here I was achieving the lowest output. Even though I was just a child, seeing my name there hit me hard emotionally. I wasn't exactly insulted, but it was difficult to take somehow.

At the factory, we would buy baked potatoes for a snack break. Someone would have to go out and buy the potatoes, so it was one of the few permitted ways to leave the factory during the shift. It wouldn't look very good if I were the only one who didn't buy a potato, so I had to add that expense into my money for round-trip train fare as well. The total came to around fifteen sen. I can't recall exactly what I earned in a day there, but since it was based on piecework, it couldn't have been enough. So I worked there for only a couple of months. Perhaps a little longer, I have forgotten. [Once they started paying according to how many boxes you assembled,] my father said I should go ahead and quit. Next, I took a job at a Chinese noodle shop that served buckwheat noodles *(soba)* and *ramen*. (39–40)

Things did not work out at the noodle shop either, so Sata went work as a maid for one year living at a restaurant called Shinryōtei. It was not easy for her living away from home. Concerned about her aunt having to work so hard, Sata wrote her father saying that she should sell her to a geisha house in order to alleviate the family's financial woes. At this point, he summoned her to Aioi, where he was working. Relieved of the need to work full-time herself, these months were among the most free of her young life.[7] While working at Shinryōtei, her favorite Uncle, Sata Hidezane, was on his deathbed and she was summoned home. But he was already deceased when she arrived.

My Uncle's Death

When I was setting off to serve as a maid, I recall my uncle looking up at me from his bed and saying, "Ah, Ineko, so you, too, are sinking down?" *(Aa, Ineko mo ochite-ikuka)* Well, I guess I was sinking down—being sent off to be in service to another family. I could agree it was a kind of sinking down, but there are much more harsh ways of sinking; at least I wasn't having to sell my body. But, I could see how, in my uncle's eyes, he would feel that I was slipping. . . . I know that he wanted to see me continue my studies. He was the first one to ever take me to the Nagasaki Library, so I am sure he had these kinds of feelings.

Much later, when I read Tayama Katai's *Country Teacher (Inaka kyōshi)*, I wept profusely. From the fall of 1934 to January of 1935, when I was writing *The Barefoot Daughter (Suashi no musume)*, I was staying alone at a lodge in Hakone. When I read about the sensitive central character whose aspirations were crushed by poverty and who died of lung disease, he became my Uncle Sata Hidezane, causing me to sob audibly and weep. I cried out loud like this because of the final memories of my uncle that I carried inside me.

When I think about the memory of my Uncle Hidezane, he was, after all, a very sad case. When I adopted his name and became Sata Ineko, it was a tribute to his memory. (52–53)

After living in Aioi with her father for a while, Sata decided to leave and return to Tokyo on her own. The year was 1920 and she was sixteen years of age. She returned to Shinryōtei and became a parlor maid (zashiki-jochū) who served food and drink directly to customers. It was while working here that she first met the writer Akutugawa Ryūnosuke. She recognized him from a photograph in the literary magazines that she had been devouring, and when word got back to him that one of the lowly maids at the restaurant recognized him, Akutagawa was impressed. Sata writes in chapter 3, "I Want to Read Books":

Apparently, Akutagawa was amused to learn that a maid knew what he looked like. In fact, I heard later on that he found it very intriguing because it was quite unusual in those days for a maid to be able to recognize a literary figure by sight. (61–62)

I think I always carried inside me a longing for culture; it was like a hunger for something that continually gnawed at me. It was not that I was necessarily yearning for something pure in my life, or something to make me fashionable. No, it was somehow different from that. I felt it was something very different. . . . I wanted to read more and more books. . . . My desire to read books was not part of some wish to study and become somebody famous. I just wanted to read books. Just as someone who is thirsty says that they want to drink water, I just wanted to read books.

For some time, there had been brewing in me this idea of immersing myself in the world of books. So I decided to quit Shinryōtei. It wasn't that I didn't like it there. But given the fact that I had no life of my own, I realized that what I wanted to do was read. There was no one there who could understand my desire to read books. There was no one there with whom I could discuss the books I had read. I doubt that anyone there had any idea of my desire to read books; there was no one with whom I could even talk about it.

I wanted my own time. I wanted to read books. I wanted my own time to read books. I did not feel any revulsion for my life there at all, but I just had these desires and therefore I felt I had to quit. So I did. (67–68)

Akutagawa Ryūnosuke was one of Japan's most important writers who participated actively in the discourse about modern Japanese literature. He engaged master storyteller Tanizaki Junichirō in an extensive debate about the meaning and value of plot for the modern novel.[8] However, Akutagawa committed suicide with his lover in 1927 while still a young man, something that had quite an impact on the young Sata, as she articulates later on. But for the time being, she was still preparing herself for life as a writer, which is why she needed to read. But since she still needed to support herself—and her desire to read—Sata took a job at Maruzen Bookstore, the largest Western-style bookstore in Japan. She read each way on her commute to and from work, and she read on her days off. A friend at Maruzen introduced her to the ideas of anarchism, and she began to think about social classes for the first time. She realized that the social order was something constructed (shikumi) and that people were born into this preconstructed social order. She also read some of Kuriyagawa Hakuson's theories on love (ren'ai ron) but had to wonder if the sublime love of which he spoke was really possible in the world she inhabited. In her own words, she began to think in a rather bold, shameless (namaiki) manner.

My ideas at that time were rather brazen. I mean I had read a lot of books, and I had worked at Shinryōtei, so I felt I knew something about how things really work in the world. I saw and heard lots of things at Shinryōtei, and, after all, there are secret, inner workings to one's life. And you can experience these workings indirectly by reading novels, and then you can develop your own way of conceptualizing how the world works. In my own personal life, I had had no real experience of love; I had not yet known a man, and even though I perhaps shouldn't have, I somehow felt that I understood life. . . . [But] in my own life, I could only paint my future gray. I was no longer able to have my dreams. Up until that time, I had wanted to read and to believe that somehow my life would be different, so I was able to keep forging ahead. But then I began to feel as though my fate was already determined. I had the feeling that I knew what my future would be, and it was increasingly hard to bear. . . .

But, in actuality, the *I* who had this feeling that I already knew where my life was headed was really being brazen and impudent. I really didn't know anything. Yet I had the impudence to think I did. Therefore, at that point I seriously thought about suicide.

Much later, people pointed out to me that I have this dark, nihilistic side. It was something that may have come from my earlier life. People often said that I had this nihilistic side to my character, and after I had become a writer, the man I married, Kubokawa Tsurujirō, also pointed it out to me. . . .

We have to work in order to live. We may work in order to live, but one can get tired from the work. So you have to begin to wonder what it means to work. If we have to work in order to live, and if you get exhausted from working, isn't death all that's left?

I was tired. Day after day after day. . . .

The same monotonous job—after two or three years, you just lose interest. It's not so much that you lose interest, you just get tired. Every morning, getting on the crowded train, arriving at the office, and before you even start working you feel tired. In addition to the emotional exhaustion, you get physically tired, and then your emotions sink even further down. Honestly, when it came time to go to work in the mornings, I thought seriously about suicide. If there were a railroad track running down the middle of the road, sometimes I would just look at that track and think about it. . . .

Human nature *(ningen so seikaku)* is extremely complex, isn't it? Even though I have often said that I am a hedonist who enjoys entertainment,

that I was a tomboy, and that I have a bright and cheerful side to my nature, I also had a nihilistic side. I guess I was not very well balanced. Perhaps everyone is like that. You cannot necessarily judge someone by the
one side of their nature that they may choose to show you. (77–79)

*These are some noteworthy ruminations on the meaning of life, work, and
human nature. It is interesting that these sorts of ideas, and her reflections
about the dark side of her nature and even about suicide, appear in the text in a
kind of muted way. The discussion is almost casual, with a tossed-off kind of
feel. This tendency to downplay, to speak casually or in a roundabout manner
about something so serious, may be a narrative strategy of the sort Long mentions. That is, the narrator was "telling it slant," setting up a tension between
the rhetoric and content of the text. The phrase "telling it slant" comes from an
Emily Dickinson poem.*

> Tell all the truth but tell it slant
> Success in circuit lies
> Too bright for our infirm Delight. . . .
> The truth must dazzle gradually
> Or else every man be blind—

*The poem refers, it would seem, to "the social constraints under which commu-
nication takes place."[9] To speak the truth too directly can be more than disturb-
ing and unsettling; it can be dangerous. Here, it is as if the narrator is aware
that giving voice to such things entails significant risk; she realizes that she is
practicing a form of trespass, that she is entering terrain upon which she must
tread lightly.*

*Despite all her complex feelings about her work and her life, though, Sata
continued to work very hard at Maruzen. Ironically, she was hailed as a model
employee. In the next passage, the narrator talks about her love of reading and
how the magazines and journals of the day were her key to making up for her lack
of formal schooling.*

Marriage, a Failed Attempt at Double Suicide, and Catastrophe

When I would spend time at home by myself, I couldn't help feeling that
not being able to go on to school was a real loss for me, and deep within I
felt very dissatisfied. Since I needed to suppress these feelings, I would immerse myself in the pages of *Central Review (Chūō kōron)*, which my father
subscribed to, as well as all the novels I could get a hold of. This was my

way of making up for not being able to go to school. Also, I had a real thirst for knowledge that made me want to absorb all I could.

In those days, I learned the word "authority." Somewhere in *Central Review* they had used this word and I had memorized it. Actually, they had used the Chinese characters for *ken'i* [権威] and then spelled out "authority" phonetically *(osorichii)* in *katakana* alongside the Chinese characters. It wasn't the other way around—that is, writing "authority" and then placing the characters for *ken'i* next to it. So I learned it that way. And as soon as I learned it, I turned around and used it. My father made some disparaging remark like, "What is this, magazine education?" How ill tempered!

I felt that in his comment there was a snide reference to the fact that I wasn't getting a formal education, as well as a sneer directed at my brazenness for using such language. So, I felt a little embarrassed, but I also felt incensed: what kind of a father was this? He was the one who wouldn't allow me to continue my education, then he makes a crack like that. I just wanted to learn, to absorb everything I could, and magazines were what were available to me.

To put it another way, I wanted to learn, and the only avenue open to me were books and journals. And this was my father's fault. In spite of this, even though there I was, a child trying to learn as best she could under the circumstances, he had to make a crack about "magazine education." But, for my part, I was brazen about showing off what I had learned. There really wasn't any need to be showing off.

Anyhow, this is how I would read his *Chūō kōron* every time I had the opportunity, and I also read more age-appropriate magazines like *A Girl's Friend (Shōjo no tomo)* and *The World of Women's Education (Jogaku sekai)*. These journals tended to have a "reader's column," where reader's submissions were published. So I thought I might as well submit something too. It wasn't so much that I was confident in my writing, but as I understood it at the time, submitting something was an opportunity to have your work evaluated in order to determine whether or not it would be printed. It wasn't that I wanted people to read my work, but just that the editorial group would take a look at it and then I would find out what other people thought about my writing. (81–84)

There is an interesting juxtaposition here. Sata is the young woman whose mother died early, whose education was cut short, and whose father sent her to work in a caramel factory when she was only eleven years old. Trying to better herself, she reads prolifically, including her father's magazines, only to be mocked by him for her "magazine education." She is shocked by her father's attitude, but in the text the incident performs a vital function. It reinforces the way in which the patriarchy insists on silencing or muting women's voices. But in this instance, all it reinforced was Sata's desire to discover her own voice as a writer. One day she returns home to find a letter from Ikuta Shungetsu waiting for her. She was quite surprised and even more so when she opened it and discovered that the journal Literary News *(Bungei tsūhō) was planning to showcase five new female authors, and she was being solicited to contribute some poetry as one of the five. It would be a special issue that would offer the opportunity to be recognized by the literary establishment* (bundan) *and perhaps launch her career. But she did not feel that she had the confidence to express herself in poetry, so ultimately she thanked the magazine and turned down the opportunity to submit. As she explained it:*

Poetry was all about selecting and placing words. There are many words one can use to capture and express one's emotions, and I enjoyed the process of giving expression to my thoughts and feelings using the structure and expressions of poetry.

However, I would really be a little embarrassed to say that I had actually composed poetry before. It was more like I had imitated other people—I had borrowed forms and expressions. It was really just a matter of fitting them into a format. Once I became a novelist, I wouldn't say that in my heart, or in my sensibilities, I had no poetic feeling at all. Writers have to have a poetic sensibility, and I do think I have such a thing. However, more than a poet, I am a prose writer. This is why I felt a connection with the proletarian literature movement. Poetry is extremely emotional, and one's feelings come across directly in poetry. Of course, one has the same thing in prose writing, but I think that in prose, more than poetry, you can express yourself through the descriptive and narrative processes. I think that in poems, it is more direct. Of course, one can think of proletarian poems, but I really did not come out of a proletarian background. The kind of environment I was raised in was more petit bourgeois, hence my uncle's admonition to me that I was "sinking down." So, when I joined the proletarian literary movement, I didn't feel that I could write poetry because I could not write proletarian poetry.

In other words, I had learned the meaning of "proletarian" through rational means. Of course, I had my background, the fact that we had fallen economically, so I could capture [the meaning of proletarian] in this sense. But in terms of my sensibilities, I was really petit bourgeois. My mother was raised with the sensibilities of an attractive young petit bourgeois woman. So I imagine that I carry over some of these same feelings. This is why, later, I had to work hard and use the process of becoming a proletarian writer in order to overcome these tendencies intrinsic to me. (88–89)

It is interesting that Sata uses this passage to establish her preference for prose narrative. She does not deny that she has poetic sensibilities—all writers must have some—but she is attracted to prose writing, for this is where she can get at the kind of truth she is interested in, the truth about the lives of working people. Poetry is better suited to the direct expression of emotions, but since she is not from the proletarian class herself, she will have to learn about their lives through "rational means"; that is, she will have to investigate and conduct research. To her, this somehow smacks of being inauthentic, which is why she believes poetry is not the appropriate way to express herself about these concerns.

Sata was frustrated working at Maruzen, where not only did work interfere with her wish to immerse herself in reading, but female employees were not even supposed to talk or make friends with other employees outside of the workplace. Perhaps her desire to extricate herself from this situation made a marriage proposal from a Keio University student, Kobori Kaizō, seem appealing. He was from a very wealthy family, and Sata thought that maybe this marriage was her reward for working hard all her life without a lot of hope for the future. Behind her back, people spoke disparagingly of her marrying into a wealthy family, "above her station." She herself would admit that she went into the marriage out of a sense of desperation. The relief and happiness she longed for was not to be found in this marriage. Viewed with suspicion by others in the family as a fortune seeker, spied upon and distrusted by her husband, Sata was extremely unhappy.

I wondered if I might be able to find happiness, but the answer was no. It was a disaster. That nihilistic part of me reasserted itself, and I turned to taking an overdose of sleeping pills. Somehow or other I managed to escape death, and people said that Kobori was very concerned about me. He was surprised and worried. He told me later that when he ran to get the doctor his wallet, which he put in his kimono, got soaked and fell apart. He was half-asleep and it just disintegrated into little pieces. That left quite an impression on me. I felt like he was really concerned that I was going to die.

That's how it was at the time. He asked if I was really going to leave him behind alone. He was a bit nihilistic himself, so he said to me that if I really wanted to die, then we should do it together. So we went to Yūga-shima to die. But the innkeeper thought our appearance was a little suspicious, so he had somebody looking out after us every time we tried to go anywhere. I was a little bit frightened of this guy, who was like a spy. If we die here, I thought, we'll end up surrounded by this guy.

So we ended up not attempting a double suicide at Yūgashima and returned to our home instead, where we took sleeping pills. . . . But our doctor was worried that something was up, so he called the police. It wound up making a big splash in the newspapers. There was an article in the Tokyo *Asahi shinbun* for February 10, 1924, which read like this:

> **Wealthy Young Couple Takes a Powerful Poison**
> **and Attempts a Double Suicide**
> In Nakameguro, Kobori Kaizō's (27) maid, worried that it was past 10:30 and the couple had not awakened, entered their room and found Kaizō and his wife Ine (22) lying with their pillows next to each other, their faces completely white. She tried to shake them to wake them up, but she got no reaction at all. Surprised, she ran quickly and reported it to the neighborhood doctor and when he examined them, it appeared that they had attempted suicide by taking the powerful drug charamela and were still in a drug-induced coma. No cause for the attempt was known. Kaizo is from a wealthy family who was thought to live a very carefree life.

If we had just died at that point, then my life would have been no more. It would not have been a matter of good or bad; I just would no longer have existed.

After all the news about the double suicide appeared in the newspapers, my father came and took me back to Aioi. There my daughter Yōko was born. I was still hopeful at that time that things might turn around for the better, that my husband's attitude might change. So I thought it best to give the marriage another try. He came to Aioi and we rented a place on the beach at Ichinatsu Akaho. But even in the little time we spent together there, I knew it would not work. I felt that this was not a healthy environment in which to try to raise a child—when a couple has a relationship like ours.

On the one hand, one thinks about not getting divorced because of the child. But, on the other hand, if the lifestyle is just not going to improve, then it becomes impossible to raise a child in a positive environment. I didn't feel I could raise my daughter satisfactorily under such circumstances, so I decided to get a divorce.

I really hoped that Yōko would one day understand my decision. . . . But [later,] when she was ill, recuperating from tuberculosis, she blurted

out something like, "Anyway, I wasn't born into a happy marital situation." It made me feel sad. But at the same time, I felt angry, too. A mother's
love for her child doesn't have anything to do with marriage. After all, I
took her with me when I left. Even though economically things were
difficult, I believed that I shouldn't be apart from my daughter, so I did
whatever it took.

At the time of our divorce, I was startled to learn from my father that
due to the patriarchal system, I should be prepared to hand the child over
to the Koboris. Yōko was an heir to the Kobori family, and it would be extremely difficult to remove her from their family register. Ordinarily, it
couldn't be done. Without someone else to replace her in the family register, it was nearly impossible. But I went to see a lawyer, and although it was
very difficult, we succeeded in removing her from the family register. And
she was formally adopted into my family. Although I was her mother, she
was formally registered as my younger sister.

My father. When I was young, he didn't seem to express much fatherly
love, but this time, with Yōko, it was clear that he really felt it. . . . So, Yōko
and I lived there with my father as well as his wife, my grandmother, and
my aunt. Including me, that was four women all living under the same
roof with my father. Being my father, he was able to avoid a lot of it, but I
knew I couldn't stay there in Aioi indefinitely. For my life, I had to get back
to Tokyo and get a job. I needed to get on with my life. So my father took
the opportunity to quit his own job and we all moved up to Tokyo to look
for work there. As soon as we landed in Tokyo, I went straight down
Dozaka Hill from Tabata Station and found a rental house where we were
able to move right in. (100–105)

Meeting the People around *Donkey*

Moving from Aioi back to Tokyo in 1926, at age twenty-two, was a new
beginning for me—not only spiritually, but physically as well. Physically,
my body felt light and refreshed after I got rid of all the extra weight from
my pregnancy, and I felt energetic and exhilarated. Spiritually, I felt the
same way. From here on, I was going to live my life the way I wanted.

If I think about how I had lived my life so far, or anyway, about how
things had turned out for me, it was pretty much as I have already related:
when I was young, I was told to marry and settle down. That's the way I believed a young woman was supposed to live. When you go to work, you are
supposed to work as hard as you can. Anyway, that was the way that society

expected us to live. . . . But I had nothing left to fear. I was not going to worry any longer about what people said or thought about me.

I was now a divorced mother who had attempted suicide. Whatever bad things people wanted to say about me had already been said. To worry about society hanging the label "bad" on you, you have to be worried about what other people think of you. But I was already in a situation where people had hung all the negative labels on me that they could. So I might as well live the way I wanted to from here on out. I resolved to no longer be constrained by what the world thinks.

It's not as though I had a clear aim in my life at this time. But I had resolved to quit trying to regulate my life according to other people's standards and expectations. Of course, I realized that starting a new life meant taking my child in my arms and moving forward with her. So, no doubt, that was in the back of my mind. That was one of the principal motivating forces propelling me forward. Otherwise, I felt good, I felt energetic. I was ready.

I have been asked if I didn't feel a little uneasy embarking on a new life like this, but I did not at all. I had worked ever since I was a child, so I had self-confidence rooted in experience. I didn't feel apprehensive at all. I knew I would have to get work right away, but that was fine. I was not thinking along the lines of a life plan where first I would do this, and then I would do that. I just knew the first thing I had to do was get a job. (106–108)

Ready to resume working, Sata found a position in the neighborhood as a café waitress. As it turned out, the experience would open up new worlds to her. As she explains:

So it was really an accident that I started working at Kōroku. But it was wonderful because that's where the group from [the journal] *Donkey* gathered, and it really was an incredible experience. There was definitely a connection between [meeting those people] and my becoming a writer later. . . . (108–109)

I started working in March (1926), and that was around the time that the first issue of *Donkey* appeared. I think they were all getting together to celebrate the publication of the inaugural issue, and they all met at Kōroku for coffee.

Of course, meeting them was pure serendipity for me, kind of like fate. Nakano Shigeharu, Kubokawa Tsurujirō, Hori Tatsuo, Nishizawa Ryūji, and Miyagi Kikuo—they were all young men at the time. It is difficult to put into words just what sort of impression they made on me, what they were like. But I can see each one of their faces so clearly, so vividly in my mind.

They were the same age as me, so they were pleasant to have as customers. Not that they were particularly good customers in terms of the café, as they usually drank only one cup of coffee. But they were so nice, and we waitresses felt like we were their friends. They were all rather poor, so they would have their one cup of coffee and drop a ten-sen coin on the table. They had no money for tips, so they really were not such good customers either for us as waitresses nor for the café itself. Before they ever showed me a copy of *Donkey*, I did not have them pegged as "literary youths." Though they did seem like young nonconformists, people who had not yet started bowing to social pressure. That is, they didn't appear to have regular jobs or anything and they seemed a little eccentric *(fūgawari)*.

After they had been coming to the shop for some time, they said, "We've just put out a little magazine," and they showed me a copy. I think it was Kubokawa [who] showed it to me. Upon looking at the inaugural issue of *Donkey* I was quite impressed and thought to myself that this was quite a little magazine. Murō Saisei (1889–1962) was one of the magazine's supporters, so of course his poetry was in there. But so were people like Akutagawa Ryūnosuke and Hagiwara Sakutarō. I was familiar with these people's names, and my impression was that Akutagawa and Murō were major writers. To feature people of this caliber in a small magazine like this was no mean feat. So I determined that this was quite an impressive effort for such a small literary coterie.

When I had met Akutagawa way back when I worked at Shinryōtei, he was quite a prominent writer. But that was already seven years ago, and he had definitely moved beyond prominent and into the ranks of the major authors of the day. Akutagawa's suicide would occur just the following year. . . .

They showed me a copy of *Donkey* because they were all excited about publishing their first issue, and because they felt proud, I am sure. But they may also have sensed somehow that I was the kind of person who would be interested in literary things. I have suggested that these *Donkey* people were not yet constrained by public opinion, that they were a little eccentric, but after all, I did not at feel alienated from those kinds of people. In fact, they probably thought that I was a little bit weird as well *(fūgawari na onna datta to omotte-ita deshō, ne)*.

So it came about that I met the *Donkey* crowd, I fell in love with Kubokawa Tsurujirō, and got married to him. Those were the days. They were the shining moment of my youth—in a number of different ways.

Whenever they came in, they always came in together, so it wasn't as though I would talk to any one of them individually. People always ask why I fell for Kubokawa, but what can I say? I felt attracted to him. When I fall for somebody, if I start to think about it, then I won't be able to be in love with them. . . .

Why did I like Kubokawa? Well, I suppose there was something about his circumstances at the time that drew me toward him. His parents were both dead and he was on his own in Tokyo, working to support himself. The rest of the group, like Nakano Shigeharu and Hori Tatsuo, were students. Nishizawa Ryūji wasn't going to school, but he was living at home. Miyagi Kikuo's circumstances were similar to Kubokawa's, but he was living on an allowance from his older sister.

Kubokawa's father had been a doctor, but he had died young. Then his mother had died, too, so he was adopted out or something to another family, but he had run away, I think. Therefore, if he didn't work, he didn't eat, so he started working at a savings bank. Not that he told me his whole life story or anything. I just gathered this information about him by talking to others. I guess I felt some kind of bond, a feeling of simpatico with Kubokawa that drew me toward him. . . . (111–115)

Meanwhile, as things progressed rapidly between Kubokawa and me, I changed jobs to a larger café in Asakusa called Shuraku and told my family that they provided housing for me. Actually, I moved in with Kubokawa. It was true that I changed jobs, but I made up the part about living at the café so that I could live with Kubokawa. Only a few months had passed since we first met, but Kubokawa was very impatient and put a lot of pressure on me. I was definitely feeling the pull toward him as well. . . .

My married life with Kubokawa was really my very first period of youthful awakening. I was in love, we were together—I had never experienced that before. At the same time, the young men around *Donkey* embraced me warmly in both a literary and a human sense. They genuinely valued us as part of life's experience. The atmosphere around *Donkey* was particularly like that. I loved reading novels, and this was a time I could make that a part of my life, and I could begin to embark in a new direction. So it was really the springtime of my youth. I was just so happy that I was able to have a period like that in my life. For that, I will always be deeply thankful to Kubokawa. (119–123)

There is a tension in the narrative as Sata reexamines this part of her life. The weight of societal expectations rested heavily upon her. Decisions that she had

*made, like marrying the young Waseda student in the first place, and then at-
tempting suicide together, marked her as an impulsive, unruly young woman
who was not afraid to trespass. Then, her decision to go to work in one of the
new cafés, which were sites of cultural resistance and countercultural energy, is
an indication that she was determined to carve out a new lifestyle for herself no
matter what others might think of her. As Silverberg points out in her article
about the role of the cafés in prewar Japanese culture, "During the modern
years, aesthetes, salaried corporate workers participating in a new white-collar
culture, and literary intellectuals sought refuge in cafés, where they imagined a
revolutionary change that would overthrow the stifling imperial order." She also
notes that there was an eroticized dimension to this kind of employment for
women because of the nature of the waitresses' interaction with male customers.*[10] *In fact, there had been flirting between the men and the waitresses, and
Sata actually put out her hand and stroked Kubokawa's hair in an impulsive
gesture that was, in her own words, both "bold and provocative" (116).*

*The young couple moving in together also broke the social rules of the day.
But the cafés were places where new ideas were hatched and new social roles were
envisioned. As Mariko Inoue notes, the number of cafés in Japan reached some
37,000 by 1933, employing over 100,000 waitresses serving young urbanites in
an atmosphere of "modernity, freedom and excitement."*[11] *Elise Tipton points out
that "contemporaries themselves . . . saw the café as a central symbol of modernity."*[12] *Tipton also observes how the number of cafés multiplied and were
"massified" (taishūka) in the years right after the Great Kantō Earthquake.*

In 1922 there were twenty cafés on the Ginza main street; in 1929, there were
fifty. In 1925 a Central Employment Agency survey counted 7319 café waitresses in Tokyo and 4230 in Osaka. According to a police survey just four years
later, the number of waitresses in Tokyo had jumped to 15,559, working in
6187 cafés and bars throughout the country and 66,840 waitresses in 1930.[13]

*If the Ginza area was the central hub of café activity, the other areas of
Tokyo like Shibuya, Shinjuku, and Asakusa, where Sata wound up working, experienced growth in the number of cafés as well. When Sata met the Donkey
group at her first job at Kōroku and later moved in with one of its members,
Kubokawa Turujirō, she was definitely partaking of the new modern life
(modan seikatsu) of the mid-1920s. The modern life was taking place in the
streets of the cities, and the cafés, "bars, restaurants, dance halls, and cinemas"
were "extensions of the streets."*[14] *Sata was therefore not only striking out in a
new direction and defying some of society's conventions along the way, but she*

was also squarely in the center of the latest trends her society had to offer. In the following section, the narrator takes up the story of how she began her career as a writer.

As a Proletarian Writer

Akutagawa Ryūnosuke committed suicide on July 24, 1927. He was thirty-seven years old. At that time, I was still working at Shuraku in Asakusa, though Kubokawa was urging me to quit and concentrate on my writing.

Kubokawa had gone over to the *Literary Arts Spring and Autumn (Bungei shunjū)* offices to check on whether a manuscript that he had submitted to the magazine *Literary Arts Spring and Autumn* at Akutagawa's urging had been accepted or not. It had not been accepted, but while he was there, he learned of Akutagawa's suicide. We were completely shocked—he was someone I had actually met back in the Shinryōtei days, and since getting together with Kubokawa and being around the *Donkey* crowd, Akutagawa was someone who was always nearby.

At that time, I had just arrived at Shuraku and was upstairs in the waitresses' room, a long, narrow room with a mirror on one wall. Underneath us was the restaurant, and I could hear some of the cooks talking. I could hear one say something like, "Akutagawa Ryūnosuke committed suicide!" I was so shocked. I remember running headlong down the stairs. I could not believe it.

Actually, just three days before I had heard from him. He wanted to talk to me, he said. I am sure he had remembered something about me from before, and he probably knew I had had an experience with suicide. Kobori was close to Akutagawa, so he might well have heard about it from him. I didn't know about that at the time, though, but when Kobori told me that Akutagawa wanted to see me, I went to Akutagawa's house with him. . . .

I had actually met Akutagawa one other time, although it was by accident. One evening I was returning home from the Shuraku café, and I was about to get off the train at Tabata Station, where Kubokawa had come to meet me, when I spotted Akutagawa. He had been on the same train with me so the three of us walked together for a bit. I was Kubokawa's wife, so I walked a little behind the men, but I don't think he recognized me as little "O-Ine-san" from the Shinryōtei. Of course, I recognized him, but I do recall thinking that he had changed somehow. When I had seen him back in the Shinryōtei days, he had cut quite the dashing figure. But this time, walking home from Tabata Station some seven years later, I had the feeling he was a little unsteady on his feet. . . . I remember thinking that this business of writing novels must really be something because it had changed Akutagawa quite substantially.

As a member of *Donkey*, Kubokawa had gone to see Akutagawa about manuscripts, and once he realized that I was the same little Ine-san from the Shinryōtei, he said that he would like to talk to me. At least that's what I thought at first.

That is, I assumed that he wanted to see little Ineko from the Shinryōtei again, since it had been such a long time, but when we met, the subject of the Shinryōtei never came up. He wanted to ask me what I had taken when I attempted suicide. I told him I drank charamela. Akutagawa himself took "veronal." Then he asked me, "After you came back to life, did you ever think about dying again?" I replied, "No, I didn't."

Anyway, I thought it was strange that he would ask me these things. . . . Just three days after we had that conversation, Akutagawa was dead by his own hand. When I heard the news, it was a terrible shock. (133–135)

Opening My Eyes to Society

Akutagawa's suicide sparked an intense debate in intellectual circles at the time. As Akutagawa's poem "From my Switzerland" suggests with his stanzas labeled Lenin One, Two, and Three, interest in Marxism and in revolutionary thought was spreading rapidly. Somehow, his death was connected with that whole discussion. So his death wasn't just the suicide of a single individual, it was related to certain intellectual trends in Japan at that time. Therefore, it was a tremendous shock.

Akutagawa had wanted to meet with Nakano Shigeharu, and I am sure he knew that Nakano was deeply involved with the Marxist movement. Nakano was also involved with the New Man Society (Shinjinkai) at Tokyo University, so when Akutagawa wanted to meet with him, the people around *Donkey* took it as a very significant step. What they may have talked about, I do not claim to know. But after their meeting, *Donkey* continued to move to the left, while Akutagawa committed suicide, so many felt that the meeting may have had a considerable affect on Akutagawa. Especially since Nakano Shigeharu himself was directly involved. (136–137)

At that time, I was also reading Engel's *[Socialism:] From Utopia to Science* and his *The Origins of the Family, Private Property, and the State*, as well as a variety of Lenin's works. I was starting to look at society in a different way as I learned to see capitalist society as a construct *(shikumi)*.

We were renting the second floor of a place where they made geta down below. I began to wonder how it was that these people worked every day from morning until night but still were poor and could barely eat. I thought that I was beginning to understand the reason why. I felt as though a veil that had covered my eyes up until now was being lifted. For this I was very thankful to Engels. I felt a real resonance with him. I liked what he had to say, though "like" may be a little strange.

As the *Donkey* group moved to the left, they began to rethink the philosophy of literature we had embraced up until that point. As a result, we became unable to write. After we put out volume ten, we took a hiatus for a year. Then we put out two more issues, and that was the end. Our lives had changed and we could no longer publish *Donkey*. When we took the hiatus, it was because we were in turmoil intellectually and had grown pessimistic about the relationship of literature to philosophy. Nishizawa and Kubokawa even took up target shooting at a place in Asakusa. (138–139)

Sata's narrative chronicles an important turning point in Japan's literary history. Writers and intellectuals were starting to grapple seriously with Japan's relationship to modernity. Critics on the left were drawn to Marxism and were seeking a more socially conscious brand of literature. At the same time, the state had already indicated its aversion to ideologies other than the emperor-centered statism promoted by the particularistic Meiji Constitution. The government had already cracked down on socialism, anarchism, and Marxism since the early twentieth century by censoring journals, arresting editors, breaking up meetings and demonstrations, and jailing leftists. Mass arrests of Communist Party members were about to begin in 1928. So the political and discursive space available to those on the left was severely limited. When Akutagawa committed suicide it sent shock waves through literary and intellectual circles. If a writer of his stature despaired, what chance was there for others? For the members of the proletarian writers' groups, the historic meeting between their leader, Nakano Shigeharu, and Akutagawa signaled a shift, a passing of the torch. For a young writer like Sata, it was a time to be inspired. She describes the process of how she became a writer in the section below.

From the Caramel Factory

At that time, I was having my eyes opened by Engels, my way of looking at society was changing, and I was getting involved in Kubokawa's work. So when Nakano Shigeharu asked me to write something, I felt that if I could do something useful for the movement, then I would. So that's how I started writing *From the Caramel Factory*.

I felt that if someone like myself, who had not been able to stay in school but had been working since they were little, could sit down and write about their experience with that sort of sensibility, and if it could benefit the movement in any way, then I ought to try my hand at writing. So even if we think of it as just writing, it was really quite a bit more than that. . . . Kubokawa encouraged me to become a writer. At that time, I figured that novels would be difficult but that an essay, dealing with something from my personal life, was something I could write. . . . *From the Caramel Factory* actually began as about an eight-page essay. But Nakano Shigeharu urged me to lengthen it and make it a novel, so I decided to do so. . . . Nakano would write later that Kubokawa Tsurujirō discovered Sata Ineko the woman, but that he had discovered Sata Ineko the writer, and, by and large, that is accurate. . . . (144–146)

From the Caramel Factory was published in *Proletarian Arts* in February 1928, when I was twenty-four years old. In 1930, it was published in book form by Senkisha as volume eight in the *Japan Proletarian Writer's Series (Nihon puroretaria sakka sōsho)*. Three thousand copies were printed, and it sold for twenty-six sen a copy. It was the first book I ever published.

What sort of reaction to *From the Caramel Factory* was there? These days, there is usually quite a bit of fanfare when a new writer publishes her first work, but at that time, they really didn't make such a big to-do about things. So there really wasn't any sort of organized response. But a columnist for the *Yomiuri shinbun* noted in passing that a certain Kubokawa Ineko had authored a piece called *From the Caramel Factory* in *Proletarian Arts*; in his opinion, though, it probably was not authored by a woman, but by a man, instead. Reading that at the time, my response as a woman was that this was quite interesting.

At the time, I took these words to the effect that it must have been a man who wrote my work as a form of praise, so I was delighted. It was the only critical notice taken of *From the Caramel Factory*.

The reason I took the notion that even though the author's name was clearly female it was probably written by a male as praise is because, in those days, the standards for male writers were much higher.

The French avant-garde female writer Marguerite Duras once said the same thing. "When I was twenty, when someone said, 'It seems like a man wrote this,' I was very happy." This was probably because she was aware that women were looked down upon and that the critical standards were higher for men, so she was delighted. When I read her remarks for the first time I felt, "So, things are exactly the same for a French woman writer!"

At that time, women's social position was quite low, and there was this attitude that it was very assertive for a woman to write. But Kubokawa himself was trying to become a writer, too, and he had high hopes for what literature could do. So if I wanted to write, he thought that was great, because he believed in literature as a whole. And then there was the proletarian literature movement, so he helped me, gave me encouragement, and tried to bring out the best in me.

The fact that I had the opportunity to meet the *Donkey* group really signaled a change in my destiny. I suppose, for their part, they were amazed to run into such a strange person as myself.

After all, my experience up to that point was limited to working at the caramel factory and the Shinryōtei at Ueno. I hadn't even finished elementary school. I had worked at Maruzen, married into a wealthy family, then attempted suicide. Then I took my daughter with me and divorced my first husband. So mine were hardly the experiences of the average young girl. No doubt, for the young men around *Donkey* my life experiences were quite intense, and it was a source of wonder to them that a woman like me would appear among them. For young people interested in literature, I imagine it was something of a stimulus. They were very interested in someone with the kind of experiences I had had. (147–149)

In the following section, Sata discusses her reflections on what it meant to become a proletarian writer.

My Activity as a Proletarian Writer

In 1928, at Yodobashi, which is now near the West Exit of Shinjuku Station, there was a group of left-wing activists who had been fired from a cigarette factory for the union activities. Guided by one of their number, I went to the factory to gather data. There were wives working there whose mothers-in-law would bring their babies to them to nurse. On one occasion, I borrowed one of these babies, strapped it to my back, and entered the factory gates and proceeded to the waiting room. So I was able to get a good look around at conditions, and I visited workers in their homes in order to listen to what they had to say. So really, more than writing about conditions in the cigarette factory, I would write about the consciousness of the workers employed there.

You might say it was presumptuous of us as proletarian writers to think that we could speak for these workers and the conditions in which they found themselves, but we felt it was our duty to try to depict the situation of the conscious worker. That is why I went to gather authentic material. In particular, I was told that it was significant to depict the lifestyle of conscious members of the working class.

To speak in this manner may sound like bragging, but I always wrote from the viewpoint of the proletarian class, even when I was writing for a regular commercial magazine. Which meant that I always was aware that if what I wrote wasn't appropriate to a proletarian writer, then it would reflect badly on the entire proletarian literary movement.

But even though I grew up with the unique experience of working since I was a child and didn't get to complete my elementary school education, my family origins were petit bourgeois. So I understood that I was not really a member of the working class. When one is writing, feelings emerge from unexpected quarters; it was inevitable that in my case, these kinds of hidden feelings that would emerge would be as a member of the petit bourgeoisie, which would not be the same as a native-born member of the working class.

The fact that we had to be aware of our lack of this feeling was a definite drawback for the proletarian literary movement. But the things that I wrote, from that point down to the present, did not really contain that working-class element. In the end, I was writing about myself, as someone who had connections to the labor movement.

If there hadn't been the proletarian movement, I probably wouldn't have written at all. If it hadn't been for the proletarian literary movement, I would never have written *The Apprentice Maid (Omemie)* or *From the Caramel Factory*. If it were just me who was feeling sad and miserable, I would not have written these works. I had probably told people that this or that thing had happened to me, but I had never thought about writing up my experiences and sharing them with the world. So, proletarian literature provided my launching pad. Without it, I would never have become a writer. I don't think I would have ever taken up writing. (153–155)

Barbara Foley's study of American proletarian fiction, Radical Representations, *offers an extensive discussion on how writers and critics struggled to define proletarian fiction. Did the author have to have roots in the working class to be authentic? Must the subject matter be exclusively proletarian? Basically four criteria were considered the most fundamental: "authorship, audience, sub-*

ject matter, and political perspective."[15] *While exceptions like Josephine Herbst's* The Executioner Waits *and John Dos Passos'* U.S.A. Trilogy *loomed prominent, it was generally accepted that proletarian literature was supposed to represent the life of the proletariat, with an emphasis on what their daily work life was like.*[16] *Clearly, as we saw above, Sata struggled with her nonproletarian social origins and went to some lengths to discuss the methodology with which she worked. According to the standards discussed by Foley and others, by virtue of the depth of her reflexiveness on her own literary processes, as well as her dedication to researching her subjects, Sata would have been judged a legitimate proletarian writer in the United States. In the following section, Sata reproduces a review of her* The Restaurant Rakuyo (Resutoran Rakuyo) *by legendary author Kawabata Yasunari.*

Resisting Oppression

When *The Restaurant Rakuyo* appeared, it was actually reviewed by Kawabata Yasunari. That was quite a privilege to get that kind of attention. I was amazed. He started the review off by saying, "In order to review *The Restaurant Rakuyo*, I would like to break out a new, different pen." I was very grateful. After all, I was a virtual newcomer. This is how the review went:

Ms. Kubokawa's *The Restaurant Rakuyo*
In order to review Ms. Kubokawa Ineko's *The Restaurant Rakuyo*, I would like to break out a new, different pen. I want to change from rough, unpolished sentences to modest sentences with hidden light. Because, in the same way, this work—especially the author's measured serenity—incites in me a feeling of deep respect.

This novel presents the truth about the life of restaurant waitresses. It is the truth as seen from within them. Recently, in literary works, waitresses have been depicted with a great deal of flair, like the blossoming of a grand flower. But these depictions have been too superficial, even focusing on the bizarre, so that there is no way the waitresses themselves would recognize these portrayals as a true representation. The truth is always the true. These words make me recall that this kind of penetrating observation, coupled with a structure which embodies a gentle, feminine awareness, is extremely rare. The flow of the lifestyle of these women as depicted here seems very lonely.

But within this loneliness, we can also feel a warm-heartedness which flows from the author's style, a style which sustains the sense of reality, while at the same time reminding us of the author's bold presence of mind.

This work appears in this journal, so I will keep my remarks brief, but I think we can say that this author has presented to the literary world a small segment of truth. It is modest, and at the same time, bold; it is detached, but at the same time, passionate.

I do not know if it really is such a well-constructed novel, but I do think that I handled the depiction of the real-life experiences of these wait-resses at a large café. And I appreciate the fact that Mr. Kawabata realized that I was not attempting to show the gaudy, outer side of their lifestyle, but, instead, to write about their lives from what was going on inside them. So I was grateful for Kawabata's insight. (161–164)

Sata goes on to discuss conditions in the "movement" in the early 1930s.

The Japan Proletarian Culture League (Nippon Puroretaria Bunka Ren-mei) was severely suppressed. First Kubokawa, then Tsuboi, Nakano, and Miyamoto Yuriko, were arrested. Those who managed to escape arrest went underground and continued their activities as part of an illegal move-ment. I also joined an illegal organization, the Japan Communist Party, and maintained underground connections with Kobayashi Takiji and Miyamoto Kenji. The following year, Kobayashi was held at the Tsukiji jail, where he was tortured and eventually murdered. It was that kind of era.

Since everyone was getting arrested, we had to carry on with our activ-ities without them, so, naturally, there was no time for one's own work. But for me, all my income came from writing, so I had virtually no money at all. I was lucky to have something to eat. . . .

Kubokawa was released from prison in October of 1933, but by then, the era had become increasingly militaristic and the suppression had be-come much more extreme and violent. In 1935, I was detained at the To-tsuka police station for thirty-eight days between May 11 and June 17 as one of the editors of the Japan Proletarian Culture League's publication, *Working Women (Hataraku fujin)*. As a reason, the authorities claimed that our content had become too radical. Miyamoto Yuriko had been arrested the day before as well.

At the Totsuka police station, I was interrogated by a police detective named Kimura. There was another Kimura who was famous for his inter-rogations, but this was a different person. But I engaged in a battle of wills with him. It was a psychological contest over the fact that I had small chil-dren. I felt that I had done nothing wrong, anyway, so I assumed that when questioning was over, I would just go home. But he refused. This was going to be interesting. Human relations are interesting, human psychology very complex. I persisted in my position and eventually he had no choice but to let me go home.

I had never been interrogated by the police before, but at one point this Detective Kimura slapped my face, saying, "Don't lie to me!" I was telling the truth, but he didn't believe me. Apparently another female activist being detained elsewhere was saying that they had gotten a copy of *Battle Flag (Senki)* from me. At that time, just reading *Battle Flag* was sufficient grounds for pursuing someone.

I told them that the other woman was lying and that they should ask her again. They did, and it turned out she had been lying, so Detective Kimura wound up feeling a little embarrassed by the whole incident. I never did say a word about my connections with Miyamoto Yuriko or my involvement in illegal underground activities, so they never knew. . . . Anyway, this was the manner in which I was prosecuted. The result was a sentence of two years at hard labor, which was suspended, plus a three-year probation period. The official crime with which I was charged was violating the Peace Preservation Law by distributing communist propaganda. Miyamoto Yuriko got virtually the same sentence, though her probation was for four years. . . . (164–174)

After I was released on bail and returned home, Kubokawa became involved with another woman. I had to struggle with the conflict between my position as a wife and continuing with my work. (185)

This issue proved to be a critical one for Sata, one that she dealt with in her autobiographical fiction extensively. Specifically, her novel of a few years later, Crimson (Kurenai) *(1936–1938), takes up the issues that arose between her and Kubokawa, which she explores below.*[17]

My Position as a Wife and My Work

In 1933, when Kubokawa got out on bail, the movement was all but destroyed. The cultural movement had been oppressed and the organization was lost. . . .

Our life had changed, also. While I personally felt that I wanted to continue to resist, the loss of our movement's shape and organization hampered my desire, a situation that persisted for the next ten years or so. . . . As far as that went, I had my writing. It was my principal work. So the first thing

I had to do was to keep expressing myself through my writing. But, in order to do that, there were many demands stemming from everyday life that I had to meet. In particular, if we were going to return to the previous shape of our lives even though the movement and organization were now gone, then I would have to make being Kubokawa's wife a significant priority.

What it came down to is whether or not my development as a writer would be compatible with my role as a wife. Living in poverty, sharing a small rental house where you cannot lock the door to your room—it creates a lot of problems. Kubokawa would be working in the larger six-mat room, while I would have the three-mat room next door. Inevitably, in cramped quarters like this, little details about everyday life were bound to arise and cause friction.

Even if you try to concentrate on things by yourself, you know that things involving your husband are going on around you. For Kubokawa, he had just gotten out of prison and was extremely eager to get on with his work. Likewise, he was very passionate about constructing his own individual self.

So we were bound to have some conflicts. Even the smallest things in everyday life, like dinner, could be a problem. If I went to the trouble of preparing something, he wouldn't show up. He was going about selfishly building up his own life. I felt that it was up to me to make my life fit in with his. This may sound like a small detail, but it was no trivial matter. At times, I would be working and eager to continue, but I would have to stop in order to prepare a meal. So I would have to stop writing and devote my time to this task. It wasn't only about meals, but numerous other household chores as well.

Something that figured largely in my thinking was that I had already lived by myself. I had already led a life of my own—on my own. For the year and a half Kubokawa was in prison, I had been living on my own, taking care of things by myself. I experienced the feeling of freedom of being in control of my own life.

But when Kubokawa returned home, it was no longer like that. I really felt frustrated with the complexities of trying to fulfill the role of wife.

As far as Kubokawa goes, I believe that he was a kind of victim. He had been incarcerated for a year and a half and all he had was his writing. So he came out of prison newly resolved to commit to his writing. Wouldn't an ordinary wife have done everything she could to support her husband and make his work as easy as possible? But as his wife, I too felt that I had to do my own work. So our attitudes were bound to clash on that front.

Writing is something individuals have to do by themselves. But it was difficult for me because Kubokawa had to operate according to his own schedule. It wasn't that I was incapable of expressing my feelings to him about it. But, looking at it practically, writing criticism really did not bring in the same kind of income that writing fiction did, so it was really my work that provided the main economic support for our household. I really needed for him to respect the fact that my work was important, too. Living together was a pretty delicate operation because Kubokawa was actually giving me a lot of encouragement and support in those days to continue with my own work.

These days, it may not seem like it is so much of a problem. But, in my case, I was probably a little old-fashioned and I had this mind-set about what being a wife entailed.

For example, when Kubokawa would be talking with his friends, and there might be people present whom I knew from my own writing as well, but because I was a woman, if I tried to join the conversation about litera-ture, to put in my two cents, well, let's just say that it very rarely went well. . . . Even though I had worked with these people in the movement and had worked actively as a writer, they still felt that way. Perhaps they assumed that I would say practically the same thing as Kubokawa. So I felt quite odd, as though they saw me as the little wife who would chime in and echo whatever her husband had to say. In the end, I wound up just shutting my mouth and serving tea not because I agreed with what Kubokawa was say-ing and therefore didn't feel the need to add anything, but because I was being denied the space in which to speak my own mind *(atashi no mono o iu ba ga nakunatchau mitai na)*. . . . Opinions are opinions and I wanted mine to be heard. Anyway, it was very complicated and messy. The "cute woman" in Chekov was able to triumphantly repeat exactly what her hus-band would say, but I wasn't that kind of "cute woman."

It was around that time that Kubokawa began to get involved with another woman. (186–189)

Complicated and messy—yet hardly an unfamiliar problem. Takamure Itsue has struggled with many of the same issues. Sata needed some space of her own and an identity of her own in order to become the writer she believed she could be. She was not willing to play the role of the "cute" and adoring wife in a Chekov play. She wanted—indeed, needed—something more. She continues:

So, I felt that I wanted to establish the grounds of my own life through my work. At the core of this was my belief in the inevitably of the work we had to do. Therefore, it was difficult for Kubokawa. I had to withdraw from him somewhat because I was the one who introduced the notion of needing to work on my own into our lives. And that gave Kubokawa cause to . . .

He said he wanted to leave me and marry another woman. He said she was like me, not just in terms of her looks, but in her character as well. . . . When he showed me a picture of her I thought she seemed like a nice young woman with a pleasant air about her. He said it was a picture taken when she was traveling with her aunt, but I felt strongly that a man had taken the picture. I have a very keen sense about these things. I don't say this out of anger. But if two women were traveling together, wouldn't they have their picture taken together? Besides, there she sat smiling in her *yukata* with an expression that could have been meant only for the person taking the photo. Kubokawa was surprised at my comments and said something like, "Yeah, maybe so."

This is the way we opened up our discussions, so the idea of separating from Kubokawa was now becoming very real, and, for the first time, it seemed like I was really going to be alone.

We had been faithfully living together ever since the early days of *Donkey*. As for myself, this was the time period in which I had grown up, working alongside Kubokawa. Our marriage had never been a very traditional one.

But, the result had been that I had developed my own work, and so we had come to this impasse. Therefore, I couldn't help but feel disappointed.

Now, I was aghast at the idea of being alone. Wouldn't being alone cause me to wither? I felt as though all my emotions and sensitivities would be exhausted. Writers need an emotional reservoir that is as rich and sensitive as possible. I was fearful that living alone might deplete that reservoir. Then, I fell into a depression over my clumsy, agitated response to my shock [at being left alone]. I thought seriously about sucking on the end of a gas pipe in the kitchen.

I felt it was my own fault that things had turned out the way they had. That's why my disappointment was so profound. In the case of my first marriage, which ended in a suicide attempt, I was told it was my fault. So it seemed that whenever there was no place left to go, it somehow always came to rest on my shoulders. . . .

But, of course, I had the children to think of and the fact that I was just beginning to emerge as a successful proletarian writer. So what impact would my suicide have in these two areas? It wouldn't be just my own self-destruction, but it would mean erasing any of the accomplishments in my life so far. If people who write in order to herald the liberation of women give up and commit suicide, then the whole movement might as well collapse. It would be a sign to the world that I was giving up. . . . (190–192)

Even today, marriages where the woman has a job and supports herself face all sorts of problems. Money is, of course, an issue, but it is not solely a money issue either. When a woman has a job, she begins to measure her own self-worth by how interesting her job is. This inevitably becomes a factor in her consciousness.

If this were not the case for me, if I hadn't focused my attention on this sort of thing, then my own writing would have been meaningless drivel. But, in fact, I had to write about what was happening to me, so our problems became the foundation of the themes in my own writing.

For the past fifty years, right down to the present, the problem for women of having to choose between work and marriage has persisted.

There are some women who forego marriage and immerse themselves in their work. But, it is not possible that men could get along without ever getting married. Men need a wife as an assistant. It's just the opposite for women. Far from getting an assistant, in most cases, women wind up sacrificing their own work for married life. Since the end of the war, I have had occasion to meet and work with a number of female reporters, but most of them remain single. I think that is pretty harsh. . . .

In our day, it just wasn't possible to have separate quarters for work so that we might have kept our marriage intact even though we might spend a lot of time apart. But the whole social system at the time could only conceive of a wife living with her husband and taking care of the household. These days, apartments are a common form of living arrangement, and there are lots of electronic appliances so that the possibility for a man to live separately and take care of himself has expanded. With all these changes in the external environment, it has been possible for people's consciousness to change as well.

But at that time, it wasn't like in America where a man might get up and fry himself an egg as though it were perfectly natural. Today, even in Japan, this wouldn't be uncommon. But back then, a man would have considered it an insult to have to prepare his own breakfast. So it was definitely a different consciousness back then.

But even today, when men may fry themselves an egg without giving it any further thought, the problems with work and marriage remain very large. (203–204)

In much the same way that Takamure Itsue confronted the conflicts in her marriage to Hashimoto Kenzō, Sata raises some of the most fundamental questions facing working couples. She pursues the discussion even further than Takamure did, however, as she delves into the basic issues confronting her marriage. Despite all that she has accomplished with her writing, her work is not taken seriously, and it is assumed that it must take second place to her husband's. Yet when he admits to having an affair and expresses an interest in divorce, the narrator is nearly paralyzed with fear. She does not know if she can face being alone. She contemplates suicide. There is a poignant moment in the text where the narrator describes looking at the photograph of the young woman with whom her husband has taken up. Given her attire and her smile, she knows that the photo was taken when they were away together somewhere. The woman's smile and her eyes reveal that whoever is taking her picture is someone with whom she is intimate.

This perception itself was painful, but infidelity is not the most significant challenge that Sata perceives in the marriage. What is at stake—and the narrator suggests that this is as it has always been for women—is who gets a space of their own within the marriage to work and grow. At one point, the discussion comes down to the narrator's perception that women can live alone and make it, but Japanese men in the prewar era were just not capable of functioning without someone to pick up after them and prepare their meals. So who is it that has to sacrifice their work for the marriage? Experience would suggest that it is not going to be the man.

In this section, the narrator has "told it messy." She has gotten right down to the details of what is at stake when two people are trying to sustain their commitment to their work. As a fiction writer, the narrator tells us, she could not do other than make these issues the stuff of her novels and short stories. She understands that for women who work, money is not the only issue, nor is independence, though both are important. A woman derives her sense of self-worth from what she does, and this is what cannot be easily sacrificed. As she agonized over what to do, even contemplating suicide, she realizes that this would not constitute any kind of solution, because not only were there her children to think about, but everything she had been working for in her life so far was at stake.

It wouldn't be just my own self-destruction, but it would mean erasing any of the accomplishments in my life so far. If people who write in order to herald the liberation of women give up and commit suicide, then the whole thing would collapse. It would be an indication to the world that I was giving up.

Erasure is something that women writers like Sata and the other autobiographers in this volume go to great lengths to overcome. When we examine her statement above and measure it against her assertion that inevitably her own marriage problems would find their way into her fiction, we see that her overarching commitment was to women's issues and "the liberation of women." Ultimately, this was something she was unwilling to compromise. Sata dealt with the break up of her marriage to Kubokawa in her novel Crimson, *so she begins the next section of her autobiography with a brief quotation from that book.*

Perpetrator or Victim

In *Crimson*, the narrator says to the character Nagami (modeled on Nakano Shigeharu), "I really think we lived well together. We both helped each other grow. But in times like these, contradictions emerged." To which the Nakano character responds, "Well, can't you reconsider and try again to work things out?" which was really about all he could say.

In fact, that's the way it was, though. It was difficult. That was the karma of women who worked. They had to operate within the limits of the existing system. These days, things are different. But in those days, we faced these kinds of limitations, and it was always my hope for the future that the possibilities for women to live a more liberated existence would expand throughout the society. However, within the limitations of the day, I was dancing very close to the edge.

> Destroying the framework of limitations.
> Rebelling against the expectations placed on wives.
> Or rebelling against the things that were personally controlling me.

But all of these things meant that I was in conflict with my own husband.

I was the one who originally talked about needing to have separate lives. So Kubokawa didn't go out and womanize. I chased him out. Therefore, Kubokawa always saw me as the perpetrator and himself as the victim. . . . On the other hand, I never experienced any consciousness of being a victim. Consequently, I never thought of Kubokawa as the perpetrator. . . . (204–205)

Crimson took as its larger theme the problem of wives and work. Subjectively, I think it had a certain meaning. But when Kubokawa began a love affair next with Tamura Toshiko, there was no other way to say it but that our relationship was irretrievably damaged. And the destruction was mutual *(otagai no haiboku to shika iiyōga nai)*.

By saying this, I am not trying to let Kubokawa off the hook by any means. But I just feel that both parties must bear responsibility for problems in the marriage and the ruin they bring to our lives *(otagai no jinsei no haibokuda to omou shika nai)*. (207–208)

In the following section, Sata begins to tell the story of her husband's involvement in a love affair with the writer Tamura Toshiko (1884–1945). Tamura had begun writing in the early 1900s, well before the feminist Hiratsuka Raichō had begun publishing the literary journal Seitō, *and before feminism had begun to exert such a powerful intellectual influence on female writers. Nevertheless, she wrote stories that explored feminine consciousness, and she had gained a solid reputation by 1913 when her best-known work,* The Mummy's Painted Lips *(Miira no kuchibeni), appeared. Married to Tamura Shōgyō, Toshiko fell in love with a younger married man, Suzuki Etsu, and after he left his wife and moved to Vancouver, British Columbia, Toshiko followed. They married and lived in Vancouver for eighteen years while Suzuki, a journalist, worked on a newspaper for Japanese immigrants,* The Continental Daily News, *and later started his own newspaper,* The People, *in order to support his labor-organizing efforts. While on a trip back to Japan in 1932, Suzuki was stricken with appendicitis and died the following year. Toshiko, who had not been writing any fiction for the past twenty years, returned to Japan in 1936, where she soon encountered the young writers Kubokawa Tsurujirō and Ineko. Sata relates the story below.*

From Kubokawa to Sata

Tamura Toshiko returned to Japan from North America on March 28, 1936, after living eighteen years in Vancouver [British Columbia]. She was fifty-one years old. . . . When Tamura was interviewed by a newspaperman at Yokohama, she was asked if she was familiar with any of the contemporary women writers in Japan. She replied that she liked Kubokawa Ineko and that she had high expectations for my work. This was reported in the newspaper. When I saw it, I felt incredibly honored and was very impressed.

I think that her reason for mentioning me was at least partly philosophical. That is, it wasn't entirely that she thought I was a great writer, but that she was interested in me because I was a proletarian writer. She had been in the movement herself, in America. At least, this is how I felt about it. . . . She never spoke much about her activities in the socialist movement in the United States. But this was a period when, given the conditions in Japan, and the circumstances we found ourselves in, the movement had all but disappeared.

At that time, Kubokawa and I were trying our best to work things out. Kubokawa had a room to work in on the second floor of his married younger sister's home, which was right in our neighborhood. Meanwhile, I was working at our house. He still bore the scars from our marital relationship, and I am sure he was very lonely.

His dissatisfaction with me, that is, his frustration over my unwillingness to meet his demands, still persisted. Somewhere deep inside, I probably felt that to some degree I had let him down. He said that his affair with the other woman was over, and he wanted to come back and try again, so we were trying to sort things out. Why, then, at just at that time, would he start going to see Tamura Toshiko at her apartment? I wondered what that was about. . . .

Even before I knew anything about their relationship, I could see the two of them together in my mind's eye. The image of Tamura Toshiko as his other woman just popped up in my mind suddenly one day. I have no idea why. But women just have a sixth sense about these kinds of things where their husbands are concerned. When a woman is suffering, her senses become peculiarly keen and can be very precise even to the point of surprising oneself. . . . (209–212)

[People always say that] "because she is a woman," she agonizes over her experiences. I felt constrained by this kind of judgment. I wanted to reject this version of the feminine; I wanted to get rid of any vestiges of it I might carry. Therefore, I cut off my long hair, and I changed how I wrote the *ine* part of my name from *hiragana* to *kanji,* employing the character for rice (稲).

I came to really dislike seeing Ineko written in hiragana. . . . As part of this overall reaction of mine, I had come to hate even my own name. . . .

Miyamoto Yuriko wrote in 1948 in *Women and Literature (Fujin to bungaku)* that Kubokawa Ineko had become Sata Ineko. With this, she continued, we may see some ideas, rooted in the period before she became a writer, which she hasn't been able to utter up till now, get expressed. This is like, she wrote, the main character in *Crimson,* who, reflecting late in life, says, "I will make every effort to continue to live my life well, making use of all my ideas as a woman."

I will end my text with the entry into my chronology, which appears in the published version of my complete works, *Complete Works of Sata Ineko (Sata Ineko zenshū),* under the entry for:

1945 (Showa 20), age 41 years
From the fall of this year, the author began to use the pen name Sata Ineko.
(236–238)

Analysis

*In this way, the narrator brings her text around full circle, to a turning point in
her life when she finally established herself as an independent woman with a
profession and an identity of her own. Tired of having her femininity defined for
her by others, she cut her hair, changed her name, and generated a new subjectivity. In doing so, she reveals to the reader what is meant by her title,* Between
the Lines of My Personal Chronology. *What may appear as a brief, innocu-
ous entry in the chronological recounting of her life is really the culmination of
all her experiences up until that point in her life when she turned forty-one.
When she changed her name to Sata she was not just reinventing herself, but
discovering a way to* re-present *herself to the world. In the official record of her
life, the one that is part of the authoritative edition of her complete works, there
is this one little entry about adopting the pen name Sata. But we readers know
there is a much more complex story behind this entry. It is the story of the family
from which she emerged, the family she tried to create and sustain, and her
need, finally, to be on her own. When she writes of these things, she knows she
is taking a risk because she is prepared to contest the sources of authority that
prevail in society.*

*As we have seen, autobiographies, by their very nature, are not only texts
that have to do with self-representation and identity, but they involve contestation and risk as well. For many feminist critics, it follows that since women's
lived experiences of life are different from men's, their attempts to reconstruct
and tell their lives will challenge assumptions about the former. Absent is a unitary, stable self; in its place is a voice that may sound more disrupted, more discontinuous, and more fragmented. Gilmore summarizes some of the points that
many feminist critics would accept with regard to the different assumptions
about how male and female autobiographies may represent the individual.*

> Insofar as feminist criticism of autobiography has accepted a psychologizing
> paradigm, it reproduces the following ideological tenets of individualism:
> men are autonomous individuals with inflexible ego boundaries who write
> autobiographies that turn on moments of conflict and place the self at the
> center of the drama. Women, by contrast, have flexible ego boundaries, de-
> velop a view of the world characterized by relationships (with priority fre-

quently given to the mother-daughter bond) and therefore represent the self in relation to others.[18]

Sata's text concludes by specifically addressing the question of how a particular individual comes to be represented in a certain way. Would it be fair to say that her narrative has emphasized her relationships with others at the expense of placing herself "at the center of the drama"? It does seem from the opening passages about the premature death of her mother that her text deals primarily *with her relationships with her mother (remembered), her father, her uncle, her husbands, her daughter, and the other people around her in the "movement." This is not to say that she leaves no room in her text to address issues and events central to her own ego. But, on balance, it does seem that relationships play an extremely significant role in her narrative.*

In the conclusion of her text, the narrator reveals to the reader why, by the time she has reached the age of forty-one, she is no longer willing to represent herself in the world either by the name of her father or her husband. She needs a name of her own. So there can be no question that Sata's autobiography deals with how she discovered her voice as a writer and how she moved herself out from under the shadow of her father and her husband in order to define her own subjectivity. That her new name comes from a deceased uncle may seem like a rather ineffectual slap at the patriarchy. But her uncle, Sata Hidezane, represented to her someone who had encouraged her to read and pursue the world of literature. His story was a part of how she became who she was. At least, this is how she has chosen to represent her identity. Even though it was her uncle's name, it was her own subjectivity that was being identified and named. Since he was no longer alive, his name need not be read as something binding Sata to the patriarchy. Rather, it operates as a trope pointing to the means by which she was able to break free from it.

Obviously, a crucial aspect of Sata's identity is her gender. Her story begins with her mother's story and unfolds amid the story of her marriages, her children, her relationships with her father, and with a variety of other people. Her story turns not on dramatic moments of heroic accomplishments, but on the unraveling of her marriage and her struggle to protect the space and time that she needs in order to write. It is the contradictions and the paradoxes of her life that structure and drive the narrative. When the narrator notes that once a woman gets a job, she derives a sense of her own self-worth from that job and that this inevitably affects her consciousness, she touches upon a profound point. For her personally, the sense of self-worth she derived from being a writer became the very foundation of the literature she created. Thus her identity as a writer was

inextricably linked with her gender and with the challenges that marriage pre-
sented to a woman who was committed to continuing to write. Gilmore notes,
"For many women writers, the community into which one is born is not, ulti-
mately, the community to which one belongs."[19] *In other words, women writing*
their lives often must abandon the familiar and the recognizable in order to cre-
ate the space they need in order to write. The narrator of Between the Lines of
My Personal Chronology *makes it clear that her journey entailed removing*
herself from her family of origin, discovering her voice amid a group of young,
idealistic leftists, marrying one of these young men, and then struggling to pre-
serve that marriage only to find in the end that she needed to escape these bonds
as well. If marriage, for a woman, means forgoing that sense of self-worth that
she had struggled to achieve, then she would have to take steps to locate herself,
and represent that self, on grounds outside of those defined, delineated, or con-
strained by men.

   De Lauretis likes to use the notion of the "space-off" from film theory—"the
space not visible in the frame but inferable from what the frame makes visible"—
in order to underscore the significance of "those other spaces both discursive and
social that exist, since feminist practices have (re)constructed them, in the mar-
gins (or "between the lines," or "against the grain") of hegemonic discourses and
in the interstices of institutions, in counter-practices and new forms of commu-
nity."[20] *Sata Ineko struggles to create just these kinds of spaces in her quest not*
only to discover her own voice, but to address the tensions that emerged between
what she calls below her "own direct experiences" and the dominant discourse.

Afterword

As a novelist, I have written works that draw mostly on my own direct experiences. If you want to say that I have made the things that happened to
me the subjects of my novels, then I guess you could say that my novels
tend toward being I-novels *(shishōsetsu)*. Since they are all about subjects
close to me, and since they pretty much follow the facts, then my past has
really already been depicted in these works. This has been my style, so I
am not about to find fault with it now. So, if my works contain all the
things that have happened to me, for a writer like myself, all that is left is
to acknowledge that.

   Therefore, I never thought that I would write an autobiography. I had
been asked to several times, but I always refused. However, one can say
that this text, *Between the Lines of My Personal Chronology*, is just such an
autobiography. Originally appearing in nine installments in special issues

of *Supplementary Issues of* Women's Review *(Bessatsu fujin kōron),* it tells of
my emergence as a writer, up through the end of the Pacific War when I
changed my name to Sata Ineko. I use the word "tells" quite literally, as I
had a listener, someone to whose questions I responded. So I literally *told*
my life. My listener was Hishida Junko, from the editorial staff of *Bessatsu
fujin kōron,* who was very skilled at eliciting my story from me, which I told
very frankly. If it seems kind of rough in places, that is why. I am a little embarrassed by the spoken quality of the language in the text. . . .

I am a little uneasy about how people will take what I have tried to say
when I tell my story in this autobiographical fashion. If there are readers
who have never before encountered Sata Ineko, then I would hope that
they could see that I am just one female writer who, for the first half of her
life, has wandered down a certain path. It is a path on which a woman,
who would probably be seen today as old-fashioned, has been plagued by
exhaustion but has continued to forge ahead, always looking, always
searching. (239–240)

*When she notes in passing that almost all of her fiction is already autobiograph-
ical, Sata inadvertently touches upon an important aspect of self-writing in Japan. If fiction is already presumed to be about the author's life and follows his or
her own experiences rather closely, what room is there, discursively speaking, for
actual autobiography itself? Since most of the autobiographies I have happened
upon do not contain a wealth of personal, intimate details, it may be argued
that Japanese readers and writers assume that such revelations are best left to
the world of autobiographical or semiautobiographical fiction. Moreover, in
terms of narrative and rhetorical style, autobiographies read very differently
from fiction. They epitomize a frank, matter-of-fact, unadorned style that addresses the reader directly. The point of autobiography in Japan seems to be to
tell the story in a forthright manner and to set the record straight, something
that is always accompanied by risks. Most of the authors we have encountered in
this volume have done something for which they are well known, perhaps even
notorious. The object of their textual excursions into the realm of self-writing is
to tell their story as best they can and situate that story in the context of the
times and of other parts of the narrator's life story. In doing so, of course, they
are not just recounting some facts about their lives and their experiences, but
they are claiming a piece of the public space as an acceptable place for women to
be and in which to discover their voice.*

*Now, Sata already had established her voice in the world of fiction, and
most of her fiction has much to say about the experiences she encountered in her*

life. But her act of finding space "between the lines" of her personal chronology
was her way to engage in what Janet Varner Gunn calls a "cultural act of self-
reading" whereby the author reads her own life and reconsiders its meaning in
the context of her encounter with her own text.[21] *A reader familiar with Sata's*
fiction can infer a great deal about what her life may have been like, but here
Sata gets to "tell it straight," engaging in the act that Gunn refers to as "taking
oneself up and bringing oneself to language."[22] *What this means for Gunn (and*
for Sata as well) is that

> What is presenced is a reality, always new, to which the past has contributed
> but which stands, as it were, in front of the autobiographer.[23]

The narrative voice that is heard in a text like Sata's is the voice of someone who
stands before the text of her own life and interprets it as she reads, displaying
another form of the so-called doubled subjectivity characteristic of women's self-
writing. She positions herself "between the lines" and writes from the margins of
hegemonic discourses, where she is able to both re-create and re-present her own
past.

6

Resisting Authority

Fukunaga Misao's Recollections of a Female Communist (*Aru onna kyōsanshugisha no kaisō*)

Fukunaga Misao. Reproduced with permission from Renga shobo.

Hatano Misao was born in Hyōgo Prefecture in 1907 and studied at Tokyo Women's College. There she became involved with a Marxist study group and secretly joined the Japan Communist Party in 1927. She married Koreeda Kyōji, editor of The Proletarian News (Musansha shinbun) *and one of the party leaders, but this marriage ended in divorce. She was arrested and imprisoned for her communist activities but refused to recant even though all the top leaders, including her husband, did so. After the war, she married Mr. Fukunaga, a writer and China specialist; she continued her studies of the* Tale of Genji *and the history of the Japanese imperial institution, which she began while she was imprisoned.*

Most of the women whose lives are examined in this volume were influenced by Marxism or other radical ideologies. Fukuda Hideko was attracted to the budding socialist movement while Takamure Itsue was drawn to anarchism. Oku Mumeo read widely in works about socialism and revolution. She knew who the leading Marxists and feminists of the day were and read their works eagerly.

Takai Toshio was introduced to feminist ideas by Hosoi Wakizō and learned about socialism and labor organization from Takai Shintarō, as well as from her own experiences working in the mills. Nishi Kiyoko thoroughly explored Marxism and socialism in her student days and considered herself a "Marx-Engels" girl. Sata Ineko owed her whole sense of what the role of a writer should be to her roots in the proletarian literature movement, and she joined the Japan Communist Party as well. But none of these women embraced Marxism or the Japan Communist Party as wholeheartedly as did Fukunaga Misao. Although she began reading about Marxism as a college student, by her own admission she was still a neophyte when she joined the party. But she continued to read Marx and Lenin and to participate in cell meetings after she joined the party. By her own definition, she was a dedicated communist. In the afterword to her autobiography, Recollections of a Female Communist, *she observes the following about her career in the party.*

I was just a rank-and-file party member without a record in the movement of any particular significance. What is special about my recollections, I believe, is the fact that I am a woman. Engels pointed out that in modern society, men were the bourgeoisie while women were the proletariat. To build upon what Engels wrote, one might say that in prewar Japan men were the slave masters and women were the slaves. We believed that the Japan Communist Party was the party that would fight for women's liberation, so we were willing to dedicate ourselves to the party. But whether or not this was actually the case, I have addressed in my text. The United States' bona fide system of slavery was abolished thanks to the Civil War of 1861–65 (an internal war among the whites), but everyone knows that more than one hundred years later, discrimination against black people has hardly been eliminated. Japanese women, thanks to defeat in war in 1945 and the policies of the occupation, were given political rights, but the reality of discrimination against women in the social life of Japanese people is something that women still experience every day. In order for women to live in this world as ordinary human beings, they must do nothing less than concentrate their efforts and persist in the fundamental self-consciousness that they are independent, autonomous human beings entitled to equality with men.

In her own words, then, what makes this narrative interesting is not what she accomplished as a young Communist Party worker in prewar Japan, but her insights as a woman in her experiences. In her view, women remain objects of discrimination in Japanese society, and, therefore, it is incumbent upon them to work to attain their independence and autonomy as human beings. It is difficult to imagine a more self-conscious declaration of the centrality of gender issues to a text. As Sidonie Smith notes, texts that "contest sovereignty" and "engage in self-consciously political autobiographical acts" deserve to be called "autobiographical manifestos."[1] Fukunaga declares here that her text will contest any claims by the prewar Japan Communist Party that it stood for female liberation.

In Part 1 of her autobiography she discusses three topics: her father, her mother, and herself as daughter. Her father was bright and studious. He gained admittance to the prestigious Second Higher School in Sendai, and from there he entered the even more prestigious law faculty of Tokyo Imperial University. He encountered the conservative legal scholar Hozumi Yatsuka, who was on the faculty, and disliked him intensely. On the other hand, he was fond of his classmate Minobe Tatsukichi, whose liberal interpretation of the Meiji Constitution became widely accepted in the 1920s (12–14). The portrait of her father in the text is, on the whole, a positive one. Fukunaga was the only daughter of her father's second wife, so she had an older stepbrother and an older stepsister. Since her father, a second son, knew quite well what it meant to be discriminated against in favor of the firstborn, he made every effort to raise his three children without showing favoritism. However, she admits that at home he was incredibly tyrannical (monosugoi "kaminari oyaji") and that her mother, his second wife, was the primary victim. She notes,

Society has long recognized that there are fathers who put on a good face in public but are terrible at home, and my father was a typical patriarch in this sense. He managed to fuse without the slightest hint of contradiction a warm face that he displayed to the public with an oppressive strictness that he reserved for his family at home.

The ultimate victim of my father's patriarchal strictness was my mother. The patriarchal atmosphere was so common in Japanese families that it hardly bears mentioning. But what was especially unfortunate for my mother was that my father was extremely knowledgeable and was capable of paying attention to the smallest details. . . . Usually my mother just followed his orders and did what Father said . . . but when his orders were simply impossible to carry out, there would inevitably be a collision between the two. The result was that in the end Mother would disappear into her room for three or four days at a time, crying, unable to emerge even for meals. But even in such circumstances, my father would not budge an inch. When I became old enough to attend girls' school my mother would sometimes turn to me and grumble, "I resolved to get a divorce any number of times, but because I did not feel I could leave you behind, I decided to persevere." (37–38)

Upon hearing this, I could not help feeling that my very existence was a burden to my mother and that I owed her a great deal. However, much later, when I was capable of thinking in terms of social categories, I realized how much of a mistake this really was. Since she was certified as a middle-school-level teacher and was capable of establishing herself as an independent person, if she really wanted a divorce, she should have been able to take me along and leave whenever she wanted to. . . .

If we examine the ideology of patriarchal absolutism from the woman's point of view, we will encounter the philosophy of "good wife, wise mother" (ryōsai-kenboshugi). Being as this was the official Ministry of Education philosophy for women's education since the Meiji era, it had been pounded into my mother's head as part of her training as a teacher. So, really, both parents subscribed to fundamentally the same ideology, and as far as their belief in sternness of character, they were not that far apart. (38–39)

The second part of her introduction takes up Fukunaga's mother, Hama, who was highly intelligent and trained as a teacher. In fact, she had taught successfully for a number of years before marrying Fukunaga's father. But when he received his first appointment as a chief justice for a provincial court in Takamatsu, she was no longer permitted to work outside the home. Fukunaga found a system that would waste someone's talents and abilities like this intolerable. She writes,

As her only daughter, I was the one who understood best what superb intelligence and talent my mother possessed as a young woman, before she got married. My father could not appreciate this about her at all. Her stepchildren—my elder brother and sister—did not really like her. The wisdom and intelligence with which she was born withered away after her marriage, and she became a shell of her former self. There was no opportunity for her abilities to blossom again. My mother's existence within the family was practically a perfect portrait of the ideal "good wife, wise mother" that the Ministry of Education policy prized so highly. When I looked at my mother, I could not help feeling that for any woman who had the desire to live life fully as a human being, this "moral ideal" was nothing but a graveyard. (53)

The narrator here presents an astute and penetrating criticism of the prewar patriarchal family system and the education system that supported it, especially the "good wife, wise mother" rhetoric forced upon females. As the narrator accurately points out, it was nothing more than a "graveyard" for women. As is the case with several of the autobiographers in Telling Lives, *Fukunaga observed her mother's fate with a certain sadness. She watched her talents "wither" and saw her denied any further opportunity to "blossom" after her marriage.*

In the third section of Part 1, "Musume," the author describes the family environment in which she was raised. In a nutshell, Fukunaga did not find her family a very interesting one in which to grow up. Her childhood, it seemed, consisted mainly of sermons and being told to shut up (55). According to Fukunaga, this was the nature of life under the patriarchal system of prewar Japan, a topic she elaborates on as follows.

In other words, under the educational ideology of the patriarchal system, the child is not permitted to make autonomous, independent decisions about anything, be it what they wear or their daily conduct. The first article of a moral education under this system was that in order to be a "good child," one must never make decisions for oneself. Rather, right down to the smallest detail we must ask our parents' permission, respect what they say, and always follow and obey their advice. If one were to "talk back," that is, to express even the slightest reservation or opposition to directions from one's parents, then one was by definition immoral and bad. Prewar Japanese children, then, had it drummed into them by the educational system that to make decisions for oneself, with one's own mind, was to be immoral, to commit a crime. (56–57)

Independence, something prized by most of the women we have examined here, was not something the prewar education system sought to cultivate. As with several others in this study, one of Fukunaga's more significant childhood memories was of the 1918 Rice Riots in the city of Takamatsu. Although it was really only one night of violence, and her parents shielded her from it, she was well aware that every rice broker in Takamatsu was broken into and their rice distributed by rampaging crowds. Fukunaga and her family moved around a great deal due to her father's postings as a judicial official. In 1919, they moved to Urawa in Saitama Prefecture, where Fukunaga graduated from elementary school. She entered Saitama Girls' Higher School, but in the midst of her second year, the family moved to Niigata. Once again, she entered a new school, the Prefectural Girls' Higher School, but in the first term of her senior year, they moved again, this time to Sapporo, where she graduated from the Hokkaido Girls' Higher School. But there were always books to keep her company as she immersed herself in the works of Natsume Sōseki and Tolstoy, along with translations of various foreign works of modern literature.

According to Fukunaga, it was the norm in prewar Japan for graduates of prefectural higher schools for girls to get married right away. Her older sister, who in Fukunaga's eyes was far more attractive than herself, followed this pattern and had a marriage arranged with a Tokyo Imperial University graduate. Apparently her father accepted the fact that things would not go as smoothly for Fukunaga. As she put it: "I think he was resigned from the outset that unlike my older sister, I did not have very good looks. I loved to study, and I had a strong spirit, but was not the type of daughter to go willingly into a marriage arranged by my parents. So it was thought that after I graduated from high school I would proceed to a first-rate university" (62–63). In those days, the only way a woman could proceed to a university was to enter a teacher's college or a women's college. Tsuda College was one possibility, as was Japan Women's College (Nihon Joshi Daigaku), but Tsuda emphasized English too much, and the latter was too strongly steeped in the "good wife, wise mother" mode to suit Fukunaga. Tokyo Women's College (Tokyo Joshi Daigaku), on the other hand, was a relatively new university, established in 1918 by American missionaries, including Edwin O. Reischauer's father, and it offered an atmosphere of academic freedom that appealed to her. She told her parents of her preference, and they did not object. So she took the entrance exam and was admitted in April 1924.

Just after beginning her first term, a poster in the dorm announcing the formation of a Social Science Research Group (Tokyo Joshi Daigaku Shakaikagaku Kenkyūkai) caught her attention. The inaugural meeting would feature Waseda professor Ōyama Ikuo as a speaker, and though she had made no friends yet, Fukunaga was eager to attend. Third-year student Watanabe Taeko, who would later join the Communist Party after graduation and marry Shiga Yoshio, another party activist, was apparently the driving force behind the study group. Highly influenced by the study of socialism as it was being practiced by members of the New Man Society (Shinjinkai) at Tokyo University, Watanabe would pique the interest of Fukunaga and others in Marxism.[2] Fukunaga notes that no one else in her family had any interest in socialism, so she posed the following question.

Since this was the case, how come I became interested in socialism immediately after entering Tokyo Women's College? I, myself, am not even sure how to answer this question. But if I have to say something, then I would say it was nothing other than the impact of the intellectual trends of the times.

The well-known works of Mushakōji Saneatsu and Kagawa Toyohiko had been out since I was in girls' school, so I had read them a long time ago. Their sentimental humanism was already thoroughly outdated by this time. As soon as I entered college, I scouted out the library, and upon discovering a translation of Kropotkin's work, I promptly checked it out and read it. Until he was dismissed from Tokyo University in 1920 for publishing an article on Kropotkin, Morito Tatsuo was a visiting lecturer at Tokyo Women's College, so I suppose that is why there were a number of Kropotkin's works on our library shelves. Although I was vaguely aware that in Japan anarchism was on the wane since Ōsugi Sakae's murder in 1923, I read [Kropotkin's work] with considerable interest. Nineteen twenty-four was the year in which the influence of Marxism grew rapidly, a year in which there was a clear transformation in Tokyo University's New Man Society and the Student Federation ("Gakuren"; *gakusei rengōkai*) movement. While I was still very young at the time and not aware of most of this, I did have a thirst for knowledge and very much wanted to learn more about this new ideology known as socialism or Marxism. Of course, at this time I had no desire as yet to directly participate in anything like the labor movement or a revolutionary movement.

With a background such as this (I suspect that the majority of participants in the study group would have expressed similar kinds of feelings), I carefully read whatever books Taeko would recommend to me. I do not remember all the titles, but I think the first thing I received from Taeko was something called "The Trick of Capitalism" ("Shihonshugi no karakuri"). It was a classic little pamphlet by Yamakawa Hitoshi that explained in simple, easy to understand language the basic ABCs of Marxian economics by posing the question, What is the mechanism by which capitalists are able to exploit laborers? Up until the mass arrests of March 15, 1928, it was customary for anyone participating in the labor movement or the student movement to first of all read this little pamphlet. After I read it, I picked up Bukharin's *The ABCs of Communism (Kyōsanshugi no ABC)* and Kautsky's *An Explanation of the Theory of Capitalism (Shihonron kaisetsu)* as soon as I could get my hands on them, although I cannot recall the precise order in which I read them. However, one thing that is very deeply etched on my memory was reading *The Communist Manifesto (Kyōsantō sengen)*, an illegal pamphlet passed on to me by Taeko. I was told that the Japanese translation was the work of Sakai Toshihiko, but in any case, the powerful lines were superbly translated. The pamphlet was typeset on rather thin, good-quality paper and was not at all bulky.

My fascination with *The Communist Manifesto* was such that I read it over so many times that I practically memorized passages from it. I did not do this just because it represented the essence of Marx and Engels' ideology. I am certain that I was not really equipped at that time to fully understand the significance of what was contained in those sentences. But, to tell the truth, what drew me to the *Manifesto* was that it was the first and only illegally printed work that I ever had in my possession.

Among some of the other works Taeko managed to get a hold of and pass along to us was an English translation of Lenin's *State and Revolution (Kokka to kakumei)*. What I felt extremely excited about when I started to read this was that being a Western book, there were not any deletions or omissions in the text at all. Relying on my dictionary, I read and reread this work over carefully a number of times. (92–94)

According to Fukunaga, 1924 and 1925 were pivotal years for the student movement. In September 1924, Tokyo University hosted the first Student Federation, to which forty-nine affiliated schools sent over seventy representatives. In July 1925, the second such conference was held, with over fifty schools represented by over eighty delegates. At this meeting, "It was determined that the fundamental policy of the Student Federation would be that the student movement should be regarded as one wing of the proletarian liberation movement, and that Marxism-Leninism would be the movement's guiding spirit" (114). Soon, the students would clash with the central government on the issue of military training on campuses, with predictable results.

[F]ierce opposition to the establishment of military training in the schools, which had emerged during the previous year, began to take shape from June of 1925. The organization that sponsored rallies and demonstrations against military education in the schools and fomented agitation was the Student Federation. It goes without saying that the significance of this mass student opposition, which confronted the pro-war militarists head-on, was considerable. Therefore, looking back objectively, the intentions of the ruling class who railroaded the Student Federation under Article 1 of the Peace Preservation Law had little to do with interpretations of law. It was clearly more a case of the ruling class being seriously threatened by the spread of the left-wing student movement. (122)

Fukunaga was particularly concerned with the role of female students within the student movement. As she explains,

It may seem unnecessary to point it out, but at that time we female students were unalterably opposed to any notion of gender discrimination. Moreover, it seems so obvious we need hardly mention it, but we naturally felt that gender equality had to be a fundamental principle of any revolutionary movement. Ever since 1919, when the principle of democracy became a feature of the post–World War I intellectual landscape, with the exception of a few conservative reactionaries, it never occurred to us that when men spoke of socialism that it might belie a deeply rooted lack of respect for women. Also, within the call for equal rights for men and women, we students believed that equal opportunity and coeducation were an integral part of our demands. Accordingly, we never anticipated that in a movement and organization built around the autonomous pursuit of the study of social science (i.e., Marxism) that there would be any need to distinguish between males and females. . . .

One could say that at the time we were young and naive, and, of course, we had no idea that the social consciousness of Japanese people incorporated such an extreme contempt for women. But the leadership of the Communist Party at that time, and its guiding philosophy, was extremely contemptuous of American-style democratic thought, which was seen as "bourgeois democracy." Also, Marxism is an ideology that aims for a far higher order of true human liberation than mere "democracy," so that if the proletarian revolution—which is the Communist Party's objective—is successfully achieved, we were told, not only workers, but all oppressed groups would be liberated; and of course, women—who have long been scorned and oppressed—would be completely liberated immediately without any debate. This was also the drift of what was written in all the books and articles we were diligently studying at this time. So we took these assertions at face value and swallowed them whole, so to speak. Therefore, we believed that however widespread the discrimination against women was in society, among people who call themselves communists or Marxists—and especially among the leadership group— there would be full recognition of the principles of human equality and equal rights between men and women. We had no reason to think that in their everyday-life attitudes they would display any kind of contempt for women or place themselves above us. (126–128)

Ultimately, Fukunaga will have much more to say about the place of women in the prewar Japan Communist Party, but for the moment she continues her narrative by focusing on her engagement with Marxist ideas and her interactions with some of the prominent personalities in the movement from the mid-1920s.

As a result of the crackdown on the Student Federation (December 1925), we had to be prudent about our contacts with various collateral groups, as I indicated above, but on our own campus, we were free to continue our research activities much as before. I believe it was in early 1926 we continued by studying Kautsky's *An Explanation of the Theory of Capitalism*. I can also recall wanting to learn a little more about basic contemporary economic theory, so I read [Rudolf] Hilferding's *A Theory of Finance Capital (Kin'yū shihonron)*.[3]

After reading *Finance Capital*—not right away, but sometime thereafter—our group took up the new edition of Fukumoto Kazuo's *The Process of Revolution against Ordinary Social Structure (Shakai no kōseinamini henkaku no katei)* (published in February 1926). Since we had previously invited Professor Inomata Tsunao to discuss his translation of *A Theory of Finance Capital* with us, we talked about approaching Professor Fukumoto to lecture us upon our completion of his text. So Taeko and I visited Fukumoto where he was staying at the time, the little Kiku-Fuji Hotel near Tokyo University's main gate, and approached him about meeting with us. He agreed readily. Thus a group of seven or eight of us visited him at his hotel on one or two occasions and he gave us some simple lectures. (134–135)

Fukunaga dwells on her contacts with Fukumoto Kazuo (1894–1983) at some length because later she will be branded a "Fukumotoist." She wants the reader to understand, therefore, that she had no special connection to the man or to his brand of Marxism. But he was the up-and-coming star of the Communist Party during these years, and it was only natural for her and her peers to give his writings their due. Fukumoto opposed Yamakawa Hitoshi's party leadership and his willingness to compromise and consider a united-front strategy. Yamakawa had emerged in the summer of 1922 as a prominent communist leader when he published his essay on a "Change in Direction" ("Hōkōtenkan") for the proletarian movement in Japan.[4] Yamakawa believed that while the destruction of capitalism was the ultimate goal, since workers wanted to address their immediate needs for improved working conditions, it was up to the party to take a practical approach and support the workers in their demands in order to prepare them for the ultimate struggle. He identified two aspects to the proletarian movement: the socialist one and the labor-organizing one. He felt that the socialists had failed the working classes by paying too much attention to theoretical principles and not enough to organizing the working class and raising their level of consciousness. This change in consciousness would occur as a direct result of labor organizers working closely with the masses.

When Fukumoto emerged to prominence in 1924, he challenged this view in favor of developing a theoretically correct position for the party. More a theoretician than a party organizer, Fukumoto sometimes alienated lower-echelon party operatives. But for a little more than a year, between 1925–1927, his ideas held sway over the party central committee. In 1927, his position was denounced by Moscow in the 1927 Theses, and his influence was nullified. But for that brief time, he was perhaps the most important figure in communist circles in Japan.⁵

At any rate, Fukunaga's narrative continues with a brief description of Fukumoto's background: a teacher at Yamaguchi Commercial High School. He had been ordered by the Ministry of Education to study abroad earlier, and his extended stays in France and Germany provided extensive exposure to Marxism. Upon his return, he became an editor of a new journal, Marxism, where he regularly published essays on Marxist theory. Among left-wing intellectuals, he soon became a shining new star. For Fukunaga's taste, his style was turgid, his argumentation confused. She claimed it was easier to read the original Marx and Lenin than to try and follow Fukumoto's tortured interpretations. However, her friend Taeko and Shiga Yoshio were among Fukumoto's staunchest supporters, so his works were required reading.

The next section in the text deals with the debate over creating a women's division of the Japanese Council of Trade Unions (Hyōgikai), which took place over three days at the Second National Meeting of the Japanese Council of Trade Unions in April 1926.⁶ What Fukunaga sees behind this issue is the growing rift between the Yamakawas—Yamakawa Hitoshi and his wife Kikue, who were both leading party theorists—and Fukumoto, who was about to usurp their position as the preeminent party theorist. Also at stake was the formation of a broader, more mainstream political organization, the Women's League (Fujin Dōmei), something the Yamakawas opposed. They did not want to see the revolutionary potential of female labor coopted by the more moderate drive to obtain political rights for women, which, as we saw in chapter 2, was being advocated by Ichikawa Fusae, Oku Mumeo, and Hiratsuka Raichō in their Women's League (138–144). The following section launches a discussion about the relationship between males and females in the underground Communist Party movement.

From Joining the Party to Arrest on March 15, 1928

One day in March of 1927, I received a message to meet someone on a street. The person was Nakano Yoshikai. I do not remember exactly which street it was, but as we walked along, he inquired very directly, "How about becoming an active member of the Communist Party?" I said something like, "I would be honored to" *(isshōkenmei yarimasu)*, and that was all there was to it. Very simple. He said, "We'll contact you again about your membership later," and left. The whole thing took less than ten minutes from start to finish—a very short procedure. (163–164)

Fukunaga also records a "strange experience" that occurred in her cell that bears an important relationship to her narrative because it reveals the attitudes of males in the party toward their female comrades. It took place after she transferred to a cell captained by Murao Satsuo.

A little more than a month had passed since I joined this cell when I began to have words with Murao-san and he sent me love letters by mail. As this was unexpected for me, I more or less had a "thanks, but no thanks" kind of feeling about it. . . . [T]o be frank, my instinctive feeling was somehow that he and I were not compatible. Of course, he was very serious, a splendid veteran party member and I was still quite young, with my head filled with a thirst for knowledge. I did not feel that I had the time to waste on fooling around with love affairs. I did not say anything as direct as that; but I just tried to politely refuse his advances without being rude or creating any hard feelings. Alas, it did not appear that I was able to get him to understand. He was very obstinate. Thinking back upon it, I probably would have been smarter just to have given him a clear, flat refusal. In other circumstances, perhaps I could have broken with him cleanly. But since he was our cell leader, I was going to have to see him once a week anyway as a regular member of a secret, illegal organization.

Since things were not going they way he wanted, Murao became increasingly irritable. . . . One day, I received a communication summoning me to Minami's place, so I visited him at his house. . . . I was wondering what it was about when I was told, "Do what Murao-san says."

This was my first time ever to meet Minami Kiichi, but I knew his reputation as a director of the Kantō branch of the Japanese Council of Trade Unions and that he was one of the top leaders of the Japanese Council of Trade Unions' brain trust, so I knew he was greatly respected as a capable organizer. Therefore, I sat for about two hours with Minami, in a room up on the second floor of his house, talking. As soon as I heard a little of what he had to say, I realized that he and I were so different that I might as well be speaking to someone from another country. We just did not live in the same world, and we could not really communicate. Even though I listened to what he had to say, I did not care for him as a person. He probably thought that I was a very disagreeable woman who might as well have been from a different world as well. It appears that he later disparaged me to Murao and Kadoya, calling me a "modern girl" *(moga)*. (177–178)

This incident has to do with how the narrator responded when older, more mature and powerful male party members were trying to exploit women for sexual favors. Murao and Kadoya had come to the party as intellectuals. They had both studied sociology at Tokyo Imperial University, where they joined the New Man Society, the Japanese Council of Trade Unions, and eventually the Communist Party. Both graduated from the university in 1926. Minami Kiichi, about ten years older than the two intellectuals, went to work in a factory after elementary school and got involved with the Communist Party through the labor movement, especially the Greater Japan Federation of Labor and the Japanese Council of Trade Unions. As the section below reveals, eventually this tendency for male party leaders to try and arrange for relationships among party members would have a profound and lasting effect on Fukunaga.

My Marriage to Koreeda Kyōji

Immediately after that final cell meeting I described above, I received a communiqué and went to meet Mr. Shiga Yoshio on the street. I had not seen Yoshio for quite a while, so I wondered what the meeting was about. As we walked, it seemed difficult for him to broach the subject, so he finally just blurted out, "This is rather sudden, but would you be interested in marrying Koreeda?" This was completely out of the blue and took me by surprise. "But doesn't he have a relationship with Ozawa Michiko?" I asked. "No," he responded, "Koreeda and Michiko have already split up." Since Shiga had responded so clearly, I did not feel it was my place to inquire further about the details of how they may have split up, so I did not say anything further. What flashed through my mind as a sudden intuition at that moment was that Shiga was not here to talk about marriage on his own volition, but rather was following a directive from the party leadership. He never said this directly, but I gathered it from his general demeanor and they way he spoke. If this were the case, it was not something I could refuse without a good reason. And, at that point, I did not really have a good reason for saying no. With this in mind, I said something along the lines of "If this is all right with Koreeda, then I don't have any objections," and with that, I parted company with Shiga and returned home.

Later on, I reflected upon this marriage discussion in the following way. While I was active in the student movement, I had not given any thought to the marriage question, and there was no reason for me to do so. I believe that was appropriate given my age, and if I had any free time in those days, I was throwing myself into reading very difficult books. But after joining the party and working for the first time with male colleagues other than those from the student movement, I became aware that in the JCP [Japan Communist Party] young, single women were often put in compromising positions where their freedom was restricted. Given the embarrassment and awkwardness surrounding the situation with Murao's persistence described above, the following vague ideas began to take shape in my mind.

Because of the contempt with which Japanese men view women, and in prewar Japan this was a common social consciousness that ran from the top to the bottom of society, we can say that this kind of discrimination against women was a peculiar feature of Japanese morality. Take, for example, the case of Minami Kiichi, which I mentioned above, who was publicly known to have several mistresses. But from his moral standpoint, this was completely justified. If a man wants to touch a single, young woman (often violently), from the point of view of his morality, it is perfectly justifiable behavior. Women like me who choose to resist are reviled as "modern girls." In other words, single women are treated as though they are like an open space into which men are free to venture in order to cut the grass (tachiiri jiyū no kusakiriba). Moreover, they do not hesitate to hurt women by making them the subject of groundless gossip. . . .

However, one common but very rigid moral position one finds among men who think this way is that they won't touch another man's wife. Especially when it comes to the wife of a colleague, or of one of the executives, they will be extremely respectful and circumspect. In this sense, a person like Minami Kiichi was extremely moral, never expressing an attitude toward the wives of his superiors that could create any unpleasantness. But this respect that these men express toward the wives of their superiors has nothing to do with respect for the wife herself. In their minds, it is because the spouse is a possession, something that belongs to the man. . . . It began to dawn on me that if I wanted to continue to be a part of the JCP and to work hard for this movement, then I really needed to find an appropriate mate and get married. . . .

I had never actually met Koreeda before this time, although I had seen him around for quite a while. He always left the impression that he was a good person. Among the New Man Society group, he was one of the friendliest and most well liked, and until the time the arrests, starting with the Kyoto Student Federation Incident, he was one of the top officials in the Student Federation. Rumor had it that these days he was finding an outlet for his intellectual gifts as editor of *The Proletarian News (Musansha shinbun)*. He was a tall, light-skinned, good-looking man who was quite popular with women. In other words, in terms of a possible marriage partner for me, there is no doubt that he would be considered an excellent prospect. . . . A few days later I heard directly from Koreeda, and after meeting alone with him several times, we decided to get married. . . .

When the decision was made to marry Koreeda, I put forth just one condition: that we obtain my father's permission and marry formally. . . . Regardless of their age, whether they had attained majority or not, until the moment they left the family to become brides, women's entire lives were always subject to the control and interference of the head of the household, be it her father or whichever male had ascended to that position, and she had to silently submit to their decisions. However, if parents send even an underage daughter over to another family as a bride, from that point forward they have absolutely no control over their daughter. That woman has come under the complete control of her husband, or the head of that household. This practice was widely accepted throughout prewar Japan virtually without protest. Accordingly, for a daughter in my situation, a proper and legal way to escape the strict controls and regulations of my parents was to complete the formal marriage procedures with a husband who would be understanding.

Therefore, the first thing I did was to go to my father's house and declare my plans to get married. After retiring as chief justice of the Utsunomiya court in 1927, my father returned to Tokyo and had just built a place to retire to in Ogikubo. As I faced him and told him that I wanted to marry this person Koreeda Kyōji, whose background I explained, he quietly listened and finally just said, "Go ahead and do as you please, but don't come back crying later." I replied that I would not. With this, the discussion ended (I intended to keep that promise, the single condition my father laid down, never to come crawling back to my family in tears). My mother just sat there quietly the whole time and never said a word (this was the way things always were in my family).

Several days after that, Koreeda went to visit my father, formally requesting permission to marry me. It seems that my father liked Koreeda from the moment they met. When my father asked about Koreeda's parents' situation, Koreeda claimed that his father in Kagoshima had happily bestowed his permission, but unfortunately he was not well, and since his mother would be looking after him, they would be unable to come to Tokyo. My father was persuaded by this and did not pursue it any further. (Actually, I never knew this until after I was arrested on March 15 [1928], but this was a big lie on Koreeda's part. Being a traditional Kagoshima man, Koreeda's father had exploded in rage when he read the letter that Koreeda sent saying he would be marrying someone from outside Kagoshima Prefecture, and later that day he collapsed. He had to retire from the National Railways where he had worked for the past thirty years and go into retirement in a little town outside of Kagoshima city.) . . .

Not long after we had set up a household together, I realized that I had misjudged the kind of person Koreeda was. As editor of *The Proletarian News* and in his work with the Student Federation and other things, he was always well liked and created a good impression wherever he went. As a tutor for study groups, he was always clear and thorough when he spoke. But around the house, he was an extremely reticent person in regards to me. He did not necessarily appear to be dissatisfied with me, but it seemed that he felt he did not have to say anything to his wife around the house. They say that there are many husbands who utter only three words to their wives: eat, bathe, and sleep. Even if a wife wants to have a face-to-face conversation with her husband at mealtimes (there were no opportunities other than mealtime to sit face-to-face in this manner), he may just open up his newspaper and neither look up at her nor reply to her comments. Koreeda was one of those types of men who have nothing to say at home unless it concerns himself. It had never occurred to me that Koreeda, who was always warm and friendly with other people, would have this type of attitude toward his wife at home.

Koreeda, who in addition to being editor of *The Proletarian News* had many other extralegal party matters to attend to, was an extremely busy person. Ordinarily, he would grab a quick bite to eat right after waking up and then run out of the house, not returning until late at night. When he was at home, he was usually writing furiously at his desk or taking party members to the back room for meetings. All of these visitors were in conjunction with illicit activities, so I was never introduced to anybody. Naturally, I never attended any of these meetings; I would slip into the small three-mat room off the entrance *(genkan)* and keep a lookout. I understood about his being busy, so I did my best not to interfere with his work. Therefore, if the situation was not of the sort I will refer to below, he was not only reticent in relation to me, but I could not help feeling isolated and lonely, as he seemed not the least bit interested in what ideas might be running around in my head. (186–194)

The Relationship between My Marriage and My Expulsion from the Party

It was in January just after Koreeda and I had set up household together. He said one day rather casually, "Since you didn't get permission to marry me, the Central Committee is going to have to expel you from the party." He seemed to feel that it was not necessary to explain the reason for my expulsion, as this was something I would already understand. I had no reply, but just fell silent. However, inside I felt that something I had secretly been worrying about ever since the cell meeting when Mitamura Shirō announced the acceptance of the 1927 Theses had finally come to pass. Needless to say, the reason I was being expelled from the party was none other than the fact that I was regarded as a female Fukumotoist, someone with petit bourgeois roots in the student movement.

I had met Mr. Fukumoto face-to-face only twice and I had read only one of his abstruse essays. . . . In 1925, the person who was looked up to the most among left-wing socialists in Japan as their leading theorist was Yamakawa Hitoshi. Ever since publishing his epoch-making 1922 essay in *Vanguard (Zen'ei)*, "A Change in Direction for the Proletarian Movement" ("Musan kaikyū undō no hōkō tenkan"), which called for the organization of legal, mass-based proletarian parties, Yamakawa had assumed a leadership position in the movement. But, in his heart, it seems he opposed the formation of an illegal revolutionary (communist) party. Since most of the leaders of the first Communist Party of Japan were all direct disciples of Yamakawa, even though secretly they felt frustrated with his lukewarm legalistic approach, there was not anyone who could speak out effectively against it. Then, in February of 1924, the decision to dissolve the party was taken without a single objection.

However, that period was a peak period for Japanese left-wing movements across the board. In the labor union movement, in October 1924, the struggle between the left and right wings of the Kantō League of the Greater Japan Federation of Labor intensified, and in May 1927 the federation split right down the middle, giving rise to the Labor Union Council (Rōdōkumiai Hyōgikai). In the student movement, the Student Federation was formed in September 1924, and it moved clearly in the direction of explicitly Marxist-oriented study groups. In April 1925, the Universal Manhood Suffrage Bill (the right to vote for males over twenty-five years of age only) passed the Diet, and there was an increasing tendency to form proletarian parties based on mass organizations like farmer and labor unions. Taking their cue from Lenin's 1902 essay, "What Must We Do?" ("Nani o nasu beki ka") many argued that in order to form a true proletarian party, it was necessary, by means of ideological debates, to ferret out the opportunists and the compromisers and distance ourselves from them, something that gave rise to the "separate and unite" movement. In this sense, Fukumoto's call for "theoretical struggle" (riron tōsō) fit perfectly with the times. It was a means for this little-known teacher from Yamaguchi Commercial High School, who had no track record in the movement, to launch a fearless frontal assault on Yamakawa Hitoshi's authority. Students and later workers and others throughout the movement began to read Lenin's "What Must We Do?" which heretofore had not been known to very many. . . . (194–196)

In 1925, the conditions of our movement were much as Lenin had described in his essay noted above. Therefore, it was very easy for us to understand. Accordingly, I never once thought of myself as a Fukumotoist. In my mind, I was a Leninist. "Theoretical struggle" became a popular phrase that was constantly on the lips of left-wing activists at that time, but there may well have been people who only partially understood the term and used it ineptly. However, the general sense of the term as it was used at that time was that one freely expressed one's opinion to anyone without reservation, engaging freely in debate and criticism. Consequently, people who did not hesitate to speak out critically against the party leadership were labeled Fukumotoists by those who did not like them. . . . I never uttered a single word of criticism against the 1927 Theses. Yet why was I being punished as a Fukumotoist? The reason was that I was a *female* Fukumotoist.

Because I was a communist, my premise was that complete liberation of women and equality between the sexes was a given, and I never once believed that women should act "femininely" (onna rashiku), defer to men, and modestly refrain from speaking out. This wasn't only me, but everyone in the women's student movement felt the same way. So, whether it was Student Federation council meetings or study groups or cell meetings, I was often the only woman among the men, but I never once hesitated to express my own ideas and opinions. At the time, I never gave it a second thought, but reflecting on it now, the fact that I was always asserting myself, expressing my opinions, and engaging the males in debate was probably a source of irritation *(mezawari)* for the men. I believe that my inclination to unhesitatingly implement the notion of freedom of debate is the reason I was looked askance at as a "woman Fukumotoist."

Therefore, the reason I was expelled had nothing do with my breaking any rules or violating any laws. . . . Probably, Koreeda had contempt for me as a woman, and perhaps it never occurred to him that I had an idea in my head. By the time I figured out that I was being expelled because I was a female Fukumotoist, I no longer had the energy to protest this attitude of contempt toward women. But that is why, when I think back upon it, that period when we were newly married was for me, regrettably, a very unsatisfactory period. (199–204)

How disillusioning to realize that the initial suggestion of a match between Koreeda, an up-and-coming party member, and Fukunaga may have been rooted in a scheme to try to muzzle her, to silence her. Many members of the left-wing movement were subjected to vicious gossip campaigns against them. It would seem that the narrator goes to great lengths to delineate the boundaries of her relationship with Fukumoto, someone she met only a few times, in order to make it clear that she was never a part of Fukumoto's inner circle. Indeed, she claims that she could barely follow his reasoning when she attempted to read his articles or discuss Marxism with him. Nevertheless, what she realizes in retrospect is that the whole marriage to Koreeda was probably a sham aimed at silencing someone whom the party considered to be an unruly woman, an outspoken female "Fukumotoist."

The following section brings up the mass arrests of March 15, 1928. This mass arrest of communists and other leftists occurred less than a month after the first election following the passage of the Universal Manhood Suffrage Bill in 1925, a bill that had quadrupled the electorate. A number of mass proletarian parties participated in the election, such as the Labor-Farmer Party, the Social Mass Party, and the Japan Farmer Party. Although the proletarian parties were unable to garner even 5 percent of the vote, the mere fact of their participation was sufficiently alarming to General Tanaka Giichi's (1863–1929) government for them to initiate a ruthless campaign of arrest, detention, and even torture of suspected leftists. Over twelve hundred people were arrested, five hundred were detained, and nearly half of those prosecuted. The following year, in March 1929, the arrest of a party member yielded a membership chart and roster. By April 16, 1929, the police were able to round up virtually every communist in the country at the time and effectively smash the Japan Communist Party's organization.

The March 15 (1928) Arrests

After March 15, as everyone knows, sweeping arrests were made at all the offices of legal left-wing organizations that the authorities were aware of and at the houses of people involved in these organizations as well. Even innocent bystanders who just happened to be at these places were hauled down to central lockup. However, unlike subsequent occasions, except for the minority of people that the Special Higher Police (Tokkō) and the prosecutor had their eyes on, most of the others were regarded as "small fries" and released in two or three days. Newspapers were forbidden to publish anything about these arrests from the outset, so unless one heard by word of mouth from the people directly involved, there was no way of knowing how widespread the arrests were. . . .

On March 16, I left my house in the morning and was following instructions as usual and moving from place to place. Then, I cannot remember exactly on whose instructions, I went to Kikuta Zengorō's house over in the Tsukiji 6-chome area. . . . The house appeared to be quiet, and everything seemed normal, so as usual, I did not call out to the people who lived below but just went straight up to the second floor to Kikuta's room and opened the door to his entryway. Inside, there were three or four plain-clothes detectives waiting to arrest me; they took me down to the Kyōbashi police station. . . . I was kept there for about a month. (214)

Fukunaga was dismayed to discover while under arrest that the police had managed to uncover a membership list for the party, a real blunder by the party leadership. It meant the virtual destruction of the Japan Communist Party. Finally, under pressure, she admitted her party membership. Detective Yamagata came by, read her confession over briefly, and signed it; she was shipped on April 20 to Ichigaya Prison (217–218). She goes on to discuss ways in which the movement exploited women.

[There was] a "special duty" demanded of female student activists: the role of housekeeper. Most of the young women, having grown up insulated from the real world *(hako-ire musume)* and familiar with very little of its workings, were babes in the woods; but they were naively willing to work hard and do whatever they could for the party in which they invested all their trust. But the whole "housekeeper" role was a popular subject for page-three newspaper articles, which not only manifested anticommunism, but heaped such scorn on these young women that it was as though they were being stripped naked and dragged through the mud for all the world to see. For most of the male leadership of the party, who had no sympathy for these women they dubbed "petit-bourgeois girls" *(koburu onnadomo)* and treated them accordingly with contempt, there was no looking back. From our point of view, when we were arrested, we expected nothing less than cruel treatment by the enemy. But the contempt of our male colleagues and leaders in whom we trusted was psychologically a damaging blow. . . . (222)

It was only natural at that time that we young female student activists, who had just read a few books on socialism, would not claim that we understood the ideas fully. But we were treated since infancy, on a daily basis, to scorn and discrimination, restrained and virtually enslaved in social terms, *simply because we were women (onna de aru dake no riyū de).* But we should have been no different from the men; after all, we were human beings too. The demands for women's liberation and equal rights with men grew naturally out of this awareness that women were human beings too. For us, this awareness was rooted in our daily-life experiences and was something self-evident that transcended any intellectualization. It was much the same way as with the outcaste *(buraku)* class, who created the Buraku Liberation Movement (Suiheisha) so that they could resist the contempt and discrimination they had experienced all their lives. By founding their own liberation movement, they could transcend the world of ideas and participate directly [in the movement]. After the founding of the Buraku Liberation Movement in 1922, the movement subsequently gained support from the labor and farmer movements and bravely forged a league of dedicated activists. The women's liberation movement should have followed along similar lines. And I suppose that it would have been most natural for those of us coming out of the student movement to have poured our energies into the democratic women's liberation movement, the Women's League, the moment we graduated or were kicked out of school.

Around 1924–25, Ichikawa Fusae formed her League for Women's Suffrage (Fusen Kakutoku Dōmei). In 1927 the Women's League was formed with Labor-Farmer Party and Japanese Council of Trade Unions support, and right around that time, the right-wing Social Democratic Women's League (Shakai Minshū Fujindōmei) and the centrist National Women's League (Zenkoku Fujindōmei), were also formed. Then, on March 21, 1928, Ichikawa created a committee to coordinate the activities of the various women's groups in order to focus on women's suffrage. . . . In other words, this was the fundamental reason why women forming their own political mass movement angered the party leadership. That is, if they did so, women would be able to step into the vanguard of the movement, and their status as ladies-in-waiting or mere servant girls at the bottom of the organization obediently following orders from the male leaders would be ended. . . .

In short, women who were inclined to support the JCP were prohibited from forming a women's-only group and so were prohibited from entering any arena of political demands on behalf of women other than those groups involved in daily economic struggles. The reason was none other than the fear on the part of the JCP leadership that if women formed their own women's league consisting of women only, then this would be the first step toward women awakening to a democratic, autonomous self-awareness. (224–228)

Fukunaga expresses genuine bitterness toward the Japan Communist Party for "helping to crush" the emerging women's league at the very moment of its inception, leaving women virtually no place to go. In its place, the party urged upon dedicated and idealistic young women the role of "housekeeper," which basically meant cooking and keeping house for male party members and possibly becoming their sexual partners. At least this was a large part of the public perception of what "housekeepers" did, as the narrator explains below.

Journalists at that time made a huge issue out of the idea that housekeeper functions included sexual relationships. This made the subject excellent material for the third-page section of newspapers, which catered to vulgar notions of women as sexual objects for males. But what made me angry about the Communist Party's custom of the housekeeper was not this aspect. The problem of sexual relationships is up to each individual to resolve. As long as it does not involve violence, the parties concerned—especially the women involved—if it is a relationship entered into freely, is not something for outsiders to become involved with. The problem is as follows. Under Japan's old, patriarchal social and family system, women are generally discriminated against and enslaved. Concerning women's issues, Engels wrote that in modern society, men are the bourgeoisie while women are the proletariat. But in Japan, generally the men constitute the slave-owning class, and women are the slaves. Marx called the modern working class "wage slaves" *(chingin dorei)*. In that sense, women in Japan are "gender slaves" *(seibetsu dorei)*. At the very stage when these pathetic women were just starting to become self-aware of their rights as human beings, the autonomously generated women's mass movement that they created, the Women's League, was crushed by despotic and oppressive orders from the top Communist Party leadership who saw it as a threat to their right of gender dominance. And what further enslaved these women who now had no political arena in which to fight their battles was the housekeeper tradition. At present, JCP top leaders and historians still have not confronted this problem nor engaged in self-criticism over this "housekeeping" issue, for it is considered a personal, love-related question for each party member to resolve on his or her own. That I have raised this whole question of the housekeeping problem here is because of my disappointment over the party's lack of self-reflexive attitude about it. (229–230)

Fukunaga is arguing that prewar Japanese women were gender slaves, and not only did the Japan Communist Party fail to live up to its promise of seeking genuine liberation for all people, but it actively conspired to preserve gender difference. It is hard to imagine a more devastating critique either of prewar society or the Japan Communist Party. Fukunaga would spend a considerable amount of time in prison over the next several years. As she describes below, these were difficult years, but one positive experience she had was to begin critically reading the Tale of Genji, *Japan's eleventh-century literary masterpiece about life at the Heian court.*

Imprisonment, Bail, and Court Battles

After describing conditions at the old wooden structure that was the women's section of Ichigaya Prison, Fukunaga turned to a discussion of how she passed her time there.

Prisoners who had not yet been convicted or sentenced led a quiet life in our cells, with nothing to do but eat and sleep, so it was, in this sense, an ideal environment for reading and studying. If I could just freely get a hold of books, then these would hardly be conditions I would complain about. However, at that time, books that we could receive as prisoners were severely restricted. As a rule, books on linguistics and literature were just about all that was permitted (later on, when the number of Communist

Party members in prison grew substantially, people demanded that the range of materials prisoners were allowed access to expanded, and over time, it was) . . . I felt as though I wanted to read some Japanese literature. But I could not think of any work of Japanese literature that I could enjoy over a several-month period. Novels were usually something I could knock off in half a day or a day at the most. Then suddenly I hit on the idea of the *Tale of Genji* and requested a copy of the Iwanami bunko edition.

At that time, the Iwanami bunko edition consisted of five volumes, a version of the text edited by Shimazu Hisamoto but without a single footnote. Various scholars had published their edited version of the *Tale of Genji*, but they were all quite expensive, so I figured that the Iwanami bunko version would be the cheapest. At that time, I had no intention of undertaking scholarly research on the Genji. Since I was just thinking of this tale *(monogatari)* as a novel that I thought I would try and read, notes and explanatory essays really were not important to me. Due to my mother's influence, I had always enjoyed classical literature since my childhood, so if I could just read the text all right, I would be able to read the *Genji* just as if it were a modern novel. Of course, without explanatory notes, there was no way I was able to recognize the source of the countless references to *waka*, Chinese poems, and other classical texts that recur in the *Genji*. But I felt that these trivial references were not absolutely necessary to appreciate the narrative in its entirety as a novel.

I had read portions of the *Tale of Genji* before, but the first time that I was able to read it all the way through was in prison. I had not read a single work of scholarship on the *Genji*, nor any simplified summaries of it. So, I was just pleased to be given the opportunity to read and reread this text in the original, with no preconceptions about it, and to take great pleasure in it. This old tale manages to skillfully bring to life on the page the experiences of several tens of women and to depict the various facets of love they experienced, along with superbly insightful human analysis that is in no way inferior to any contemporary novel. Moreover, the author, in spite of the fact that she was born more than a thousand years ago, at a time when the genre of the novel did not exist anywhere in the world, managed to create a work that, with its classical balance and its independent structure, we most certainly would have to call a novel. The author of this mysterious masterpiece was a woman, and as I was also a woman, I read this text in a natural, unforced way through the eyes of a woman.

Ever since that time, even well into the postwar era, whenever I have been sick or needing rest and did not care to read something difficult, I simply take up the *Genji* and read it for pleasure. I have also taken up reading the scholarship on *Genji*. I have been surprised that all the famous *Genji* scholars—and they are all males—treat Hikaru Genji as the main character of the tale, and interpret the *Genji* as a text about Hikaru Genji. If you think about it, research on Japanese literature was revived in the Tokugawa era, an era when Japanese society was rigidly differentiated from top to bottom and men gained the right to oppressively control women, who were virtually enslaved by this system. In ancient Japanese society, women did not live such a despicable existence. Until around the eleventh century, when the *Tale of Genji* was written, women still had the respect of men, and it is even depicted in the text that men often deferred to women and allowed them to go first (ladies first). Therefore, if we are to take the *Tale of Genji* as a forerunner of the modern novel, then its protagonist cannot be Hikaru Genji. He does not have the consistency of character to sustain him as the protagonist throughout this long novel. The youthful Genji is hardly portrayed as an unfaithful rake; rather, he is depicted as a pure and loyal man. So, Hikaru Genji, with his multiple love affairs, is inconsistent as a character, representing a highly fragmented psyche, someone who cannot be treated as one individual human being. I doubt that the author ever intended to depict Genji as a single, unified character. Rather, I think she created him as a link in order to connect the disparate short love stories that constitute the *Genji,* much as the *"mukashi otoko"* functions in the *Tale of Ise (Ise monogatari).* The real protagonists of this tale are the various women. Each of these women possesses her own unique individuality and a strong measure of self-respect that makes each one lively and animated. No modern novelist in the post-Meiji literary world attempts to depict characters like this. (232–236)

Fukunaga is making an argument that, for its time, was quite unique. She maintains that this long, complex text, written by a woman, could not really be about the nominal hero, Prince Genji; rather, it must really be an occasion for the voices and the perspectives of the numerous female characters to come alive and be celebrated.

Getting Released from Prison with a Suspended Sentence, Giving Birth, and the Written Report on Dissolution of the Party

It turned out that Fukunaga was pregnant when she was incarcerated, so when it was time for her to give birth, her sentence was suspended and she was

released into the care of her parents. Her parents had a very difficult time ac-
cepting Fukunaga's radical beliefs. Her text describes the situation as follows.

[M]y father seemed to feel that the only way to recover his good standing
was to make efforts to enable his daughter to do penance. . . . While living
in such circumstances day in and day out, suddenly, around June of 1929,
I believe, I received a summons from the office of the prosecutor. So I had
my mother take care of my infant, and I departed for the prosecutor's office
in Sakuradamon, where I was ushered into a small interrogation room. I
was shown by a clerk a document of several pages purported to be a written
report by the so-called "dissolution faction" and told to read it. As I recall,
it was supposed to be the work of Mizuno Shigeo, Koreeda Kyōji, Asano
Akire (or Hikaru), Kadoya Hiroshi, Murao Satsuo, and Murayama Toshirō.
At the time, it was felt that among these men, the ones who had the greatest impact on the content were Mizuno and Koreeda.

The thrust of what was being advocated by the "dissolution faction"
was, to me, incredibly shocking. In terms of the various things articulated
in this document, such as detailed criticism of the concrete political policies and guidelines for political activism that the JCP had followed to this
juncture, there were many points on which I could willingly agree. What
was shocking was the central conclusion of the report, that is, that the imperial household was at the core of the Japanese people's racial unity, and
therefore the appeal to "overthrow the monarchy" should be withdrawn.
Our objective, then, should be to overthrow the landlord-capitalist class
and establish a labor-farmer government that would pursue a socialist
revolution within the framework of the monarchical system. Therefore,
the JCP should be dissolved and a new mass-based workers party should
be created. In the instant that I read this, what leapt into my mind in a flash
as an intuitive, illogical *(rikutsunuki)* response was that to call for a socialist
revolution that recognized the centrality of the imperial institution was
virtually indistinguishable from the "national socialism" being advocated
by the extreme right wing. I never imagined in my wildest dreams that
leaders from the middle echelon of the JCP, whom I had come to admire
and trust since I first became active in the movement as a student, could
ever support this kind of idea. It was like a lightning bolt out of the blue.
(240-243)

As the narrator notes later on numerous occasions, the experience of being con-
fronted by this document was a severe psychological shock (seishinteki shō-

geki). *She reiterates how much this was not so much a logical response dictated by ideology or by party theses but her gut response.*

At the time, what moved me decisively in the direction of opposing the "dissolution faction" was not the guiding ideology of the Communist Party, or any of its theses. Rather, it was something I felt deep down in my heart, something beyond logic. It was my opposition to the cruel and barbaric political oppression by this entity known as the emperor system *(tennōsei)*. In my view, the emperor system could only be the direct enemy of the Japanese working class, and if we refused to confront it as our enemy head-on, then by what logic could we claim to represent the interests of the working class? (244)

There was perhaps no more fundamental question for Marxists in Japan, but, in fact, the majority of prewar Marxists renounced their beliefs and embraced the ideology of the emperor system in its stead. Of course, they did this under the pressure of imprisonment, interrogation, and, in some instances, torture. Nevertheless, the lack of resistance was, on the whole, shocking. The shock, of course, was accentuated for Fukunaga because her husband was a principal in this philosophical reorientation that she could not abide. And, of course, party assumptions about the role of a spouse was clearly that, first and foremost, she was expected to support her husband. So not only was she bucking party leadership, but she was going against expectations for her role as a spouse. Apparently, Koreeda realized the error of his ways and distanced himself from the document almost immediately so that the issue did not become a serious one in their marriage. Meanwhile, though, with almost everyone she knew being incarcerated and her parents still pressuring her to recant, saying that they would support neither her nor her child if she did not do so, Fukunga began to contemplate killing herself and her child (248–249).

She went to visit Koreeda to say good-bye, and he came up with the idea of sending her to his family in Kagoshima. She went willingly to escape her parents, whom she felt did not really love their grandchild. She was warmly received by Koreeda's family in their small fishing village in Taniyamamachi outside of Kagoshima City. Although she was treated very well by the family, she had the opportunity to see firsthand how entrenched was the Kagoshima attitude of contempt for women. She concluded, "If I could have known how deeply in his consciousness this 'Kagoshima man' attitude was imbedded, I wonder if I ever would have married him. But when you notice something like this only after the fact, it becomes a matter of reaching awareness 'too late'" (254).

My Study of History and Koreeda's Bail

The traumatic experience of the document about dissolution of the party sparked Fukunaga to undertake some reading on Japanese history, in particular on the role of the imperial institution. She read Mikami Sanji and Kuroita Katsumi, *but the historian who had the greatest impact on her was Tsuda Sōkichi, especially his* Studies on the *Kojiki* and the *Nihon shoki* (Kojiki oyobi Nihon-shoki no kenkyū) *and* Studies on the Age of the Gods (Shindaishi no kenkyū). *Tsuda demonstrated in these works that the* Record of Ancient Matters (Kojiki) *and* Chronicles of Japan (Nihon shoki) *were works that dated from the eighth century and no earlier and that the imperial line could be traced back only as far as the sixth century. So Tsuda argued against the idea of a twenty-six-hundred-year-old monarchy in favor of one approximately fourteen hundred years old. And he demonstrated that the creation myths were less an assemblage of folk stories and myths generated by the people than they were the construction of the early imperial court trying to legitimize itself. Inspired by Tsuda's work, Fukunaga took up reading the* Record of Ancient Matters *and the* Chronicles of Japan *herself.*

From her own reading, she became convinced that the modern emperor system was not linked in any significant way to Japan's ancient past, but rather was the construction of a modern state (256–257). She summarizes her conclusions below.

Therefore the modern imperial state *(kindai tennōsei kokka)* to which the Meiji Restoration gave rise was in no sense a holdover from feudalism. Nor could it in any way be considered a successor or a revival of the archaic and barbaric monarchical state of ancient Japan. The question arises that even though it might incorporate remnants from a fossilized social hierarchy based on the ideology of the samurai class and be adorned with linguistic elements and apparel from the prefeudal ancient period, shouldn't it be acknowledged that the actual reality of this modern emperor system is rooted firmly in the political structure of modern Japanese capitalist society?

At the time, this was only a vague question in my mind. I lacked the basic background in history to proceed any further with this question, nor did I have the time and resources to undertake my own research. In my youth, all I possessed was a very random sort of knowledge gleaned from my unfocused reading. But even so, I found Tsuda Sōkichi's works to be wonderfully illuminating. I only hoped that since a former Waseda professor like Dr. Tsuda could carry out this kind of pioneering research without benefit of any revolutionary ideology, but rather out of a love and respect for the discipline of history, that younger researchers specializing in history would be able to carry on his work and help further elucidate Japanese history. . . . However, the prewar JCP, even though they put forth the slogan "overthrow the emperor system," it was just a slogan, and no efforts were made to explore such basic questions as "What *is* the emperor system?" Nor was there any sign of research that might challenge the official Ministry of Education–created version of Japanese history.

For me, personally, the upshot of this interest in history was that I read probably more than one hundred books dealing with historical materialism. Thanks to all this reading, I was able to get through Sano [Manabu] and Nabeyama [Sadachika]'s ideological recantation *(tenkō)* three years later, as well as the entire Pacific War, without wavering in my intellectual convictions. That I was able to take the time to do that kind of reading was due to the fact that I had this period when I was staying with my family at home while I worked to secure Koreeda's bail. (260–261)

Koreeda eventually was released on bail because he had contracted tuberculosis in prison, although his case was not severe at the time. Fukunaga notes in passing that they never once spoke about the whole party dissolution debacle. In the summer of 1929, Koreeda, along with eight or nine others, was publicly expelled from the Communist Party and their names published on the front page of Red Flag (Akahata). *"Koreeda felt that his expulsion was a tremendous source of shame, and it seems he continually agonized over it. I could well understand those feelings and had no desire to pour salt in this psychological wound, so I never raised the subject with him" (262).*

The problem with this arrangement was that since the "dissolution" issue was so closely tied up with the 1927 Theses issue and the whole history and future direction of JCP policies, there was little else we could speak about together. Avoiding conflict as we did, we may have appeared to be a happy couple, but in reality a gulf between us was widening.

Thinking about the whole thing from a present perspective, the basic problems that existed between us as a couple may have had little to do with such an external problem as Koreeda's expulsion from the party. Deep in his heart, he may have been bothered by the fact that when he joined the "dissolution faction," I opposed his point of view directly, and everybody in that faction and in the Central Committee knew this very well. . . . That his colleagues in the party knew about my opposition may have been the greatest burden of shame he had to bear.

At the time, I really did not understand how deeply rooted in the consciousness of Japanese males was this notion of the husband's face *(men-tsu)*, which dictated that as long as the wife was a wife, she must obey her husband unconditionally and that his honor was linked to his ability to control her and force her obedience. When I was a child, I never accepted the idea that a man had the right to be arrogant just because he was male. Actually, in elementary school, when education was still coeducational, there were not any boys who had the ability to get the best of me, anyway. At Tokyo Women's College, as far as I was concerned, the idea of gender equality was such a natural and basic part of modern democratic thought that I took it as a given. Therefore, I naturally assumed that the Communist Party, which looked down upon American-style democracy as vulgar and fiercely attacked it, would be critical of a feudalistic outlook that elevates men over women and supports a system in which husbands are authoritarian and would want to see these eliminated. By revoking his own support for the report calling for dissolution, Koreeda himself affirmed that his wife's opinion, which opposed his, was the correct one. But he never uttered one word to me about this, nor about the whole "dissolution" issue. The fact that he did not may have been indicative of how deeply concerned he was about it. (262–264)

Once again, the narrator has focused her attention on the role gender plays in these theoretical disputes within the party. Her former position about dissolving the party had been the correct one, and she knew it. Now it was being acknowledged publicly, but no male in the party would deign to admit this to Fukunaga, least of all her husband.

In April 1931, after spending six months in Kagoshima, Koreeda and Fukunaga were summoned back to Tokyo to stand trial. They were among a group of 230 or so defendants put on trial from the March 15, 1928, arrests. Meanwhile, first Koreeda and then Fukunaga petitioned the party to be reinstated. Koreeda was reinstated provisionally, and because his reinstatement was only provisional, Fukunaga's reinstatement could not be acted upon until his was decided. When Koreeda told her this, she was deeply disappointed and could say nothing.

Of course, if I could have met face-to-face with some of the Central Committee members whom I had previously met, like Sano Manabu, Shiga, and Tokuda, I would never have kept my silence. I was certainly just a minor party functionary, but since joining the party in April 1927, I have no recollection that I ever violated any rules or regulations. Nevertheless, at the end of 1927 the party leadership decided, just because I was a woman, that if I did not agree to marry Koreeda, I would be expelled from the party. Now, this interim Central Committee, consisting of some of the very same people, was saying that just because I was Koreeda's wife, my name was to be removed from the party rolls. What kind of an illogical decision was that? Didn't all the people on the Central Committee, along with the prosecutor's staff and the dissolution faction themselves, know full well that I had clearly and publicly opposed the dissolution manifesto when it was issued around June 1929? So where in my own party record was there a reason for punishing me for my involvement with Koreeda? I would have loved to confront these people with this sort of question. But they were all in prison, so what was I to do? Ask for a visitation and then under the gaze of the supervisory officials give voice to my criticisms? (265–266)

From Sano and Nabeyama's Ideological Recantation to My Re-imprisonment

First, in June 1933, two of the Japan Communist Party leaders, Sano Manabu (1892–1983) and Nabeyama Sadachika (1901–1979), "recanted," which is to say that they issued declarations of recantation from their jail cells. In other words, they renounced Marxism and the Japan Communist Party and endorsed the ideology of the emperor system. Specifically, they recognized the special position of the emperor in Japanese history and society and the unique national polity (kokutai) that characterized Japan. Several days later, other top party members announced their concurrence with their leaders' decision. After several more weeks passed, Koreeda followed suit as well. This behavior was far from uncommon, as the overwhelming majority of the nearly twenty-five hundred people arrested under the authority of the Peace Preservation Law by 1943 had issued some form of political or ideological recantation. On the occasion of his renouncement, Koreeda wrote Fukunaga with some specific instructions he wanted carried out. Fukunaga found the whole tone and content of his letter troubling.

Koreeda's Ideological Recantation

Around the middle of July [1933], I received a short and very unexpected letter from Koreeda. It was a simple letter the contents of which, in brief, were that he had made up his mind to renounce the party himself. He then told me to vacate the apartment and return to my father's house. Also, he said I should sever any and all connections with party members. I should see no one and just remain ensconced in my family home. He said that he would let me know what I was to do next, so I should just wait until he gave me further instructions. I had never witnessed such a frighteningly high-handed attitude in a letter before in my life.

I want to make it clear that the reason I was angry at that time was not because of the intellectual recantation *(tenkō)* itself. If he had just written a simple letter saying that he had decided to renounce the party and that he knew I would be upset but that he just wanted me to think it through carefully and decide for myself, then I probably would not have gotten angry. I do not know what kind of treatment he had been getting since his trial had begun, being tried with a group of other defendants, but he never said anything about it to me. But from what I could see, I think I could understand it if he began to feel deep down inside that it was stupid to sacrifice himself for a party like this. . . .

The right of individual freedom of thought was something many Japanese people learned about for the first time after their defeat in the Pacific War, as taught to them by the Occupation authorities, so it may be thought of as "American democracy" (or bourgeois democracy). But ever since I had entered Yasui Tetsuko's Tokyo Women's College at seventeen years of age, I had come to accept this notion as something as natural as the air we breathe around us. For me, it was something that preceded my exposure to communism. Considering this idea from the point of view of global history, individual freedom of thought was born much earlier than the birth of the republic of the United States. It was part of the birth of modern thought itself. . . . (313–314)

As mentioned above, Koreeda's letter to me did not just communicate his plan to renounce the party. He high-handedly ordered me to unconditionally obey him as his wife and follow his lead in the recantation matter, telling me it was my duty to obey him. As far as I was concerned, this was a fundamental human issue that preceded the advent of communist thought. As soon as he turned his back on communism, he was clearly reverting to behavior of a stereotypical Japanese male. I almost felt as though I could hear the old Kagoshima adage, "Woman, don't turn your back on your duty" *(Onamera, gi o koku na)* leaping off the back of his letter. . . . [N]ow, I am forced to conclude that from the outset he basically had contempt for me as his wife and did not consider me worthy as an intellectual adversary for him. Now that he is in prison, he thinks that he is free to write about his wish to renounce the party and distribute it wherever he pleases, but that I have no business writing even a single line opposing his views on this matter.

Since Koreeda was a communist, of course he had read Marx and Lenin on the liberation of women, and he had never mentioned in passing any opposition to equal rights for men and women. However, the moment he renounced the party and reverted to type as a Japanese male, his ideas changed and he adopted fully the belief that a wife had to submit slavishly and unconditionally to her husband. For my part, I felt it would be not only foolish, but meaningless [as well] to try and argue against him. So my only choice was to point out that if I were not his wife, I would have no obligation to obey him, so let us end the marriage. . . .

Therefore, I made up my mind and went to see Koreeda in jail and told him I had no wish to oppose his recantation, but that I wanted to have the freedom to do my own thinking for myself. Therefore, I told him, I wanted to separate from him in order to have that freedom. I indicated that I did not really care about the legal procedures, but that in terms of reality, I wanted to initiate efforts to bring about our separation. Interviews at the jail were limited to five minutes, and the guards were always standing nearby, so obviously we did not have the opportunity for a detailed discussion. Needless to say, even though we were talking about separating, since he had been in prison, we had not really been living together as man and wife anyway. I had just been arranging for things he needed in jail, visiting him, and so on.

Afterward, Koreeda sent me a particularly long three-part letter dated July 11, July 13, and July 15. In it, he explained in detail his reasons for the recantation, but there was really nothing new there other than some very stalwart but critical language about the decay and "bourgeoisification" of the party. There was none of the theoretical spark and rigor of presentation evident in the written report at the time of the 1929 dissolution affair. The only noteworthy thing was that at the end of each of the three letters he had added a postscript that he would like my father to read each one.

When I saw that I speculated that, in his original letter, his high-handed ordering of me to sever relations with people in the movement and to return to my father's house was simply a device to use my father in order to expedite getting bail. Now, if it meant obtaining his freedom a little sooner, he was apparently still interested in using my father. This might be a bother to me. However, if Koreeda were going to deliver his beloved daughter to my father, then he would probably be very grateful and do everything in his power to help Koreeda make bail. But how was I to understand who was being used in this situation? It certainly poured cold water on any idealistic notions about feelings of love between husbands and wives I might have held.

So I returned to the jail and asked to see Koreeda. I told him that the only thing I wanted was to separate from him and establish myself as a single, independent person. I said to him clearly: "I do not want to receive any more letters from you. If I get them, I may not even read them." That was the last time I ever saw Koreeda. (316–321)

The patriarchy was aligning its considerable forces against Fukunaga. She had to face her husband, her father, and the criminal justice system. Despite the fact that the pressure was on, she was determined to stand her ground. Silence on the part of her husband during their married life together had been construed optimistically by Fukunaga as recognition of her right to hold her own views. Now she realized it was only an expression of his contempt. It did not seem to matter that they had read the same Marxist texts, which clearly called for the liberation of women. These ideas apparently did not penetrate into Koreeda's thinking.

Koreeda's Arrest and Death in Prison

At this time (1934), the arrests of JCP members became more and more intense. People were being picked up for the slightest thing so that at the Shibuya police station's lockup it was virtually filled with people being held for having "dangerous ideas" *(shisōhan)*. . . .

At the end of June I was summoned to the interrogation room and told by the Special Higher Police, "Your older brother came and said that Koreeda has died in the Sakai Prison in Osaka and that we should pass that on to you." (This was after they turned my brother back who had asked to see me in order to give me the news; the Special Higher Police disliked me intensely, as I refused to give in to them.) When I first heard what they had to say I cried out, "You are lying!" It was news I never dreamt I would hear. But after I was returned to my cell, the reality of it began to sink in, tears welled up, and I could not say anything. For several days after that I could not even say anything to my cellmates. I just cried silently. (324–325)

As stated above, at the time of Koreeda's death I was not allowed to know any of the circumstances other than that he had died. Later on, in

1937, after I had been released due to illness, I heard from my father for the first time the circumstances surrounding his death. On June 25, after he had died, the prison authorities notified both my father, in Tokyo, and Koreeda's family in Kagoshima. My father set out right away and arrived at the Sakai Prison the following day. Koreeda's older sister arrived another half-day later from Kagoshima. When my father met with the warden, he admitted that, yes, he had the authority to release a prisoner who was gravely ill. However, the prison doctor did not in fact think that Koreeda's tubercular condition was that severe at the time. On the morning of that day, Koreeda requested water to wipe his body down, and a sink full of water was specially put into his cell. He cleansed himself and said how wonderful it felt. It was only shortly after that that his condition deteriorated rapidly. My father examined the body very carefully and only noted that he was terribly emaciated. Afterward, my father assisted Koreeda's sister, who arrived later to make arrangements with the crematorium and to have his remains properly boxed for shipment back to Kagoshima. (327–338)

While in Ichigaya Prison, Fukunaga was moved to her own cell. Shortly thereafter, her immediate neighbor, one Kumazawa Mitsuko, committed suicide. This, combined with her own declining health, was an occasion for her to reflect morosely on her life, her involvement with the Japan Communist Party, her frequent imprisonment, and her own apparent imminent death. She concluded,

Prison is a home for dead people. While I was in prison, just like a dead person, I had no relationship with the real world. Therefore, all I tried to do was describe the fantasies I had in my sickbed and be aware of them as fantasies quite divorced from reality.

When I was free, I did not do anything particularly significant. However, it was my misfortune to be born a woman in a disagreeable country like Japan *(kono Nihon no yō na iya na kunide, onna ni umareta koto ga watashi no fuun datta)*. This was not my fault. Therefore, I have no regrets, no reason to feel sorry. This was how I resolved to feel. My fever and coughing up of blood only got worse. I thought that the end was near, so there was no need for me to contemplate suicide. If I was going to die anyway, it was better not to have to see my family's morose faces. All I wanted to do was to die quietly in prison, without anyone even knowing. (336)

It is not uncommon for autobiographers to look back over their lives and claim that they have no regrets, but it is rare in my experience to encounter a woman who was willing to denounce male chauvinism and the emperor system as thoroughly as Fukunaga Misao does. To say that it was her misfortune to be born a woman in such a disagreeable country as Japan is a very strong statement. In this volume, there are numerous instances of misfortunes, disrupted lives, death of spouses and children, and all manner of economic deprivation and hardship. But no one denounces the hypocrisy of the prewar patriarchy as thoroughly as Fukunaga does. To be sure, hers is a text that manifests a "fierceness with reality."

She continues with her account of her own illness and how it was ultimately sufficient to warrant her release from prison. She writes of that occurrence.

When I was released from prison in 1937, the world had changed so much that I was startled. I was not able to get many details, but I did know that the JCP, for all intents and purposes, had ceased to exist in 1934. Up to that point, I had believed that the party would never disappear, so it was unexpected. Until I was sent back to prison in 1934, I felt that the comrades I would see were, for the most part, keeping strong and would not lose their fighting spirit. I thought perhaps they [were] just faking their recantations and would reconstitute the party the first opportunity they were given. However, once the party organization is gone, there is not much anyone can do. Not only did the party disappear, [but amid] the circumstances of Japan's rapid turn to fascism after the February 26, 1936 Incident, there was virtually no room for mass movements to exist. Even those the party had viewed with hostility and periodically attacked, like the Farmer-Labor faction (Rōnōha) and the middle-class parties, along with scholars and literary people, were being arrested under the Peace Preservation Law. Virtually all progressive cultural movements and artistic activity had lost their arena of operations. I guess that my old colleagues felt that in these very dark times, all one could do was grit one's teeth and keep one eye on the situation, for it was really not possible to carry out any activities.

The recantation problem had just ceased to be an issue. If you don't have an organization, no matter how vicious and illegal the pressure one is under, there is no way to raise one's voice in protest. The most common response to this complete collapse in the face of fascist control was just to say that human faith had been eclipsed everywhere and obliterated in everyone. Everyone was suspicious of the next person and had to be hesitant about revealing one's true thoughts and feelings. This was a special psychological feature of Japanese society during those dark ten years between 1935–1945. In this psychologically unbearable dark and gloomy society, people had to put on a serious face whenever they spoke or wrote something, even though others might wonder whether this was how they really felt deep down inside. Japan was so bad at this time it is even unpleasant just to recall it.

Why had Japan become such a horrible place? Of course, at the time I was unable to discover an answer to this query. But I have continued to ponder this problem for a long time afterward. Finally, in the current postwar era, I have been able to formulate the following response to which I would like to turn my attention briefly.

Most people believe that these dark ten years came about in Japan because fascists (the military and extreme right-wing groups) seized political power. This is a very shallow, superficial understanding. The extreme right always exists in any society anywhere. The question is how—by what means and as a result of what causes—did these hateful people suddenly expand their power and seize political control of all of Japan?

Politics, whenever and wherever we find it, is driven by a relative balance of power among various contenders for political influence. That fanatically pro-war militarists bent on invading others, and the right-wing extremists who tagged along with them, were able to swiftly expand was because there was no viable political entity to challenge them frontally. In other words, it was because the labor movement, the farmer's movement, the democratic student movement, the women's movement, the various cultural movements, and other mass revolutionary movements and mass organizations were all weakened.

The people of my generation, that is, of the post–World War I era of the 1920s, raised their voices in favor of democracy, peace, and reduction of military expenditures, and we can recall that it was during this period that the labor movement spearheaded the growth of democratic and revolutionary mass movements. Our own JCP came into being at this time and operated under the direction of Moscow's Comintern during the 1920s. Therefore, from the outset, we carried the burden of trying to operate while embracing the major flaws of the Comintern, which are known today as Stalinism. The most basic feature of Stalinist thought was that the Communist Party is the only class organization that can represent the working class. Accordingly, starting with labor organizations and proceeding to all other labor and mass organizations, they were all required to obey and submit to the authority of the party. (These ideas are expressed in one of Stalin's representative works, *The Foundations of Leninism [Reninshugi no kiso]*.)

Therefore, the party heaped abuse on all those political parties and labor organizations that refused to obey it, labeling them fundamental enemies of the working class. As long as the party persisted in this self-righteous attitude, even though it may have paid lip service to the idea of a united front, in reality it was incapable of forming across-the-board coalitions among the working classes and other revolutionary mass organizations. Internal conflicts within popular movements conformed to the expectations of the ruling classes. The JCP and the labor organizations under their immediate control (the Japanese Council of Trade Unions and All Japan Federation of Labor) called for a united front, but in reality they caused mass organizations to fall apart. Indeed, isolated but bravely struggling along as they were, they were easy targets for the ruling classes. (344–347)

Move to Tochigi

After convalescing at home for three years, Fukunaga was contacted again by the prosecutor in early March 1940 to see how her health was doing. She had never written a word of denunciation against the party and had no intention of doing so now. So she preferred to return to prison and complete her sentence rather than recant. The old Ichigaya Prison had been abolished, so she was sent to a newly constructed, modern facility in Tochigi Prefecture. Later the same year, she was released and sent home thanks to some lobbying by her father. Her father offered to set her up in a law practice if she would just give up her resistance and declare her opposition to communism, but she still would not take the bait. She went to work as a seamstress instead.

In the early postwar years, her father died. Shortly after, she met her husband, Fukunaga, a man who had studied Chinese at the university and had served as a correspondent in Tientsin during the war. He came to live at the Hatano household when his family and their home had been destroyed by Allied bombing. He was very helpful at the time of her father's death and proposed to her formally thereafter. Her first marriage had been a bittersweet experience, but she blamed it on societal attitudes that denied women status as autonomous human beings. The concluding lines of the final chapter of her text read as follows.

The biological distinction between male and female should have no special meaning except as pertains to individuals' needs for love and sexual relations. Before speaking in terms of "woman" all the time, we must think first of each woman as an individual human being. I believe that embracing this notion is an indispensable condition for establishing a genuinely human society. (372)

Analysis

The narrator here makes a very simple but central point: women's experiences are diverse, and something may be lost when we try to reduce them to a single category, "woman." But the most important thing is that women be regarded for who they are as individual human beings. There are a number of ways in which Fukunaga Misao's narrative parallels those of other social activists of her day: she experienced difficulties in marriage, harassment by the police and the Special Higher Police, frequent arrest, interrogation, mistreatment, and, in some cases, witnessed the deaths of comrades in prison. Few women, however, have written so frankly about their involvement in the Japan Communist Party, nor have many leveled such a harsh and thoroughgoing attack at the party. Fukunaga Misao's text is a "manifesto" in Sidonie Smith's sense of the term, that is, "a public declaration or proclamation . . . for the purpose of making known past actions," and therefore can be read as "a revolutionary gesture posed against amnesia and its compulsions to repetition."[7] As Smith characterizes a manifesto,

Purposeful, bold, contentious, the autobiographical manifesto contests the old inscriptions, the old histories, the old politics, the *ancien regime*.[8]

There can be very little question that the purpose of Fukunaga's text is to contest, to lay bare the hypocrisy and androcentrism of the Japan Communist Party, and to assert that top party leaders, including her husband, caved in rather readily under pressure and renounced the party.

The narrator, herself imprisoned and harassed, was able to stand her ground, and she would have the reader believe that it was precisely her tendency to think for herself, to argue with comrades, to "talk back," as it were, and to stand up to the police that made her anathema to the party leadership. Moreover, she makes a convincing case that the chauvinism of the party leadership made a mockery of the party's claim to speak for the liberation of all human beings. Her own marriage to Koreeda, she concludes, must have been conceived by the party hierarchy as a way to control her, to keep her in check. The final straw comes for her when her husband writes her a letter from prison ordering her to be silent, to return to her family and await further instructions—this after he had turned his back on party ideology and renounced the very principles that were central to Marxism. When she was participating in all these discourses, as well as when she tells her story later on, Fukunaga had to take great risks, and her text reveals that she paid the price for taking these risks many times over.

But Fukunaga's text does not stop here. She raises a question fundamental to modern Japan's historical development: why was the military able to seize control over civilian cabinets and government policy so completely? The answer, she finds, is not only in the rise of right-wing nationalism, but is also in the Stalinist-style tactics employed by the prewar Japan Communist Party that set out to discredit and weaken all other organizations that it could not control itself, thus fatally weakening the "left" in prewar Japan. This is a powerful indictment.

There were two other features of her narrative that represent something quite extraordinary. While in prison, she turned to the Tale of Genji *and developed— without the benefit of existing research on the* Genji—*a feminist reading of this text well in advance of anyone else. This sprawling narrative of over a thousand pages depicts the life of courtiers in tenth-century Japan and seemingly centers around the life of a "shining prince," Hikaru Genji. But Fukunaga tells us that*

> [t]he author of this mysterious masterpiece was a woman, and as I was also a woman, I read this text in a natural, unforced way through the eyes of a woman.

Her reading compels her to look beyond the notion that it is really a text about a male courtier and to see it as a narrative of female strength and power. "The real protagonists of this tale," she writes, "are the various women. Each of these women has her own unique individuality and a strong measure of self-respect that makes them lively and animated." Prince Genji is too fragmented and too inconsistent to stand up as a central character. Rather, he is the link that joins the narratives of the various female characters who populate the text. In 1990, Fukunaga published a book of her Genji *criticism titled* The Women of the Tale of Genji and the Writer (Genji monogatari no onnatachi to sakusha), *which includes chapters on each of the principal female characters such as Lady Kiritsubo, Utsusemi, Yūgao, Fujitsubo, Oborozukiyo, the Rokujō Lady, Princess Asagao, the Akashi Lady, and others.[9] If this perspective on the* Genji *seems ordinary today, it was rather unique when she first began to develop her ideas in prison in the 1930s.*

The other intriguing feature of her narrative is her depiction of her interest in ancient history, which she developed while in prison and which led her to the works of Tsuda Sōkichi. As a young, budding Marxist, she was critical of the Communist Party for failing to come to grips with the question of the imperial institution, or the emperor system (tennōsei) as it is better known. In the scholarly work of Tsuda she discovered the grounds for a solid critique of the official, Ministry of Education version of the origins of the imperial household, a version that showed the monarchy to be much younger than official histories asserted, and that the creation of the myths had been the result of a concerted effort to by the aristocratic leadership to support its claims to legitimacy. As with her arguments about the Genji, the narrator raises the question that if these kinds of materials are accessible to her, without any substantial academic background, why hadn't literary scholars and party leaders pursued these avenues of inquiry more vigorously? There should have been no more question central to Marxists than the nature of the Japanese monarchical system—the tennōsei—but there was an apparent lack of will to confront the history of this institution.

When women ask these kinds of questions, they transgress. Not only did Fukunaga transgress the boundaries of what was expected of a good party functionary, but she challenged her husband's authority over her as well. In doing so, she not only ran up against centuries of unquestioned patriarchal authority, but also the particularly virulent sort of male chauvinism associated with the men from Kagoshima, the southernmost tip of the island of Kyūshū. Takamure Itsue had encountered similar behavior from her husband, Hashimoto Kenzō, who also hailed from Kyūshū. But the irony, to which the narrator keeps returning, was that when she joined the movement as a student at Tokyo Women's College, it was precisely because she believed that communism's aim was the creation of a completely egalitarian society. She had assumed, or at least hoped, that the men in this movement would be different and could rise above their enculturation. When she realized that the Communist Party actually reconfigured the patriarchy and institutionalized most of its values in its "contempt for women," she had no choice but to denounce it. That she could do so at the same time she ridiculed the leadership for renouncing the party in 1929 must have been all the more difficult for her male colleagues to bear. Hence, the risks for speaking out were great.

We have seen that female autobiographers are often writing in order to save themselves from erasure. Fukunaga encountered resistance and attempts at erasure at every turn. Both the Communist Party and her husband wanted to control and silence her. Even her father, mortified at the way the rest of society would regard his daughter, wanted to silence her as well. She was anathema to the authorities who wanted her to renounce her beliefs. Even though her in-laws supported her, she found the whole chauvinist mentality of southern Japan, the island of Kyūshū, unbearable. Pressured from all sides, the narrator often felt conflicted and contradictory. Not many others could have withstood the enormous pressures that Fukunaga Misao encountered, but she would neither bend nor break. Her text, Memoirs of a Female Communist, is her way of "talking back," of asserting her own subjectivity by means of a ferocious attack on those who derided and demeaned her.

7
Conclusion

Self-writing is a marvelous place for readers and writers alike to explore the spaces that exist between the narrator and the narrated, between memory and experience, and between genre and gender. Autobiographies are able to offer valuable insights into the experiences of people who lived through tumultuous times, but since women's historical experiences have been so often omitted from the historical record, female self-writing is particularly useful for enhancing our understanding of how women lived their lives and of the kinds of choices with which they were confronted in a given era. It is in this sense that the texts examined here offer valuable insights into the discursive processes at work in the prewar years that made this agency possible even though it was virtually proscribed.[1] Are there "differences" that one would expect to find in the self-writing of men and women? Certainly, one assumption deeply lodged in feminist criticism holds that because the lived experiences of men and women are different, these differences ought to be reflected in their self-representational writing. Moreover, many critics believe that when women write their lives—when they engage in the act of finding their own voice and telling their own story—it can provide an important link to agency. Specifically, it is argued that when women resist the "objectification" that self-writing can impose, it marks a place of agency for them. That is precisely why, even within dominant discourses, there can "exist unruly subjects" who manage to take responsibility for their own agency and subjectivity.[2]

This volume has demonstrated convincingly that modern Japanese women who have written their lives have earned the appellation "unruly subjects." Their texts not only constitute a challenge to gender subordination, but they signify the emergence of an oppositional ideology that had its roots in the interwar years. Willing to take risks and to contest their subordinate position, the five women examined here offer narratives that manifest a distinctive "fierceness" in relation to the world and to the dominant discourses that they were compelled to confront. Moreover, the autobiographies examined in *Telling Lives* also display tensions, paradoxes, and ambiguities. Gilmore believes that since feminist theory conceives of women as "objects of exchange," it is valuable to examine "how women use self-representation and its constitutive possibilities for agency and subjectivity to become no longer primarily subject to exchange but subjects who exchange the position of object for the subjectivity of self-representational agency."[3] I argue that each of the texts examined in this volume manifests—along with a strong sense of "contestation and risk"—that element of exchange whereby the narrator escapes the definitions and expectations placed upon her by society and by her family in order to embrace her own agency. By claiming the right to speak for themselves instead of being spoken for, they succeed in exchanging their position as objects for the position as subject of their own discourse.

Since virtually no agreement exists among critics concerning any of the main constituents of self-writing—what an individual is, what a self may be, what subjectivity is, or, indeed, even what an autobiography is—there is really no easy pathway to understanding what constitutes female self-writing in Japan. But the attempt to discover this pathway is well worth the effort, for as Betty Bergland reminds us, self-writing is an extremely useful way "to examine the effect of discourses on subjects, both those that seem to guarantee prevailing social relations and those that critique them."[4] By exposing their readers to a variety of discourses, the five Japanese women whose texts we have examined here generate narratives that critique prewar political structures and the status of gender relations.

For the most part, the texts examined here were written with one eye squarely on the historical record. Oku Mumeo, Nishi Kiyoko, and Takai Toshio, for example, indicate clearly in their texts that they were concerned about the ability of future generations to understand what those who had gone before had accomplished in order to make things better for women. It could also be argued that Takai, Sata Ineko, Fukunaga Misao, and Oku as well manifest a strong commitment to social justice in general and gender equality in particular in their texts. But perhaps the most important thing these texts share in common is a willingness to contest patriarchal authority and the subordinate position of women in the family and in society. We can review briefly how this willingness to contest authority is manifested in each text

Oku Mumeo's narrative is a lengthy and detailed treatment of the range of possible modes of activism open to Japanese women. Her goal was always to make a difference in the everyday lives of Japanese women. In order to do so, she formed organizations, networked, published journals, campaigned for proletarian parties, and spoke at rallies. Since no single strategy or mode of activism—no ideology—was superior to any other, nor appropriate for all times and places, Oku had to experiment, to discover her own path by means of trial and error. This is often a painful and disruptive process, one that may leave the narrator endorsing contradictory strategies. Oku wrestled with guilt over always being on the run, attending meetings and rallies, instead of being with her children, but asserting the right of women to take control over their lives was her highest priority. It kept her fires burning.

Takai Toshio's narrative is clearly driven by a desire to set the record straight, to let readers know what she had meant to Hosoi Wakizō and what his legacy should mean to young people today. Bullied by floor managers, company executives, policemen, and editors who would deny her standing as Wakizō's spouse, Takai learned to stand her ground. Her message is clear: while society's laws may be aligned against women, women must do what they can to contest the inequities of patriarchal rule. Nishi Kiyoko's story has everything to do with gender and the challenges women confront when they seek to establish their financial and political independence. It poignantly addresses the ghosts of an antiquated family system that still haunt the corridors of her household. The old institutions, the families, as well as the corporations, may not wish to see women stand on their own, but it is incumbent upon women to do what they can to contest their authority.

Sata Ineko makes it clear to her readers how important independence and identity can be to a writer and how difficult it is for a woman to create the literal and discursive space necessary to sustain them. In a prominent way, her autobiography points to the moment in which the narrator renames herself, rejecting the authority of fathers and husbands in favor of a beloved uncle who had introduced her to literature. In this way, she makes clear how in writing from the margins and "between the lines" of her chronology she is able to create and sustain her own subjectivity. Finally, Fukunaga Misao challenges her readers to appreciate how even the most progressive social and political ideology of the day can be thoroughly engendered and deny women any room to develop as individuals or to operate with any degree of agency. She places on display all the regimes of authority that would silence her: her husband, her father, the Communist Party, and the authorities. But her voice remains strong and her intentions clear: she writes to contest the practices—discursive and actual—that would silence and repress women.

The self-representational narratives of the five women examined here, then, are very much centered on the process of "grappling" with important issues. There is a final question worth posing: what role does autobiography theory play in helping us read and interpret women's self-representational narratives? For one thing, it helps us appreciate that autobiography is a literary construct that privileges a post-Enlightenment version of the individual along with notions of truth and power that are rooted in male experience. Feminist critics argue that the male experience is foundational[5] and that men are seen as "autonomous individuals with inflexible ego boundaries who write autobiographies that turn on moments of conflict and place the self at the center of the drama."[6] When women write their lives, then, they must do so with a doubled subjectivity, what Sidonie Smith refers to as a "double-helix of the imagination."[7] In chapter 1 it was indicated that one of the principal aims of this study would be to attend to the "cultural specificities" of the autobiographies under examination. What cultural specificities can we legitimately claim are shared by these five texts? Clearly, all of them feature a narrating "I" that is produced in relation to *institutions* (families, schools, marriages) and to *discourses* (individualism, feminism, socialism, Marxism), and this narrating "I" engages in the act of interrogating how these institutions and discourses have operated upon it. In so doing, they courageously and vigorously contest many of the concepts underlying the dominant discourse, particularly with regard to gender equality.

Likewise, the autobiographies examined here manifest a tendency to understate, to be self-effacing, to "tell it slant." In this way, the contestatory tone can be muted, and the humble posture can belie a fierce undertone. But it is not the case that all of the assumptions from Western feminist criticism that we have discussed apply equally to Japanese texts. For example, in the earliest stages of the development of feminist autobiography criticism, Jelinek made the argument that compared with male autobiographers, women "emphasize to a much lesser extent the public aspects of their lives, the affairs of the world, or even their careers, and concentrate instead on their personal lives—domestic details, family difficulties, close friends, and especially people who influenced them."[8] This view was echoed recently by Sanders in her study of Victorian women's recollections of girlhood, where she argues that most of these women tended to "invert the usual patriarchal value-system and put domestic and childhood events at the centre of their writing."[9]

However, nothing could be further from the case of Japanese women writing their lives in the late twentieth century. Except, perhaps, for Jelinek's point about the role of influential figures in their lives, Japanese women's autobiographies offer little in the way of domestic events in their narratives. Rather, it is the "public aspects of their lives" and "the affairs of the world" that are the principal subject of these texts. Relationships may be discussed, but these relationships are primarily with other women who operated in the same circles as the narrators. Details on more personal relationships are usually lacking in these texts. When marriages, affairs, or messy divorces *are* discussed, it is precisely because something about the relationship was already public knowledge and possibly a subject of some notoriety. Takai's relationship with Hosoi and Sata's marriage to Kubokawa were not only matters of public record, but were tinged with scandal. Fukunaga's marriage to Koreeda was not so much a matter of public notoriety, but his ideological recantation definitely was, and her insights into what the whole marriage might have meant and her own refusal to renounce the Communist Party herself stand out as important currents in the narrative. On the other hand, Oku and Nishi divulge virtually nothing about their spouses; and Fukunaga has little to say about her second husband. Marriages are usually mentioned quite abruptly, with no indication how a couple may have met or gotten to know one another. On the whole, then, these autobiographies are scarcely concerned with details of domestic life at all.

It would be my contention, however, that Western feminist criticism on self-writing does have much to offer students of Japanese autobiography. It can be argued convincingly that each of these texts, in its own way, displays the telltale signs of being what Gilmore and Scott regard as "site[s] of resistance."[10] As we saw in the epigraph to chapter 1, Gilmore believes that self-writing can be a political act, an act of resistance by which women assert their own agency.[11] Abundant evidence was uncovered in the texts we examined to support the idea that these narrative voices were more than capable of challenging and subverting prevailing ideologies. This is perhaps especially so in the case of narrators such as Takai or Fukunaga, both of whose texts bear the mark of a "manifesto" in Sidonie Smith's sense of the term. That is, they "contest sovereignty" and "engage in self-consciously political autobiographical acts." But it can be argued that all five of the autobiographies functioned as places where "crucial political and cultural contests are enacted" to recall Scott's phrase. Scott defends her idea of looking at women's lives as "sites" because she believes that

> [t]o figure a person—in this case a woman—as a place or location is not to deny her humanity; it is, rather, to recognize the many factors that constitute her agency, the complex and multiple ways in which she is constructed as an historical actor.[12]

By examining the narratives of Oku Mumeo, Takai Toshio, Nishi Kiyoko, Sata Ineko, and Fukunaga Misao, we are able to appreciate "the complex and multiple ways" in which the discourses and institutions they encountered shaped their lives. It is in this sense that feminist autobiography criticism offers us the opportunity to read Japanese women's self-writing in exciting and productive ways. At the same time, the "cases" that their narratives represent enrich our body of knowledge about self-representational writing in general and about the relationship between lived experience and representation that is so central to this type of writing. But in the end, a careful reading of these texts also suggests that the discursive circumstances in which Japanese women found themselves were not so very different from those experienced by women elsewhere in the world.

Notes

Introduction

1. Stephen Greenblatt, *Shakespearean Negotiations: The Circulation of Social Energy in Renaissance England* (Berkeley: University of California Press, 1988), 1.

2. Ibid; italics added.

3. John Eakin Paul, *Fictions in Autobiography: Studies in the Art of Self-Invention* (Princeton, N.J.: Princeton University Press, 1985), 3.

4. Sidonie Smith and Julia Watson, eds., *De/Colonizing the Subject: The Politics of Gender in Women's Autobiography* (Minneapolis: University of Minnesota Press, 1992), xvii.

5. See Doris Sommer, "'Not Just a Personal Story': Women's Testimonies and the Plural Self," in Bella Brodzki and Celeste Schenck, eds., *Life/Lines: Theorizing Women's Autobiography* (Ithaca, N.Y.: Cornell University Press, 1988), 111.

6. Laura Marcus, *Auto/biographical Discourses: Theory, Criticism, Practice* (Manchester and New York: Manchester University Press, 1994), 16.

7. Estelle Jelinek, ed., *Women's Autobiography: Essays in Criticism* (Bloomington: Indiana University Press, 1980), ix.

8. Ibid., 17.

9. Domna Stanton, ed., *The Female Autograph: Theory and Practice of Autobiography from the Tenth to the Twentieth Century* (Chicago: University of Chicago Press, 1984).

10. Ibid., 13.

11. Ibid., 15.

12. Sidonie Smith, *The Poetics of Women's Autobiography: Marginality and the Fictions of Self-Representation* (Bloomington: Indiana University Press, 1987), 44.

13. Ibid., 50.

14. Bella Brodzki and Celeste Schenck, eds., *Life/Lines: Theorizing Women's Autobiography* (Ithaca, N.Y.: Cornell University Press, 1988).

15. Other works worth mentioning are Carolyn Heilbrun, *Writing a Woman's Life* (New York: Ballantine, 1989); Françoise Lionnet, *Autobiographical Voices: Race, Gender, Self-Portraiture* (Ithaca, N.Y.: Cornell University Press, 1989); Personal Narratives Group, eds., *Interpreting Women's Lives: Feminist Theory and Personal Narratives* (Bloomington: Indiana University Press, 1989); Felicity Nussbaum, *The Autobiographical Subject: Gender and Ideology in Eighteenth-Century England* (Baltimore, Md.: Johns Hopkins University Press, 1989); and Regenia Gagnier, *Subjectivities: A History of Self-Representation in Britain, 1832–1920* (1991). Sidonie Smith contributed two other important studies in the early 1990s: *De/Colonizing the Subject: The Politics of Gender in Women's Autobiography*, ed. Smith and Julia Watson (Minneapolis: University of Minnesota Press, 1992); and *Subjectivity, Identity and the Body: Women's Autobiographical Practices in the Twentieth Century* (Bloomington: Indiana University Press, 1993). The late 1990s also saw a number of new critical studies of self-writing from the feminist perspective such as Diane Bjorkland's *Interpreting the Self: Two Hundred Years of American Autobiography* (Chicago and London: University of Chicago Press, 1998); Suzette Henke's *Shattered Subjects: Trauma and Testimony in Women's Life-Writing* (New York: St. Martin's Press, 1998); and Martine W. Brownley and Allison Kimmich, eds., *Women and Autobiography* (Wilmington, Del.: SR Books, 1999). Other important works include Judy Long, *Telling Women's Lives: Subject, Narrator, Reader, Text* (New York: New York University Press, 1999); Martha Watson, *Lives of Their Own: Rhetorical Dimensions in Autobiographies of Women Activists* (Columbia: University of South Carolina Press, 1999); Kristi Siegel, *Women's Autobiographies, Culture, Feminism* (New York: Peter Lang, 1999); and Alison Donnell and Pauline Polkey, eds., *Representing Lives: Women and Auto/biography* (New York: St. Martin's Press, 2000). A useful survey of feminist critical writing on autobiography up through 1990 is Sidonie Smith's "The [Female] Subject in Critical Venues: Poetics, Politics Autobiographical Practices," in *a/b: Auto/Biography Studies* 6.1(1991):109–130. For a broader and more updated review of the literature, see "Introduction: Situating Subjectivity in Women's Autobiographical Practices," in Sidonie Smith and Julia Watson, eds., *Women, Autobiography, Theory: A Reader* (Madison: University of Wisconsin Press, 1998), 3–52.

16. Long, *Telling Women's Lives*, 25.

17. Ibid., 53. Gilmore makes a similar point in her preface when arguing that gender is produced in discourses of self-representation: "Autobiography is positioned within discourses that construct truth, identity, and power, and these discourses produce a gendered subject." Leigh Gilmore, *Autobiographics: A Feminist Theory of Women's Self-Representation* (Ithaca, N.Y.: Cornell University Press, 1994), xiv.

18. Long, *Telling Women's Lives*, 27.

19. See Saeki Shōichi, comp., *Nihonjin no jiden* [Japanese autobiographies], vol. 6 (Tokyo: Heibonsha, 1900), 1–74.

20. Janet V. Gunn, *Autobiography: Towards a Poetics of Experience* (Philadelphia: University of Pennsylvania Press, 1982), 3.

21. See my article, "Is There a Woman in the Text? Gender in Fukuda Hideko's *Warawa no hanseigai,*" in Julie Ann Carson and John Rehm, eds., *In the Pacific Interest: Democracy, Women and the Environment,* Willamette Journal of the Liberal Arts, Supplemental Series no. 4 (Salem, Oreg.: Willamette University, 1991), 73–86. Note that Vera Mackie also attaches a high level of significance to Fukuda's text in her book, *Creating Socialist Women in Japan: Gender, Labour and Activism, 1900–1937* (New York: Cambridge University Press, 1997), where she argues that "the questions raised by her attempt to forge a political identity—to create herself as a socialist woman—are relevant to a succession of individuals and groups in early twentieth-century Japan"—groups and individuals that are the subject of her pioneering study. If Mackie sees Fukuda's story as a point of origin for the story of socialist women in Japan, she also finds intriguing the answers that Fukuda's text may offer to questions about "why a young woman from a low-ranking samurai family would rebel, become involved with the extremist elements of the liberal movement, and even after her release from imprisonment identify herself with the socialists—a group whose ideas were beyond the pale of acceptable political discourse in Meiji Japan" (*Creating Socialist Women in Japan,* 2).

22. See Fukuda Hideko, *Warawa no hanseigai,* in Saeki, comp., *Nihonjin no jiden* [Japanese autobiographies], vol. 6 (Tokyo: Heibonsha, 1980), 3–4.

23. *Warawa no hanseigai,* 73–74.

24. For a detailed examination of Takamure's text see my essay, "Female Self-Writing: Takamure Itsue's *Hi no kuni no onna no nikki,*" *Monumenta Nipponica* 51.2 (summer 1996):153–170.

25. See E. Patricia Tsurumi, "Visions of Women and the New Society in Conflict: Yamakawa Kikue versus Takamure Itsue," in Sharon A. Minichiello, ed., *Japan's Competing Modernities: Issues in Culture and Democracy 1900–1930* (Honolulu: University of Hawai'i Press, 1998), 335–357.

26. See Saeki, comp., *Nihonjin no jiden,* vol. 7, 3–324, for the edition of *Hi no kuni no onna no nikki* used in this chapter. The quote is from 224.

27. Takamure Itsue, *Hi no kuni no onna no nikki,* in Saeki, comp., *Nihonjin no jiden,* vol. 7, 224–225.

28. Ibid., 226.

29. Ibid., 284–287.

30. Rita Felski, *Beyond Feminist Aesthetics: Feminist Literature and Social Change* (Cambridge, Mass.: Harvard University Press, 1989), 14.

31. Ibid., 164; see also 96–97 and 154–155.

Chapter 1. Producing Writing Subjects: Women in the Interwar Years

1. See Barbara Sato, *The New Japanese Woman: Modernity, Media, and Women in Interwar Japan* (Durham, N.C., and London: Duke University Press, 2003), 13.

2. An excellent piece of scholarly work by Vera Mackie on the emergence of

socialist women in prewar Japan precedes my work. See her *Creating Socialist Women in Japan.*

3. Sato, *The New Japanese Woman*, 7.

4. Ibid., 152–156.

5. Ibid. Sato states clearly, "The modern girl, the housewife, and the professional working woman had neither the desire nor the intention to clash with the system. They shunned radical change. Had there been an organized women's movement, they probably would not have joined it. The small-scale resistance these women conducted in the Taishō and early Shōwa periods focused on areas of life considered more private and individual."

6. Joan W. Scott, *Only Paradoxes to Offer: French Feminists and the Rights of Man* (Cambridge, Mass.: Harvard University Press, 1996), 16.

7. We may think of Dilthey as the grandfather of modern autobiography criticism because it was at his urging that his student and son-in-law Georg Misch undertook the first systematic study of autobiography as a form. Laura Marcus, in her book *Auto/biographical Discourses*, notes how Dilthey placed "lived experience" *(Erlebnis)* and "the understanding of life-expressions" on a par with one another in his quest to see "[e]xperience, which in this sense is distinct from the mere registration of facts or states of affairs" as "the source of worthwhile literary works and the basis of their value" (*Auto/biographical Discourses*, 136–137).

8. Scott, *Only Paradoxes to Offer*, 16. Studying four French women who agitated for suffrage in eighteenth- and nineteenth-century France, Scott notes that "it is tempting for historians to correct the record treating feminism as a form of heroic resistance to injustice by locating this resistance in the wills of individual women. I have been arguing throughout this book that the issue is far more complicated than that. Feminism is not a reaction to republicanism, but one of its effects, produced by contradictory assertions about the universal rights of individuals, on the one hand, and exclusions attributed to 'sexual difference,' on the other. Feminism is the paradoxical expression of that contradiction in its effort both to have 'sexual difference' acknowledged and to have it rendered irrelevant. Feminist agency is constituted by this paradox. . . . Although feminists have been 'women who have only paradoxes to offer,' they have nonetheless done so in fundamentally different terms." (168)

9. Miguel A. Cabrera has addressed this question of the relationship between new language and vocabulary, and the emergence of social activism. See his "On Language, Culture, and Social Action," *History and Theory Theme Issue* 40 (December 2001):82–100.

10. See page 6 in the introduction to this volume or Long, *Telling Women's Lives*, 27.

11. Gilmore, *Autobiographics*, 63.

12. Ibid.

13. See Scott, *Only Paradoxes to Offer*, 17.

14. The expression "Every life has a story" is a popular advertising slogan for the magazine *Biography* and the Arts and Entertainment channel's television program of the same name.

15. Some critics would see memoirs as decidedly less than autobiography—less introspective, less sweeping in their scope, and less intrinsically interesting. However, I have not found the distinction between *kaisō* and *jiden* to be of this nature.

16. See Helen Bruss, "A Feminist Revision of New Historicism to Give Fuller Readings of Women's Private Writing," in Smith and Watson, eds., *Women, Autobiography, Theory*, 222–231. Stephen Greenblatt writes cogently and passionately about the historian's "desire to speak with the dead." See page 1 in the introduction to this book. Bruss' cautionary remarks remind us that all too often, women's voices have been erased from the record or were never included to begin with.

17. Cabrera, "On Language, Culture, and Social Action," 88.

18. Valerie Sanders, ed., *Records of Girlhood: An Anthology of Nineteenth-Century Women's Childhoods* (Aldershot, Hampshire, and Burlington, Vt.: Ashgate Publishing, 2000), 3.

19. Scott, *Only Paradoxes to Offer*, 17.

20. Ibid.

21. Paul Schalow and Janet Walker, eds., *The Woman's Hand: Gender and Theory in Japanese Women's Writing* (Stanford: Stanford University Press, 1996), 5.

22. Harry Harootunian, *Overcome by Modernity: History, Culture, and Community in Interwar Japan* (Princeton, N.J., and Oxford: Princeton University Press, 2000), xxiv.

23. Saeki Shōichi, "Autobiographical Literature In Japan," *Japan Echo* 10.3 (autumn 1983):69–75.

24. Lynne Miyake, "Woman's Voice In Japanese Literature: Expanding the Feminine," *Women's Studies* 17.1–2 (1989):87–100.

25. Terry Kawashima, *Writing Margins: The Textual Construction of Gender in Heian and Kamakura Japan* (Cambridge, Mass.: Harvard University Press, 2001), 214.

26. See the epigraph to chap. 1 in Rebecca Copeland, *Lost Leaves: Women Writers of Meiji Japan* (Honolulu: University of Hawai'i Press, 2000), 7.

27. Ibid., 4–5.

28. Kishida Toshiko (1863–1901) popularized the phrase *"hako-ire musume"* in the early 1880s to describe how unmarried daughters were virtually kept in boxes by their parents while they were being raised, isolated and protected from the harsh realities of life. Kishida, a popular rights activist and later a fiction writer, was renowned for her political speechmaking and was credited by Fukuda Hideko with inspiring her to become politically active. See Yukiko Tanaka, *Women Writers of Meiji and Taishō Japan: Their Lives, Works and Critical Reception, 1868–1926* (Jefferson, N.C., and London: McFarland and Co., Inc., 2000), where

it is noted that "Toshiko concluded her speech by saying that if young women are placed in small, suffocating boxes, they will try and find a much larger box called *sekai*, the world" (23).

29. Andrew Gordon, *Labor and Imperial Democracy in Prewar Japan* (Berkeley: University of California Press, 1991), 144.

30. Ibid., 158ff.

31. Harootunian, *Overcoming Modernity*, xi.

32. See John Benson and Takao Matsumura, *Japan, 1868–1945: From Isolation to Occupation* (Essex, U.K.: Pearson Education Limited, 2001), 96–97.

33. See Michael Lewis, *Rioters and Citizens: Mass Protest in Imperial Japan* (Berkeley: University of California Press, 1990), xvii.

34. See "From Sedentary Culture to Mobile Culture" ("Suwaru bunka kara ugokubunka e") in Kano Masanao, *Taishō demokurashii* [Taishō democracy], *Nihon no rekishi* [Japanese history], vol. 27 (Shogakkan, 1976), 304–306.

35. See Elise Tipton and John Clark, eds., *Being Modern in Japan: Culture and Society from the 1910s to the 1930s* (Honolulu: University of Hawai'i Press, 2000), 7.

36. Jordan Sand, "The Cultured Life as Contested Space: Dwelling and Discourse In the 1920s," in Tipton and Clark, eds., *Being Modern in Japan*, 99–118.

37. Harootunian, *Overcoming Modernity*, 17.

38. Tanaka, *Women Writers of Meiji and Taishō Japan*, 155.

39. See chap. 2, page 64.

40. E. Taylor Atkins, *Blue Nippon: Authenticating Jazz in Japan* (Durham, N.C., and London: Duke University Press, 2001), 101–102.

41. Kano Masanao, *The Undercurrents of Taishō Democracy: The Reappearance of a "Folkloric" Spirit [Taishō demokurashii no teiryū: "Dozoku" teki seishin e no kaiki]*. Nihon hōsō shuppan kyokkai (Tokyo: NHK Bukkusu, 1973), 14–18. Kano refers to a second usage of "reconstruction" that had ominous implications for the era: Kita Ikki's adoption of the term in his plan for the reconstruction of the Japanese state.

42. See Elise K. Tipton, *Modern Japan: A Social and Political History* (London and New York: Routledge, 2002), 103.

43. Atkins, *Blue Nippon*, 102.

44. Sato, *The New Japanese Woman*, 48.

45. Ibid., 49.

46. Sato, *The New Japanese Woman*, quotes essayist Kitazawa Shūichi on 57–58.

47. See Paul John Eakin, ed., *On Autobiography/Philippe Lejeune*, trans. Katherine Leary (Minneapolis: University of Minnesota Press, 1989).

48. Each of these three scholars has made important contributions to the study of female self-writing in Japan. Saeki Shōichi's contribution is of major proportions. He is one of the few Japanese scholars to pay any attention to the study of Japanese autobiography at all. His two books, *Japanese Autobiography [Nihonjin no jiden]* (Tokyo: Kōdansha, 1974), and *Modern Japanese Autobiography [Kindai Nihon no jiden]* (Tokyo: Kodansha, 1981), are pioneering works. He also oversaw the

compilation of the twenty-five-volume anthology of autobiographies, *Japanese Autobiographies [Nihonjin no jiden]* (Tokyo: Heibonsha, 1981–1983) and edited a collection of essays, *The World of Autobiographical Literature [Jiden no sekai]* (Tokyo: Asahi shuppansha, 1983). Some of Saeki's essays have appeared in English as well: "Autobiographical Literature in Japan" and "The Autobiography in Japan," *Journal of Japanese Studies* 2.2 (1985):357–368. It is interesting to note that in an essay on Fukuda's autobiography in *Modern Japanese Autobiography*, Saeki detects something he refers to as a *nijūsei* (a "dual structure") at work in female self-writing in Japan. Because of its resonance with the language of feminist critics who speak of double identifications and "double voicedness," Saeki's choice of the term *"nijūsei"* is particularly intriguing. But Saeki's *nijūsei* is not identical with the notions of contemporary feminist critics. As much as anything, Saeki sees the dual structure as a product of Fukuda trying to straddle two worlds: the political and the literary. What Saeki finds "deeply imbedded" in the narrative structure of Fukuda's text is "a delicate inner rhythm rooted in her individuality," which "floats to the surface of its own accord," contrasting with the events she narrates (189). This rhythm to her prose may persist as an undercurrent or it may generate dramatic tension in the text, such as when she confesses to being a "sinful person," one who has transgressed (197).

A feminist reading of *nijūsei* would see the notion of sin or transgression rather differently from Saeki. Fukuda's real sin was that she dared to transgress political and sexual boundaries, but also that she dared to write her life. In other words, she dared to use the language of the patriarchy to attack its structures. Saeki nearly makes this point himself when he contrasts the prefaces of *Warawa no hanseigai* and the *The Gossamer Years (Kagerō nikki)*, the eleventh-century diary of a lady of the imperial court. He argues that Michitsuna's mother's narrative voice originates in a thoroughly enclosed, private space, while Fukuda's infuses such private or subjective concerns as love, marriage, betrayal, and suffering with the concerns and the fiery rhetoric of the political activist (200–202). But the critical difference for Saeki remains that Fukuda is straddling two worlds, one public, one private, one political, and one literary. He does not see that as a female writing her life, Fukuda must write as a woman, but that she must tell her story to men. She must use some approximation of the language and narrative structure of traditional autobiography, with its essentialist assumptions about the self and individual identity, for that is all that is available to her. To be sure, she could have looked to the *Kagerō nikki* or the diaries of other Heian women as her model. But we must recall that it is not the work of her Heian foremothers, but Benjamin Franklin's *Autobiography* that she cites in her preface. As she composes her life, then, she struggles with the reality that she is writing in a voice and in a form that implicitly marginalizes her, which is why the act of remembering and writing must be so painful.

Marilyn Jeanne Miller published the only English-language monograph on self-writing by Japanese women, *The Poetics of Nikki Bungaku* (New York and London:

Garland Publishing, Inc., 1985), which deals with the classical era, while Livia Monnet's lengthy two-part essay, "'In the Beginning Woman Was the Sun': Autobiographies of Modern Japanese Women Writers—1 and 2," is the only substantial study
of modern and contemporary women autobiographers. Monnet examines autobiographies by Hiratsuka Raichō, Takamure Itsue, and Ishimure Michiko. See *Japan
Forum* 1.1 and 1.2 (April and October 1989):55–81, 196–233. Miller's work was ex-
perimental and applied structuralist techniques to classical Heian texts. Monnet
takes what she calls a "flexible feminist stance" in her article but states plainly that
she believes "literary texts to be indelibly gender-marked, and autobiography to be
one of the most telling instances of sexual difference in the *ecriture*" (56). But beyond a page or two, there is not a great deal of discussion of either feminist or critical
theory in this otherwise excellent scholarly essay.

Other works in the Japan field that relate to women's self-writing include
Richard Bowring's provocative essay on the diaries of the Heian court women,
"The Female Hand in Heian Japan: A First Reading," in Stanton, ed., *The Female
Autograph*, 49–56, in which he argues that although Heian court diaries may be
characterized as "among the earliest examples of the attempt by women living in
male-dominated society to define the self in textual terms," they should hardly be
characterized as an instance of "woman triumphant." Rather, he finds a troubling
"sexual grammar" embedded in these texts in which "[m]an is at the very center
of the world, and women define themselves almost exclusively in relation to this
all-powerful other. . . . Woman, the passive center of the narrative, cannot initiate
passion, but rather generates it in the other. Male and female always live apart,
and woman is the object of desire whose thoughts are concentrated on the man's
next visit" (51). Lynne Miyake argues in her review of Bowring's book, *Murasaki
Shikibu: The Tale of Genji*, that Bowring may be overstating his case while mini-
mizing the significance of Heian women's poetry, diary writing, and imaginative
texts, particularly in terms of empowerment and the sense of female solidarity
their writing may have forged. See *Monumenta Nipponica* 44.3 (autumn
1989):349–351. Miyake also has written an important essay, "Woman's Voice in
Japanese Literature: Expanding the Feminine." In a very distinct but related field
is Tomi Suzuki, *Narrating the Self: Fictions of Japanese Modernity* (Stanford: Stanford University Press, 1996), which is a useful companion to Edward Fowler's
discussion of the "I-novel" in Japan, *The Rhetoric of Confession: Shishōsetsu in Early
Twentieth-Century Japanese Fiction* (Berkeley: University of California Press, 1988).

49. See Stanton, ed., *The Female Autograph*, 49–56.

50. See Sharon L. Sievers, *Flowers in Salt: The Beginnings of Feminist Consciousness in Modern Japan* (Stanford: Stanford University Press, 1983), 110–113.

51. See, e.g., Tōkyōto fujin jōhō sentaa shozō, comp., *A Record of Holdings in
the Tokyo Municipal Center for Information on Women [Shiryō mokuroku]* (Tokyo:
Fujin jōhō sentaa, 1987), 23–45, for a listing that includes the autobiographies
held in this collection. See also Joseigaku kenkyūjo, ed., *A Guidebook to Women's*

Studies [Joseigaku bukku gaido] (Tokyo: Ibundō, 1987), 103–190, for an annotated listing of biographies, autobiographies, and other materials on Japanese women. Another useful bibliographic source is the supplementary volume *(bekkan)* 25 of the Heibonsha series (Saeki, comp., 1981–1983), Kano Masanao, ed., *Japanese Autobiographies: 300 Selections [Nihonjin no jiden: 300 sen]* (Tokyo: Heibonsha, 1982), an annotated listing of three hundred autobiographies by Japanese men and women.

52. No recent visitor to libraries or bookstores in Japan, with their women's issues *(josei mondai)* sections, can fail to notice the significant number of Japanese women's autobiographies that have appeared on the shelves in the last dozen years. Most of these texts narrate the struggles—personal, institutional, societal, and political—in which women engaged in order to discover their voices and recount their lives. Apparently, a primary motivation for these authors is to have their readers, especially other women, gain an appreciation for what others have gone through in previous generations in order to establish political and civil liberties for Japanese women. In this sense, their texts initiate what Mary Catherine Bateson calls a "dialogue of comparison and recognition, a process of memory and articulation that makes one's own experience available as a lens of empathy"; see Bateson, *Composing a Life* (New York: Penguin Books U.S.A, 1989), 6. According to Rita Felski, this impulse to tell one's story in the hope of building a sense of community and solidarity with others is a significant attribute of female self-writing; see Felski, *Beyond Feminist Aesthetics*, 154ff).

Chapter 2. Politics Rooted in Everyday Life: Oku Mumeo's *Fires Burning Brightly (Nobi aka aka to)*

1. See Akiko Tokuza, *The Rise of the Feminist Movement in Japan* (Tokyo: Keio University Press, 1999).

2. Oku Mumeo, *Fires Burning Brightly: The Autobiography of Oku Mumeo [Nobi aka aka to—Oku Mumeo jiden]* (Domesu shuppan, 1988). Also of interest to English-language readers is Narita Ryūichi's essay, "Women in the Motherland: Oku Mumeo through Wartime and Postwar," in Yasushi Yamanouchi, J. Victor Koschmann, and Ryūichi Narita, eds., *Total War and "Modernization"* (Ithaca, N.Y.: Cornell East Asia Series, 1998), 137–158.

3. Kuriyagawa Hakuson published an essay in *Women's Review [Fujin kōron]*, "On Modern Love" ["Kindai ren'ai ron"], in 1920 that put forth a modern view of love and marital relationship that greatly influenced young women at the time. It held up as an ideal a mutual relationship in which both men and women had the opportunity to develop themselves and cultivate their souls within the bonds of a marriage between equals.

4. Nihon Joshi Daigaku, or Japan Women's University, was founded in 1901 by Naruse Jinzō. At that time women were not allowed to attend most four-year institutions of higher learning in Japan. According to the university's on-line materials,

Naruse believed that the first goal of the university was "to educate women as human beings." He also promoted "the idea of educating students as women and as citizens." See www.jwu.ac.jp/ gn/message.htm (December 12, 2002).

5. On Tanaka Ōdō, see Sharon Nolte, *Liberalism in Modern Japan: Ishibashi Tanzan and his Teachers, 1905–1960* (Berkeley: University of California Press, 1987).

6. For middle-class women during the interwar years, the notion of self-cultivation *(shūyō)* was compelling. Oku's description of her thirst for knowledge, her account of spending her college years following her own reading program at the library while resisting the *ryōsai-kenbo* program of the women's college, her attraction to Zen, her fondness for the writings of Kuriyagawa Hyakuson and Tomonaga Shunsui, and her involvement with Ōsugi Sakae and his followers all point to a young woman serious about exploring her ideas and her philosophy of life as she seeks a way to situate herself in the world.

7. For more on the Sekirankai, see Mikiso Hane, trans. and ed., *Reflections on the Way to the Gallows: Rebel Women in Prewar Japan* (Berkeley: University of California Press, 1988), 125–174.

8. For more information on Yamakawa Kikue, see Hane, *Reflections on the Way to the Gallows*, 161–164; and Mackie, *Creating Socialist Women in Japan*, 102–105.

9. Sano Manabu (1893–1953) was a leading Marxist theoretician and Japan Communist Party leader.

10. For details on the *iede-jiken*, see my article, "Female Self-Writing: Takamure Itsue's *Hi no kuni no onna no nikki*," *Monumenta Nipponica* 51.2 (summer 1966):153–170.

11. Sidonie Smith, "Construing Truths in Lying Mouths: Truthtelling in Women's Autobiography," *Studies in the Literary Imagination* 23.2 (fall 1990):145–164. The quote is from 145.

12. Scott, *Only Paradoxes to Offer*, 16.

13. Narita, "Women in the Motherland," 151–152.

Chapter 3. Changing Consciousness: Takai Toshio's *My Own Sad History of Female Textile Workers (Watashi no jokō aishi)*

1. Martha Watson, *Lives of Their Own: Rhetorical Dimensions in Autobiographies of Women Activists* (Columbia: University of South Carolina Press, 1999), ix.

2. Ibid., 12.

3. See Sato, *The New Japanese Woman*, 7ff, for details on the three principal varieties of new Japanese women.

4. See E. Patricia Tsurumi, *Factory Girls: Women in the Thread Mills of Meiji Japan* (Princeton, N.J.: Princeton University Press, 1990), who draws on some of Hosoi's findings in her chapters on the cotton mills. Included is an example from Hosoi's study of a young woman who, while being punished, was pushed by a male supervisor and fell into the spinning machinery, where she was crushed to death (146–147).

5. Yoshino Sakuzō (1878–1933), a professor of politics at the prestigious Tokyo Imperial University, was a forceful advocate for parliamentary democracy and worker's rights. A Christian with sympathies toward socialism, Yoshino tried to make the notion of democracy and popular sovereignty compatible with the emperor system by coining the phrase *"minponshugi"* (government based on the people) as opposed to *"minshūshugi"* (the people as sovereign), which was the standard Japanese equivalent for the term "democracy." Since the Meiji Constitution firmly lodged sovereignty in the person of the emperor, the idea of sovereignty residing in the people was not legally viable. But Yoshino tried to maneuver around this legal obstacle by insisting that the people's welfare be the basic goal of government. To this end he advocated universal manhood suffrage, civilian control over the military, the transformation of the House of Peers to a popularly elected body, and an active social welfare program. Although he spoke of socialism in positive terms, he stopped short of endorsing left-wing ideologies, as he found their materialism and atheism personally repugnant. In 1924 he resigned his post at the university in order to write full time for the daily newspaper, the *Asahi shinbun*. A very popular and influential figure in his day, his combination of Christian socialism, trade unionism, and Confucian morality did not attract the kind of following that Marxism, socialism, and the proletarian literature and arts movements would in the latter half of the 1920s. For more on Yoshino, see Peter Duus, "Yoshino Sakuzō: The Christian as Political Critic," *The Journal of Japanese Studies* 4.2 (summer 1978):301–326.

6. Tokyo Muslin, where Hosoi Wakizō once worked, was the site of a major labor dispute in 1914 that heralded the coming age of frequent labor-management conflicts. It also sparked the formation of a union at the company. See Gordon, *Labor and Imperial Democracy in Prewar Japan*, 76–77.

7. Ibid., 176–181. As Gordon notes, labor organizers, along with political radicals like anarchist Ōsugi Sakae and his feminist partner Itō Noe, who were also murdered by police at this time, were considered to have "skirted or crossed the edge of legitimate thought and action as defined by the keepers of order in early imperial Japan. The police and the soldiers in Kameido maintained grim consistency in their extreme acts, offering an emphatic statement of the relationship between the political system and social activists" (181).

8. See Stephen S. Large, *Organized Workers in Socialist Politics in Interwar Japan* (Cambridge: Cambridge University Press, 1981), 53.

9. Ibid., 47.

10. Surveys at the time queried working women on their motivation for seeking employment outside the home, and for most it was to achieve economic independence. But as Sato points out, "economic independence" had more than one meaning: it meant relieving the burden the young women might impose on their families as well as actually achieving financial independence (*The New Japanese Woman*, 130–131). Here, it is quite evident that Toshio did not send money

home to help her family, and, more important, she did not hesitate to spend her hard-earned money on consumer goods for herself.

11. Self-cultivation *(shūyō)* was another important reason propelling women, especially those with a higher-school education, into the workforce. "Self-cultivation" could mean many things—spiritual growth, cultural development, character training, etc. While there might be a variety of ways to accomplish this kind of character training, reading and attending lectures were among the primary avenues. For more on self-cultivation and Japanese women in the interwar period, see Sato, *The New Japanese Woman,* 134–141. In this passage, and in a section below where she describes her life with Wakizō, the narrator indicates the way in which she tried to cultivate her humanity.

12. For a brief account of the strike included as part of a biographical sketch of one of the participants, Iijima Kimi (1911–1935), see Kano Masanao, *Individual Personalities in History [Rekishi no naka no koseitachi]* (Yuikaku sensho, 1989), 33–54.

13. See Miriam Silverberg, "The Café Waitress Serving Modern Japan," in Stephen Vlastos, ed., *Mirror of Modernity: Invented Traditions of Modern Japan* (Berkeley: University of California Press, 1998), 208–225. As Silverberg notes, "The Japanese café was new; it was not to be confused with the Japanese coffeehouse, the first of which was established as early as 1888. . . . The café, in contrast, was considered a modern successor to the Taishō-period milk halls." And the café waitresses, she points out, "served food, poured the drinks, and joined in the drinking as they made conversation with their customers. These young women were spectacularized in the print media, in the movies, and in movie song lyrics" (212–213).

14. Yamamoto Sanehiko was an innovative and influential editor. His journal, *Kaizō,* first appeared in April 1919 and was dedicated to introducing readers to all the newest currents—currents that owed little or nothing to the older world of Meiji and early Taishō. The word "Reconstruction," which also appeared in red, roman letters on the magazine's cover, captured the sense that a new Japan was in the making. See Kano Masano, *The Undercurrents of Taishō Democracy.* See also Matsubara Kazushige's biography of Yamamoto Sanehiko, *Yamamoto Sanehiko and the Kaizōsha [Kaizōsha to Yamamoto Sanehiko]* (Nanpō shinsha, 2001). As Professor Kano points out, the term *"Kaizō"* captured something of the atmosphere of the times and was used in a variety of contexts. For example, in August 1919, a group of young reform-minded liberals formed the Reconstruction League (Kaizō Dōmei) in order to transform Japan so it would become more like the victorious democracies of World War I. On this subject, see also Sharon Minichiello, *Retreat from Reform* (Honolulu: University of Hawai'i Press, 1984).

15. Yamamoto Senji (1889–1929) was a fascinating person. He was best known and admired as a pioneering sex educator and birth-control advocate. He grew up in a Christian family in Kyoto but left Japan as a youth and lived for four and a half years in Canada. When he returned to Japan to resume his education, he was older than his fellow students and did not graduate from the University of

Tokyo until he was thirty-two years old, something almost unheard of even today. He published books on biology, sex education, and birth control. In 1928 he ran for election to the Diet from one of Kyoto's wards as a member of one of the many proletarian parties that appeared after the passage of the Universal Manhood Suffrage Act. Yamamoto was elected but was assassinated in 1929 by a member of the right wing because he opposed the death penalty for violations of the Peace Preservation Law. For more on Yamamoto, see Kano Masano, *A Guide to Modern Japanese Thought [Kindai Nihon shisō annai]* (Iwanami bunko, 1999), 217–220.

16. Kagawa Toyohiko (1888–1960) was a charismatic Christian social reformer who walked the slums of Kobe and Osaka spreading the gospel and trying to help people. He was active in the labor movement as well.

17. Felski, *Beyond Feminist Aesthetics*, 14.

18. Ibid., 91–96.

19. Long, *Telling Women's Lives*, 28.

20. Judith Fetterley, *The Resisting Reader: A Feminist Approach to American Fiction* (Bloomington: Indiana University Press, 1978), viii.

21. Gilmore, *Autobiographics*, 45.

Chapter 4. Her Mother's Voice: Nishi Kiyoko's *Reminiscences (Tsuioku)*

1. See Sato, *The New Japanese Woman*, 32.

2. Ibid., 46.

3. See Harootunian, *Overcome by Modernity*, 95.

4. Sato has written in detail about the impact of these and other sensational incidents as reported in the media. Sato comments on how "Byakuren's behavior was even more shocking than that of Yoshikawa Kamako. Kamako had at least attempted suicide. Byakuren 'brazenly' lived with the man she loved. Moreover, she contributed an open letter to the October 22, 1921, Tokyo *Asahi* stating why she had acted as she did. Byakuren's letter recounted a ten-year loveless marriage to a man twenty-seven years her senior, the nouveau-riche owner of a coal mine in Kyūshū. She described an emotionally barren life at the mercy of an incorrigible womanizer." Sato, *The New Japanese Woman*, 111. Clearly, these kinds of events had an impact on young women of the day. In this case, it strengthened Nishi's resolve to avoid a loveless arranged marriage.

5. See Miriam Silverberg, "Constructing a New Social History of Prewar Japan," in Masao Miyoshi and H.D.Harootunian, eds., "Japan in the World," *Boundary 2* 18.3 (fall 1991):61–89.

6. Ōyama was emblematic of the age. Originally a fervent supporter of Taishō democracy, he grew disillusioned with the mainstream political parties in the 1920s and threw himself into the proletarian party movement. Since the liberal parties were too absorbed in maintaining their own grip on power, only the proletarian parties could address the needs of the masses. For more on Ōyama, see Peter Duus, "Ōyama Ikuo and the Search for Democracy," in James W. Morley, ed.,

Dilemmas of Growth in Prewar Japan (Princeton, N.J.: Princeton University Press, 1971), 423–458.

7. Fukumoto Kazuo (1894–1983) was a Tokyo Imperial University graduate who emerged as a primary theoretician for the Japan Communist Party in the 1920s. He believed that the theoretical struggle was as important for raising proletarian consciousness as organizing efforts among the workers. His views enjoyed prominence during the mid-1920s. More will be said about Fukumoto in chapter 6.

8. Sakai Toshihiko was a prominent socialist and friend of her uncle's who had provided a letter of introduction for Kiyoko to facilitate her interview with Ishibashi.

9. Joe Moore, *Japanese Workers and the Struggle for Power 1945–1947* (Madison: University of Wisconsin Press, 1983), 52.

10. Ibid., 55.

11. See Mark Gayn, *Japan Diary* (New York: William Sloane Associates, Inc., 1948).

12. Gilmore, *Autobiographics*, 85.

13. Long, *Telling Women's Lives*, 36–41.

14. Scott, *Only Paradoxes to Offer*, 16.

15. Ibid., 17.

Chapter 5. Re-presenting the Self: Sata Ineko's *Between the Lines of My Personal Chronology (Nen'pu no gyōkan)*

1. See Miriam Silverberg, *Changing Song: The Marxist Manifestoes of Nakano Shigeharu* (Princeton, N.J.: Princeton University Press, 1990), 40–41. Nakano was an enormously important figure in the prewar left. He was a man of letters, a poet, a novelist, an intellectual, a Marxist critic, and a revolutionary. As Silverberg says of her own study of Nakano:

> It offers an image of Nakano Shigeharu as Marxist critic, and in the process it suggests a new way of positioning the Japanese Marxist vision within the prewar culture of Taishō Japan. . . . It is the history of the changing consciousness of one Japanese Marxist, whose life spanned the three imperial reigns of Japan's modern era, the Meiji (1868–1912), Taishō (1912–1926), and Shōwa (1926–1989) years. (3)

2. Ibid., 61.

3. In David Madden, ed., *Proletarian Writers of the Thirties* (Carbondale: Southern Illinois University Press, [1968] 1979), 173–174.

4. Constance Coiner, "Literature of Resistance: The Intersection of Feminism and the Communist Left in Meridel Le Sueur and Tillie Olsen," in Bill Mullen and Sherry Linkon, eds., *Radical Revisions: Rereading 1930s Culture* (Urbana: University of Illinois Press, 1996), 144–166.

5. Charles Eisenger, "Character and Self in Fiction on the Left," in Madden, ed., *Proletarian Writers of the Thirties*, quoted in Barbara Foley, *Radical Representations: Politics and Form in U.S. Proletarian Fiction, 1929–1941* (Durham, N.C.: Duke University Press, 1993), 27.

6. Jo Malin, *The Voice of the Mother: Embedded Maternal Narratives in Twentieth-Century Women's Autobiography* (Carbondale: Southern Illinois University Press, 2000), 1.

7. She wrote of these years in Aioi in a later novel, *Barefoot Girl (Suashi no musume)*.

8. See Noriko Mizuta, *Reality and Fiction in Modern Japanese Literature* (White Plains, N.Y.: M. E. Sharpe, 1980), 55–69.

9. Cited in Long, *Telling Women's Lives*, 37.

10. See Silverberg, "The Café Waitress Serving Modern Japan," 208–225. The quote is from 208. According to Tipton, contemporary researcher Maruboshi Takanobu "acknowledged the sexual attraction of the waitresses," but "he denied the café's primary function and appeal as a place for arranging sexual assignations. In his view the young generation was interested in 'platonic' and 'romantic' love, not sex, so it was as atmosphere of love *(ren'ai)* that brought young people to the café." Quoted by Tipton in "The Café: Constested Space of Modernity in Interwar Japan," in Elise K. Tipton and John Clark, eds., *Being Modern in Japan: Culture and Society from the 1910s to the 1930s* (Honolulu: University of Hawai'i Press, 2000), 127–128.

11. Mariko Inoue, "The Gaze of the Café Waitress: From Selling Eroticism to Constructing Autonomy," *U.S.-Japan Women's Journal* 15 (1998):78–106. The quoted material is found on 81.

12. Tipton, "The Café: Contested Space of Modernity in Interwar Japan," 119.

13. Ibid., 122.

14. This assessment by Gonda Yasunosuke is quoted by Tipton, ibid., 123.

15. Foley, *Radical Representations*, 87.

16. Ibid.

17. See an interesting essay by Hillaria Gössman, "Writing as a Means of Liberation: Women Writers' Autobiographical Works in Proletarian Literature," in Susanne Formanek and Sepp Linhart, eds., *Japanese Biographies: Life Histories, Life Cycles, Life Stages* (Vienna: Der Osterreiischen Akademie der Wissenschaften, 1992), 99–112.

18. Gilmore, *Autobiographics*, xiii.

19. Ibid., 4.

20. See Teresa de Lauretis, *Technologies of Gender: Essays on Theory, Film, and Fiction* (Bloomington: Indiana University Press, 1987), 26.

21. Janet Varner Gunn, *Autobiography: Towards a Poetics of Experience* (Philadelphia: University of Pennsylvania Press, 1982), 8.

22. Ibid., 16.

23. Ibid., 17.

Chapter 6. Resisting Authority: Fukunaga Misao's *Recollections of a Female Communist (Aru onna kyōsanshugisha no kaisō)*

1. Sidonie Smith, "The Autobiographical Manifesto: Identities, Temporalities, Politics," in Shirley Neuman, ed., *Autobiography and Questions of Gender* (Portland: Frank Cass, 1991), 186–212. Quote is on 189.

2. See Henry D. Smith, *Japan's First Student Radicals* (Cambridge, Mass.: Harvard University Press, 1972). Although originally more populist and democratic in its leanings, in the mid-1920s the New Man Society became a major site for investigating and disseminating information on Marxism.

3. Rudolf Hilferding (1877–1941) published one of his most influential works, *Finance Capital,* in 1910, and it drew extensive commentary from Lenin, Kautsky, and Bukharin. He joined the Social Democratic Party and served as finance minister on two occasions. A Jew, Hilferding fled Hitler's Germany only to be handed over to the Gestapo by Vichy authorities in 1941. He died in Paris in the Gestapo dungeon at Le Santé, apparently after taking an overdose of veronal. See William Smaldone, *Rudolf Hilferding: The Tragedy of a German Social Democrat* (De Kalb: Northern Illinois University Press, 1998).

4. See Peter Duus and Irwin Scheiner, "Socialism, Liberalism, and Marxism, 1901–1931," in Peter Duus, ed., *The Cambridge History of Japan,* vol. 6 (Cambridge: Cambridge University Press, 1988), 698ff.

5. For more information on Fukumoto and his position in the Japan Communist Party, see Germaine Hoston, *Marxism and the Crisis of Development in Prewar Japan* (Princeton, N.J.: Princeton University Press, 1986), 3–54.

6. The Japanese Council of Trade Unions (Hyōgikai, short for Nihon rōdō kumiai hyōgikai) was the more militant and Marxist rival of the Greater Japan Federation of Labor (Sōdōmei), the more moderate union that grew out of Suzuki Bunji's Friendly Society (Yuaikai). While the Greater Japan Federation of Labor emphasized negotiation and cooperation with management, the Japanese Council of Trade Unions, run by prominent Marxists, put its faith in militant struggles against capitalism and readily endorsed strikes as an effective way to promote class consciousness and encourage union membership. In 1928, the Japanese Council of Trade Unions was dissolved by the government for being too Marxist and "antistate." See Koji Taira, "Economic Development, Labor Markets, and Industrial Relations in Japan, 1905–1955," in Peter Duus, ed., *The Cambridge History of Japan, Vol. 6: The Twentieth Century,* 606–653. See also Stephen S. Large, *Organized Workers and Socialist Politics in Interwar Japan,* 84–100.

7. Smith, "The Autobiographical Manifesto," 208.

8. Ibid., 189.

9. See Fukunaga Misao, *The Women of the Tale of Genji and the Writer [Genji monogatari no onnatachi to sakusha]* (Renga shobō shinsha, 1990).

Chapter 7. Conclusion

1. This recalls Scott's remarks about the importance of becoming aware of "discursive processes—the epistemologies, institutions and practices—that produce political subjects, that make agency (in this case, the agency of feminists) possible even when it is forbidden or denied" as noted in chap. 1, p. 18. See Scott, *Only Paradoxes to Offer*, 16.

2. See Gilmore, *Autobiographics*, 12, where she argues that

[t]he subject of autobiography, upon which so much scrutiny has recently focused, can be more accurately described as the object of production for the purpose of cultural critique. . . . Thus the ways in which an autobiographer variously acknowledges, resists, embraces, rejects objectification, the way s/he learns, that is, to interpret objectification as something less than simply subjectivity itself marks a place of agency. It is in this act of interpretation, of consciousness, that we can say a woman may exceed representation within dominant ideology. She exceeds it not because she possesses some privileged relation to nature or the supernatural. Rather, the discourses and practices that construct subjectivity through hierarchy must always be defended, their boundaries guarded, their rights maintained. Within these discourses exist unruly subjects who are unevenly objectified and who represent identity in relation to other values and subjectivities.

3. Ibid. Gilmore takes the notion of "objects of exchange" from Claude Lévi-Strauss; see the footnote on p. 43.

4. See Betty Bergland, "Postmodernism and the Autobiographical Subject: Reconstructing the 'Other,'" in Kathleen Ashley, Leigh Gilmore, and Gerald Peters, eds., *Autobiography and Postmodernism* (Amherst: University of Massachusetts Press, 1994), 162.

5. Long, *Telling Women's Lives*, 25. Long asserts that autobiography criticism "assumes a male subject," and she characterizes autobiography "as a discourse of institutionalized androcentrism" (15).

6. Gilmore, *Autobiographics*, xiii.

7. Sidonie Smith, *The Poetics of Women's Autobiography*, 51.

8. Ibid., 7–8.

9. Sanders, *Records of Girlhood*, 18.

10. Gilmore, *Autobiographics*, 80. Scott explains her notion of women as "sites—historical locations or markers—where crucial political and cultural contests are enacted" in *Only Paradoxes to Offer*, 16.

11. Gilmore, *Autobiographics*, 40.

12. Ibid.

Bibliography

Autobiography Criticism: General

Bates, E. Stuart. *Inside Out: An Introduction to Autobiography.* New York: Sheridan House, 1937.

Bruss, Elizabeth. *Autobiographical Acts: The Changing Situation of a Literary Genre.* Baltimore, Md.: Johns Hopkins University Press, 1976.

Burr, Anna. *The Autobiography: A Critical and Comparative Study.* Boston: Houghton Mifflin, 1909.

Delany, Paul. *British Autobiography in the Seventeenth Century.* London: Routledge and Kegan Paul, 1969.

de Man, Paul. "Autobiography as De-Facement." *Modern Language Notes* 94.5 (1979):919–930.

Eakin, Paul J. *Fictions in Autobiography: Studies in the Art of Self-Invention.* Princeton, N.J.: Princeton University Press, 1985.

———. *Touching the World: Reference in Autobiography.* Princeton, N.J.: Princeton University Press, 1992.

———, ed. *On Autobiography/Philippe Lejeune,* trans. Katherine Leary. Minneapolis: University of Minnesota Press, 1989.

Fleishman, Avrom. *Figures of Autobiography: The Language of Self-Writing in Victorian and Modern England.* Berkeley: University of California Press, 1983.

Goodwin, James. *Autobiography: The Self-Made Text.* New York: Twayne Publishers, 1993.

Greenblatt, Stephen. *Shakespearean Negotiations: The Circulation of Social Energy in Renaissance England.* Berkeley: University of California Press, 1988.

Gunn, Janet Varner. *Autobiography: Towards a Poetics of Experience.* Philadelphia: University of Pennsylvania Press, 1982.

Gusdorf, Georges. "The Conditions and Limits of Autobiography." In James Olney, ed., *Autobiography: Essays Theoretical and Critical.* Princeton, N.J.: Princeton University Press, 1980, 28–48.

Jay, Paul. "Being in the Text: Autobiography and the Problem of the Subject." *Modern Language Notes* 97.5 (1982):1045–1063.

———. *Being in the Text: Self-Representation from Wordsworth to Roland Barthes.* Ithaca, N.Y., and London: Cornell University Press, 1984.

Lejeune, Philippe. *Le Pacte Autobiographique.* Paris: Seuil, 1975. [An English version of his essay, "The Autobiographical Contract," can be found in Tsvetan Todorov, ed., *French Literary Theory Today.* Cambridge and New York: Cambridge University Press, 1982, 192–222.]

———. *On Autobiography.* Minneapolis: University of Minnesota Press, 1989.

Lentricchia, Frank, and Thomas McLaughlin, eds. *Critical Terms for Literary Study.* Chicago and London: University of Chicago Press, 1995.

Mehlman, Jeffrey. *A Structural Study of Autobiography: Proust, Leiris, Levi-Strauss.* Ithaca, N.Y.: Cornell University Press, 1974.

Misch, Georg. *The History of Autobiography in Antiquity.* 2 vols. (Reprint). Westport, Conn.: Greenwood Press, 1973.

Olney, James, ed. *Autobiography: Essays Theoretical and Critical.* Princeton, N.J.: Princeton University Press, 1980.

———. *Memory and Narrative: The Weave of Life-Writing.* Chicago: University of Chicago Press, 1998.

Pascal, Roy. *Design and Truth in Autobiography.* Cambridge, Mass.: Harvard University Press, 1960.

Shapiro, Stephen. "The Dark Continent of Literature: Autobiography." *Comparative Literature Studies* 5.4 (1968):421–454.

Spengemann, William C. *The Forms of Autobiography.* New Haven, Conn.: Yale University Press, 1980.

Todd, Jane Marie. "Autobiography and the Case of the Signature: Reading Derrida's Glas." *Comparative Literature* 38.1(1986):1–19.

Todorov, Tzvetan, ed. *French Literary Theory Today: A Reader.* London and New York: Cambridge University Press, 1982.

Weintraub, Karl J. "Autobiography and Historical Consciousness." *Critical Inquiry* 1.4 (1975):821–848.

———. *The Value of the Individual: Self and Circumstance in Autobiography.* Chicago and London: University of Chicago Press, 1978.

Female Self-Writing and Feminism

Ashley, Kathleen, Leigh Gilmore, and Gerald Peters, eds. *Autobiography and Postmodernism.* Amherst: University of Massachusetts Press, 1994.

Bateson, Mary Catherine. *Composing a Life.* New York: Penguin Books U.S.A, 1989.

Belsey, Catherine. *Critical Practice.* London and New York: Methuen, 1980.

Benstock, Shari, ed. *The Private Self: Theory and Practice of Women's Autobiographical Writings.* Chapel Hill: University of North Carolina Press, 1988.

Bergland, Betty. "Postmodernism and the Autobiographical Subject: Reconstructing the 'Other.'" In Ashley, Gilmore, and Peters, eds., *Autobiography and Postmodernism*.

Brodzki, Bella, and Celeste Schenck, eds. *Life/Lines: Theorizing Women's Autobiography*. Ithaca, N.Y.: Cornell University Press, 1988.

Brownley, Martine W., and Allison Kimmich, eds., *Women and Autobiography*. Wilmington, Del.: SR Books, 1999.

Bjorkland, Diane. *Interpreting the Self: Two Hundred Years of American Autobiography*. Chicago: University of Chicago Press, 1998.

Butler, Judith, and Joan W. Scott, eds. *Feminists Theorize the Political*. New York: Routledge, 1992.

Cabrera, Miguel A. "On Language, Culture, and Social Action." *History and Theory Theme Issue* 40 (December 2001):82–100.

Clyman, Toby, and Judith Vowles, eds. *Russia through Women's Eyes: Autobiographies from Tsarist Russia*. London and New Haven, Conn.: Yale University Press, 1996.

Cosslett, Tess et al., eds. *Feminism and Autobiography: Texts, Theories, Methods*. London and New York: Routledge, 2000.

de Lauretis, Teresa. *Technologies of Gender: Essays on Theory, Film, and Fiction*. Bloomington: Indiana University Press, 1987.

Donnell, Alison, and Pauline Polkey, eds. *Representing Lives: Women and Auto/biography*. New York: St. Martin's Press, 2000.

Egan, Susanna. *Mirror Talk: Genres of Crisis in Contemporary Autobiography*. Chapel Hill: University of North Carolina Press, 1999.

Evans, Mary. *Missing Persons: The Impossibility of Autobiography*. New York and London: Routledge, 1999.

Felski, Rita. *Beyond Feminist Aesthetics: Feminist Literature and Social Change*. Cambridge, Mass.: Harvard University Press, 1989.

Fetterley, Judith. *The Resisting Reader: A Feminist Approach to American Fiction*. Bloomington: Indiana University Press, 1978.

Foley, Barbara. *Radical Representations: Politics and Form in U.S. Proletarian Fiction, 1929–1940*. Durham, N.C.: Duke University Press, 1993.

Friedman, Susan S. "Women's Autobiographical Selves: Theory and Practice." In Benstock, ed., *The Private Self*, 34–62.

Gagnier, Regenia. *Subjectivities: A History of Self-Representation in Britain, 1832–1920*. New York: Oxford University Press, 1991.

Gilmore, Leigh. *Autobiographics: A Feminist Theory of Women's Self-Representation*. Ithaca, N.Y.: Cornell University Press, 1994.

Gooze, Marjanne E. "The Definition of Self and Form in Feminist Autobiography Theory." *Women's Studies* 21.4 (1992):411–429.

Heilbrun, Carolyn G. *Writing a Woman's Life*. New York: Ballantine, 1989.

Henke, Suzette. *Shattered Subjects: Trauma and Testimony in Women's Life-Writing*. New York: St. Martin's Press, 1998.

Hirsch, Marianne, and Evelyn Fox Keller, eds. *Conflicts in Feminism*. New York and London: Routledge, 1990.

Jelinek, Estelle. *The Tradition of Women's Autobiography from Antiquity to the Present*. Boston: Twayne Publishers, 1986.

———. *Women's Autobiography: Essays in Criticism*. Bloomington: University of Indiana Press, 1980.

Lionnet, Françoise. *Autobiographical Voices: Race, Gender, Self-Portraiture*. Ithaca, N.Y.: Cornell University Press, 1989.

Long, Judy. *Telling Women's Lives: Subject, Narrator, Reader, Text*. New York: New York University Press, 1999.

Malin, Jo. *The Voice of the Mother: Embedded Maternal Narratives in Twentieth-Century Women's Autobiographies*. Carbondale: Southern Illinois University Press, 2000.

Marcus, Laura. *Auto/biographical Discourses: Theory, Criticism, Practice*. Manchester and New York: Manchester University Press, 1994.

McConnell-Ginet, Sally, Ruth Borker, and Nelly Furman, eds. *Women and Language in Literature and Society*. New York: Praeger, 1980.

Miller, Nancy K. "Women's Autobiography in France: For a Dialectics of Identification." In McConnel-Ginet, Borker, and Furman, eds., *Women and Language in Literature and Society*, 258–273.

Neuman, Shirley, ed. *Autobiography and Questions of Gender*. London: Frank Cass, 1991.

Nussbaum, Felicity. *The Autobiographical Subject: Gender and Ideology in Eighteenth-Century England*. Baltimore, Md.: Johns Hopkins University Press, 1989.

Personal Narratives Group, eds. *Interpreting Women's Lives: Feminist Theory and Personal Narratives*. Bloomington: Indiana University Press, 1989.

Polkey, Pauline, ed. *Women's Lives into Print: The Theory, Practice and Writing of Feminist Auto/Biography*. New York: St. Martin's Press, 1999.

Scott, Joan W. "Experience." In Smith and Watson, eds., *Women, Autobiography, Theory*, 57–71.

———. "Gender: A Useful Category of Historical Analysis." *The American Historical Review* 91.5 (December 1986):1053–1075.

———. *Only Paradoxes to Offer: French Feminists and the Rights of Man*. Cambridge, Mass.: Harvard University Press, 1996.

Sanders, Valerie, ed. *Records of Girlhood: An Anthology of Nineteenth-Century Women's Childhoods*. Aldershot, U.K.: Ashgate Publishing, 2000.

Sellers, Susan, ed. *The Hélène Cixous Reader*. New York: Routledge, 1994.

Siegel, Kristi. *Women's Autobiographies, Culture, Feminism*. New York: Peter Lang, 1999.

Smith, Sidonie. "The Autobiographical Manifesto: Identities, Temporalities, Politics." In Neuman, ed., *Autobiography and Questions of Gender*, 186–212.

———. "Construing Truths in Lying Mouths: Truthtelling in Women's Autobiography." *Studies in the Literary Imagination* 23.2 (fall 1990):145–164.

————. *The Poetics of Women's Autobiography: Marginality and the Fictions of Self-Representation.* Bloomington and Indianapolis: Indiana University Press, 1987.

————. *Subjectivity, Identity, and the Body: Women's Autobiographical Practices in the Twentieth Century.* Bloomington: Indiana University Press, 1993.

Smith, Sidonie, and Julia Watson, eds. *De/Colonizing the Subject: The Politics of Gender in Women's Autobiography.* Minneapolis: University of Minnesota Press, 1992.

————. *Getting a Life.* Minneapolis: University of Minnesota Press, 1996.

————. *Women, Autobiography, Theory: A Reader.* Madison: University of Wisconsin Press, 1998.

Stanley, Liz. *The Auto/Biographical I: Theory and Practice of Feminist Autobiography.* Manchester and New York: Manchester University Press, 1996.

————. "The Knowing because Experiencing Subject: Narratives, Lives, and Autobiography." *Women's Studies International Forum* 16.3(1993):205–215.

Stanton, Domna. *The Female Autograph: Theory and Practice of Autobiography from the Tenth to the Twentieth Century.* Chicago and London: University of Chicago Press, 1987.

Steedman, Carolyn. "Women's Biography and Autobiography." In Helen Carr, ed., *From My Guy to Sci-Fi: Genre and Women's Writing in the Postmodern World.* London: Pandora, 1989.

Watson, Martha. *Lives of Their Own: Rhetorical Dimensions in Autobiographies of Women Activists.* Columbia: University of South Carolina Press, 1999.

Japan-Related and Other Materials

Atkins, E.Taylor. *Blue Nippon: Authenticating Jazz in Japan* (Durham, N.C.: Duke University Press, 2001).

Benson, John, and Takao Matsumura. *Japan, 1868–1945: From Isolation to Occupation* (Essex, U.K.: Pearson Education Limited, 2001).

Bernstein, Gail Lee. *Recreating Japanese Women 1600–1945.* Berkeley: University of California Press, 1991.

Bowring, Richard. 1987. "The Female Hand in Heian Japan: A First Reading." In Stanton, ed., *The Female Autograph.*

Duus, Peter. "Ōyama Ikuo and the Search for Democracy." In James W. Morley, ed., *Dilemmas of Growth in Prewar Japan.* Princeton, N.J.: Princeton University Press, 1971.

————. "Yoshino Sakuzō: The Christian as Political Critic." *The Journal of Japanese Studies* 4.2 (summer 1978):301–326.

————, ed. *The Cambridge History of Japan, vol. 6: The Twentieth Century.* Cambridge: Cambridge University Press, 1988.

Duus, Peter, and Irwin Scheiner. "Socialism, Liberalism, and Marxism, 1901–1931." In Duus, ed., *The Cambridge History of Japan.*

Eisenger, Charles. "Character and Self in Fiction on the Left." In David Madden, ed., *Proletarian Writers of the Thirties*. Carbondale: Southern Illinois University Press, [1968] 1979.

Foley, Barbara. *Radical Representations: Politics and Form in U.S. Proletarian Fiction, 1929–1941*. Durham, N.C.: Duke University Press, 1993.

Fowler, Edward. *The Rhetoric of Confession: Shishōsetsu in Early Twentieth-Century Japanese Fiction*. Berkeley, Los Angeles, and London: University of California Press, 1988.

Fukunaga Misao. *The Women of the* Tale of Genji *and the Writer [Genji monogatari no onnatachi to sakusha]*. Renga shobō shinsha, 1990.

Gayn, Mark. *Japan Diary*. New York: William Sloane Associates, Inc., 1948.

Gordon, Andrew. *Labor and Imperial Democracy in Prewar Japan*. Berkeley: University of California Press, 1991.

Gössman, Hillaria. "Writing as a Means of Liberation: Women Writers' Autobiographical Works in Proletarian Literature." In Susanne Formanek and Sepp Linhart, eds., *Japanese Biographies: Life Histories, Life Cycles, Life Stages*. Vienna: Der Osterreiischen Akademie der Wissenschaften, 1992.

Hane, Mikiso, trans. and ed. *Reflections on the Way to the Gallows: Rebel Women in Prewar Japan*. Berkeley: University of California Press, 1988.

Harootunian, Harry D. *Overcome by Modernity: History, Culture, and Community in Interwar Japan*. Princeton, N.J., and Oxford: Princeton University Press, 2000.

Hirakawa, Sukehiro. *When Progress Was Still Longed For [Shinpo ga mada kibō de atta koro]*. Tokyo: Shinchōsha, 1984.

Hoston, Germaine. *Marxism and the Crisis of Development in Prewar Japan*. Princeton, N.J.: Princeton University Press, 1986.

Hunter, Janet. "Factory Legislation and Employer Resistance." In Tsunehiro Yui and Keiichirō Nakagawa, eds., *Japanese Management in Historical Perspective*. Tokyo: University of Tokyo Press, 1989.

———. "Labour in the Japanese Silk Industry in the 1870s: The Tomioka Nikki of Wada Ei." In Gordon Daniels, ed., *Europe Interprets Japan*. Kent, England: P.Norbury Publications, 1984.

Inoue, Mariko. "The Gaze of the Café Waitress: From Selling Eroticism to Constructing Autonomy." *U.S.-Japan Women's Journal* 15 (1998):78–106.

Iwamoto, Yoshio. "Aspects of the Proletarian Literary Movement in Japan." In Berand Silberman and Harry D. Harootunian, eds., *Japan in Crisis: Essays on Taisho Democracy*. Princeton, N.J.: Princeton University Press, 1974.

Jansen, Marius B. "Ōi Kentarō: Radicalism and Chauvinism." *The Far Eastern Quarterly* 2.3 (1952):305–316.

Joseigaku kenkyūjo, ed. *A Guidebook to Women's Studies [Joseigaku bukku gaido]*. Ibundō, 1987.

Kano Masanao. *Consciousness of Order at the Time of the Formation of Capitalism [Shihonshugi keiseiki no chitsujo isshiki]*. Chikuma Shobo, 1969.

————. *Individual Personalities in History [Rekishi no naka no koseitachi]*. Yuikaku sensho, 1989.

————, ed. *Japanese Autobiographies: 300 Selections [Nihonjin no jiden: 300 sen]*. Tokyo: Heibonsha, 1982.

————. *Taishō Democracy [Taishō demokurashii]. Japanese History [Nihon no rekishi]*, vol. 27. Shogakkan, 1976.

————. *The Undercurrents of Taishō Democracy: The Reappearance of a "Folkloric" Spirit [Taishō demokurashii no teiryū: "Dozoku" teki seishin e no kaiki]*. Nihon hōsō shuppan kyokkai (NHK Bukkusu), 1973.

————. *A Guide to Modern Japanese History [Kindai Nihon shisō annai]*. Iwanami bunko, 1999.

Kano Masanao and Horiba Kyoko. *Takamure Itsue*. Asahi Shinbunsha, 1977.

Kawashima, Terry. *Writing Margins: The Textual Construction of Gender in Heian and Kamakura Japan*. Cambridge, Mass.: Harvard University Press, 2001.

Kinoshita, Naoe. *Zange* [1906]. In Kano and Saeki, comps. *Nihonjin no jiden*, vol. 3 (1981–1983), 267–370.

Large, Stephen S. *Organized Workers and Socialist Politics in Interwar Japan*. Cambridge: Cambridge University Press, 1981.

————. "Revolutionary Worker: Watanabe Masanosuke and JCP 1922–28." *Asian Profile* 3.4 (August 1975):371–390.

————. *The Rise of Labour in Japan, Yuaikai 1912–1919*. Tokyo: Sophia University Press, 1972.

————. "The Romance of Revolution in Japanese Anarchism and Communism during the Taishō Period." *Modern Asian Studies* 11.3 (July 1977):461–473.

Lewis, Michael. *Rioters and Citizens: Mass Protest in Imperial Japan*. Berkeley, Los Angeles, and Oxford: University of California Press, 1990.

Loftus, Ronald P. "Female Self-Writing: Takamure Itsue's *Hi no kuni no onna no nikki*." *Monumenta Nipponica* 51.2 (summer 1996):153–170.

————. "In Search of Japan's First Modern Autobiography." *biography* 6.3 (1983):256–271.

————. "Is There a Woman in the Text? Gender in Fukuda Hideko's *Warawa no hanseigai*." In Julie Ann Carson and John Rehm, eds., *In the Pacific Interest: Democracy, Women and the Environment*, Willamette Journal of the Liberal Arts, Supplemental Series no. 4. Salem, Oreg.: Willamette University, 1991, 73–86.

Mackie, Vera. *Creating Socialist Women in Japan: Gender, Labour, and Activism, 1900–1937*. Cambridge: Cambridge University Press, 1997.

————, ed. *Feminism and the State in Modern Japan*. Melbourne: Japanese Studies Centre, 1995.

Matsubara Kazushige. *Yamamoto Sanehiko and the Kaizōsha [Kaizōsha to Yamamoto Sanehiko]*. Nanpō shinsha, 2001.

Miller, Marilyn Jeanne. *The Poetics of Nikki Bunqaku*. New York and London: Garland Publishing, Inc., 1985.

Minichiello, Sharon A., ed. *Japan's Competing Modernities: Issues in Culture and Democracy, 1900–1930*. Honolulu: University of Hawai'i Press, 1998.

———. *Retreat from Reform*. Honolulu: University of Hawai'i Press, 1984.

Miyake, Lynne. Book review of Richard Bowring, *Murasaki Shikibu: The Tale of Genji*. *Monumenta Nipponica* 44.3 (autumn 1989):349–351.

———. "Woman's Voice in Japanese Literature: Expanding the Feminine." *Women's Studies* 17.1–2 (1989):87–100.

Mizuta, Noriko. *Feminism in the Distance [Feminizumu no kanata]*. Kodansha, 1991.

———. *Reality and Fiction in Modern Japanese Literature*. White Plains, N.Y.: M.E. Sharpe, 1980.

Monnet, Livia. "'In the Beginning Woman Was the Sun': Autobiographies of Modern Japanese Women Writers—1 and 2." *Japan Forum* 1.1 and 1.2 (April and October 1989):55–81 and 196–233.

Moore, Joe. *Japanese Workers and the Struggle for Power 1945–1947*. Madison: University of Wisconsin Press, 1983.

Narita, Ryūichi. "Women in the Motherland: Oku Mumeo through Wartime and Postwar." In Yasushi Yamanouchi, J.Victor Koschmann, and Ryūichi Narita, eds., *Total War and "Mobilization."* Ithaca, N.Y.: Cornell East Asia Series, 1998.

Nishikawa Yuko. *The Sorceress of the House in the Woods [Takamure Itsue: Mori no ie no fujo]*. Regurusu bunko, 1977.

Nolte, Sharon. *Liberalism in Modern Japan: Ishibashi Tanzan and his Teachers, 1905–1960*. Berkeley: University of California Press, 1987.

Orr, James J. *The Victim as Hero: Ideologies of Peace and National Identity in Postwar Japan*. Honolulu: University of Hawai'i Press, 2001.

Raddeker, Helene Bowen. *Treacherous Women of Imperial Japan: Patriarchal Fictions, Patricidal Fantasies*. London: Nissan Institute/Routledge Japanese Studies Series, 1997.

Saeki, Shōichi. "Autobiographical Literature in Japan." *Japan Echo* 10.3 (autumn 1983):69–75.

———. "The Autobiography in Japan." *Journal of Japanese Studies* 2.2 (1985):357–368.

———. *Japanese Autobiography [Nihonjin no jiden]*. Kodansha, 1974.

———. *Modern Japanese Autobiography [Kindai Nihon no jiden]*. Kodansha, 1981.

———, comp. *Japanese Autobiographies [Nihonjin no jiden]*. Heibonsha, 1981–1983.

———, ed. *The World of Autobiographical Literature [Jiden bungaku no sekai]*. Asahi Shuppansha, 1983.

Sato, Barbara. *The New Japanese Woman: Modernity, Media, and Women in Interwar Japan*. Durham, N.C.: Duke University Press, 2003.

Schalow, Paul, and Janet Walker, eds. *The Woman's Hand: Gender and Theory in Japanese Women's Writing*. Stanford: Stanford University Press, 1996.

Shea, George T. *Leftwing Literature in Japan*. Hōsei University Press, 1964.

Sievers, Sharon L. *Flowers in Salt: The Beginnings of Feminist Consciousness in Modern Japan*. Stanford: Stanford University Press, 1983.

Silverberg, Miriam. "The Café Waitress Serving Modern Japan." In Stephen Vlastos, ed., *Mirror of Modernity: Invented Traditions of Modern Japan*. Berkeley: University of California Press, 1998, 208–225.

———. *Changing Song: The Marxist Manifestoes of Nakano Shigeharu*. Princeton, N.J.: Princeton University Press, 1990.

———. "Constructing a New Social History of Prewar Japan." In Masao Miyoshi and H.D. Harootunian, eds., "Japan in the World," *Boundary 2* 18.3 (fall 1991):61–89.

Smaldone, William. *Rudolf Hilferding: The Tragedy of a German Social Democrat*. Dekalb: Northern Illinois University Press, 1988.

Smith, Henry D. *Japan's First Student Radicals*. Cambridge, Mass.: Harvard University Press, 1972.

Suzuki, Tomi. *Narrating the Self: Fictions of Japanese Modernity*. Stanford: Stanford University Press, 1996.

Taira, Koji. "Economic Development, Labor Markets, and Industrial Relations in Japan, 1905–1955." In Peter Duus, ed., *The Cambridge History of Japan*, 606–653.

Tanaka, Yukiko. *Women Writers of Meiji and Taishō Japan: Their Lives, Works and Critical Reception, 1868–1926*. Jefferson, N.C., and London: McFarland and Company, Inc., 2000.

Tipton, Elise K. "The Café: Contested Space of Modernity in Interwar Japan," in Tipton and Clark, eds., *Being Modern in Japan: Culture and Society from the 1910s to the 1930s*, 127–128.

———. *Modern Japan: A Social and Political History*. London and New York: Routledge, 2002.

Tipton, Elise K., and John Clark, eds. *Being Modern in Japan: Culture and Society from the 1910s to the 1930s*. Honolulu: University of Hawai'i Press, 2000.

Tokuza, Akiko. *The Rise of the Feminist Movement in Japan*. Tokyo: Keio University Press, 1999.

Tōkyōto fujin jōhō sentaa shozō, comp. *A Record of Holdings in the Tokyo Municipal Center for Information on Women [Shiryō mokuroku]*. Fujin jōhō Sentaa, 1987.

Tsurumi, E. Patricia. *Factory Girls: Women in the Thread Mills of Meiji Japan*. Princeton, N.J.: Princeton University Press, 1990.

———. "Visions of Women and the New Society in Conflict: Yamakawa Kikue versus Takamure Itsue." In Minichiello, ed., *Japan's Competing Modernities*, 335–357.

Yoneda Sayoko. *Modern Japanese Women's History [Kindai Nihonjoseishi]*, vol. 1. Shin Nihon shuppansha, 1972.

Index

About the Author

Ronald P. Loftus was born in Washington, D.C., and grew up in many places around the world, including India, France, Italy, and Thailand, where he graduated from the International School of Bangkok. He received his doctorate in modern Japanese history from Claremont Graduate School. Professor Loftus currently serves as chair of the Department of Japanese and Chinese at Willamette University and teaches language, history, and literature.